RELIGIOUS LIFE IN THE U.S. CHURCH

The New Dialogue

PAULIST PRESS
New York, N.Y./Ramsey, N.J.

Cover design by Morris Berman.

Library of Congress
Catalog Card Number: 84-61868

ISBN: 0-8091-2683-4

Published by Paulist Press
545 Island Road, Ramsey, N.J. 07446

Printed and bound in the
United States of America

CONTENTS

DEDICATION AND ACKNOWLEDGMENTS

FOREWORD

I

POPE JOHN PAUL II

II

ADDRESSES OF THE PONTIFICAL DELEGATE, JOHN R. QUINN, D.D.,
ARCHBISHOP OF SAN FRANCISCO

III

IN THE SERVICE OF THE CHURCH: CONFERENCE FOR BISHOPS AND
MAJOR RELIGIOUS SUPERIORS ON RELIGIOUS LIFE IN THE
UNITED STATES (Papers of the June 20-22, 1984 Conference
at Boston College

V

TOWARD THE FUTURE

DEDICATION AND ACKNOWLEDGMENTS

This volume is dedicated to those to whom it owes its existence: the countless members of the Communion of Saints, past and present, whose lives have formed the reserve of experience and wisdom on which the contributors to this book have drawn. Some of their names are mentioned in these pages, but most are not, nor would space allow us even to begin to list them. However, justice requires at least some few acknowledgments.

First, a profound debt of gratitude is owed to the Pontifical Delegate, Archbishop John R. Quinn, D.D. and to the joint committee made up of the Commission of Bishops and the Committee of Religious for the Study of Religious Life in the United States. Without their enlightened leadership the dialogue might not have begun as constructively as it has. Then there are the many who have responded to this call to dialogue. The most conspicuous of these, in terms of what is presented here, are those at Boston College and the Weston School of Theology on the east coast, and at the University of San Francisco and the Jesuit School of Theology at Berkeley on the west coast, who responded by organizing the conference and lecture series from which most of this book is drawn. Particular thanks is due to the vision and generosity of the administrators of Boston College whose encouragement guaranteed from the beginning the support needed both to organize a conference and see to the publication of its papers. In the course of that conference, several dozen people--students, religious, administrators and staff--generously provided the general and particular assistance which helped make the conference and its papers successful. Similar support on the west coast helped assure the success of the San Francisco lecture series.

As for the actual and unusually rapid publication of this book, special thanks are due to Paulist Press which agreed not only to publish the book but also, in order to save time, to place the final editing and printing entirely in the hands of its general editor. Finally, the technical planning and production of the book fell almost entirely to Lisa Foley, the administrative assistant of the Boston College theology department. That the book got through the penultimate stages of production at all was due largely to her ability to handle this massive new assignment in addition to her regular responsibilities.

Finally, we must humbly acknowledge the limitations of this book. Having chosen to bring it out quickly, we did not have the normal time for carefully editing and revising the manuscript. For the occasional stylistic and typographical lapses which may still remain, the authors and editors request the reader's indulgence.--R.J.D.

FOREWORD

In the summer of 1983, the Church in the United States experienced an unprecedented intervention of the Pope. John Paul II summoned the American bishops to an extensive involvement with religious communities in the United States, an involvement whose purpose was the strengthening and encouragement of religious life and whose signature was "special pastoral service."[1] When Archbishop John R. Quinn, the Pontifical Delegate appointed to direct this episcopal ministry, attempted to couch in a single sentence the mission entrusted to the bishops, he summarized: "In short, our pastoral service is cast in terms of a dialogue of salvation."[2] With this phrase, the Archbishop deliberately subsumed the papal mandate under that interchange which Paul VI had made a purpose of his pontificate: "To impress upon the internal relationships of the Church the character of a dialogue between members of a body, whose constitutive principle is charity."[3] To the religious of the United States, Archbishop Quinn formulated a similar appeal: "For over the past twenty years, as you moved through this period of experimentation, your partners in dialogue have been the members of your own congregation and other congregations. Now what the Holy See is asking for is an extension of this dialogue to a larger group, to the bishops and the Church as a whole."[4] Thus, to a degree unparalleled at least in recent Church history, the papal intervention has called the Church in the United States to the inauguration or to the renewal of communication between bishops and religious, and between religious and the Church as a whole. It has meant the widening of the dialogue.

"Dialogue" comes into contemporary usage out of an ancient tradition rich in its accomplishments, and it carries meanings or purposes as diversified as mutual inquiry, reciprocal arguments, fictional narratives, and the written report of any of these. Every subject and every humane discipline has been explored and furthered in dialogue: mechanics by Galileo, atheism by Mersenne and Diderot, philosophy by Berkeley, painting by Vincenzo Carducci, and theology by Augustine, Gregory of Nyssa and Methodius of Olympus. In its debased forms, dialogue has covered unresolvable controversies and even concealed instruction. In its finest forms, it has moved towards the resolution of seeming contradictions by eliciting the truth in positions

ix

initially poised in conflict. For all of these multiple topics and differing forms of dialogue reach back to Plato and the Socratic dialogues that have given the subsequent centuries both inspiration and a model for discussion. Over these twenty centuries, dialogue has come to mean many things, but all of them in some way embodied discussion, a mutuality of communication. Dialogue is more than self-expression; it is even more than communication. It adds to communication many voices; it adds reciprocity. Dialogue has always involved such communical interaction as conversation, argument, deliberation, exchange, debate, and colloquy. However varied the dialogue--whether the question and answer of Socrates or the extended speeched of Cicero and Hume--dialogue points to a profound reciprocity of knowledge, an agreement to discuss, a seriousness about the opinions of others, and a common commitment to come to the truth. Dialogue presupposes a community of discussion, a community constituted by discussion, and that is almost the definition of a university.

The call of the Pontifical Delegate for dialogue makes a twofold claim upon the Catholic university; one, because it is a university, and the other because it is Catholic. It was singularly appropriate for Catholic universities to answer that call.

Discussion is the life of a university. The assembly of faculty and of students is not simply for the research of one and the individual growth of the other. They come together because both growth and research are a participative, collaborative process, and the commitment to that process creates whatever life the university possesses. The interchanges of knowledge--of the perspectives out of which it comes, the evidence to which its judgments appeal, and the reflections by which its nature and worth are assessed--form the unity of a university. The life of a university is only as vital as the discussions it fosters. A university which is Catholic offers the Church this unique service: that in this forum for discussion, the issues which confront the Church can be given the serious attention of the inquiring mind. They may be explored in scientific and professional disciplines brought into collaboration precisely to investigate a common problem. The Church, in posing such issues, actually furthers the intrinsic life of the university, while the university, in discussing them, puts at the service of the Church that multiform inquiry which can advance knowledge and test conclusions for their soundness.

The contemporary meaning and direction of religious life is such an issue. Two Catholic universities sponsored its exploration during the summer of 1984. Boston College, in collaboration with the Weston School of Theology, submitted this topic to a symposium, a conference extending over three days in which scholars from different academic disciplines discussed with bishops and religious superiors the implications of religious life in the American Church. The University of San Francisco, in collaboration with the Jesuit School of Theology at Berkeley, contributed a different university form: the lecture and responsive discussion in a series that lasted over six weeks and was offered for a more general audience of faculty, students and religious of the area. Both forms of university discussion, the conference and the series, fed into the greater conversation either in the immediate responses which they elicited or in the informal exchanges that often bring both seminar and lecture to their fulfillment.

Dialogue, whether in the Church or in the university, possesses only a fragile life, one constantly threatened by the extremes of fanaticism and skepticism. Discussion bears upon problems whose importance engages the reflection of serious human beings and whose complexity requires the help of many different perspectives, areas of experience and academic fields. It means that all claims must appeal to criteria and evidence, and it assumes that each member of the dialogue has something to contribute and something to learn. Few human beings say things that are simply silly, and even fewer say things that are exhaustively true. If the evidence for a conclusion or the criteria for an evaluation are not evident, it is the purpose of discussion to discover this and to amend either the argument or its conclusions. Discussion, in presupposing that there are things that can profitably be submitted to rational, impartial discourse, poises the dialogue in countermovement to both fanaticism and skepticism.

Fanaticism holds a persuasion so intensely that every discussion is closed. Skepticism rejects the possibility of any assured conclusions so that discussion is never engaged. Under appeals to loyalty or the eager fervor of enthusiasms the fanatic disparages rational or academic interchange with its moderation of assertions and its pedestrian insistence upon grounds for statements. "What is there to discuss?" comes with a rush of fidelity to the past or insistence upon action now. The skeptic, distant or disillusioned, claims to know that argumentation comes to nothing and that one conclusion is as defensible as another. "What is the use of discussion?" has a ring of realism about it, or world-weariness. Paradoxically, however, both groups hold a number of characteristics in common: They place serious questions beyond discussion.[5] They dismiss those engaged in dialogue as foolish, weak or dishonest. They are easy prey for the rhetoric of the right or of the left as they tend to turn authority into violence, distending it to settle the issues which they have removed from rational discourse. Over the centuries they have had their harsh day when they made the university an impossibility and distorted the teaching office of the Church.

The conference at Boston College and the lecture-series at the University of San Francisco attempted to move the issue of religious life beyond the reach of either fanaticism or skepticism and into the realm of academic dialogue. Variant positions were represented in the papers and discussions. One will notice that the speakers addressed their subject neither from the right nor from the left; those are ultimately political distinctions. The diversity in a university and in these papers is that of different disciplines: history and theology, psychology and sociology, canon law and literature. And these are met and furthered by those experienced in religious life and engaged in its leadership. Disagreements were respected, and an effort made to realize the truth inherent in any position irrespective of its command of public opinion. Both in the breadth of fields represented and the frankness of their interchange, the conference and series attempted to realize the axiom of the great Cardinal Newman: "As to the range of university teaching, certainly the very name of university is inconsistent with restrictions of any kind."[6]

The following pages reflect in their sequence the genesis of the two university discussions. First: the letter of the Pope which carried his charge to the American bishops and constituted the Pontifical Commission. Together with that letter came the document, Essential Elements, placed here in appendix because of its great length. Second: the several addresses of the Pontifical Delegate in which the meaning of the papal intervention was determined and the dialogic nature of its mandate specified. Third: the papers from the conference in mid-June at Boston College in which the Delegate's appeal for dialogue was answered by bishops, religious superiors, and the academic community. Fourth: the papers from the series of lectures over the summer at the University of San Francisco in which this discussion was further extended to religious and laity in the Church.

Finally: Sister Bette Moslander's reflections, joined to those of Sister Helen Flaherty and Father Howard Gray, to guess and to hope and to caution about the future.

A conference and a series of lectures, however, have their intrinsic limitations of time and space. Neither can claim to be more than partial in the subjects it explores and in the inquiries it fields. Further, both forms of university discussion are, in this case, initial attempts to take up the challenge offered by the Pontifical Delegate, and they may well bear the additional limitation of early efforts. These papers do not present the dialogue that they occasioned; they do not even report it. But they carry much of that dialogue with them in their final form, and they indicate the materials which were presented for the discussions over those days. We present them, joined with the Papal Letter, the document, Essential Elements, and the several addresses of the Pontifical Delegate, both as a serious exploration of important issues and as a stimulus to further discussion.

The Editors

NOTES

1. "Letter of Pope John Paul II to the Bishops of the United States," April 3, 1983, no. 3 (See below in Part I).
2. Archbishop John R. Quinn, "Special Pastoral Service: A Shared Pilgrimage," Address to the NCCB, November 15, 1983, no. II (See beolw in Part II).
3. Pope Paul VI, Ecclesiam Sanctam 14. This section is cited by the Pontifical Delegate in his address to the NCCB, n. II (See below in Part II).
4. Archbishop John R. Quinn, "Extending the Dialogue about Religious Life," Address to the National Assembly of the LCWR, August 16, 1983, no. III (See below in Part II).
5. Cf. Ch. Perelman and L. Olbrechts-Tyteca, The New Rhetoric: A Treatise on Argumentation (trans. John Wilkinson and Purcell Weaver; Notre Dame: University of Notre Dame Press, 1983) 62.
6. John Henry Cardinal Newman, "University Teaching, Discourse II," The Idea of a University (Image Books; Garden City, New York: Doubleday, 1959) 61.

I

POPE JOHN PAUL II

Pope John Paul II

Letter to U. S. Bishops on Religious Orders*

1. In this extraordinary holy year which has just begun,
the whole church is seeking to live more intensely the mystery
of the redemption. She is seeking to respond ever more
faithfully to the immense love of Jesus Christ the redeemer of
the world.

In the bull of indiction of the jubilee, I pointed out
that "the profound meaning and hidden beauty of this year. . .
is to be seen in the rediscovery and lived practice of the
sacramental economy of the church, through which the grace of
God in Christ reaches individuals and communities" (Aperite
Portas Redemptori, 3). While these words have a personal
meaning for everyone, they are particularly relevant to
individual men and women religious and to each religious
community. It is my profound hope and ardent prayer that the
grace of the redemption will reach religious in great
abundance, that it will take possession of their hearts, and
become a source of Easter joy and hope for them—that the holy
year will be a fresh beginning for them to "walk in newness of
life" (Rom. 6:4).

By their very vocation, religious are intimately linked
to the redemption. In their consecration to Jesus Christ they
are a sign of the redemption that he accomplished. In the
sacramental economy of the church they are instruments for
bringing this redemption to the people of God. They do so by
the vitality that radiates from the lives they live in union
with Jesus, who continues to repeat to all his disciples: "I
am the vine, you are the branches" (Jn. 15:5).

Religious bring the people of God into contact with the
redemption by the evangelical and ecclesial witness they bear
by word and example to the message of Jesus. Their communion
with their local churches and with the universal church has a
supernatural effectiveness by reason of the redemption. The
important collaboration they give to the ecclesial community
helps it to live and perpetuate the mystery of the redemption,
especially through the eucharistic sacrifice in which the work
of the redemption is repeatedly actuated.

---

*Origins 13.8 (July 7, 1983) 129-133.

The church presents the Year of the Redemption to all the people of God as a call to holiness, a call to renewal and a call to penance and conversion, because "there is no spiritual renewal that does not pass through penance and conversion" (Aperite Portas Redemptori, 4). But this call is linked in a particular way with the life and mission of religious. Thus the jubilee year has a special value for religious; it affects them in a special way; it makes special demands on their love, reminding them how much they are loved by the redeemer and by his church. Especially relevant to religious are these words of the apostolic bull: "The specific grace of the year of the Redemption is therefore a renewed discovery of the love of God" (No. 8).

In this regard, as pastors of the church, we must proclaim over and over again that the vocation to religious life that God gives is linked to his personal love for each and every religious. It is my earnest hope that the Holy Year of the Redemption will truly be for religious life a year of fruitful renewal in Christ's love. If all the faithful have a right—as they do—to the treasures of grace that a call to renewal in love offers, then the religious have a special title to that right.

2. During this Jubilee of the Redemption you will be coming to Rome for your ad limina visits, and I shall have an opportunity to consider with you some of the aspects of religious life as you see them. This makes my thoughts turn at this time in a special way to the religious of the United States. In reflecting on their history, their splendid contribution to the church in your country, the great missionary activity that they have performed over the years, the influence they have exerted on religious life throughout the world, as well as on the particular needs which they experience at the present time, I am convinced that, as bishops, we must offer them encouragement and the support of our pastoral love.

The religious life in the United States has indeed been a great gift of God to the church and to your country. From the early colonial days, by the grace of God, the evangelizing zeal of outstanding men and women religious, encouraged and sustained by the persevering efforts of the bishops, have helped the church to bring the fruits of the redemption to your land. Religious were among your pioneers. They blazed a trail in Catholic education at all levels, helping to create a magnificent educational system from elementary school to university. They brought into being health care facilities

4

remarkable both for their numbers and quality They made a valuable contribution to the provision of social services. Working toward the establishment of justice, love and peace, they helped to build a social order rooted in the Gospel, striving to bring generation after generation to the maturity of Christ. Their witness to the primacy of Christ's love has been expressed through lives of prayer and dedicated service to others. Contemplative religious have contributed immensely to the vitality of the ecclesial community.

At every stage in its growth, the church in your nation, marked by a conspicuous fidelity to the See of Peter, has been deeply indebted to its religious: priests, sisters, brothers. The religious of America have also been a gift to the universal church, for they have given generously to the church in other countries; they have helped throughout the world to evangelize the poor and to spread Christ's Gospel of peace. This generosity has given evidence of a strong and vital relgious life, ensured by a steady flow of vocations.

3. And because I have stressed the pastoral character and the full participation of the local churches in the celebration of the holy year, I now turn to you, the bishops of the United States, asking you during this holy year to render special pastoral service to the religious of your dioceses and your country. I ask you to assist them in every way possible to open wide the doors of their heart to the redeemer. I ask that, through the exercise of your pastoral office, as individual bishops and united as an episcopal conference, you encourage the religious, their institutes and associations to live fully the mystery of the redemption, in union with the whole church and according to the specific charism of their religious life. This pastoral service can be given in different ways, but it certainly includes the personal proclamation of the gospel message to them and the celebration of the eucharistic sacrifice with them.

It will likewise mean proclaiming anew to all the people of God the church's teaching on consecrated life. This teaching has been set forth in the great documents of the Second Vatican Council, particular in Lumen Gentium and Perfectae Caritatis. It has been further developed in Evangelica Testificatio, in the addresses of my predecessor Paul VI and in those which I myself have given on many occasions. More recently still, much of this doctrinal richness has been distilled and reflected in the revised Code of Canon Law promulgated earlier this year.

The essential elements are lived in different ways from one institute to another. You yourselves deal with this rich variety in the context of the American reality. Nevertheless there are elements which are common to all forms of religious life and which the church regards as essential. These include: a vocation given by God, an ecclesial consecration to Jesus Christ through the profession of the evangelical counsels by public vows, a stable form of community life approved by the church, fidelity to a specific founding gift and sound traditions, a sharing in Christ's mission by a corporate apostolate, personal and liturgical prayer, especially eucharistic worship, public witness, a life-long formation, a form of government calling for religious authority based on faith, a specific relation to the church. Fidelity to these basic elements, laid down in the constitutions approved by the church, guarantees the strength of religious life and grounds our hope for its future growth.

I ask you, moreover, my brother bishops, to show the church's profound love and esteem for the religious life, directed as it is to the faithful and generous imitation of Christ and to union with God. I ask you to invite all the religious throughout your land, in my name, and in our own name as bishops, in the name of the church and in the name of Jesus, to seize this opportunity of the holy year to walk in newness of life, in solidarity with all the pastors and faithful, along the path necessary for us all--the way of penance and conversion.

In their lives of poverty, religious will discover that they are truly relevant to the poor. Through chastity they are able to love with the love of Christ and to experience his love for themselves. And through obedience they find their deepest configuration to Christ in the most fundamental expression of his union with the Father--in fulfilling his Father's will: "I always do what pleases him" (Jn. 8:29). It is especially through obedience that Christ himself offers to religious the experience of full Christian freedom. Possessing peace in their hearts and the justice of God from which that peace flows, they can be authentic ministers of Christ's peace and justice to a world in need.

In those cases, too, where individuals or groups, for whatever reason, have departed from the indispensable norms of religious life or have even, to the scandal of the faithful, adopted positions at variance with the church's teaching, I ask you my brother bishops, sustained by hope in the power of Christ's grace and performing an act of authentic pastoral service, to proclaim once again the church's universal call to conversion, spiritual renewal and holiness. And be sure that the same Holy Spirit who has placed you as bishops to shepherd the church (cf. Acts 20:28) is ready to utilize your ministry to help those who were called by him to a life of perfect charity, who were repeatedly sustained by his grace and who have given evidence of a desire--which must be rekindled--to live totally for Christ and his church in accordance with their proper ecclesial charism.

In the local churches the discernment of the exercise of these charisms is authenticated by the bishops in union with the successor of Peter. This work is a truly important aspect of your episcopal ministry, an aspect to which the universal church, through me, asks you to attach special priority in this jubilee year.

4. As an expression of my solidarity with you in this area of your pastoral service, acknowledging the special links between religious life and the Holy See, I am hereby appointing Archbishop John R. Quinn of San Francisco as pontifical delegate to head a special commission of three bishops whose task it will be to facilitate the pastoral work of their brother bishops in the United States in helping the religious of your country whose institutes are engaged in apostolic works to live their ecclesial vocation to the full. Associated with him in the commission are Archbishop Thomas C. Kelly of Louisville and Bishop Raymond W. Lessard of Savannah.

Working in union with the Sacred Congregation for Religious and Secular Institutes and following a document of guidelines which the congregation is making available to them and to you, the commission has authority to set up a suitable program of work which, it is hoped, will be of valuable help to the individual bishops and to the episcopal conference. I would further ask the commission to consult with a number of religious, to profit from the insights that come from the experience of religious life lived in union with the church. I am confident that the religious of contemplative life will accompany this work with their prayers.

In asking the commission to be of assistance to you in your pastoral ministry and responsibility, I know that it will be very sensitive to the marked decline in recent years in the numbers of young people seeking to enter religious life, particularly in the case of institutes of apostolic life. This decline in numbers is a matter of grave concern to me--a concern which I know that you and the religious also share.

7

As a result of this decline, the median age of religious is rising and their ability to serve the needs of the church is becoming increasingly more limited.

I am concerned that, in a generous effort to continue manifold services without adequate numbers, many religious are overburdened, with a consequent risk to their health and spiritual vitality. In the face of this shared concern, I would ask the commission, in collaboration with religious, utilizing the prayerful insights of individual religious and major superiors, to analyze the reasons for this decline in vocations. I ask them to do this with a view of encouraging a new growth and a fresh move forward in this most important sector of the church's life.

And in addressing the many issues affecting the consecrated life and ecclesial mission of religious, these bishops will work closely with you, their brother bishops. Besides having as an aid the document on the salient points of the church's teaching on religious life prepared by the Sacred Congregation for Religious and Secular Institutes, you and they will have my full fraternal and prayerful support. The ad limina visits of the American bishops will truly offer an excellent opportunity for you and me to speak personally about the pastoral service that we wish to render together in the name of Jesus, chief shepherd of the church and redeemer of the world.

By requesting that this call to holiness, to spiritual renewal and to conversion and penance be initiated during the Jubilee Year of the Redemption, I am trusting that the Lord Jesus, who always sends laborers into his vineyard, will bless the project with his redeeming love. The power of the Holy Spirit can make this call a vital experience for all who respond to it, and a sign of hope for the future of religious life in your country. May Mary, the patroness of the United States, the first of the redeemed and the model of all religious, support your episcopal ministry with her motherly prayer, so that it may come to fruition, bringing renewed joy and peace to all the religious of America, and offering ever greater glory to the most holy Trinity.

From the Vatican, the Solemnity of the Resurrection, April 3, 1983.

8

II

ADDRESSES OF THE PONTIFICAL DELEGATE,

JOHN R. QUINN, D.D., ARCHBISHOP OF SAN FRANCISCO

1

Archbishop Quinn Discusses the Commission on
Religious Life

(An Interview Conducted by the San Francisco
Archdiocesan Office of Information)

Q. Archbishop, could you explain in a general way this action of the Holy Father?

A. Yes, I think so. Since the Second Vatican Council, the Religious in the United States (and indeed, throughout the world) have been engaged in an intensive period of renewal. In 1966 Pope Paul VI gave the religious a special mandate to update and rewrite their constitutions. In order that these constitutions might reflect the lived experience of the religious, a period of almost 20 years was given for experimentation. Now with the submitting of constitutions and the promulgation of the new Code of Canon Law, this unique time of experimentation is ending. But with the ending of the period of special experimentation, the pope has asked the American bishops to enter into the process in order to support and to second the efforts of the religious to strengthen and to renew their communities.

Q. Archbishop, what has occasioned this action of the Holy Father?

A. I think that this call for renewal has been typical of the Holy Father. When he visited Latin America or the Philippines, he said that he hoped that his visit would be a call for the Christian renewal of the church in those countries. These were almost the first words that he spoke when he visited Poland for the fist time as pope. The renewal of the church is very much on his mind and there are many ways in which he urges it. Sometimes by these extraordinary visits, as in Latin America or Poland, at other times in his addresses to national hierarchies, and more recently by the announcement of the holy year whose purpose is "a call to holiness, a call to renewal, a call to penance and conversion."

In this context, it is not so extraordinary that he would also address the religious in the church. By their vocation, they are crucial to this whole attempt to renew the church. They are both consecrated to Christ through their vows to be a sign of the redemption, and they are among the indispensable means by which this renewal would come into the lives of all the members of the church. If the church is to be renewed, it is reasonable that the pope would make this call strongly and directly to the religious within the church. As I remarked, this is only to support and strengthen a process of renewal which religious themselves have been engaged in for some time.

Q. Why does the pope single out the religious not only for this mission, but for renewal themselves?

A. Because they minister to the Gospel in a very special way. This lies at the heart of the Catholic theology of ministry. Ministry in the church does not consist in the professionally good condescending to help those who are sinners. We are all sinners, and we all stand in need of the forgiving grace of God. You will notice in the lives of the saints, Saint Theresa is a good example, a pervasive sense of sin and forgiveness in their own lives. All of us need to be challenged and called to a deeper holiness, to a more authentic living of the religious vision of our lives--especially those whose ministry in the church involves and specifies their entire lives. We need to be called continually and insistently to what the pope has termed "a fruitful renewal in Christ's love."

The papal appeal for holiness to those whose lives are at the service of the Gospel is part of Catholic tradition from its beginning. The pope's call upon religious finds its parallel, for example, in the Pauline demand of Timothy: "You must aim to be saintly and religious, filled with faith and love, patient and gentle." (1 Tm. 6:11)

Q. But this seems so massive . . .

A. Yes it does. But would you like to draw up a list of things the pope does in a small way!

Seriously, however, the magnitude of the papal action indicates something of the unique value that the church places on religious life. The church presents religious life as a profound vocation, as a way in which one follows Christ more intensely. It is a special form of consecrated life, one which gives witness to a total commitment to God through the evangelical counsels. Now that in itself is quite massive!

12

Implicit in all of this are certain elements, essential elements, which must be present for any community to be recognized as "religious" in the canonical sense of that term, that is, as a life confirmed in its soundness by the church as an authentic way of seeking and finding God. This is a very serious action of the church, to confirm and to foster such a religious life, and it deserves the attention of those who minister to the church in leadership, specifically the bishops. As the Holy Father and Lumen Gentium remind us, "Religious life is not your property, no more than it is the property of an institute. It is a gift of God which the church has received from the Lord and which by his grace she always safeguards."

The document presented by the Sacred Congregation for Religious is an outline of these essential elements as drawn from the teaching of the church, especially since Vatican II. These elements are uniquely enfleshed by each religious community with its own special charism and within each cultural context.

Q. Granted that it is appropriate to call religious continually to renewal, why single out American religious?

A. I think that the answer is complex. It involves both the American bishops and American religious.

First of all, the pope is not only calling religious to a renewal of their consecration to a life of holiness, he is also calling upon us American bishops to meet our own responsibilities in this matter. He reminds us of what so many of us take for granted, the enormous contributions which religious have made to the church in this country, and he directs us during this holy year to render them special pastoral service. Now during this year, the American bishops are slated to make their ad limina visit to Rome. (The "ad limina" is a visit which each Catholic bishop makes to the Holy See once every five years to discuss the state of his diocese with the Holy Father.) The pope wants to use this time to discuss with American bishops some aspects of religious life. Hence, if the pope wants to call the bishops to their pastoral responsibility to the religious in their diocese, this is the time.

Second, however, there is more here than just appropriate timing. There is the point insisted upon by the Holy Father in his letter. The religious have been a major influence in shaping the present features of the church in the United States. They have founded, maintained and directed a vast school system unmatched by anything in the Catholic world. Catholic hospitals, orphanages and convalescent centers mark every American city. Religious have led the church in catechetical reform, evangelized both children and adults of every age, and minister as members of parish teams everywhere in the United States. Their leadership has been evident in the integration of social justice into the church's mission to evangelize. Many, many religious lead the way in a care for the oppressed and indigent, which is a tangible continuation and embodiment of the compassion of Christ.

Third, the influence of American religious, not only in the United States but throughout the world, is massive. This is a point that must be understood by American religious, and the pope mentions it twice as an operative consideration. One gets the impression that he considers them as important for the international church as for the church in the United States. This means that the holiness of the contemporary church calls very much for the holiness of American religious.

Q. But does this action mean that the pope thinks that there is something wrong, pervasively wrong with American religious?

A. That is exactly what I am afraid that some fringe voices on either the radical right or the radical left will affirm, but they are wrong.

If you read the papal letter carefully, you will find that its purpose is to draw the bishops into a pastoral service of the religious. Now what kind of service? The pope lists five things.

First, the ministry of the word of the eucharist: "This pastoral service can be given in different ways, but it certainly includes the personal proclamation of the gospel message to them and the celebration of the eucharistic sacrifice with them."

Second, the bishops' service involves explaining religious life to the church as a whole. It is striking that the pope says that this should be done "to all the people of God" and not specifically to the religious. It is the church that needs to come to a renewed understanding of religious life.

Third, the bishops are to invite the religious in the name of the church to use the opportunity to deepen the vitality of their Christian life "in solidarity with all the pastors and faithful, along that path necessary for us all--the way of penance and conversion."

Only fourth does the pope mention particular departures from the indispensable norms of religious life or even from the teaching of the church whether these are by individuals or by groups.

Let me say just a word about this fourth point before going on with my analysis of the letter. Over the past 17 years, American religious have been involved in an intensive period of experimentation. Their accomplishments have been impressive. Of course there have been problems, misunderstandings, difficulties and failures. These incidents have been simply inevitable. You are talking about 150,000 people, perhaps more. Where there is serious experimentation, there will also be failures; just as where there is life, there are problems. But they do not compare with the achievements.

The problems are not to be ignored--religious life is too important for that--but neither are they to be irresponsibly exaggerated. The pope goes out of his way twice to underline the spectacular contributions of religious to the church. The papal call to all religious is for the deepening of their life, not just the correction of isolated aberrations. Finally the pope brings up the drastic decline among the number of American religious and asks the commission of bishops to work with the religious to analyze the reasons for the decline in vocations.

There is nothing in any of this that indicates that something is pervasively wrong with religious life in the United States. There are five ways in which the bishops of the United States are to aid the religious, and only in one of them--the issue of the drastic numerical decline--does the pope call for a study of its causes.

Q. You mentioned the numerical decline of the religious in the United States. Is this a concern of the Holy Father?

A. There is no question that it is a paramount concern. In his letter to the bishops, this is the only issue that he singled out as such for serious analysis by the commission and religious. His letter gives a general call for renewal and for the pastoral care of those who have departed from what is essential in religious life.

When he deals with the numerical decline, his language becomes more personal and more urgent: "This decline in numbers is a matter of grave concern to me--a concern which I know that you and the religious also share. As a result of this decline, the median age of religious is rising and their ability to serve the needs of the church is becoming increasingly limited."

Similarly, in the document on the essential elements of religious life, the Congregation for Religious and for Secular Institutes lists as the first three problematic areas: "rising median age, fewer vocations, diminishing numbers." In my opinion, the pope, the bishops and the American religious have every reason to be concerned.

The numerical decline of religious in the United States which has already taken place and even the more drastic one which is projected in the years ahead forces the church to recognize that a situation of crisis exists. In the past 17 years, since Ecclesiae Sanctae, the number of religious brothers has fallen to a little over 60 per cent of what it was. The number of religious sisters has decreased from 181,421 to 121,370, about two-thirds of what it was in 1966. While the number of religious priests has remained about the same, the loss in their membership is registered in the significantly fewer men who have entered their novitiates or who are in the long process of preparation for ordination.

There are smaller religious communities which are threatened with disappearance if these trends continue, and even among the very large religious orders there is often found a great uncertainty about the future of their form of life and apostolic commitments.

Religious men and women have carried a great deal of the burden for ministry within the church in the United States. It would be impossible for the church to see this life continue to diminish numerically without giving this diminishment very serious study. It is imperative for all of us in the church in the United States to do what can be done to foster and strengthen religious life during this decade.

Q. Archbishop, granted this analysis of numerical decline mandated by the Holy Father, what are the general questions that will fall within it?

A. Serious questions are inevitably raised by this phenomenon of numerical decline among American religious.

First, no reflection upon it can be done except against the background of contemporary changes in the American society, in American religious consciousness and in the Catholic Church itself. Let me give you an example of each of these questions: Are we dealing with a diminishment that is part of the cultural shifts in American society in general and in American religious sensitivity in particular? What does it say about the church in the United States that such a life is no longer attractive to so many as before? How significantly have attitudes toward the church itself altered in 17 years? These, I would say, are "background questions" of critical importance.

Second, then, there are those that touch upon religious life more immediately. For example, what does it say about religious life and its witness that it does not possess the same drawing power within the lives of so many young people? Why is it, for instance, that so many young men and women are dedicating themselves to some form of Christian ministry, something for which years of theology are required, and at the same time fewer are interested in living out a religious life according to the evangelical counsels? To consider carefully the essential notes of religious life and how they can and should be embodied in the contemporary American church could result in a better understanding of the current phenomenon and produce a much more effective long-term response to it than either ignoring the issue or accepting it with a debilitating loss of hope or mounting a well-intentioned but mistaken reaction. This study will involve this kind of consideration.

Still further, it must also be peacefully but frankly asked whether those of us who hold roles of authority in the church are of sufficient sensitivity to the issues which contextualize religious life in the United States. We have to ask ourselves whether we are aware of the pressures and questions with which religious must live, aware enough so that we can meet our obligations to promote this life and support it with the kind of encouragement which our culture and the pope demand.

Finally, how significant is this numerical decline, how should it be evaluated in terms of the future apostolic commitments of the church?

All of these questions enter into the more general topic of the numerical decline among American religious and the consequent mandate of the Holy Father.

Q. Why, then, has the Congregation for Religious and for Secular Institutes sent this document on the guidelines of religious life?

A. That is fairly common and useful procedure in any work such as this. It simply summarizes past documentation on the nature of religious life and makes it available to the religious and the bishop and the church in general. The letter from the Holy Father directs the bishops to "proclaiming anew to all the people of God the Church's teaching on consecrated life." I don't think it would be unfair to say that many bishops do not feel expert on religious life nor well read in all of the documentation that supports religious life today. I suspect that many religious might find themselves in a similar situation.

As Sister Sharon Holland recently wrote: "It is difficult for a diocesan bishop to become familiar with the charism, spirit and characteristic works of 10 or 20 religious congregations in the diocese. Similarly, it is difficult for a major superior to become familiar with the pastoral plans of the 10 or 20 dioceses in which the religious are serving."

This paper from the Congregation for Religious and Secular Institutes makes the central documents of the church on religious life available in a manner in which they have not been available before. This is helpful because many aspects of religious life will come up, not only when bishops interpret religious life to the Catholics in their diocese, but also when they and the religious explore the causes for the numerical decline in religious life.

Finally such a document is very helpful if the bishops are to encourage religious and call them to continual growth in holiness.

Q. How rigid or inflexible are these norms presented by the Congregation for Religious?

A. It is important to note from the outset that these norms do contain the essential elements for religious life. They are neither framed nor understood in an inflexible manner. Religious life has had and continues to have vastly different expressions. Further, any kind of realization of an abstract set of norms will always be analogous, that is, realized by each religious community in its own way. The pope stresses this in his letter, especially in terms of the American situation. "The essential elements are lived in different ways from one institute to another. You yourselves deal with this rich variety in the context of the American reality."

Q. Archbishop, your appointment comes at a time of some concern about the handling of the mandate to Agnes Mansour. Is there any conection? Did this issue prompt this further response from Rome?

A. To take your last question first, the answer is no. The papal appeal to the bishops of the United States has been many months, perhaps years, in the offing. Nor is there any connection between the directive given to Agnes Mansour and the setting up of this commission. Further, this commission has nothing to do with any individual disciplinary decision by religious superiors or by the Holy See. I really insist upon this separation because the appointment of this commission could be read as a further response to one or another individual problem in the United States. It is not nor will it be!

Another way of answering this question in a more general form would be to see what the pope is not asking for. Despite the fearful anticipations of some and the requests of others, the pope is not calling for an investigation of religious life in the United States. The Holy Father is not even calling for a prolonged and elaborate study of religious life, comparable with the study of the American seminaries presently underway. Rather there is a profound call to the bishops to encourage and strengthen religious life in its own authentic renewal. A concrete theme that the bishops and religious are asked to study is the numerical decline of religious.

Q. Why is the pope the one to issue this call for religious renewal?

A. The central ministry of the pope is to call the entire church to holiness, to become a community which embodies the Spirit of Christ. What is asked for in this Holy Year is a common effort by both the bishops and the religious of the United States. The Christian responsibility of the pope is precisely to call for this kind of unity from various sections of the church, especially in an issue that is of concern not simply to religious, but to the whole church.

Pontifical institutes enjoy exemption from local episcopal government in their internal life and the bishop of one diocese is independent of the directives of another bishop, yet all of us are most closely bound to the Holy Father. It is his ministry to summon us beyond our immediate, even parochial interests, to that which is the critical focus of the whole church—and nothing is more critical than the grace which should be witnessed in our lives. There is no one else in the church who could call upon the bishops to offer to religious the "encouragement and the support of our pastoral love."

And as I have said before, when you consider both the national and international influence of American religious—in the example of their inculturation of religious essentials within American society, in their education of religious from other countries and in their apostolic presence all over the world, the Holy Father's concern for the entire church would very naturally include them in a special way.

Q. Why did the pope write directly to the bishops "to render special pastoral service to the religious of your diocese and your country?"

A. Because it is the function of the bishops collectively, in collaboration with the Holy Father, to represent the church's concern that religious life should flourish. The concern about the quality of religious life and the numerical strength of religious is not just of interest to religious; it is one that the entire church shares. The normal way of communicating and dealing with an issue in a country is through the bishops.

There is a second reason: In this matter, the bishop in each diocese is to serve as a principle of unity. The bishop is to bring members of different orders to consider religious life in the United States today. The bishop is the only one

20

in a particular diocese who has this kind of authority or presence.

The pope has referred this general concern to the national hierarchy in his letter to the bishops and he has also established a commission of bishops. He has appointed me as pontifical delegate to head this commission. The pope has directed this commission to enter into serious consultation with American religious, and I have established a committee of leaders of religious communities for this purpose. In addition, there will be two religious who will act as consultants.

Q. How can your commission and the bishops be of aid to religious?

A. I think that we have touched on a good deal of this already. We are dealing with a matter of enormous concern to those who have dedicated themselves to the following of Christ in this way. To encourage this life, to support its authenticity, to explain it to the church as a whole, and to analyze its numerical decline--these are all significant attempts of the bishops to put themselves at the service of religious life, to support the religious in the renewal which they have long since begun.

To add something to this, however: The purpose of the present action of the pope is to enable American religious to surface and to reflect on the various ways in which they have developed since Vatican II. It will enable them to review their experiences and structural changes in the light of the teaching of the church on religious life and in the light of the religious witness they are giving in the American context. Since this will be conducted within the context of each local church, religious will have a concrete situation in which to evaluate their experience of the past 20 years in terms of the items I have mentioned: the American religious experience, the reality of the local church and the teaching of the church on religious life.

There is one major advantage in this: Through this collective contact with their bishops, religious will have the opportunity to present their findings in a totally American context. The Holy Father is anxious for this communication, and it would provide a foundation for a more fruitful dialogue in the future.

Q. What kind of commission will you chair as pontifical delegate?

A. The pope has not tried to handle at a distance this pastoral concern which involves the church in the United States. He has appointed a pontifical delegate, myself, from the American hierarchy and two other American bishops to form a commission of bishops. The Holy Father has directed that this commission work in serious collaboration and consultation with American religious, and I, as pontifical delegate, have appointed a committee of outstanding religious leaders from various religious communities for this purpose. This joint group will meet this week to begin its task.

I have further appointed two American religious to serve this group as consultants. The two American bishops appointed by the Holy Father are Archbishop Thomas C. Kelly, OP, of Louisville, and Bishop Raymond Lessard of Savannah. The religious are Sister Alexa Suelzer, SP, Father Alan McCoy, OFM, Sister Clare Fitzgerald, SSND, Brother Thomas More Page, CFX, and Sister Bette Moslander, CSJ. The consultants will be Sister Sharon Holland, IHM and Father Michael J. Buckley, S.J.

Q. What will be the procedures of this commission? How will it work?

A. This Saturday, June 25, 1983, the joint commission will meet to address this very question. Our initial meeting will have two tasks: first, to achieve a common understanding of the mandate of the Holy Father; second, to begin to set up procedures or a process for carrying out this mandate. Obviously, this second task will only begin with this meeting.

I have written to the presidents of the Leadership Conference of Women Religious, the Conference of Major Superiors of Men, and the National Conference of Catholic Bishops to ask for their suggestions how we should accomplish the job the pope has given us. As pontifical delegate, I will also be in contact with the proper offices of the Holy See. In the meantime, I can assure you, it is the subject of a great deal of prayer.

2

Extending the Dialogue About Religious Life

(Address to the Leadership Conference of Women
Religious Assembly, August 16, 1983)

You have honored me by asking that I speak with you. For
the church recognizes in your lives as religious the
continuation of the poverty, the chastity and the obedience of
Christ. What is more: In and through your leadership
thousands and thousands of your sisters are in this room with
us this morning, present through the care you have for the
consistency and holiness of their unique form of Christian
living and present because of their choice that you should
bear the profoundly sacred responsibility of leadership among
them.

It is no light burden that you carry. The future and the
integrity of American religious life lie greatly under the
influence of your own lives: Your own union with God, your
own humility and integrity, your courage and vision will tell
historically upon your communities. The mystery of your lives
is inextricably bound up with the mystery of the lives of the
sisters whom you love and whom you serve in this ministry. It
is finally one mystery: a form of life in which Christ is
followed with such intensity and at such a level of
renunciation that to follow becomes to imitate him concretely
and historically in his chastity, his poverty and his
obedience even to the death of the cross. The gravity and the
demands of this leadership of communities toward a life of
holiness would be hard to exaggerate. That is why you honor
me by asking me to speak with you about it.

I know that you have asked me to be with you today
because the pope has appointed me pontifical delegate to head
a special commission of three bishops whose task is to foster
the pastoral service bishops are to offer American religious.
In a lengthy interview that many of you have read, I have
already commented upon this appeal of the Holy Father to the
bishops and on the constitution of a joint group of bishops
and religious. Rather than repeat those remarks I should like
to extend them, but only in the context of the mystery of
religious life and the history of American religious over the
past 20 years.[1] You know that I am no expert in these
matters, but what I think I put before you as an invitation to

your own reflections. I hope that these remarks will amplify several important subjects touched upon in the interview.

My reflections, then, fall into four parts:

--The vision which the church possesses of your life.

--The paschal mystery as you have experienced it in the past 20 years.

--The papal appeal to the bishops of the United States.

--The papal charge to this episcopal commission with its committee of religious.

The Church's Vision of Your Life

I make no apologies for beginning with the call that the church recognizes as yours. It alone provides the context or the horizon in which any other aspect of religious life can be evaluated or discussed. It is not that religious alone are called to holiness. You know that all Christians are called to holiness. But religious are called to that holiness which consists in a total consecration to God expressed in the unique continuation and embodiment of his life of poverty, chastity and obedience: Not to copy it, but to imitate it--that is, to transpose it into the situation of the 20th century--so that this form of life would not die within the church, that it would be a continual reminder to the entire church in as public a witness as possible of the holiness to which every Christian is called.

Not every Christian is called to leave father and mother, husband and wife, children and relatives, to abandon personal property and private career, and to follow Christ in the direction of one's life as that voice is concretized in the church and in this given community of disciples. But every Christian is called to that detachment and love which give an absolute priority to Christ as the communication of God, and the public vows of religious are a constant sacramental reminder of this absolute claim that Christ makes upon us all. Religious life is essentially sacramental in the sense that it is an explicit, historical and tangible manifestation of the victorious grace of God emerging to its completion in human signs and actions. And we can never really understand it except as sacramental.

24

It is classically true that every human being has to struggle for her integrity, not simply in the sense that a commitment to the truth is always costly, but in the more basic sense of keeping some consistency, some focus in her life that gives unity to everything else, that makes sense out of diversity. What is true for the individual is also true of a religious community or a way of life. The demands upon your time, the conflicting claims for your attention, are infinite and sometimes irreconcilable. Not that any one of them is illegitimate, but that all of them together constitute an impossibility.

The expectations in which a religious community lives can be multiple, endless and even mutually contradictory. One can feel surrounded and fragmented by their press, wondering at the end of a busy day what was actually accomplished, seemingly more reacting to incessant demands than peacefully moving through them with a cumulative sense of purpose, even beginning to wonder in her darker moments if this way of living has any value or has kept its meaning. A religious or even an entire community can feel eroded, burnt out, because one cannot meet all the demands, and what slips away almost imperceptibly is the vision that makes sense even of the frustration.

It is simply imperative for a religious—as for any human being with a serious Christian vocation—to have a fundamental focus for her way of life, one that is not negotiable, one in terms of which everything else is negotiated. So the church over and over again reminds religious what they are for the whole church, the vision and the call that is theirs: You are those consecrated by the call of God to follow Christ in the mystery of the church by continuing his chastity, his poverty and his obedience for the sake of the kingdom of God. It is an enormous gift that is yours, and it is a gift for the whole church.

The Past 20 Years

Sisters, I know that these have been hard and demanding years since the Vatican Council. The opportunities have been glorious and the achievement of your communities have been obvious and remarkable—but at what an enormous cost! Let me speak a bit about the history of the past 20 years.

One of the staggering parts of this cost over these years has been the numerical diminishment of the congregations of American sisters. Following the directions of the council and

25

in obedience to subsequent papal documents such as Ecclesiae Sanctae, enormous efforts were brought to bear in a sincere and seriously considered move to renew and adapt religious life in light of worldwide cultural transformation and in the spirit of the church. Yet this tremendous enterprise was followed by striking numerical disintegration.

Where novitiate classes had been 30, now there were three--if any at all. Convents and institutions were closing all over the nation. The average age of the sisters was going up steadily. Some of the elderly began to fear that there would be no one around to take care of them, while tens of thousands were either leaving or had already left for possibilities and for a future which seemed to them more secure and more promising. You and many other religious may have lived with a sinking sense of loss as close friends with whom you shared this form of life left.

At the same time American sisters were exposed to an unprecedented level of misrepresentation and attack from both the right and the left. Sisters who had for so long lived as the object of an almost uncritical awe within the church now were exposed to two implacable critics: shrill accusations that their catechetics were destroying the church, that their every change was a betrayal of their heritage, that they had become worldly, compromised women who deserve their own decline. Or from the left came the arch suggestions that religious life could only attract the sexually stunted, the socially and economically insecure, an unenlightened and declining remnant from a dated church. There are the recent plays on Broadway that dismiss them as unsophisticated fanatics and some "Catholic" publications make a practice of continual harping criticism exaggerating every conflict out of all proportion. There are circles in which to be a woman religious today is to walk into an atmosphere of the joke half-told, of suspicion of unconscious arrogance sometimes on the part of clerics, of the question that waits for no answer, of the unrelenting and constant demand for justification.

As in every other group, priests or lay people, so among religious there are no doubt some who give foundation for justifiable criticism and concern. But Sister--you who are present here today and others who are not with us at this meeting--you have sustained the cost of these years and nothing you have accomplished, no matter how great and obvious, matches what you have accomplished in living in fidelity to your vocation through these difficult years of tensions from outside sources as well as from internal

26

divisions, misunderstandings and polarization. Indeed, many faithful American women religious, and not the least those in positions of responsibility, truly passed through a profound experience of the paschal mystery.

I suspect that this experience has yet to register in all its valence within the reflection of American religious. You will find any number of works that counsel religious to count their gifts and number the aptitudes they bring to the church. This is certainly sound advice. But there is very little written about the collective experience of entering into the rejection and humiliations and loss that configured many of you with the passion--and even less about how profound a fulfillment this experience is of the vocation that is yours, the public witness to the whole church of the life and destiny of Christ.

When Victor Frankl reflected upon the horror of his experience of Auschwitz and Dachau, he summarized his own survival with a single line from Nietzsche that those who have purpose and vision can bear with almost any manner of existence; "The person who has a why to live for, can bear with almost any how."[2] There is a clear and profound sense of identity in many American religious born of prayer, faith and a deep love for the church, which has enabled them to live through these years of deflated expectations and even searing personal disappointment. And that identity lies with their configuration to Christ. The great St. Mechtild of Madgeburg, speaking of a single person, wrote what has been the history of a number of religious congregations during these past 20 years:

"God leads his chosen children on extraordinary paths. This is an extraordinary path, a noble road and a sacred way. God himself has trod it."[3]

And so it is true that these years, difficult though they have been, have been rich in their accomplishments and productive as religious community after religious community, responding to the challenge of the council, moved into structures that were more life giving and into more mature forms of community. In many ways over these years American women religious found themselves coming of age, an experience of resurrection. Many American women religious have deepened their lives of prayer, their social compassion for suffering and exploitation, their sense of the international mission of the church. Granted that all this is true, still the question must be asked: What is the source of this new depth if it is not both the church from which the challenge came and what American women religious have endured and suffered during these 20 years?

Our experience of the resurrection emerges from the experience of the passion. The life of authentic Christians has always combined them: "that I might know Christ and the power of his resurrection and may share his sufferings, becoming like him in his death, that if possible I may attain the resurrection from the dead" (Phil. 3:10-11). That is why I believe it is excessive to see in the present as some do "the cluster of the signs of breakdown in virtually all communities." It is my conviction that we must keep clearly before our minds the great and moving words of Pope John XXIII at the opening of the council:

"In the daily exercise of our pastoral office we sometimes have to listen, must to our regret, to voices of persons who, though burning with zeal, are not endowed with too much sense of discretion or measure. In these modern times they can see nothing but prevarication and ruin. They say that our era, in comparison with past eras, is getting worse, and they behave as though they had learned nothing from history, which is, nonetheless, the teacher of life. They behave as though at the time of former councils everything was a full triumph for the Christian idea and life and for proper religious liberty.

"We feel we must disagree with those prophets of gloom, who are always forecasting disaster, as though the end of the world were at hand.

"In the present order of things, divine providence is leading us to a new order of human relations which, by humanity's own efforts and even beyond their very expectations, are directed toward the fulfillment of God's superior and inscrutable designs. And everything, even human differences, leads to the greater good of the church."[4]

Certainly, then, the "numerous defections and decreasing number of new members" cannot be denied.[5] But if you understand religious life as this profound imitation of Christ and share the marvelous vision of faith articulated by Pope John, then rejection or abandonment or crisis or pain or threat is not just a breakdown, but also for those who live by faith a more profound entering into the meaning and identity of religious life. Juliana of Norwich put it very simply: "So was our Lord Jesus afflicted for us; and we all stand in this way of suffering with him and shall till we come to his bliss."[6]

This is really the second point I want to make. If religious life is a persistent and public reminder to the church of the life of Christ then the drastic numerical decline and threatened extinction of some religious communities is not something completely outside of that witness, but within it. Yes, "history is the teacher of life." Each time religious life has entered into this night that can be so dark--the Reformation and the French Revolution come to mind--it has risen from suppression, persecution and virtual extinction with a deeper ecclesial sense and stronger and more effective than before.

For example, when Mother St. John emerged from the prison of St. Didier in 1794, she rebuilt with new resilience from the Terror of the French Revolution the Sisters of St. Joseph. But does anyone think that her years of suffering in prison had nothing to do with forming this "strong-souled woman to whom the community owed its regeneration?"

Mary Ward, foundress of the Institute of Mary, endured the condemnation of her community and even imprisonment in Munich, but her religious genius and her deep faith finally prevailed and continues to influence the formation of communities even through our time.

In her last letter to Antonio Filicchi, the dying Elizabeth Ann Seton wrote: "Could you but know what has happened in consequence of the little, dirty grain of mustard seed you planted by God's hand in America!"[7] For the seed to grow, it had to pass into the death that was the end of her marriage, the violence which followed her conversion, the endless and seemingly hopeless contradictions, the betrayal of friends, the death of those very dear to her and the shameless indifference of her son William.

All of these lived by faith and had an unshakable fidelity to the church. In their story each religious community could trace a similar history from its own tradition. You and I both know that the religious accomplishments of the two previous centuries developed from beginnings that were desperate in their poverty or persecution, ridden with the forebodings of some, but fostered by a few religious women of profound courage, integrity and endurance. The successes were not in spite of the suffering any more than we are saved in spite of the cross. In the mysterious working of providence, one actually leads into the other.

This, then, is my key to understanding much that religious have undergone over these years of renewal. Constitutions, chapters, serious analysis, arduous discernment, regrouping of forces, creative efforts at experiment--all of these had done what they could. But that they would have their effect, God gifted them with the cross, brought them into communion with the passion of the Lord.

I am obviously not saying that the past 20 years have been absolved from mistakes and errors. That would be to parody my remarks. It would be sheer fantasy to imagine that in times so complex such far-reaching efforts at renewal of such magnitude could go forward without some mistakes and perhaps some of serious proportions here and there.

But what I am saying is that through it all you have sought to be faithful to the call of the Lord and you want to love him and service him in his church for the glory of the Father. It is in the paschal mystery, in fidelity in the face of suffering, that all human efforts are purified and all human faults and failings are healed and all things that are ours are gathered by their resurrection into God. The renewal of all religious realities is only through the passion.

This is how I see the mystery of your religious life, and it is the light in which I read the past 20 years. It provides the religious context in which I see the task to which the Holy Father has called the American bishops: "To render special pastoral service to the religious of your dioceses and your country . . . to assist them in every way possible to open wide the doors of their heart to the Redeemer."

The Papal Appeal to the U.S. Bishops

So now let me pass to the papal response both to what you are and what you have undergone.

To understand the action of the Holy Father, we must attend to an event which has been given great significance in Rome but not yet grasped sufficiently everywhere: the anniversary of our redemption. In the mystic symbolisms and approximations by which we number the centuries, 1,950 years ago the great paschal mystery of Christ took place, the passion, death and resurrection of Jesus by which the world is justified, sanctified and saved. To underline this moment as we move toward the third millenium, the pope proclaimed the extraordinary Holy Year, the jubilee of our redemption. This action of the pope was profoundly and religiously serious. Christ as redeemer has been a theme of his preaching and his pontificate, and it formed the subject of his first encyclical. Through this year jubilee he is calling the whole church to live more intensely the central human-divine event which gives it meaning. It would be impossible to understand many papal initiatives this year unless the centrality and urgency of the redemption is grasped.

It is within that context that he calls religious especially to renewal. Not just religious. The call is to the whole church. But especially religious. And why? Because of this event, the redemption of the entire human race by the action of God in Jesus Christ, they are both witness and intermediary. They are both signs to the world of what Jesus Christ has done in human life--as they continue in a following of him that becomes a profound configuration--and they are means, instruments, by which this redemption of Christ reaches into this Holy Year and into this nation. What the pope is saying is simply staggering in its implications: that the redemption which Christ offers will have its presence in our times and its efficacy determined in great part by the quality of holiness, of union with God, in the lives of religious. The religious either augments or limits the effective mercy of God within her culture.

This is not an abstract statement of speculative theology; it is a concrete reading of what religious have become for the church. Look at your own personal histories. For many persons whose religious gifts developed at an early age, the most influential persons in their lives were those women religious whose insightful goodness and care touched their lives more formatively than either was aware of. Look at contemporary Catholic challenges to the social structures of our nation, or at the repeated efforts to reform catechetics, or at the person who is often among the most resourceful in parish ministry or at the person from whom people spontaneously expect a quality of sympathy and understanding unavailable elsewhere--and you will very often find the American sister.

In general the history of our church in the United States shows religious women to have lived lives of frugality and prayer, of persistent service to others even at enormous personal cost and of providing support for those who needed that support—whether this was in education, in medical care or in social works. To cite the papal letter, "Working toward the establishment of justice, love and peace, they helped to build a social order rooted in the Gospel, striving to bring generation after generation to the maturity of Christ." To read our history is to find the American nun at its center,both as a sign and as the channel of the redemption.

The contemporary reflection upon religious life is just beginning to assimilate what has been the actual place of religious in the church for centuries, certainly the church in the United States. It has been a theological commonplace to say of the bishop or of the priest who assists him *agit in pesona ecclesiae*, that he acts in the name of the church, that he represents the church. Now increasingly this is being said of the religious, that the religious represents the church. But this is just theology catching up with what the average American Catholic has always known.

The bishop represents the church in its unity, its unity of doctrine, of communion and of sacramental life. To see the bishop is to be reminded of this unity whose source is the Spirit of God and which is made real by communion with the successor of Peter. But the religious represents the church in its evangelical holiness. The church is not only realized in their lives, but witnessed by these lives. What Teresa of Avila said of herself, "I die a daughter of the church," was extended by the great Elizabeth Seton to her daughters in almost her last words to them: "I am thankful, Sisters, for your kindness to be present in this trial. Be children of the church, be children of the church."[9]

It is not that Teresa of Avila or the Sisters of Charity are the only daughters of the church. All religious by the public witness of their lives are a reminder of that ecclesial discipleship to which we are all called. The religious is not the only one who represents in public witness the holiness of the church, but she is the one who does in this unique way—through the open, countercultural profession of the evangelical poverty, chastity and humble obedience of Christ. When the church talks about the public witness of religious life, this is what she is talking about: not that presentation or witness proper to the church in its hierarchy, but the visible manifestation of the church in its holiness. Just as the unity of the church is not simply for the bishops but for all the disciples of Christ, so the holiness of the church is not just for religious but for all the disciples of Christ. But it is crucial for the church that both its unity

32

and its holiness be strongly represented to all, and that is why we have both a hierarchy and religious life. Another way of putting the same point is the papal statement:

"By their very vocation, religious are intimately linked to the redemption. By their consecration to Jesus Christ, they are a sign of the redemption that he accomplished. In the sacramental economy of the church, they are instruments for bringing this redemption to the people of God."

What, then, has the pope asked of the bishops? He has called upon all the bishops of the United States to place themselves at the pastoral service of the religious of their diocese. Let me be more specific. You know, far better than I, that since **Perfectae Caritatis** and **Ecclesiae Sanctae**, the religious in the United States have engaged in an intensive period of renewal. General chapters have been held which took this as their principal object. Constitutions have been revised, and these general laws of religious institutes submitted to the Holy See for confirmation. National unions of the major superiors of men and women have been formed or have been strengthened and now flourish. New forms of religious and academic formation and of ministerial training have been introduced into almost every apostolic religious congregation.

These changes have exacted great expenditures of energy and time and have found their fulfillment many times in a deepening of prayer, apostolic creativity and the sharing of life that characterizes religious communities. The question that religious have had to deal with, the central one according to the distinguished Jesuit theologian, Father Thomas E. Clarke, S.J., has been this issue:

"How are we to disengage Christian faith from the time-bound cultural expressions and vehicles of the past without a loss of integrity? This is indeed the question at the heart of the anguish, tensions and polarizations characteristic of a period which has turned out to be as much a new passion as a new Pentecost. No group in the church has had to deal with the question with greater seriousness than members of religious communities and particularly of American communities of religious women."[10]

Father Clarke wrote those lines some 10 years ago, and without attempting a defense or an evaluation of each one of them, I think it would be fair to say that these last 10 years have continued this experience: the effort to articulate a form of life that is evangelical in its public ecclesial consecration yet American in the inculturation of this consecration. As this period of "special experimentation" comes to its close--the period, that is, in which new constitutions were drafted, the Holy Father has asked th American bishops to enter into this process in order to support and to second the genuinely heroic efforts of the religious to strengthen and renew their communities.

How are the bishops to do this? The pope speaks generically of aiding religious in every way possible and lists seven particular ways in which this generic support can be realized. If I had to summarize all seven, I would do it with a single word: communication.

The bishops are to communicate to the whole church by preaching and catechesis on the nature of religious life and, more particularly, on the link between a religious vocation and the love of God for each and every religious. The bishops are to communicate sacramentally and liturgically with religious; they are to extend and support the invitations to renewal in solidarity with the bishops and the faithful; "in those cases too where individuals or groups, for whatever reason, have departed from the indispensable norms of religious lie or have even, to the scandal of the faithful, adopted positions at variance with the church's teaching," they are "to proclaim once again the church's universal call to conversion, spiritual renewal and holiness."

The bishops are to communicate with religious in a mutual program of work to be established by the episcopal commission of which have been appointed papal delegate and which has been strengthened by an appointment of a committee of religious to act in concert with them. Finally, the bishops are to communicate their findings to the Holy Father on the occasion of their ad limina visits this year.

It is only in this context that we can ask ourselves the genuinely hard questions which bear upon the future of religious life in the United States. One question which the pope singles out as of immense concern: Why this drastic numerical decline? And under this question, perhaps the most important issue: Why are so very few American women and men interested in becoming religious today? What does that say about our national character, about our church and about religious life itself? Is there any truth in the diagnosis of religious life made by the authors of Shaping the Coming Age of Religious Life that the "crises set in from within religious life due to the loss of identity and the inroads of the secularizing process."[11] Finally, it must be asked whether we bishops and priests have been of sufficient sensitivity to the issues which contextualize religious life in the United States.

All of these and other important issues can be addressed fruitfully if they are asked by bishops and religious together and asked in such peace and mutual trust that they admit of answers rather than with the kind of accusatory rage that inhibits any ability to answer anything. These are profound issues on which we must communicate. They touch on a problem that is common to us all yet larger than any of us, and we expect to be mutually challenged by them. For it is not only the problem that is common to us all, but the process as well. It is one that we can only address together.

Why this insistence upon communication? Because there has been too little of it. Historically, any process of renewal and any process of inculturation have been open to misrepresentation, misunderstandings and mistakes. I could take examples from the history of dogma, from the history of rites and ritual, but let me take them from the history of religious life itself. For decades the mendicant orders lay under the suspicion that their form of life was not canonically religious because they were not confined to a monastery. The foundation of the Society of Jesus was opposed because this order did not engage in the choral office and admitted some members whose vows were not solemn. There was enormous opposition to the original provisions of Angela Merici despite the solemn approval of Paul III and these provisions eventually gave way to conventual life and monastic enclosure. The original plans of St. Francis de Sales and St. Jane Frances de Chantal that the Visitation would be a congregation in which only simple vows would be pronounced and visiting the sick would be the special work of its members also yielded to solemn vows and enclosure. But eventually the inculturation of active orders of women religious did occur, and they dominated the extraordinary evolution of religious life in the 19th and 20th centuries.

Inculturation is an exigency of the incarnation. It is an indispensable condition for the development and vitality of the church, and it is inevitably attended by its share of divisions and struggles and even by mistakes.[12] But if these inevitable struggles are exacerbated by arrogance or impatience, by the attribution of false motivation or by party interests, then disintegration or alienation results.

Attempts at inculturation die only when communication is stilled, and that is why I welcome the efforts of the Holy Father to foster communication in all of its forms.

For over the past 20 years as you moved through this period of experimentation, your partners in dialogue have been the members of your own congregation and other congregations. Now what the Holy See is asking for is an extension of this dialogue to a larger group, to the bishops and to the church as a whole. For there is much incomprehension here, either about what the religious have accomplished or why they have gone in the directions they have chosen, as well as some confusion about what the church has been asking of relgious since the council. Through the bishops, the religious orders can engage all of the church in this renewal of religious life: those whom they serve, those with whom they serve, and the bishops in union with the pope whose ministry it is to confirm and validate this service.

There is no question that inculturation carries its own dangers. For instance, the adoption of Stoic and neo-Platonic terminology during the patristic period, terms with such far-reaching implications and ambiguity as apatheia as used by Clement and Origen, or the eons, nous and the five fundamental gnoses of Evagrius Ponticus, all these seriously endangered the entire monastic movement.[13] I doubt further if anyone would care to resurrect the secular military activity of the Templars as an appropriate work for religious. So also today. There is always a danger of having religious life become co-opted as just another version of the American way of life, and the challenge given both by the traditions of the order and by the judgments of the Holy See are necessary and critically important if religious are to embody the essentials of religious life in an American setting effectively and authentically.

This question has been with us since John Carroll, and it is not surprising that it continues to be with us now. It is inevitable in a church so universal and with cultures and perspectives that are so divergent. That is why this extension of the dialogue is so critical, both to explain the achievements of the past 20 years, but also to receive serious, supportive and critical challenge.

For there is a healthy and continual dialectic which is always at work within the church: between the Gospel and its cultural expression, between authority and prophecy, between the unity of the church and its manifold cultural forms. And the life of the church can never be won by suppressing one or another of these moments or by an impatient destruction of the very process. All organic forms of life consist in a sustained balance between various and seemingly contradictory elements. Yet if they are seen by faith and in their historic interactions, they do not contradict one another but at a deeper level support one another. Thus Freud maintains that the desire to live without tensions--the desire to live in unchallenged comfort--is actually a disguised form of the death wish. The tension of balanced contradictions is essential to life.

But tension does not necessarily make for life. It can also be a destructive disintegration of life. The difference lies with living faith and with communication. Does this moment of tension open to a deeper communication or to the closing of all communications?

The Papal charge to the Commission

And this brings me to the fourth point I wish to register: for this is the reason that the Holy Father has not only sent a letter to the American bishops, but has established an episcopal commission to aid the bishops in their service of religious and to analyze the reason for the decline in religious vocations. For each of these tasks the Holy Father has challenged the commission to work in close collaboration with American religious, to profit from their experience and to assimilate their insights. To facilitate this communication I have appointed a committee of religious who will work with the commission of bishops in a collaborative effort to foster and to encourage religious life in any way that is open for us.

We will also be consulting experts in various disciplines not represented on our committee such as psychology, sociology, anthropology and history. Further, I have sent a letter to the presidents of the Leadership Conference of Women Religious, Conference of Major Superiors of Men and the National Conference of Catholic Bishops asking for any suggestions these groups might have to further this work. All of us have something to learn from one another, and the papal initiative provides an occasion for this mutual ministry.

It would be unrealistic to expect of this renewed effort at communication that all disagreements would cease and all misunderstandings be erased. There are too many differences in cultural background, in religious-life history and even in the critical perspectives on contemporary issues. However, what we can achieve and what we must be seeking is reverence and respect for one another, a compassion for mutual suffering, the building of a sense of trust and the comprehension of an underlying common mission in the church and from the church as portrayed in all its doctrinal richness in Lumen Gentium.

What we can pray for is that we may all find a continually greater degree of freedom from harsh judgments and stereotyping, irrespective of what misunderstandings remain to be eliminated. But how very difficult this will be, Sisters, to touch the skepticism and the anxiety, the suspicions and the misunderstandings that have woven themselves into the fabric of our histories over these years. Whatever their causes, they have become part of its texture and seem indistinguishable from our expectations and hopes. They inhibit communication and they inspire the most pejorative reading of motives, while the memories of past wrongs rise periodically to reinforce their presence.

But what is stronger, please God, is what we share together. For if members of the church cannot work together to reconcile our histories and our differences, how could we possibly preach forgiveness and reconciliation to a world whose checkered histories and whose differences beggar those in the church by comparison. It is patient and loving work that we are about to do together, but your president has wisely written: "Reconciliation is the patient and loving weaving of threads of tension into a peaceful background in which the Spirit is free to imprint the design."[14]

May this Spirit then be with us in our work. In hope for this new phase of our history we pray with the Psalmist:

"You will guide me with your counsel and afterward you will receive me into glory. Who have I in heaven but you? And there is nothing upon earth that I desire in comparison with you. My flesh and my heart may fail, but God is the strength of my heart and my portion forever" (Ps. 73:24-26).

And so, "To him whose power now at work in us can do more than we ask or imagine—to him be glory in the church and in Christ Jesus through all generations forever and ever. Amen" (Eph. 3:20-21).

NOTES

1. For the understanding of religious life which pervades this address, cf. the recent document of the Sacred Congregation for Religious and Secular Institutes, "Essential Elements in the Church's Teaching on Religious Life as Applied to Institutes Dedicated to Works of the Apostolate," May 31, 1983. This document is itself a "clarification and restatement" of the church's teaching on the essential elements of religious life. This prior teaching has been articulated in the documents of the Second Vatican Council, especially Lumen Gentium, Perfectae Caritatis and Ad Gentes, in the apostolic exhortation Evangelica Testificatio of Pope Paul VI, in the addresses of Pope John Paul II and in the documents of the Sacred Congregation for Religious and Secular Institutes, especially, Mutuae Relationes, "Religious and human promotion" and "The Contemplative Dimensions of Religious Life" and in the new Code of Canon Law. "Essential Elements" is the latest attempt of the Holy See to fulfill the mandate enunciated by Lumen Gentium: "Church authority has the duty, under the Holy spirit, of interpreting these evangelical counsels, of regulating their practice and finally of establishing stable forms of living according to them" (42).

2. Victor E. Frankl, Man's Search for Meaning, translated by Ilse Lasch (New York: Simon and Schuster, 1962) xi, 76 and 104.

3. Cf. H.A. Reinhold (ed.), The Soul Afire: Revelation of the Mystics (New York: Pantheon Books, Inc., 1951) 206.

4. Walter Abbot, S.J., and J. Gallagher, The Documents of Vatican II. An Angelus Book. (Guild Press, 1966) 712-713.

5. Lawrence Cada, S.M., et al., Shaping the Coming Age of Religious Life. A Crossroad Book. (New York: The Seabury Press, 1979) 49 and 43.

6. Juliana of Norwich, Showings, Translated from the critical text with an introduction by Edmund Colledge, O.S.A., and James Walsh, S.J., The Classics of Western Spirituality. (New York: Paulist Press, 1978) Chap. 18, p. 211.

7. Joseph I. Dirvin, C.M., Mrs Seton: Foundress of the American Sisters of Charity (New York: Farrar, Straus and Cudahy, 1962) 448.

8. Gerard Manley Hopkins, S.J., "The Wreck of the Deutschland," no. 24, The poems of Gerard Manley Hopkins, W.H. Gardner and N.H. MacKenzie, eds. 4th ed. (London: Oxford University Press, 1970) 59.

9. William Thomas Walsh, Saint Teresa of Avila (Milwaukee: Bruce Publishing Co., 1943), p. 579; Dirvin, op. cit. 453.

10. Thomas E. Clarke, S.J., New Pentecost or New Passion? The Direction of Religious Life Today (New York: Paulist Press, 1973) 1.

11. Cada, et al., op.cit. 43.

12. For the development of the church's teaching on inculturation, cf. Lumen Gentium, 13 and 17, Ad Gentes, 16-18, 22, 26, Gaudium et Spes, 53-58, Populorum Progressio, 65, and Evangelii Nuntiandi, passim.

13. Cf. Louis Bouyer, The Spirituality of the New Testament and the Fathers (New York: Desclee Co., 1960) 260-302, 369-394. Despite Father Bouyer's sympathetic treatment of Evagrius Ponticus, he finds hismself forced to conclude: "Whatever precise meaning his own mysticism may have had for Evagrius, it would be difficult to deny that his expressions introduced a lasting threat into the Christian mystical tradition: the fatal attraction of pure abstraction. A neglect of scripture, of dogma, in favor of a 'contemplation' that runs the risk of being no more than a state of psychological vacuity is not, as experience has abundantly shown, for minds nourished on the tradition which we can now call Evagrian, a merely chimerical danger" ibid. 393. For the division of monasticism into two camps, cf. ibid. 380.

14. Sister Helen Flaherty, S.C., "The Presidents Reflect--After Two Years"; in Women: Weavers of Peace, Leadership Conference of Women Religious, Conference Report, 1982-1983, p. 6.

3

Dialogue and the Bishop's Pastoral Service to
Religious

(A Report to the U.S. Bishops, November 15, 1984)

Last April, on the feast of the Lord's resurrection, the
Holy Father addressed a letter to each of us. In that letter
he enunciated a new and fundamental concept that gives meaning
to everything else in his letter and which explains the task
we are to accomplish:

> I now turn to you, the bishops of the United States,
> asking you during this Holy Year to render special
> pastoral service to the religious of your dioceses and
> your country.[1]

Before I deal with the meaning of this special pastoral
service, I would like to say something about our role as
bishops, which is the foundation of this service.

I

The Vatican Council and postconciliar documents of the
magisterium have elaborated in some detail the doctrine of
episcopal collegiality. And the Holy Father has emphasized
this concept of speaking to us. Christus Dominus puts it this
way: "By divine institution and by virtue of their apostolic
office, all of them (the bishops) are jointly responsible for
the church"[2]

And in his address to the bishops of the United States on
Sept.Sept. 19, the pope, speaking of this special pastoral
service, said:

> I am deeply grateful to our Lord Jesus Christ
> that this initiative . . . is seen for what it is, an
> application--an extremely important application--of
> the principle of collegiality, a principle so
> forcefully enunciated by the Second Vatican Council.
> In proposing this initiative to your pastoral zeal, my
> first intention has been to affirm collegial
> responsibility for the state of religious life, which

is intimately linked to the mystery of the church and to the mystery of the episcopate.

He then adds, "This pastoral endeavor is of such importance that it could be fulfilled only by a full collegial commitment on the part of the bishops of the United States."

This special pastoral service, then, is primarily a manifestation of episcopal collegiality: The successor of Peter, head of the episcopal college, is calling us, his brothers, to this service of religious, which is an aspect of our own office as bishops.

Speaking of the episcopal office, the council teaches:

> The Spirit dwells in the church and in the hearts of the faithful as in a temple. In them he prays and bears witness to the fact that they are adopted sons and daughters. The Spirit guides the church into the fullness of truth and gives her unity of fellowship and service. He furnishes and directs her with various gifts, both hierarchical and charismatic, and adorns her with the fruits of his grace.[3]

And because the charisms and gifts of the Spirit are not dispersed in some random manner, but in a certain ordered relationship, the council states:

> There is only one Spirit, who, according to his own richness and the needs of the ministries, distributes his different gifts for the welfare of the church. Among these gifts stands out the grace given to the apostles. To their authority, the Spirit himself subjected even those who were endowed with charisms.[4]

Thus, according to Catholic faith, while the apostolic office is indeed a gift or charism of the Spirit, it is not simply one among many co-equal charisms. It is for this reason that the document Mutuae Relationes affirms:

> Bishops, in union with the Roman pontiff, receive from Christ the head the duty of discerning gifts and competencies, of coordinating multiple energies and of guiding the entire people in living in the world as a sign and instrument of salvation. They, therefore, are also entrusted with the duty of caring for

religious charisms, all the more so because the very indivisibility of their pastoral ministry makes them responsible for perfecting the entire flock. In this way, by fostering religious life and protecting it in conformity with its own definite characteristics, bishops fulfill a real pastoral duty.[5]

Perfector totius gregis, the bishop by reason of his office, has pastoral responsibility for the religious in his diocese.

This deeper understanding of our role as bishops, however, raises certain questions for us and for religious. One of these is the relationship between our pastoral responsibility and the internal autonomy of religious. In this connection the document on the relationship between bishops and religious affirms, "Institutes then have an internal organization all their own which has its proper field of competency and a right to autonomy even though in the church this autonomy can never become independence."[6]

Likewise, Canon 586 of the new Code of Canon Law states: "A true autonomy of life, especially of governance, is recognized for each institute . . . Local ordinaries have the responsibility of preserving and safeguarding this autonomy."

I think it is true to say that in the past at least we have judged that because most institutes were of pontifical right that they were the exclusive concern of the Holy See. There was good will, but a large measure of distancing from religious communities in the belief that religious communities were not part of our responsibility. Because of this, both religious and bishops came to assume that there were only two possible relationships: either control by the bishop or detached good will.

It is precisely the adequacy of this dichotomy which the mandate of the Holy Father has called into question. Autonomy or control do not exhaust the possible relationships between religious and the local bishop. There is a third possibility which the pope sees inherent in our episcopal office—beyond control, beyond detachment—it is called "special pastoral service."

And so nowhere in his letter or in the document "Essential Elements" is the canonical autonomy of religious denied or mitigated. Bishops are not constituted major superiors of the religious congregations in their dioceses.

43

In fact "Essential Elements" deals at some length with the ex officio religious authority in religious institutes and conferred on them by the church. The pope is not abrogating this authority, and he insists that he is only calling the bishops to something which is "in the precise area of episcopal competence."[7]

Because all of this touches on the fundamental issue of ecclesiology, it seems to me appropriate here to say something about what are called "differing ecclesiologies." I think we all recognize that from the New Testament through the Fathers and the ensuing history of theology there has been a variety of legitimate ecclesiologies. Lumen Gentium itself, especially in Chapter I, witnesses to this variety. At the same time it is important to recognize with equal clarity that all authentically Catholic ecclesiologies are rooted in and are expressions of a single more basic reality—the living church—which is both Trinitarian and incarnational and whose objective reality always involves the compenetration of the visible and the invisible, the human and the divine, the charismatic and the hierarchical.

This legitimate variety becomes defective, however, when the institutional component of the church is considered separable from the spiritual or when the apostolic-hierarchical element is considered separable from the charismatic. One can sin against the integrity of the ecclesial mystery by affirming the hierarchical and rejecting the charismatic or, equally, by affirming the charismatic and rejecting the hierarchical-apostolic office in the church. When in the Creed we profess our faith in one, holy, catholic and apostolic church, we declare our belief in the total reality of the church at once charismatic and hierarchical.

We may indeed speak of various models of the church. But in the final analysis, models are an intellectual construct articulating in limited human terms an objective ecclesial reality, apostolic in structure and doctrine, charismatic and spiritual, which lives and moves through history and which in all models, is gathered into a single incarnate mystery by the Holy Spirit.

Thus, by reason of the apostolic structure of the church, bishops have a responsibility for religious life in their churches. As a matter of fact, every religious institute comes into existence through the action of the charismatic and hierarchical factors in the church. The Holy Spirit gives a certain gift to a foundress or founder and only through canonical recognition of that gift does the religious institute as such come into being in the church. On the other hand, it is this very canonical recognition which guarantees the continuing integrity of the charism of each religious institute, including its "true autonomy of life, especially of governance.

II

In light of this, just what does this special pastoral service mean? Just what is the Holy Father asking of us?

In his letter to us, the Holy Father lists six ways we are to carry out this pastoral service:

1. Through the preaching of the Gospel and the celebration of the eucharist with them, the bishop is to give a special invitation to religious to walk arm in arm with him "in living fully the mystery of the redemption in union with the whole church and according to the special charism of their religious life."

2. Catechesis to the entire church on the church's teaching on consecrated life.

3. Special invitation to religious to share with the pastors and the faithful in the holy year of redemption through the path of conversion and penance.

4. Fraternal admonition of individuals or groups who for whatever reason have departed from the indispensable norms of religious life or who have adopted positions at variance with the church's teaching.

5. Appointment of the pontifical delegate and the commission of bishops and the committee of religious.

6. Analysis of the reasons for "the marked decline in the numbers of young people seeking to enter religious life."

In his address, which he directed to all the bishops of the United States, on Sept. 19, the pope further elaborated what he is asking of us by this special pastoral service. I will not here repeat the content of that important address, but I would note that the Holy Father describes our task in words such as: call, dialogue, explain, proclaim, remind, help speak to religious, emphasize the feminine role of women religious, manifest our love to the religious, confirm them in

45

their charism, encourage the religious.

In short, our pastoral service is cast in terms of a dialogue of salvation. This is a service which is eminently positive as it is eminently pastoral. It cannot be accomplished without our willingness to devote an important amount of quality time to personal contacts with our religious. It cannot be fulfilled as the Holy Father envisions it merely by letters or even exclusively by massive gatherings of our religious for a one-time event.

For this reason, it cannot be accomplished in many larger dioceses in the space of a few months. It will take time. And it is to be accomplished in the context of prayer and faith. Thus in his letter the Holy Father urges us to celebrate the eucharist and to preach the word of God to our religious.

And so, what does dialogue mean? As you know, Paul VI conceived the whole life of the church in terms of dialogue. In his first encyclical letter, Ecclesiam Suam, he spoke of his desire "to impress upon the internal relationships of the church the character of a dialogue between members of a body, whose constitutive principle is charity."[8]

Noting that this dialogue is not a denial of the apostolic-hierarchical element of the church nor a denial of the need for obedience in the church, he went on to say, "It is our ardent desire that this conversation . . . should be full of faith, of charity, of good works, should be intimate and familiar."[9]

Affirming that "dialogue is a method of accomplishing the apostolic mission . . . an example of the art of spiritual communication," Pope Paul outlined the characteristics of dialogue in the church:

1. Clearness: "to review every angle of our language to guarantee that it be understandable, acceptable and well-chosen."

2. Meekness: "The dialogue is not proud, it is not bitter, it is not offensive. Its authority is intrinsic to the truth it explains, to the charity it communicates, to the example it proposes; it is not a command, it is not an imposition. It is peaceful; it avoids violent methods; it is patient; it is generous."

3. Trust: "Trust, not only in the power of one's words, but also in an attitude of welcoming the trust of the interlocutor. Trust promotes confidence and friendship. It binds hearts in mutual adherence to the good, which excludes all self-seeking."

4. Prudence: Pedagogical prudence, which esteems highly the psychological and moral circumstances of the other . . . prudence strives to learn the sensitivities of the hearer and requires that we adapt ourselves and the manner of our presentation in a reasonable way lest we be displeasing and incomprehensible to the other. In the dialogue conducted in this manner, the union of truth and charity, of understanding and love is achieved."[10]

Having noted these characteristics which should mark the dialogue in the church, I would like to note two other points of some importance which Paul VI underlines. First he says, "The dialectic of this exercise of thought and patience will make us discover elements of truth also in the opinions of others, it will force us to express our teaching with great fairness."[11]

Then he comes to a point of the greatest wisdom, noting:

Before speaking, it is necessary to listen, not only to the other's voice, but to the heart. The other must first be understood; and where he merits it, agreed with. In the very act of trying to make ourselves pastors, fathers and teachers . . . we must make ourselves their brothers. The spirit of dialogue is friendship and, even more, is service. All this we must remember and strive to put into practice according to the example and commandment that Christ left us.[12]

And so we are to enter upon this dialogue not from some exalted place. Yes, we are to do it in the profound confidence of the sacred, apostolic office we have received from Christ through the church. But we are also to accomplish it with apostolic humility and gentleness, recognizing the religious as our partners in the dialogue. Pope John Paul touches on this in his Sept. 19 address:

In the very moment in which we bishops recognize our own need for conversion, the Lord asks us to go out to others--humble and repentant, yet courageous and without fear--to communicate with our brothers and sisters. Christ wants to appeal through us, to invite and call his people, especially his religious, to conversion.

The document on the relationship of bishops and religious states the same idea:

> All pastors, mindful of the apostolic admonition never to be a 'dictator over any group that is put in (their) charge, but (to) be an example that the whole flock follow' (1 Pt. 5:3) will rightly be at the same time leaders and members; truly fathers, but also brothers; teachers of the faith, but especially fellow disciples of Christ; those indeed responsible for the perfection of the faithful, but also true witnesses of their (own) personal sanctification.[13]

Dialogue, then, is a manifestation of a fundamental quality of the church, organic ecclesial communion and mutuality. Our pastoral service, then, is not one in which we give but do not receive, speak but do not listen, teach but do not learn. For this reason _Lumen_ _Gentium_ states: "Christ continually distributes in his body, that is, in the church, gifts of ministries through which, by his own power, we serve each other unto salvation so that, carrying out the truth in love, we may through all things grow up into him who is our head"[14]

III

Our guide in this pastoral service to our religious is the document "Essential Elements." I would now like to offer some orientation for interpreting it.

Having listened to what I have just said about dialogue, some may experience the concern that there is no clear or binding teaching about religious life, that dialogue means everything is an open question. It is, then, important to recall what Paul VI says in developing his thought on dialogue:

> The danger remains. The apostle's art is a risky one. The desire to come together as brothers must not lead to a watering down or subtracting from the truth . . . it will be for the wise, attentive government of the church to determine, from time to time, the limits and forms and paths to be followed in maintaining a living and fruitful dialogue.[15]

First of all, then, it is evident that "Essential Elements" is not a statement of something new. It does not intend to state some new direction or a new policy. Thus the final sentence of the introduction states, "In the present text addressed to institutes dedicated to apostolic works, this sacred congregation confines itself to a clarification and restatement of these essential elements."[16]

"Essential Elements" is a compilation from conciliar and other magisterial documents and from the new Code of Canon Law. In order to interpret the meaning of any point in this document, therefore, the source document must be consulted both in its text and context. "Essential Elements," therefore, cannot be correctly understood only by a superficial reading or without reference to the source documents which are clearly indicated in the text.

Second, the binding force of "Essential Elements" is derived from two things: from the magisterial and canonical sources from which it derives, but also and importantly from the fact that this compilation has been mandated by the Holy Father and has been sent by him to the bishops following upon his approval of the document.

It is also important to keep in mind that this document cannot be applied blindly and without regard for the long-standing principle governing the interpretation of magisterial and canonical documents. Religious life is simply not a univocal reality in the church. There are many differences, for example, between the religious life of the Daughters of Charity and Maryknoll, between Dominicans and Jesuits. Hence in understanding and applying this document the law of analogy must be operative. "Essential Elements" itself embodies this sense of analogy when, in treating of community, it states:

> The style of community life itself will relate to
> the form of apostolate for which the members have
> responsibility and to the culture and society in which
> this responsibility is accepted. The form of
> apostolate may well decide the size and location of a
> community, its particular needs, its standards of
> living.[17]

The document "Essential Elements" is then a binding document, but it cannot be interpreted without recourse to the source documents and without application of the accepted principles of interpretation and without recognition of the

49

principle of analogy.

IV

Our pastoral service exists in the context of the dialogue of salvation and is guided by the document "Essential Elements." This pastoral service, then, involves discernment.

Every Christian, of course, has the obligation of trying to discern the action of God and the action of the spirit of evil. Our discernment as heirs of the apostolic office in the church, however, is beyond that personal, individual level. We are charged by our very office to discern in the church what is and what is not in keeping with the Gospel as it has been handed on in the church. This discernment is twofold: to hold to what is good and to reject what is evil. But this is no easy task. And so the document on the relationship of bishops and religious states:

> Every authentic charism implies a certain element
> of genuine originality and of special initiative for
> the spiritual life of the church. In its surroundings
> it may appear troublesome and may even cause
> difficulties, since it is not always and immediately
> easy to recognize it as coming from the spirit.[18]

Nor is true discernment a unilateral function. What is authentic discernment after all but an effort to recognize the true action and voice of the Holy Spirit? No real discernment is possible, then, without listening to the voice of the Spirit, who is superior both to bishops and religious yet who works in both. Discernment includes careful weighing of and listening to the lived experience of religious and especially the lived experience of the past 20 years during which the great body of religious have made heroic efforts to respond to the call of the council for reform and renewal.[19]

In keeping with this function of ecclesial discernment is the apostolic duty of correction or admonition. This is referred to only once in all the documents we have received. Yet we must honestly confront the challenge. In his letter to us the Holy Father puts it this way:

> In those cases, too, where individuals or groups,
> for whatever reason, have departed from the

indispensable norms of religious life or have even, to the scandal of the faithful, adopted positions at variance with the church's teaching, I ask you my brother bishops, sustained by hope in the power of Christ's grace and performing an act of authentic pastoral service, to proclaim once again the church's universal call to conversion, spiritual renewal and holiness.[20]

We are not asked to condemn. We are asked to invite those relatively few, among the larger number of faithful religious, who may be living in conflict with the church's norms or teaching, to walk together with us anew the journey of conversion, spiritual renewal and holiness of which we all stand in need.

If bishops are called to show the humility of Christ in the exercise of their office, religious too are called to the same humility in recognizing possible mistakes and internal contradictions.

V

We are called to a special pastoral service involving dialogue and ecclesial discernment. One final aspect of our mandate remains to be considered: The numerical decline of religious life. Of this the Holy Father says:

In asking the commission to be of assistance to you in your pastoral ministry and responsibility, I know that it will be very sensitive to the marked decline in recent years in the numbers of young people seeking to enter religious life, particularly in the case of institutes of apostolic life. This decline in numbers is a matter of grave concern to me--a concern which I know that you and the religious also share.[21]

One obvious reason for this concern is, of course, that the decline in numbers of religious places in jeopardy the many indispensable apostolic works through which they have shaped and sustained the church in the United States. But a far more important reason for concern about the decline in numbers of those entering religious life is the prospect of losing the public witness of their consecrated life among us. It is their unique, public, ecclesial witness of the poverty, obedience and chastity of Christ which is their first and highest contribution to the church. If we were not concerned about this decline it would be a statement that to us the religious life is but a trivial or marginal factor in the church's life. We must, then, with utmost seriousness examine the resons for this decline. But this will take time and professional assistance.

VI

Shortly Archbishop Kelly, on behalf of the pontifical commission, will present to you a practical model of a process which you may find helpful in carrying out this pastoral service in your dioceses.

As we take up this great work of service to religious life, we do so in the awareness of our communion in faith and charity with the successor of Peter. It is he who has called us to this service, and he accompanies us with his concern and his prayers. We do so also with a deep-felt sense of gratitude to and love for the religious in our dioceses and in the awareness that we are bishops "for them" but disciples "with them." Thus we have every confidence that rich fruit will attend our work since we believe that the Holy Spirit is at work in this enterprise precisely because it is an action of the church. To us it may at times seem overwhelming. But we rely not on human strength or cleverness. We rely on Christ, who is ever with us and who strengthens our weakness by his power.

NOTES

1. Letter of Pope John Paul II to the bishops of the United States, April 3, 1983, no. 3.
2. *Christus Dominus* 7.
3. *Lumen Gentium* 4.
4. *Ibid.* 7.
5. *Mutuae Relationes* 9c.
6. *Ibid.* 13c.
7. Pope John Paul II, Address to American Bishops, Sept. 19, 1983.
8. Paul VI, *Ecclesiam Suam* 14.
9. *Ibid.* 113.
10. *Ibid.* 81.
11. *Ibid.* 83.
12. *Ibid.* 87.
13. *Mutuae Relationes* 9d.
14. *Lumen Gentium* 7.
15. *Ecclesiam Suam* 88.
16. "Essential Elements" 4.

17. Ibid. 21.
18. Mutuae Relationes 12.
19. Cf. Letter, 4; "Essential Elements" 4.
20. Letter of Pope John Paul, 3.
21. Ibid. 4.

III

IN THE SERVICE OF THE CHURCH

CONFERENCE FOR BISHOPS AND MAJOR RELIGIOUS SUPERIORS

ON RELIGIOUS LIFE IN THE UNITED STATES

(Papers of the June 20-22, 1984 Conference at Boston College)

To Share and To Learn: A Keynote Address

by

James Hennesey, S.J.

Two hundred years ago this month, on June 9, 1784,
Cardinal Leonardo Antonelli, who was then Prefect of the
Sacred Congregation de Propaganda Fide, took quill pen in hand
and signed the appointment of Father John Carroll as Superior
of the Mission in the thirteen United States of North America.
With that stroke of the pen, the church in the new American
republic was officially released from the jurisdiction of the
English Vicar Apostolic of the London District and began life
as a distinct entity -- "an ordinary national church," John
Carroll called it -- in communion with the Bishop and Church
of Rome. Carroll was later, in 1789, elected by the priests
first Bishop of Baltimore and in 1808 Pope Pius VII named him
archbishop.

We have known a remarkable two hundred years. The
Catholic community in our nation has grown from a relatively
homogeneous 25,000 people, most of them British or German, to
somewhere in the neighborhood of fifty million today, of every
race and national origin. We here tonight are heirs of a long
line of women and men who over the years have come from that
community and have freely chosen to return our lives in
ministry to it. We do not meet as strangers. We meet as
brothers and sisters. We come of the same families. We
belong to the one Body of Christ, to the one People of God.

Vatican II's Constitution on the Church, Lumen Gentium,
emphasized that "all Christ's faithful ... are called to the
fulness of Christian life and to the perfection of love," to
holiness. All of us, the Constitution continued, "must use
the strength with which we are gifted by Christ to mold
ourselves in his image, to seek God's glory and the service of
our neighbor."[1] That is the common vocation we share with
all Christians. Our particular roles among God's people
differ, but our vocation is one: to follow Christ, that one
day we may partake of his glory.

When we come together in a graced moment like the one
which has brought us here tonight, I suggest we can do no
better than to model our assembly on that first Christian
community which met in the joy of the Risen Lord at Jerusalem
after the great event of Pentecost. "Repent, be baptized, and

you will receive the Holy Spirit," Peter told them.[2] Let us come together in humility to share and to learn, confident that the Holy Spirit will be with us. The Jerusalem Christians remained faithful to the teaching of the apostles, to their company, to the breaking of the bread and to the prayers.[3] It is a good prescription for us. These are days designed for companionship. We share living space and meals and conversation. We listen together. We discuss together. We question together. And we pray together.

If there is any constant which has marked the Christian community which is the Church down through the ages, it is that we have met for the breaking of the bread and for prayers, as they did in Jerusalem nearly two thousand years ago. Our oneness is symbolized, represented and brought about in the Eucharist we share, "the blessing cup that we bless is a communion with the blood of Christ and the bread that we break is a communion with the body of Christ. The fact that there is only one loaf means that, though there are many of us, we form a single body because we all have a share in this one loaf.[4] So Paul reminded the Corinthians, in an image taken up again in that early Christian writing, the Didache: "As this broken bread, once dispersed over the hills, was brought together and became one loaf so may your church be brought together from the ends of the earth into your kingdom."[5] Let us pray together tonight that we may begin in that union of genuine companionship, that love for one another by which we will be known to be Christians.

We, you and I who are here tonight, have been called by the Lord in a particular way to lives of service, service to him and to his people. Our meeting these three days has no purpose except to examine how we may better accomplish that service. We propose to do that by praying together, by living in community, and by honest and open discussion of our joys and hopes, our pains and fears. We hope to come to know one another better, to share our concerns, to find inspiration for greater love and service, and to do it as sisters and brothers in the Lord.

I began by mentioning the anniversary of John Carroll's appointment as Mission Superior. Those of you who know me are aware of what may politely be termed my obsession with Bishop Carroll. I turn to his life and writings regularly for guidance and counsel. He was not given to what I call "ecclesiastical positivism": such-and-such is right or wrong, good or bad because I say it is. Rather, he searched the Scriptures and he searched the tradition and he weighed what he found in the balance of contemporary reality before he came to a decision. That kind of personal study of the sources was the way he had learned to do theology.[6] Where better then to begin my preparation for this introductory talk than by studying the forerunner of tonight's session, the very first-ever meeting of minds between the nation's one-and-only bishop and its one-and-only religious superior?

I have sadly to report that Bishop Carroll let me down! It happened in 1793.

There were no male religious communities in the United States at that time. There had been Jesuits from 1634 until 1773, but after that they were temporarily ex-Jesuits, thanks to the benevolence of Pope Clement XIV of blessed memory. There were the occasional wandering monks and friars, true gyrovagues in St. Benedict's term, many of them good zealous priests, but generally of the type for whom superiors gladly provide one-way passage to distant shores. The Augustinians would start a community in Philadelphia in 1796, and Edward Fenwick came home in 1804 and brought the Dominicans with him. But in 1793 the only religious superior in the United States was Ann Matthews, Mother Bernadine Teresa of St. Joseph, Discalced Carmelite, of the monastery established three years earlier at Port Tobacco, Maryland.

Bishop Carroll had welcomed the Carmelites, but, even before their arrival, he confided to a friend, "I wish rather for Ursulines." Maryland Catholic girls had for generations gone to convents in Flanders for their education; Carroll wanted a school for them at home, to match the new boys' academy at Georgetown. But Carmelites came, and Ursulines did not. The bishop had a solution. He wrote to Cardinal Antonelli: "They would be far more useful . . . if they undertook the education of girls." Antonelli replied with a dispensation from Pope Pius VI, allowing the Carmelites to open a school.[7]

You will notice that in this exchange, which took several years to complete, intercontinental communication being what it was, somebody had been left out. The bishop perhaps did not wish to disturb the contemplative atmosphere at Port Tobacco until he had the pope's dispensation in hand. Then he announced it in a triumphant letter to Mother Bernadine. Here there is a lacuna in the correspondence. We only know that, seven years later, John Carroll was still nursing his wounds. "They will not," he wrote, "undertake the business of female education, tho' the late pope recommended it earnestly to them."[8]

So much for my turning to John Carroll for guidance and counsel! He did do better, later on, with the Visitation nuns and with St. Elizabeth Seton and her sisters.

Apart from the salutary lesson which history always teaches, that clay feet are not the exclusive property of any one generation, there are other lessons taught by the episode of Bishop Carroll and Mother Bernadine: the need to know and to respect the charism of each institute and above all, the need for communication that is honest and open. I cannot help but think that an episcopal horseback ride to Port Tobacco would have helped mightily back in 1793.

A caution here. I do not at all mean to suggest that failure in dialogue is an episcopal preserve. No one can think that who remembers how, in 1823, an agent of the restored Jesuits protested to U.S. Secretary of State John Quincy Adams that a papal brief supporting the Archbishop of Baltimore in a property dispute with them was unwarranted foreign interference in American affairs. Nor how, five years later, two prominent Dominicans enlisted Secretary of State Henry Clay's aid when they were ordered to move from Philadelphia to the wilds of Cincinnati.[9] Dialogue is always a two-way street; failure runs both ways.

I have tried so far to make two points:

(1) that our coming together should be marked by a sense of community, of the communio, that koinonia, that companionship so characteristic of authentic Christians; and that we foster it in our common²prayer, the life we will be sharing, and in the Eucharist, and,

(2) that we work with one another to foster good communication, speaking not to, at, or around one another, but with one another.

I would make two final points:

(1) we need to isolate tradition from traditions. Here my model is chapter two of Vatican II's Dei Verbum, on the transmission of divine revelation, with its emphasis on living, growing, developing, dynamic tradition, as opposed to the static view which promotes antiquarianism, and, (2) a

final postscript on the makeup of our assembly, which has much
to say to the focus of the Pontifical Commission's work.

In a recent article on the frequency of the Eucharist,
Robert Taft wrote that "history shows the past to be always
instructive, but never normative. What is normative is
tradition. But tradition, unlike the past, is a living force
whose contingent expressions . . . can change."[10] The
"tradition" of which we speak here is, I think, that we
religious "devote ourselves with all our being to the glory of
God and the service of our neighbor," in accordance with the
particular charism of our individual institutes. The
historian can say how that has been done in the past. Today
we religious must ask, how best can we do it as we move toward
the 21st century; the bishops must ask, how best can they
extend their pastoral to us as we do it.

American religious life grew in political and social
circumstances vastly different from those which obtained in
19th century Europe. We were not driven again and again from
our schools and hospitals, as were our opposite numbers across
the Atlantic. Rather we were drawn into them. They became
the spinal cord around which we fashioned our religious life.
That is important to remember when we have to deal with
theories of religious life born of different histories than
our own. We found a great deal of our identity in our
institutions, and our financial support also, meager as it
sometimes could be. But those American circumstances,
whatever the pure theoretician may think, took our institutes
and shaped them, not always to the good.

An example. St. Ignatius Loyola's vicar general, Jerome
Nadal, dramatically portrayed the apostolic mobility which is
the authentic Jesuit tradition when he wrote that we have four
types of houses: novitiates, colleges, pastoral centers, and
"journeys" Yes, that's right: journeys, apostolic missions,
the freedom to go where sent for spiritual purposes and the
will to go. These last, Nadal claimed, were "the
characteristic and most perfect house of the Society."[11] In
the case of my religious order, that is the authentic
tradition against we measure what we do today and tomorrow.
You have similar experiences as you cut away encrustations and
dismiss the temptation to absolutize the contingent
realizations of previous generations and rediscover beneath
them your authentic tradition, seeking for our age its
appropriate embodiment. It is a process eminently corrective
of the mindset where preoccupation with preserving the forms
of the past has let initial commitment to a good work harden

into a stultifying sense of possession, or of being possessed, by outdated manifestations.

I used the metaphor of the spinal cord. If it is cut or removed, obviously we have problems. So do we if it is atrophied. But metaphors go only so far. We are talking of living men and women. As Raymond Hostie has pointed out in his recent study on The Life and Death of Religious Orders, we have always the option of seeking contemporary realization of the authentic tradition.[12] It is when we freeze some contingent realization from the past that we are in trouble.

There are other areas which need historical exploration and which will not necessarily yield the results some expect, for example, the role of practices more properly monastic in an apostolic community or externals such as dress. One topic which occurs in several of the documents we must consider is the relationship of contemplation and action. There is there emphasis on what we are, rather than on what we do. Recognizing the integrity of both poles, do we tend toward dichotomy or toward dynamic union of the two? There are different spiritualities: the medieval way, which sees action graced by contemplation as by an overflowing well, is not that of Vincent de Paul instructing the Daughters of Charity that to nurse the sick is to pray.[13] His approach sounds a theme common to the Counter-Reformation spiritualities seminal in active apostolic communities, where prayer and work do not so much alternate as fuse. As one raised to "find God in all things," and "no less devotion in works of charity and obedience than in prayer and meditation," I confess to some unease in what I see set down as normative in terms of ecclesial identity and in the consequences drawn therefrom. In any case, these are some of the areas in which we search, bishops and religious, for the signs of the times.

I have only a brief last point. We are all in this together, men and women, members of contemplative institutes and of apostolic institutes. None are excluded, nor in the process should any be allowed to slip away. "We have all," Paul told the Corinthians, "put on Christ as a garment. There is no such thing as Jew or Greek, slave or free. We are all one in Christ Jesus."[14] This is true for all Christians. It is true for us. This does not mean that there are not concerns more immediate with some than with others. But everyone's concerns are all our concerns. We can and should learn from each other as we face the challenge of the contemporary church and the world it serves.

We are gathered in community. We pray and share the Eucharist together. We learn together. There will be speeches to set the context of religious life and of its American experience, to help us meditate theologically and to understand sociologically the phenomenon of which we are part. Above all, we need to share our needs and hopes, to express them openly and frankly, to pray about them, to grow together "to the fullness of Christian life and to the perfection of love."

NOTES

1. Lumen Gentium 40.
2. Acts 2:38.
3. Acts 2:42.
4. 1 Cor 10:16-17.
5. Didache 9.
6. James Hennesey, "An Eighteenth Century Bishop: John Carroll of Baltimore," Archivum Historiae Pontificiae, 16 (1978) 171-204; id., "The Vision of John Carroll," Thought, 54 (1979) 322-333; id., "Grasping the Tradition: Reflections of a Church Historian," Theological Studies, 45 (1984) 153-163.
7. Thomas O'Brien Hanley, ed., The John Carroll Papers (3 vols.; Notre Dame, 1976) 1.312; 2.32; 2.84-85.
8. Ibid., 2.319.
9. John P. Marschall, "Diocesan and Religious Clergy: The History of a Relationship, 1789-1969," in John Tracy Ellis, ed., The Catholic Priest in the United States: Historical Investigations (Collegeville MN, 1971) 386-389; Victor F. O'Daniel, The Dominican Province of St. Joseph: Historico-Biographical Studies (New York, 1942) 135-138.
10. Robert Taft, "The Frequency of the Eucharist throughout History," Concilium, 152 (1982) 21.
11. John W. O'Malley, "To travel to Any Part of the World: Jerome Nadal and the Jesuit Vocation," Studies in the Spirituality of Jesuits, 16 (1984) 6-7.
12. Raymond Hostie, The Life and Death of Religious Orders: A Psycho-Sociological Approach (Washington DC, 1983).
13. Pierre Coste, The Life and Works of St. Vincent de Paul (trans. Joseph Leonard; 3 vols.; Westminster MD, 1953) 1.356.
14. 1 Cor 11:11-12.

Memory, Vision and Structure:
Historical Perspectives on the Experience
of Religious Life in the Church

by

John W. Padberg, S.J.

Introduction

The central content of this paper is a series of major historical forms in which a personal religious vision of a commitment to the life and memory of Jesus Christ has been lived out in communities of men and women in the church. That content includes memory, vision and structure.

The central question to ask ourselves is how the knowledge of those communities might illuminate our own understanding of the essential elements of religious life today. To repeat from the keynote address to this conference: "What is normative is tradition. But tradition, unlike the past, is a living force whose contingent expressions...can change." To illustrate by only two examples of contingent expressions of religious life, what could be more different today than the monks and hermits of Mount Athos living in absolute isolation on a Greek monastery island forever barred to all females, and the Medical Missionary Sisters conducting hospitals in the middle of million-inhabitant cities. Yet, both are examples of religious life.

To move in this talk so quickly in space and time over so vast and varied a phenomenon will necessarily mean broad strokes. I hope that they will, however, give the basic lineaments of that religious life. I shall, in addition, use examples to illustrate some important phenomena.

The major divisions of the talk follow the major ways in which in its history the church has experienced religious life. There are the first ages of religious life; then, monasticism in East and West; thirdly, canons regular, mendicant orders and lay groups; fourth, clerics regular and directly apostolic institutes; next, religious life in the centuries of Tridentine Catholicism; sixth, revolution and restoration; and, finally and briefly, the immediate past of our present conciliar age, Vatican II, with its charter of renewal.

The First Ages of Religious Life

Religious life had its origins in the desire to provide an organized and systematic pursuit of holiness for groups living in some way in common. The church itself obviously was such a group, awaiting at first the imminent coming of the Kingdom.

In late New Testament times, the first implicit beginnings of religious life existed in the small organized groupings of lay women who were either widows or virgins living in community. The widows engaged in a rudimentary apostolic life; the virgins lived a secluded life of prayer and asceticism.

The phenomenon of such small groups self-consciously pursuing holiness in an organized way started sometime between the years 250 and 300. It began in the Eastern lands of the church with a planned separation from the world. Anthony of the Egyptian Desert is the first and most famous example of this type. As his fame and that of others spread, disciples came to be directed personally by them. But there were at best only embryonic communities and no stable rule. Such a rule, simple and primitive, came from another desert father, Pachomius. It had become clear that the asceticism of people who pursued holiness by sitting on pillars or loading themselves with chains or living on all fours or deliberately cultivating decay needed some regulation, especially of the delusion-prone self-will that many of these extravagant ascetical practices came from.

It is important to recognize how much this first movement of religious life was lay-inspired and how much such a planned separation from the world turned to an indifference to the world, then a protest against the world and then a suspicion of the world and a contempt and hatred of it. In many instances, too, it was a protest against a church seen as too worldly and over-institutionalized. It was a particular restatement of gospel teaching (For instance, "If you would be perfect, go sell what you have and come follow me.") albeit in changed social circumstances.

Here begins the prophetic role of religious in calling members of the church back to the core of the gospel. It is a grace but also a temptation, both for the church not to listen and for religious to cut themselves off from the mainstream of the life of the church.

Monasticism in East and West

The insertion back into that mainstream was especially the work of two great legislators, Basil in the East and Benedict in the West. There were other early attempts to bring this inchoate religious life back into such a mainstream, by people such as Martin of Tours or John Cassian in Gaul. The latter, Cassian, is especially important because he became the conduit to Western Europe for the teachings of the desert fathers and for some of the neo-Platonic mistrust of matter, of the world, of the body and especially of sexuality.

But it is Basil and Benedict who most importantly took the memory of the gospel of Jesus and of these previous individual attempts to live it out, who had the talent to enable groups to incarnate that vision and who established in changing circumstances structures to make it possible. For example: living absolutely alone, the eremitical life, was at first regarded as essential; now it gave way to living in community, which in its turn became an essential element for the centuries to come.

Here, too, even before Benedict, women were among the first to be gathered into communities of consecrated virgins. There is the evidence for this, for example, from Jerome in Rome and Bethlehem, and from ancient rules for such communities in France and Spain. Very often those rules for women were the counterparts of the rules for men, adapted by monastic legislators for women who were their sisters or mothers. The most famous such relationship in the West, of course, was that of Benedict and his supposed sister, Scholastica. Benedict in the early 500's did not start out to found a community. He fled the licentiousness of Rome to live as a solitary in a cave at Subiaco in Italy. But he attracted followers to Subiaco and with followers eventually came disagreements. About 525 he went off with a small band of adherents to Monte Cassino and there, too, further followers came. For these men who were laymen he, also probably a layman, wrote one of the most influential documents of Western history, the Rule.

That Rule contained both a vision of the principles of religious life and the structure of details on how to live it in community. This was a rule for a community life of prayer and labor internal to the monastery; it was not for apostolic activity, not for the spread of the Gospel externally into the world. But what happened is a good example of the needs of the time helping to shape the life of an order. So it was Benedictines, because there were no others, who deeply implanted Christianity in so many places. As in earlier communities and with Benedict's first followers, so later Benedictines for a long time were predominantly lay persons; the overwhelming clericalization of the male religious order was yet in the future.

In the several centuries of chaos and decline of civilization which took place from about 500 to 750 A.D., the evil times infected the Benedictines, too. By the late 700's another Benedict, this one of Aniane, undertook a reform under the direction of Charlemagne who as emperor had no doubt whatsoever that reform was his responsibility as much or even more than it was the pope's. The emperor as civil ruler had responsibility for Christendom just as did the pope, and most priests and bishops thought the same. None of us, today, would think that a president, even if Catholic, should be reforming religious houses.

The great change in monasticism, however, came in the 10th century, when for the first time a centralized organization of monasteries under one superior general took place. Cluny in Burgundy built the greatest and grandest order up to that time, with eventually more than a thousand houses dependent on the mother abbey at Cluny. The abbey in turn was directly dependent on the pope, the first major religious group to acquire exemption from the control of the territorial bishops, the ordinaries of the place. Cluny was in great part admired by the diocesan clergy and, perhaps unfortunately, helped to monasticize their lives and duties, too. Cluny inspired the reforming popes, especially Gregory VII, Hildebrand, in his crusade against simony and for the imposition of clerical celibacy. Exemption, too, was part of the fundamental changes in the old relationships of pope and hitherto much more independent bishops which had existed from time immemorial in the church. That change reached its culmination centuries later at Vatican I, of course, in the definition of Papal primacy as ordinary, immediate and universal jurisdiction of the Pope in every diocese in the world.

For centuries the Benedictine rule held sway in Europe as the rule for religious life. There were two major exceptions. The first was the rule of the Carthusians which attempted to combine in a monastic community both the very ancient solitary or eremitical and the contemporary communal or cenobitical element. The other was the rise of canons regular in the 12th century. Examples would be the Norbertines or the Croziers. They were essentially clerics, priests, attached to parishes, who took vows according to a specific rule of life usually adapted from the so-called Rule of St. Augustine. In some ways they were, without recognizing it, a bridge to the newer forms of religious life soon to come.

But before we go to them, let me return to the development of religious life among women. After 600 A.D. the Benedictine Rule gradually became almost exclusively the rule for women religious, and remained so for at least the next six centuries. It was easily adapted for women; by the middle 700's various national and local councils and assemblies, both ecclesiastical and civil, prescribed the Benedictine Rule for all monks and nuns. There were even some "double orders" of Benedictine monks and nuns living under the rule of one single religious superior. Surely the most striking example of the differing structures of religious life was the "double order" at Fontevrault in France, founded in 1100 by Robert d'Arbrissel. It had several separate congregations, for men and for women in the traditional Benedictine forms, for the care of pilgrims, for the sick and for penitent women. (Apparently men never became penitent enough to be public about it.) What made it most striking, however, was that from the foundation of the house in 1100 to its destruction almost 700 years later in the French Revolution, all of these groups at Fontevrault, both men and women, were governed in common by an uninterrupted succession of women major superiors or abbesses.

The various reform Benedictine groups through the centuries regularly established women's branches, too, for example the Cistercian nuns. So, too, in the 12th century the Canons Regular had female branches, almost always called Canonesses Regular and following the rule of St. Augustine. It is that rule which is at the remote basis of some of the more modern orders such as the congregations of Notre Dame de Namur or the School Sisters of Notre Dame.

Canons Regular, Mendicant Orders and Lay Groups

To move on, what happened in the twelfth and through the thirteenth century? Quite simply Europe recovered from the long ages of turmoil and isolation since the end of the Roman Empire seven centuries before. For the religious needs of the rise of cities again new structures of religious life arose. I have already mentioned the canons regular. The most famous of the new orders, of course, were and are the Franciscans and the Dominicans.

Not rural but urban; not bound by stability to one house but easily sendable to many; not localized as an individual house but a collection of houses called a province; not relying on landed property for support but rather on begging and almsgiving; these orders were surely different in what had long been regarded as absolute hallmarks of religious life.

Both the Franciscans and Dominicans illustrate well the interplay of charism and structure in religious life. Both Francis and Dominic strongly impressed their particular vision of religious life, their talents, their qualities on their respective orders. For the Dominicans, the devotion to sound doctrine and to public preaching came to be hallmarks everywhere. Maybe less well known, but equally important then and later was the Dominican commitment to careful organization and to participatory and representative governing processes inside the order. The regular, orderly, free election of delegates to provincial chapters, and from there to a general chapter (the major founding ones were held in 1220 and 1221) and the election of superiors within the order, without outside arbitrary interference, were greatly to influence later orders.

For the Franciscans, the imprint of Francis was perhaps even stronger. In some instances it was so strong that it became divisive. Look, as an example, at what happened in the matter of poverty, so dear to Francis. The rule insisted on an absolute poverty, personal and corporate. How did one square absolute poverty with the need for settled houses and with plans for training the immense flow of recruits? Two viewpoints emerged and for a hundred years you had Spirituals (a minority insisting on absolute poverty) against Conventuals (a majority insisting on facing the needs of the times and of the order). Perfectly good men with totally stubborn passions argued and fought for generations. In 1317-18 the then Pope, John XXII, decided in favor of the Conventual view that the order could have corporate ownership of possessions. Some of the Spirituals fled and became the schismatic Fraticelli whom church authorities hunted down as heretics and whom civil authorities of the emperor protected. (The current best-selling novel, The Name of the Rose, vividly portrays a part of that bitter split.) With consequences for more modern times, some Franciscans among the victors in the Pope's decision on poverty began to develop and urge the doctrine of papal infallibility in order to make sure that a later pope could not reverse what the current pope, John XXII, had decided in their favor.

The foundation and the first-century history of the two orders furnish excellent examples of new forms of religious life arising to meet new religious and social demands and of the ongoing tensions in and between charism and structure. When does an initially liberating charism become a dead weight in changed circumstances? How does a carefully organized structure produce and then continue to foster a freedom of spirit?

The same questions, of course, can be asked of any order at any time. And at this time other mendicant orders, too, came into existence such as the Augustinians and the Carmelites. The latter insisted in their early existence that they really went back in foundation to the times of Elijah and the sons of the prophets on Mount Carmel (as recounted in scripture in the second book of Kings). This is a good example of a misplaced concern for supposed scriptural origins of religious life.

If the thirteenth century was the height of medieval civilization, the fourteenth century with the Black Death in all of society and with the Great Schism in the Church was the beginning of the disintegration of that medieval synthesis. The scandal of two and then three men claiming to be pope and the evidence at times not clear as to which really was the pope was immense. The Black Death and the Great Schism brought wholesale disruption and increasing laxity in the old orders. There was great heroism within them, too, and within new groups of lay followers of the Lord, dedicated to the plague-stricken, the dying, the rooting out of clerical abuse, the cultivation of a deeper Christian life. Such a lay group, for example, were the Brethren of the Common Life, one of whose members was Thomas a Kempis, author of the most influential devotional book ever published, The Imitation of Christ. Another such group were the Cellites, later to be known as the Alexian Brothers.

Clerics Regular and Apostolic Institutes

Abuses high and low, in head and numbers, in religious orders, in the hierarchy and in the scandalous conduct of the worldly, money-grubbing renaissance papacy were utterly evident. Those abuses were steps through the late 15th and early 16th centuries on the road to a reformation in the church of Christ which everyone knew was needed and to a split

in the church of Christ which no one at all at the beginning
in 1517 wanted.

At the same time there were forces for change in the
church at work both before and during the Protestant
Reformation. In the crisis of that event, they became even
more ardent and active. Among those forces for reform was a
new type of religious life which began in the 1500's, the
clerics regular. Among the new orders of this type were the
Theatines, the Barnabites, the Sommaschi,the orders of the
Mother of God, of the Ministers of the Sick, of the Pious
Schools, and the Society of Jesus. Clerics regular were, from
their beginnings, not congregations or orders of laity as most
earlier orders had been at their foundation, but right from
the beginning orders of priests, and they were directly
dedicated to apostolic work as their very reason for
existence.

What rapidly became the largest and most influential of
these new orders, the Society of Jesus, introduced certain new
and unheard of characteristics and eliminated older elements
which had long been regarded as central to religious life.
For example, there was to be no obligatory choir or chanting
of the divine office. Another innovation was to have both
solemnly and simply vowed members, quite unheard of up to that
time. The practical import of this change might be clear from
a single example. The common canonical practice of the time
was that a person with solemn vows was never absolved of them.
A common teaching was that not even the pope could absolve
from such vows. One result was a horde of ill-suited
religious, unfitted for the life, irremediably stuck in it,
who fled their monasteries or convents or lived there
discontentedly, making life impossible for others unless the
malcontents were put in the prison of their order. With a
long period of simple vows, the Jesuits could easily dismiss
the unfit. When the Society was seeking initial approval, one
of the Cardinals is supposed to have asked where in the
Constitutions was the then usual provision for imprisoning
recalcitrant members. Ignatius is said to have responded:
"There is no need for a prison when we have the door." This
provision for both simple and solemn vows is only one example
of an innovation, and of its consequences.

Far more important were the high centralization of
governing authority in the general superior, the very close
bonds between members all over the world, the extended period
of training before final admission into the Society, the

direct commitment to be at the disposal of the pope in order
to be more available for worldwide apostolic purposes.

Most important were the specific spirituality of the new
Society, flowing out of the Spiritual Exercises and the
apostolates which followed upon that spirituality. It was a
spirituality which saw God at work in all things; it put
Christ at the center of a man or woman's personal love and
commitment; it regarded the world as inherently good but not
of itself good enough and so yet to be brought to God through
prayer and apostolic activity; and it lived out that apostolic
activity itself as a prayer because personal holiness and
apostolic activity were not to be separate items in a member's
life, but necessarily flowing out of and into each other.
These characteristics are so familiar to us today. However,
they were very new at the time and especially new in their
linkage. In addition, those elements of a spirituality have
become very characteristic of many apostolic orders of men and
women, each in its own way, founded since then.

There was a two-fold social circumstance in which this
and other new orders arose in the following two centuries,
orders such as the Christian Brothers, the Passionists, the
Redemptorists, the Daughters of Charity, the Visitation nuns,
the Institute of the Blessed Virgin Mary, the Sisters of St.
Joseph, and some congregations such as the Vincentians or
Sulpicians with either private vows or—a new thing—simple
promises. First there was the immediate counter-reformation
internal to the church. It brought an outpouring of zeal and
piety and intelligence. Then there was the overwhelmingly
important and long-term influence of the greatest monument of
the counter-reform, the Council of Trent.

We have, all of us, lived in a post-Tridentine church
right up to Vatican II. We have much for which to thank that
Council. Our problems have arisen when we thought that Trent
was the only norm, present and future, unconditioned by its
circumstances.

With extraordinary devotion, zeal and imagination the
church pulled itself out of one of its gravest crises, and
historians regularly note that the three central factors in
doing so were the Council of Trent, reform-minded popes and
bishops and the new and reformed religious orders.

In one area, however, imagination failed grievously. It
was the area of women's religious congregations. In the
sixteenth and seventeenth centuries, extraordinarily

imaginative women and men tried to fashion specifically apostolic congregations of women, dedicated to work outside the cloister. Up to this time the cloister had been the only place in which women could undertake even a very limited apostolic activity. The record of innovation is impressive: for example, Angela Merici with the first Ursulines; Jane de Chantal and Francis de Sales with the Visitation nuns; Mary Ward with the Institute of the Blessed Virgin Mary, Vincent de Paul and Louise de Marillac with the Daughters of Charity. The problem lay with those who had to approve and make use of the orders. Every one of these religious congregations of women was forced back into the cloister, with the sole exception of the Daughters of Charity. They succeeded in working externally only because Vincent de Paul and Louise de Marillac devised a way by which the Daughters of Charity were not formally religious but only laywomen who annually took promises to live and work together. In all the other cases, the church, in both its men and women, could not summon up the imagination to see women other than in protected cloisters. Even so great a churchman as Charles Borromeo, nephew of Pope Pius IV and at the age of twenty-two Archbishop of Milan and Cardinal, prominent at Trent, one of the most influential of the reformers and a model bishop of his time, was one of the people who gradually forced the Ursulines into the cloister where they then had to live and work in a way quite different from their founding charism and from the conception that Angela, the foundress, had had of them. There was no lack of good will or intelligence here; there surely was a lack of imagination. Only in the nineteenth century, as we shall see, did externally apostolic orders of women come into being on a significant scale.

Revolution and Restoration

Before that nineteenth century arrived, there came the revolution, specifically the French Revolution in 1789, finally ending with the defeat of Napoleon in 1815. Americans today have almost no sense of what that event did to the thousand-year-old structures of Europe. The churches, schools, hospitals, abbeys, convents of a millenium and a half of Christendom, much of the physical, political, social, economic structure on which the church had relied for 1500 years, all--at the end of the Revolution--were gone or in utter disarray.

The same was true of religious orders. Let me give only two such examples. First, no male religious order of brothers or priests founded before the French Revolution has ever again

after the Revolution right up to our own day, been as large as
it was before the Revolution with only the two exceptions of
the Society of Jesus and the Christian Brothers. Second,
before the French Revolution there were in Europe some two
thousand Benedictine houses. Some were large, some small;
some rural, some urban; some lax, some strict; some rich, some
poor; some male, some female. But two thousand! In 1815, at
the end of the revolution, there were in Europe twenty
Benedictine houses in existence. This was all distressingly
extraordinary.

What was even more extraordinary and beyond all
expectation was the rebirth of the church, and yet more
amazing the rebirth or new birth of religious life in the
nineteenth and twentieth centuries. It was a phoenix arising
from its ashes. Without going into details, it is probably
true that in the nineteenth and twentieth centuries, in the
150 years from 1815 to 1965, more religious congregations were
founded than in any period twice that long in the history of
the church; more women's religious congregations and
congregations of brothers were founded; more apostolic and
missionary congregations came into existence, and more men and
women in total numbers entered religious orders. Most of us
today came to expect as normal what was a totally
unprecedented experience of religious life. Most of the
centuries old religious orders have survived and flourished in
the whole history of the church on far less recruitment and
membership than we came to regard as normal and expectable.

All of this began to take place, however, in a church
deeply suspicious of change and intransigently conservative.
But what would we ourselves have done in the early nineteenth
century if as committed Catholics living through the
revolution we had experienced churches burned, convents
pillaged, nuns degraded, priests killed, Christians exiled,
all in the name of liberty, equality, fraternity, democracy?
Pius VII, pope at the end of the revolution, tried to get his
curia to understand that change had become inevitable. But
when he died the tide of reaction rolled in. At the same
time, equally suspicious and conservative were most Catholics,
laity and religious and clergy. The few who tried to
enunciate principles that we embrace today, such as in the
declaration of Vatican II on religious liberty, were silenced
or ridiculed or ignored by most other Catholics. Religious
orders, at the service of the church and made up of men and
women who came from among the ordinary members of the church,
could hardly be otherwise. So they, too, were often very
suspicious of change and very conservative. There were

precious few people around to tell them how, under the externals of established tradition, they were, sometimes without recognizing it, really establishing quite new traditions and new characteristics.

Among those new characteristics, the most striking was the rise of women's apostolic orders. Their members might be wearing the habit of seventeenth or eighteenth century origin or might devise one from a nineteenth century foundress. But at the same time women religious were for the first time leaving the cloister to engage in the apostolate. Which apostolates? Interestingly, the only two allowed to women by the larger society of the times, teaching and nursing. We have grown accustomed to seeing these as the traditional external apostolates of women's orders. The tradition, glorious in what has been accomplished within it, is nonetheless only a century and a half old. Knowing that, we can recognize that for our day other external apostolates may be just as important, even if they are new for us now, as nursing and teaching were new then.

The new foundations for men were also in the overwhelming majority apostolic institutes. Some of the contemplative orders were revived or took on new vigor. That new contemplative vigor was especially true in the United States after World War II.

The main apostolates of religious orders and congregations of men and women, clerical and lay, over the last century and a half have been education, health care, the preaching of missions and retreats, and the foreign missions. The ministries of interiority such as spiritual direction and directed retreats, except for religious colleagues, are a very new phenomenon. As for the foreign missions, just as in the sixteenth and seventeenth century, they followed the flags of Spain and Portugal and France, so in the nineteenth, they went to the new colonies of France, or Belgium, or Germany, or Britain. No longer a colony itself, the United States was incomparably important for that collection of what might be called ethnic colonies, the result of the tidal waves of immigration. To minister to them came religious orders from every country of Europe, and those orders grew enormously in this country. The historical perspective on the experience of American religious is the subject of the next presentation at this conference.

The other most distinctive mark of religious orders in the last one hundred and fifty years has been the increasing direct centralization of the orders under the authority of Rome. This is not an isolated phenomenon but simply an instance of such an increasing centralization of the church under the authority of the Holy See ever since the revolution all the way up until Vatican II. Again let me cite just two examples. When Pius VII and Napoleon signed a concordat in 1801, one of its provisions was that every single French bishop was to resign, with some former ones to be reappointed and some new ones to be ordained and appointed. That in itself was unusual. More unusual was the provision that the pope would depose from their sees any and all bishops who did not wish thus to resign. Never in the entire history of the Church had a Pope done that; not even Innocent III or Boniface VIII, the most ardent proponents of papal authority in the Middle Ages, would ever have thought they could do it. Another example: More formal doctrinal pronouncements came from the Holy See in the 150 years from 1815 to 1965 in the form of encyclicals, decrees of Vatican congregations, briefs and solemn declarations than probably in any other previous five hundred year period. Where before the nineteenth century bishops had often spoken doctrinally for their own dioceses and had turned to the Catholic faculties of theology in their countries for commentaries on such matters, now they increasingly turned to Rome.

The religious orders did so too. More and more they moved their headquarters there, not a common situation until after the mid-nineteenth century. More and more they centralized decisions in those headquarters rather than at the national or province level. More and more those general headquarters turned to the Roman congregations for advice or rulings and more and more the congregations took on such legislative activity. All of this culminated, of course, in the code of canon law of 1917, one of the most impressive, ordered, universal, legislative codes, civil or religious, ever put together. The doctrinal underpinnings of all of this, of course, were the decrees of Vatican I on primacy and infallibility. It was not that the Pope explicitly exercised those ministries of infallibility and primacy very often. It was rather that they were there as the ultimate bulwark for the lesser but increasingly pervasive legislation of the Holy See.

Such were some of the circumstances in which a reinvigorated church and reestablished religious orders labored in this last century and a half. And a magnificent labor it was. One has only to look at what was accomplished to see that, especially in the United States where the number of religious men and women grew as never or anywhere before, where the variety of apostolates was extraordinary, where new communities such as the Maryknolls, both women and men, or the Paulists or the Xaverians arose. Inevitably with the success came the problems such as a preponderance of structure over vision, of canonical enactments over memory of the Lord in whose name they were promulgated, of routine over charisma. We all can recall the problems. We ought also to recall the graced times, the heroic lives, the extraordinary results, the love of the Lord which imbued that century and a half.

Since Vatican II

Vatican II brought change, not in everything, not everywhere. But a vision of the Lord and church and world and person was born out of a return to the sources of tradition in the church and out of a simultaneous move forward into new structures, new sensibilities, new understandings of the gospel and of the way it is to be lived.

I could go on for as long a time as I already have simply in detailing what has happened in these last twenty years in religious life. But those two decades are so recent that they are not yet history but rather current events.

To return, as I conclude, to the beginnings of this presentation: the major historical forms of religious life have moved from private to public, from monasticism to canons regular, to mendicant orders, to clerics regular, to modern apostolic congregations. Except for the clerics regular those forms have regularly included both men and women. With the clerics regular, it is not in the particular ordained character of its members but rather in their apostolic activities that the apostolic orders of women have been similar. This is a change from a much older pattern of similarity in character rather than in activity which yet needs much historical investigation and theological analysis. But whatever the particular major historical forms of religious life, those communities in general have embodied the memory of the Lord in vision, in structure and in activity within the larger community of a church which accepts this service.

These are among the essentials which make up the history of religious life. But by far the most important things which go into every example of religious life and religious community are well summed up in the titles of the three documents which since Vatican II have been the charters of renewal: <u>Perfectae</u> <u>Caritatis</u> and <u>Evangelica</u> <u>Testificatio</u> and <u>Mutuae</u> <u>Relationes</u>. We all know what those Latin phrases mean: "Wholehearted Love" and "Gospel Witness" and "Mutual Relationships." In their myriad forms over fifteen hundred years of history, at the center of religious communities and of the lives of men and women in those religious communities of the church, have been wholehearted love of the Lord and of each other, and gospel witness in word and deed to the values which Jesus came to live out for us and with us. In our own times we now recognize that we are all in this together, that interrelatedly religious and clerics and bishops and laity should be at the mutual service of each other for the sake of the kingdom of God. I am confident that it is these elements, wholehearted love and gospel witness and service of each other for the sake of the kingdom which are still at the center of what is essential to religious life and that they will, thank heaven, also be at the center of its memory, vision and structure for the years to come.

Historical Perspectives on the Experience of Religious Life in the American Church

by

Karen M. Kennelly, C.S.J.

One has to be either foolhardy or ignorant (or both) to approach this topic, given its complexity and profundity. I am cheered as I take up the task by the old story which defined three things known only to the Holy Spirit. The first is how much the Dominicans know; the second, how much the Jesuits think they know; and the third, how many congregations of religious there are in the world!

Being neither Dominican nor Jesuit is assumed to give me the proper historian's objectivity to deal with this topic. And being only human, I can be excused for not having exact statistics to report concerning numerical aspects of the experience of American religious.

With the hope of focusing attention on historical developments which are crucial for the evolving experience of religious life in the United States, I have organized my explorations around four periods of time: missionary beginnings to around 1830; the early immigrant experience from 1830 to 1900; the time of maturing as part of an immigrant church from 1900 to 1940; and a period of emerging American traits from 1940 to 1965. Topically I propose to examine what religious communities of women and men experienced in terms of the spirit and purposes of religious life in the United States church, and what their collective experience was regarding such specifics as membership, community life, prayer and ministry, governance, and finance. I will lean heavily on a few communities to exemplify generalizations and to give flesh and blood to what might otherwise be an abstract, speculative, assessment.

Two features strike us as we examine our beginnings in what is now the United States of America: the precariousness and impermanency of early missionary efforts, and the absence of women religious until well toward the end of this period. The period itself is long, stretching from the middle of the sixteenth century when Franciscans and Jesuits began their missionary apostolates in this country, to 1830 when European emigration triggered a series of changes which were to transform a colonial into an immigrant church.

The chart I have prepared (see end of article) identifies the religious communities whose experience spans the first several centuries of European contact with present-day United States: various male branches of the Franciscan Order (First Order friars, Recollects, Capuchins, Third Order); Jesuits; Sulpicians; Ursulines—the first women religious; Carmelites; Augustinians; Visitandines; Poor Clares; and Dominicans.

Regular clergy by far outnumbered secular or diocesan clergy during these missionary and colonial years and down through the early independence era. Sulpicians, a society of diocesan clergy; and priests from the Quebec Seminary constituted significant exceptions.

Among the experiences of religious during the missionary phase were: untimely death from violence or sickness; physical hardship and spiritual deprivation; loneliness; a deepened sense of following Christ by bringing the Good News to those who had not heard it. Theirs was a very direct apostolate, marked by a spontaneous and unquestioned adaptation of community customs to individual circumstances and by frequent failures and occasional successes in their work. Virtually all religious were European-born and trained. Mission was not so strongly colored by awareness of nationality and ethnic consciousness as would be true in the nineteenth century. Cultural disparities and language differences severely challenged the ability to evangelize the American Indian, however, and gave rise to many profound insights into intercultural questions. Shifts in colonial control and treatment of Indians often halted missionary efforts, as when the Louisiana Territory changed hands, when Spain lost control over its American colonies, and when tribes of Indians were forced to migrate or were decimated by wars and disease.

Religious had a close relationship to bishops in the sense that most of the early bishops were themselves religious. On the other hand, there were very few bishops to whom to relate. The southwest missions came under San Juan, Puerto Rico and later Mexico City. The vast Louisiana Territory came first under Quebec and then under San Juan and later still, under Santiago de Cuba. The former English colonies received their first resident bishop in the person of John Carroll of Baltimore in 1789.

The early years of the eighteenth century saw the initial breaking up of these huge jurisdictions with the according of episcopal status to New Orleans, New York, Boston,

Philadelphia, and Bardstown (Louisville), the last-named including the old Northwest Territory. The first cluster of six bishops included two Jesuits, a Dominican, a Franciscan, a Sulpician, and the incomparable John Lefebvre de Cheverus of Boston from the ranks of the French diocesan clergy. This pattern began to alter with the next series of episcopal appointments, although replacements, and appointments to new sees created in the 1820's and 30's, included a majority of religious from the above-named communities and from the Vincentians.

The initial absence of women religious is a reflection of role expectations in early modern European society and of the Tridentine requirement of cloister for women. We have already noted the arrival of the Ursulines in New Orleans in 1727; their New World history actually reached back to 1639 when they came to Quebec. A Sister of St. Joseph, Anna Maria Javouhey, set the stage for a widespread participation of women in overseas missions in 1817 and 1819 when she sent a group of Sisters to Reunion Island and Senegal (Jedin, ed. History of the Church, VII, 198). By then, the impulse to religious vocation among women in the United States was expressing itself in a way that was to accelerate the differentiation of European from American modes of living the religious life. The women founded religious congregations in the United States, most of which established no governance ties to a European motherhouse even though European Rules were utilized.

The trend began with a few Catholic women in Maryland who, lacking the opportunity to become religious in the colonies, entered a Carmelite monastery in Flanders. The French Revolution compelled them to return to Maryland where they became the nucleus for an American Carmelite community, the majority of whose members continued to be American-born. As of 1850, 41 of their 53 entrants had come from Maryland families (Barbara Misner, "Highly Respectable and Accomplished Ladies: Early American Women Religious, 1790-1850," University of Notre Dame Working Paper Series, Series 8, No. 1, Fall, 1980, p. 23 and Table 3a).

By the end of the missionary-colonial period, eight permanent communities of women religious had been established. Although each eventually adopted a traditional rule, each was formed by a core of American-born or by immigrant women who had not been trained in an existing European community. In addition to the Maryland Carmelites, there were the Visitation Sisters of Georgetown, the three Kentucky communities, the

Oblates of Baltimore (first among communities for Negroes), the Sisters of Charity of Emmitsburg, and the Sisters of Charity of Our Lady of Mercy in Charleston.

The Emmitsburg community illustrates much of what can be said about the experience of these American women religious. Elizabeth Seton, whose saintliness has now been recognized by canonization, felt herself to be called to live a vowed religious life. She attracted other women to do this with her. They supported themselves by teaching children, and, upon the advice of Sulpician priests and Bishop Carroll, adopted the rule used by the Daughters of Charity as the framework for their life together. Again at the advice and with the support of Carroll, they began teaching in a tuition-free parish school setting, thus initiating what would become a parochial school system in the United States.

An early consideration of affiliation with a French motherhouse was deferred for nearly forty years because of Mother Seton's apprehensions, a sense that French customs might contradict American needs, and an inclination toward autonomy. Concerned lest affiliation would deprive her of the latitude she needed within the religious life to continue to mother her own children and to direct her community to meet American needs, and satisfied that the Emmitsburg community was developing as a truly religious and blessed undertaking independent of France, Mother Seton died in 1821 without pursuing the affiliation which was finally to come in 1850.

Meantime, growth enabled the community to send members to Philadelphia, New York, Boston, and somewhat later to Cincinnati in response to the request of bishops in these cities. There the sisters opened schools, orphanages, and hospitals. They settled into a daily horarium of prayer, meals, and recreation accommodated to their work; kept silence during certain times of the day and in certain parts of their simple houses as the main vestige of cloister retained in the rule and customs of the Daughters whom St. Vincent had told "let the rooms of the sick be your cloister." They wore a common dress, and covered their heads with a simple bonnet not too dissimilar from the ladies' fashion of the day--habits became more elaborate as and when European custom asserted itself. Bishops found these religious a marvelous addition to their flock, indispensable for initiating or continuing parochial schools and tending to the needy within their dioceses.

Men religious were much in demand also, to complement the women as teachers of older boys and to take charge of parishes and dioceses. Not all bishops would have completely concurred with Archbishop DuBourg of New Orleans writing to the Propagation of the Faith in 1826: "It is scarcely possible to realize how contagious even to the clergy and to men otherwise well disposed, are the principles of freedom and independence imbibed by all the pores in these United States. Hence I have always been convinced that practically all the good to be hoped for must come from the Congregations or religious Orders, among which flourish strict discipline" (DuBourg to Peter Caprano of the Propagation, 1826, cited by Ewen, The Role of the Nun in Nineteenth Century America, 72). His remarks underline the enthusiasm with which religious were recruited even before large numbers of immigrant Catholics began to transform the parishes of the port cities and of the river-canal routes to the interior.

The discipline DuBourg admired among religious was to undergo a severe test when congregations began assimilating bold and democratic Americans, utterly lacking in a proper sense of social class distinctions and disrespectful toward authority. The fact that discipline and traditional concepts of obedience and government were upheld is indicative of the limits of adaptation and assimilation in the nineteenth century.

The men and women religious in existence in the United States by 1830, whether European or American-born, were part of an Anglo-American church which was about to be transformed into a church of immigrants. A glance at statistics suggests the enormity and pace of change: 250,00 Catholics came in the 1830's; 700,000 in the 1840's; 1,000,000 in the 1860's. The decades of heaviest immigration came after that, at a pace of 1,000,000 per decade from 1880 to 1920 (over 2,000,000 in the 1901-10 decade alone), with a resultant increase in Catholics from 6,259,000 to 16,363,000. The 1880 to 1920 influx moved the Catholic population from less than 1/10 to approximately 1/5 of the national census. Eastern and midwestern cities absorbed the bulk of the newcomers. By the end of the century, immigrants or children of first generation immigrants constituted 4/5 of New York City's residents. Even by 1840, the impact was enormous: the eight lay-taught parish schools of Manhattan were utterly inadequate to educate the estimated 20,000 Catholic immigrant children whose language and religion inhibited their entrance into the common school system (Dolan, The Immigrant Church, 99-111; Hennesey, American Catholics, 116-127).

Hinterland cities and dioceses were worse off. Matthias Loras, as first bishop of Dubuque in 1837, assumed episcopal responsibility for a territory reaching from Missouri to Canada with the grand total of one priest to help minister to Indians, French-Canadians, and other assorted settlers. Of course, it did help that the priest was the zealous and experienced Dominican, Samuel Mazzuchelli. Loras lost no time trying to recruit religious to join him and succeeded within a few years in bringing a group of Irish Trappist monks and the nineteen women (mostly Irish immigrants) who comprised the entire community of the Sisters of Charity of the Blessed Virgin Mary. The account of the BVM's journey from their first home in Philadelphia to their new mission on the bluffs of the Mississippi reads like a guidebook to the migrations of religious communities in the mid-nineteenth century. Leaving Philadelphia in 1843, the women broke their trip to stay with the Emmitsburg Sisters of Charity in Pittsburgh, and again with the Nazareth Charities in Louisville, whose habit they seem to have imitated when they adopted a common garb in the 1850's. The last leg of their trip allowed for a stayover with the Emmitsburg sisters again, this time in St.Louis where seven communities were by then resident: besides the Emmitsburg Charities there were the Visitandines, Madames of the Sacred Heart, Sisters of St. Joseph, Jesuits, Victorians, and Vincentians.

From the broader perspective of the seventy-year period 1830-1900, it was an era of remarkable expansion of religious communities more or less following the streams of immigration and the elaboration of ecclesiastical structure in the nation. Approximately 220 religious communities made foundations. Women's communities continued to show a striking difference from men's with respect to having European motherhouses, only a third of their foundations being governed from Europe compared to four-fifths of the men's. Continuing a trend begun in the 1820's, religious foundations by women outnumbered those of men by more than four to one.

Communities which were independent of Europe had this status because of their original autonomous position as American foundations or because efforts to maintain a link with the founding European motherhouse either were not made or were unsuccessful. As has been noted, one American community, the Sisters of Charity of Emmitsburg, reversed the autonomy of early years by affiliating with the Paris Daughters of Charity.

You can appreciate the complexity involved in gaining an historical perspective on the experience of religious in the United States during this period. The bewildering number of distinct orders and congregations; the progressive intermingling of European and American membership in many; the rapidity with which new foundations were made in diverse urban and rural settings and among diverse ethnic groups; and the paucity of narrative sources which could illuminate the ways in which Rule books were observed,--all conspire to render this a difficult if not impossible task. Rather than attempting to generalize on the basis of my admittedly sketchy knowledge, I have concentrated my perspective on certain themes, and on a representative religious community, the Sisters of St. Joseph. In this way, I hope to identify experiences which probably have broad validity for the period.

Themes which I regard as of key importance for understanding American experience of religious life in the nineteenth century are: the resolution of canonical questions, particularly those relating to papal or diocesan status and cloister regulations; spirituality and interpretation of the Rule; and ministry.

The Sisters of St. Joseph, alluded to earlier in the person of Anna Marie Javouhey and the Cluny group, is typical of post-Tridentine congregations which afforded women the opportunity to be religious while taking only simple vows and engaging in active works of the apostolate. As such, it is an early example of its kind, having been established in France in 1651 after communities with similar intentions, such as those begun by Angela Merici, Jane Francis de Chantal and Francis de Sales, Vincent de Paul, and Mary Ward, had been forced to observe cloister or to employ pious subterfuges--avoiding the title of Sister and replacing perpetual vows with annual promises--in order to retain their freedom of movement.

Dispersed by the French Revolution and refounded in the early eighteenth century, the Sisters of St. Joseph of Lyons were persuaded by the Vincentian Bishop Rosati in 1836 to send Sisters to St. Louis. St. Louis, actually the settlement of Carondelet south of the city, became the mother site for numerous daughter houses beginning with Philadelphia (1847) and continuing, in chronological order of foundation, with St. Paul, Toronto, Wheeling, Buffalo, Brentwood, Albany, Erie, Baden, Rochester, Rutland, Boston, Tucson-Los Angeles, Watertown, Springfield, Concordia, Wichita, Tipton, Nazareth, and LaGrange, all before 1900. Additional St.Joseph foundations were made directly from France, (from the diocesan congregations of Bourg and Chambery) in New Orleans (1855) and in West Hartford (1885). More would be made after 1900 by Carondelet's daughters and directly from France.

Only two of these foundations, St. Paul and Albany, responded to Carondelet's invitation in the mid-eighteenth century to consider a form of central government; the bishops of Buffalo, Toronto, Philadelphia, Brooklyn, and Wheeling insisted on submission to diocesan episcopal jurisdiction. All of Carondelet's progeny remained independent of European motherhouses. Americanization was accelerated by this action, as well as by early acceptance of American-born novices, almost no personnel from Europe, early translation of the Rule into English, and work among diverse ethnic groups (Byrne, "The Sisters of St. Joseph: The Americanization of a French Tradition," unpublished ms. 1982, 5-1).

The Sisters of St. Joseph pattern had parallels in many communities of this period. It exemplifies an experience which women's communities had with the hierarchy, one marked by the bishops' desire not only to recruit religious but also to control where they would work. The annals of communities are replete with instances of bishops persuading, conniving, even forcing adoption of diocesan status. Most bishops came to agree with Bishop Martin Spalding's opinion that, "It is well that each diocese should have a motherhouse and a novitiate" (letter of 1856, cited Ewen, 129). Most communities, intent upon meeting the needs of the local church where they had begun to put down roots, freely cooperated with bishops. The net effect of this process was to insulate communities from European influence and to narrow the scope of their nineteenth century expansion to within the boundaries of dioceses to which they had become attached during the initial dispersion phase.

The pluralism to which this trend could have led was checked by the commonality of the Rule and customs followed by each "family" of related foundations, by the traditions handed on by living members of each congregation, and by accountability to Rome. Although the jumble of canonical laws and regulations produced since the thirteenth century was not reduced to any kind of order until the codification of 1917, Pius IX and Leo XIII fostered such centralizing measures as the 1860 Norms for new congregations and a model rule, and review of constitutions as a prelude to the granting of pontifical right. Pius X reorganized the curia in 1908 to bring religious communities of men and women under the new

Sacred Congregation for Religious. The Sisters of St. Joseph of Carondelet submitted their Rule for papal approval in 1863 and were granted pontifical right in 1877.

The Rule followed by the Sisters of St. Joseph derived from the so-called Rule of St. Augustine, thoroughly adapted to the purposes of an active religious community. Its flexibility with respect to vows, prayer, cloister practices, ministry, clothing, government, and finances partially relieved the Sisters of St. Joseph of the tensions which permeated the experience of other communities.

Many other congregations of women, such as the Benedictines, Franciscans, and Dominicans, had monastic or semi-monastic rules premised on observance of cloister and extensive hours of choir prayer. Faced with intractible financial circumstances; uncomprehending or desperate bishops; members whose health could not support the combined demands of nocturnal prayer, a full day of teaching or caring for the sick or for orphaned children, farm and house work; in a word by general incompatibility of cloister regulations and their American milieu, these groups went through years of seeking dispensations and clarifications before reconciling their rule with their lives and environment.

Much of the tension arose from the Tridentine mentality, from which the Sisters of St. Joseph and like communities did not completely escape, of considering cloister and solemn vows as necessary elements for the religious life. Ambiguities persisted regarding the status of persons making simple vows, and concerning the need for active congregations to imitate a monastic horarium. This mentality, reinforced by a moralistic spirituality which laid great stress on personal salvation, deeply affected the experience of American religious. Adaptation to the United States milieu was traumatic and prolonged, with outcomes which are only today becoming evident. The spontaneity and free adaptation to frontier conditions yielded to a highly regimented form of community living. This tendency was aggravated by the frequent organization of very large houses, a circumstance which made it possible for one twentieth century philosopher to analyze religious communities using the prison as a model.

Although I have concentrated my remarks on women's communities, men were not immune from similar tensions and needs to adapt. It may surprise us to learn, for example, that the Rule of Alphonsus Ligouri observed by Redemptorist priests who began their work in the U.S. in 1850, designated most areas of their rectories as off-limits to parishioners, forbade them to visit homes of parishioners alone, and even when accompanied, only for purpose of comforting the sick and dying. Permission of the superior was required before parish social events could be attended; contacts with women were strictly prohibited, as was also smoking in public.

Nothing had a greater impact on the experience of American religious during this period than their ministry, particularly the absorption of women religious in the evolving parochial school system. The story of the maturing of religious life from 1900 to 1940 is very much intertwined with the parish school growth, as well as with the institutionalization of the roles of religious in parishes and in various charitable works.

Broadly viewed, the history of religious communities during the first part of the twentieth century is one in which regular clergy yielded to the diocesan clergy many parish and most episcopal roles. Men religious dedicated most of their apostolic energies to the preaching of missions and retreats, and to secondary and higher education for men. Women assumed the staffing of most of the charitable institutions of the United States church, including hospitals and schools, and established colleges for the education of women.

Entrants into the religious life continued to exceed numbers lost by separation or death, the great majority of recruits coming from first and second generation immigrant families with an average of eight children. (Catholic University Masters theses 1950-52; see, for example, Blanchette, A Study of the Environmental Factors of Vocations to the Congregation of the Sisters of St. Joseph of Carondelet St. Paul Province, 1954, based on survey of entrants pre-1900 to 1952). The resultant experience of religious was that of a relatively youthful membership expressing its apostolic zeal through pastoral care, education, other charitable works, or, in the case of contemplative groups, through a life of intensive prayer.

Approximately 180 congregations established houses in the United States during this era, women's foundations outnumbering men's by more than three to one. The women reversed their previous tendency to sever ties with European motherhouses and to generate brand new communities in the United States. Four-fifths of all foundations initiated at this time retained a European motherhouse; very few indigenous congregations were begun. This pattern, plus the fact that the new foundations were initiated by European members which frequently did not speak English extended into the twentieth century the process of adapting European to American modes of interpreting the religious life. At the same time, the question of canonical status which had troubled American religious in the previous century was resolved by the canon law codification of 1917. Room was found at last in the juridical definition of religious life for persons taking simple as well as solemn vows. By a rather strange quirk of juridical fate, no Benedictine woman in the United States could be accorded the title and functions of an abbess, this office being restricted to communities whose members took solemn vows. The religious life was portrayed in the 1917 code as a higher and better way for the baptized Christian to earn salvation, an expression of scholastic and Tridentine theology of religious life which was not to be questioned for some decades yet to come.

A closer examination of one community's history during this period can, as before, help exemplify these generalizations in specific terms. I have again focused on the Sisters of St. Joseph, this time on its diocesan branch in Boston. Here, a recently published study of religious and parochial schools of the archdiocese permits us to trace the impact of ministry on a twentieth century American congregation. (Oates, "Organized Volunteerism: The Catholic Sisters in Massachusetts, 1890-1940," American Quarterly, 1978, 652-680).

When the Sisters of St. Joseph came to Boston in 1873, the archdiocese incorporated most of the state of Massachusetts. Immigration had drastically altered the Anglo-American complexion of the state's Catholic population from 1830 onward; introduction of parochial schools had been slow, reflecting the reluctance of Bishop Williams to develop such schools and the scarcity of resources with which to do so. A handful of religious communities, with men and women in approximately equal numbers, made up the church's labor force in Boston as of 1870.

Although seventeen different communities had established houses in Boston by 1900, there was a pronounced tendency for one or two communities, in this case, the Sisters of Notre Dame de Namur and Sisters of St. Joseph, to predominate, and for women's communities to concentrate on parochial school teaching as their chief and well nigh sole apostolate. This latter tendency was induced by the demand for women religious as teachers and by the compatibility between their teaching and their religious vocation.

The movement from diverse occupations to the single one of teaching can be detected already by 1880. By 1940, two-thirds of all Sisters in the archdiocese of Boston were to be found in the occupation of parochial school teaching; the proportion reached over 95% for the Sisters of St. Joseph. Numbers in hospital work, social work, academies and boarding schools were minuscule. We are struck by the fact that this trend gained momentum and persisted at the very time that women's work in the United States was becoming more, rather than less diversified. And this in a religious congregation such as the Sisters of St. Joseph whose primitive constitution identified as part of its charism "to provide for all spiritual and temporal needs of the beloved neighbor," and "to practice all the spiritual and corporal works of mercy of which woman is capable." It is not too hard to imagine that the Church's later appeal to religious communities to return to their charism would cause some soul-searching and provoke some thoughtful reassessment of ministry in this and other congregations.

Scrutiny of the finances of the Boston parochial school system has much to tell us about the experience of American religious and sheds light on the strong push toward women teachers in this and other diocesan systems. Statistics show that salaries accounted for nearly two-thirds of expenses in Boston's public schools in the late nineteenth and early twentieth centuries. Parish experience can be assumed to match this fairly closely, with the consequence that the feasibility of maintaining a parish school system rested largely upon the ability to control salaries. Taking their cue from the prevalent labor practice of paying women half of what men were paid, parishes employed women religious for half the salary paid to men religious, namely, to the Christian Brothers, who, in turn, were hired at half the salary paid to lay men in the public school system. Put another way: Christian Brothers received twice the payment given to Sisters, but only half what their lay colleagues received. The amount paid to Sisters came to about three-fifths of the estimated living wage for women workers in Boston.

This situation was repeated wherever dioceses strove to implement the Council of Baltimore's injunction to build a school in every parish. By some astounding slight-of-hand, religious managed to subsist. The women, particularly hard pressed, found ways to supplement teaching income by charging tuition in academies and collecting fees for art and music lessons. They began to receive lay salary equivalents as hospital employees in the 1930's when third party payment came into the picture and it became advisable to attach a cash figure to every employee's work in order to secure equitable reimbursement for costs.

In addition to setting financial precedents which congregations could tolerate only so long as a majority of their members were young and able to earn, the segregation of religious personnel in parochial school teaching affected the kind and number of vocations and formation programs. An increasingly larger percentage of those who entered religious life during this period came after having had some formal Catholic education; many who came did so with an attraction for the apostolates in which specific congregations were engaged. In part, this attraction sprang from the obvious dedication with which religious were living out their charism of performing the works of mercy. Schools and hospitals served the poor in a very direct manner, as did also other works taken care of by religious. Nobody but the poor went to hospitals in the early days when Sisters opened such institutions; the same could be said for many an immigrant parish school.

In their rush to supply the demand for teachers, and with little money to spare, religious communities were very slow to modify formation programs. For the women, this meant a one or at most a two-year novitiate, frequently with admission to perpetual vows at the conclusion of the two-year novitiate and part-time teaching for the second year novice. Years went by before Sisters were given opportunities to prepare themselves for teaching by formal studies beyond high school. The first baccalaureate degree earned by a Sister of St. Joseph of Boston was in 1921. The struggle to up-grade Sisters' education to better prepare them for the classroom and, as time went by, to meet state certification standards, replaced canonical status and autonomy as the signle greatest source of tension between bishops and communities in the first half of the twentieth century.

Monastic communities participated in this struggle to the extent that they took up pastoral and educational responsi- bilities which did not always accord well with their monastic calling. Strictly contemplative groups, on the other hand, succeeded in maintaining their vocation intact. The first part of the twentieth century was, for them, a time of slow growth in numbers and expansion to parts of the United States from which they had been absent in the previous century. Although I have not probed the subject, I have the impression that episcopal attitudes toward contemplative religious had changed by the 1900's from one of doubtful toleration to warm acceptance.

John Carroll's reaction to the Carmelites in 1790 was certainly of the doubting sort--as Carroll said to Antonelli of the Propaganda Fide in a letter of 1792, the nuns were edifying to their neighbors, winning the admiration even of non-Catholics, but "they would be a far greater benefit in the future if a school for the training of girls in piety and learning were begun by them" (letter cited Ewen, 37, as given in Guilday, The Life and Times of John Carroll 1735-1815, 490). The nuns declined to use the teaching dispensation Carroll secured for them; he finally got his teachers in the person of Elizabeth Seton and her companions as well as in the Visitandines and the Ursulines.

The attitude Carrol expressed was slow to die, as witness Bishop Martin Spalding's relations with the Gethsemani Trappists in the 1850's. He gave the monks permission to hold a fund drive if they would build primary schools in the diocese. The monks held the drive, built a school on their property, and persuaded five local women to become religious and teach in the school (an initial try to keep the school going with lay teachers failed). To make a long story short: the five completed a novitiate under the Oldenburg Franciscans and returned to begin a new community near Gethsemani. Having taught for a time, they conceived of a desire to become Trappistines. The then-bishop McCloskey refused their request, and forced them to move their motherhouse from Gethsemani grounds to Shelbyville, a safe distance from Trappist influence! ("Franciscans," portion contributed by M.A. Welch, New Catholic Encyclopedia, VI, 62). Incidents of this kind become a rarity as dioceses and bishops grew in wisdom, age, and grace, and as contemplatives acclimated themselves to the American environment.

The separatism which characterized communities in the nineteenth century, even among those sharing the same Rule, was modified from 1900 to 1940 by means of federations and unions. Typical of this trend were the Benedictine federations, the Sisters of Mercy Union, the Ursuline unions, the Visitation federations, and federations participated in by Franciscans, Dominicans, and Sisters of St. Joseph.

This evidence of growing communication among congregations brings me to the themes which characterize the last period upon which I wish to comment, namely, the years from 1940 to 1965. As I try to gain some historical perspective on those years, they seem to me to have been both a culminating and germinal period for American religious life. Culminating in the sense that the experiences of the immigrant era now had overt consequences; germinal in the sense that many experiences still lay imbedded in the lives of religious, awaiting full expression until the next generation. The adaptation of religious communities to an immigrant American Church was complete; their adaptation to American society and culture had only just begun.

European, Canadian, and Latin American congregations continued to establish houses in the United States. The pace of new foundations accelerated in the 1950's and dropped off sharply after that; total numbers reached over 80 for the women and over 50 for the men. Among congregations with a long United States pedigree, concern over the preparation of religious for life and ministry led to a restructuring of formation programs and to the Sister Formation movement. Advanced study in the key area of theology presented a particularly frustrating problem for women religious, important as it was for growth in the spiritual life and for the teaching of religion, and closed as it was to the feminine sex. No Catholic university offering advanced degrees in theology admitted women to these programs; that seminaries were closed to women goes without saying. Leadership within the Sisters of the Holy Cross offered a partial solution to the dilemma by introducing graduate studies in theology at St. Mary's college in 1943.

Those who gave papal documents a serious reading perceived in <u>Mediator Dei</u> and <u>Mystici Corporis</u> the seeds of a revitalized theology of religious life, one that would replace the Tridentine emphasis on personal salvation and a hierarachy of states of perfection with an understanding of a common baptismal call to holiness and to participation in a community of the faithful. Liturgical reform and scriptural scholarship watered these seeds.

The ground was well cultivated by the time Pius XII convened the General Congress on the State of Perfection in Rome in 1950 and urged religious to return to the spirit which had animated their founders and to adapt outmoded customs to the demands of the day. Saintly founders and foundresses had incarnated Christ in their own time and country. The theme of the congress was "accommodata renovatio," or the renewal of the primitive spirit of religious institutes adapted to needs of the present day.

American religious heard this message and began to respond. They also responded as to a wind of the Spirit when Pius XII enjoined them to look beyond their dioceses and their American abundance by assigning 10% of their personnel to third-world missions. United States congregations selected sites and began sending members to missions in Latin America, Asia, and Africa. The movement begun by the Maryknoll society in 1911, only three years after the United States was itself removed from mission status, now had its marvellous consequences.

In a related development, a subtle shift was taking place among religious away from a traditional concept of social reform. Having for years labored to carry out the works of mercy so as to alleviate the sufferings of the ignorant, the poor, the sick, the hungry and the homeless, religious now began to reflect on the necessity for structural change and social activism if the church was to be true to its Gospel mission.

In the end, it was a Belgian, Cardinal Suenens, who crystallized these conceptual movements among American religious into a call for action on the eve of the Second Vatican Council. His central thesis, set forth in a 1957 book, The Gospel to Every Creature, and further explicated in The Nun in the World published in 1962, was that all Christians and certainly all religious, excepting the strictly contemplative, had an obligation to exercise the direct apostolate, that is, to spread the gospel by direct personal action.

It was the best of times, it was the worst of times. Religious community membership had reached numerical levels which have been declining ever since. American congregations were on the brink of a crisis from which they are still emerging. I will leave it to later speakers at this symposium to probe the dimensions of the changes which were gathering momentum as religious communities of sisters, brothers, and priests completed an era of adaptation to the American immigrant church and began an era of adaptation to American society.

MISSIONARY ERA	IMMIGRANT AND INDIGENOUS
1550-1789	COMMUNITIES
	1790-1860

Franciscans

Jesuits

Sulpicians   1790-1829

Quebec Seminary   Carmelites
Priests   Maryland

Ursulines   Augustinians
                                                    Philadelphia

Carmelites   Visitandines
                                                    Georgetown

                                                    Dominicans
                                                    Kentucky

                                                    Poor Clares
                                                    Baltimore

                                                    Sisters of Charity
                                                    of Emmitsburg
                                                    Baltimore

                                                    Sisters of Loretto
                                                    Kentucky

                                                    Sisters of Charity
                                                    of Nazareth, Kentucky

                                                    Madames of the Sacred
                                                    Heart
                                                    St. Louis

                                                    Vincentians
                                                    Arkansas, Missouri,
                                                    Illinois (upper
                                                    Louisiana missions)

                                                    Sisters of Charity of
                                                    Our Lady of Mercy
                                                    Cincinnati

1830-1839	1840-1849	1850-1859
Jesuits Maryland Province	Sisters of Providence Terre Haute	Daughters of the Heart of Mary Massachusetts
Sisters of Charity of the Blessed Virgin Mary Philadelphia/Dubuque	Sisters of Notre Dame de Namur Cincinnati	Benedictines St. Mary's, PA
Sisters of St. Joseph of Carondelet St. Louis	Holy Cross Indiana	Passionists Pittsburg
Priests of Mercy New York	Sisters of the Holy Family New Orleans	Sisters of Charity of the Incarnate Word Texas
	Sisters of Mercy New York	Sisters of the Presentation of the Blessed Virgin Mary San Francisco
	Marianites of the Holy Cross New Orleans	Sisters of Providence Seattle
	Good Shepherd Kentucky	Congregation of the Holy Humility of Mary Pennsylvania
	Sisters of the Precious Blood Missouri	Daughters of the Cross Louisiana
	Franciscans Friars Minor Cincinnati	Sisters of Our Lady of Charity of the Refuge Wisconsin
	Brothers of the Christian Schools Baltimore	Sisters of St. Agnes Wisconsin

1830-1839 (cont.)	1840-1849 (cont.)	1850-1859 (cont.)
	Servants of the Immaculate Heart of Mary Monroe	Franciscan Brothers of Brooklyn
	Benedictines St. Vincent's, PA	Paulists New York
	School Sisters of Notre Dame Pennsylvania	Sisters of the Holy Names of Jesus and Mary Oregon
	Brothers of the Sacred Heart New Orleans	
	Cistercians (Trappists) Kentucky	
	Franciscan Sisters Milwaukee; LaCrosse	
	Missionary Oblates of Mary Immaculate	
	Marianists Cincinnati	

Sources: James Hennesey, American Catholics
Barbara Misner, Early American Women Religious, 1790-1850
Catholic Almanac, 1984
Catholic Encyclopedia
New Catholic Encyclopedia

The Theology of "The Essential Elements"
in the Teaching of the Church

by

John Manuel Lozano C.M.F.

I have been entrusted with a delicate task: to attempt a formulation of the theology and spirituality of the religious life, as delineated in the church's most recent magisterial documents relating to this theme. Before I proceed directly to the theme itself, allow me to interpose a few important reflections.

1. Preliminary Observations

1.1   If theology as a whole is an historical undertaking, not only because it is a human activity carried out in the context of certain cultural suppositions, but also because it deals with the way the divine is historically revealed to human beings and experienced by them, then the theology of the religious life is, if possible, even more historical since its object is a type or, rather, several types of Christian existence which have been created by the Holy Spirit in history. Religious life, broadly speaking, is a form of Christian discipleship which has continued to develop historically in response to the action of the Risen Lord: a response that is intimately conditioned by particular cultural and ecclesial horizons. This accounts for the rich variety of forms it has taken, as well as the wealth of interpretations it has been given by the church's ministers and by theologians in different times.

1.2.   We cannot adequately understand what the church is teaching about the religious life today, unless we understand the various levels at which the church not only discerns the action whereby the Holy Spirit creates the religious life, but also attempts to assimilate that life by interpreting it.

1.2.1.   That the Lord Jesus, by sending his Spirit, calls some of the faithful to certain concrete forms of following him, is in itself an ecclesial fact (LG 43b, PC 1b). The church as the Communion of the Saints is already present in the vocation of Anthony of Macrina, Scholastica or Benedict, Louise de Marillac or Vincent de Paul, Catherine McAuley or Edmund Rice.

1.2.2. Secondly, the church, as the community of the disciples of Jesus, asserts its presence by recognizing in these facts, the action and fruits of the Spirit, when its ministers (the bishops or the pope) approve the kind of life, ministry and rule which serves as their source of inspiration and stability (LG 45, PC 1b). The official documents in which the church's pastors have acknowledge these various forms, have almost always been concrete in nature. They approve this or that religious family in particular. It is obvious, however, that when they approve new Institutes with profoundly new characteristics (Franciscans, Jesuits, the Company of Our Lady, etc.), these ecclesial acts, which create the religious life on the canonical level, either confirm or broaden our understanding of the religious life. they are creative acts on the canonical level (although on a more primordial level their creation begins in the Holy Spirit and in the souls of Founders and Foundresses), but they are also, in an incisive yet implicit way, acts of magisterium. Much more sporadically, there have been church acts of a more general character, as when one pope (Innocent IV) stated that the three vows are essential elements of all religious life, or another (Boniface VIII) proclaimed that cloister is essential for women's religious life, or yet another (Pius XII), moving beyond the religious life in the strict canonical sense, acknowledge the existence of secular institutes.

1.2.3. Thirdly, in the realm of the church's explicit teaching activity, we have the doctrinal documents of Vatican II, as well as those of Paul VI and John Paul II. It would obviously be wrong to begin at this third stage, or to read those documents which, because of their rather general character, cannot include the entire spectrum of the rich variety of forms of the religious life, without first taking into account all that the Spirit and the Bride have been doing throughout the ages. Documents that refer to such a variety of vocations as that of a Trappist, a Benedictine, a Carmelite Nun, a Christian Brother and a Sister of Loretto, must perforce limit themselves to a generic vision of the religious life and certainly do not intend to do away with the by no means small differences between them. The pope has referred to these differences in his Letter (no. 3).

1.3. Finally, among the church's recent teaching documents suggested for our consideration, "The Essential Elements," Perfectae Caritatis, Evangelica Testificatio and Mutuae Relationes were mentioned. To these, we would have to add chapter 4 of Lumen Gentium and, more recently, Redemptionis Donum by John Paul II. It should be noted, however, that merely listing these documents in this fashion could be misleading, since the value of "The Essential Elements" is, both canonically and theologically speaking, quite different from that of the two conciliar texts or from the two Apostolic Exhortations or even, for that matter from Mutuae Relationes. For the pope did not take official responsibility for it by signing it, in contrast to Evangelica Testificatio and Redemptionis Donum, nor is it an Instructio or Decretum officially promulgated by Roman Congregations and signed by their Cardinal Prefects, as was Mutuae Relationes. In his letter, the pope refers to the unsigned text as "a document of guidelines" (no. 4) and "the document on the salient points of the church's teaching on religious life" (no. 4). The text itself claims to represent a synthesis of the recent magisterium of the church concerning religious life. It is not, therefore, a new official act of the magisterium as, more recently, Redemptionis Donum was. It should be read as an authoritiative synthesis of the church's teaching, prepared by the Congregation of Religious, in order to serve as a working document for the revision of life asked of apostolic communities and for the committee appointed by the Holy Father. Precisely because this is a summary of other works put together for practical purposes, in any attempt at explaining it theologically, one can do no less than return periodically to those other official documents of the magisterium which the text in hand aims at summing up and expressly citing. Since the document in question expressly states that it is a synthesis or summary, the attention of the theologian trained in the analysis of texts, will naturally be moving back and forth between the summary itself and the magisterial texts which it purports to summarize.

2. The Intent of the Document

2.1.   The "document of guidelines" presents itself as "a clear statement of the Church's teaching regarding the religious life at a moment which is particularly significant and opportune" (Ess. El. 2). That is to say, its redactors have composed this synthesis with an eye to the present circumstances of the religious life and as the title itself reveals with the current situation of apostolic Institutes in mind. And although it is of a rather general character, it has been sent just to the bishops of our country.

2.2.   The reason for this is stated in the letter of John Paul II to the North American Bishops, where he manifests his concern that "individuals and groups . . . have departed from the indispensable norms of religious life" (Letter, April 3,

1983, no. 3). We believe, then, that the document is by way of a response to this problem as it is perceived in Rome. The pope does not spell out just which groups or norms he means, but since he chooses to remedy the situation, not by an apostolic visit to one or more Institutes, but rather by calling all apostolic Institutes to a revision of life and by appointing a committee of bishops to see to it, we can readily see that the "departure from the norms" is viewed as being closely related to some general trends. The pope is evidently concerned that some of these general trends may be present in the apostolic religious communities of the United States. Certain recent events, such as the visitation of seminaries and the withdrawal of some imprimaturs, reveal that the concerns of Rome are not merely limited to North American religious.

3. The Crisis of Religious Life

3.1.   That the religious life has passed through a serious crisis during the last ten years, is a fact so obvious that we hardly need to be reminded of it.[1] The abandonment of the religious life by large numbers of persons has been, throughout the centuries, a clear indication of a crisis in institutions. Individuals tend to withdraw from institutions when the latter lose their meaning or begin to lack cohesion. In general, these crises in institutions of religious life have come about when civil society is undergoing a crisis which, in turn, affects the church on a deep level.[2] It is well known, however, that the term "crisis' does not have an exclusively negative denotation. Historically, crises in institutions of religious life have always been the culture medium in which vigorous new forms or families of religious life have sprung to life. Our institutes, we may say, are all products of a crisis in civil and ecclesiastical society, because they have been born in response to needs for which the existing secular, ecclesial or religious institutions were unable to provide a satisfactory answer. A situation of deep crisis can be noted above all when new forms of religious life make their appearance: the anchorites, Benedictine monasticism, the canons regular, the mendicants, the radically apostolic life of the Jesuits and the lay communities of men and women.

3.2.   The crisis of American religious life is far from being an isolated phenomenon. The whole First World and a good part of the the Third World is passing through it.[3] No: it was not caused by Vatican II. The new type of society, the laity's new awareness of their mission in the

101

church, the growing affirmation of women in American society, the high professional competency demanded of us in our ministries, the consciousness-raising of a good part of the Third World and the heightened sense of social awareness in the First World--all of these were bound sooner or later to provoke a profound crisis. The old model of religious community that was forged in the 18th and 19th centuries could not have withstood the ravages of time. But the Second Vatican Council called us not only to a spiritual renewal but also to an adaptation of life and structures, and the spirits began to escape from the bottle--those spirits (the demons of history) which we are now trying to exorcise.

3.3.   In America, too, the crisis is already beginning to reveal itself as a positive reality, the mother of new life. I am convinced of one fact: that here and now, in these United States toward the close of the 20th century, for the first time in history there is appearing a radically apostolic form of religious life for women, which heretofore had been possible for men only--a life characterized by professionalized personal ministries, and by small and flexible communities. The regimented conventual routine which used to be followed by communities of women devoted to apostolic works is beginning to disappear or to be greatly limited. Naturally, under the motto of renewal and adaptation, and the subsequent fall of a certain tenor of life and not a few structures, many things have been done, some of them excellent, some of them good, and some of them less than good.[4]   Naturally, too, Peter and his brothers in the pastoral ministry are concerned. The religious life is something important for the whole church. We religious can do no less than take this concern seriously.

3.4.   But precisely because we have to take it seriously and respond to it with an attitude of faith and a process of discernment, we cannot avoid facing an historical fact. Periodically throughout the centuries, the concern of the church and above all of its ministers vis a vis what was happening in institutions of religious life, arose not only from phenomena that history would later qualify as illusory, but also from their alarm about new forms of religious life that did not seem to fit into the mold of the theology or canonical norms inherited from the past. The faithful were so scandalized when a group of priests began living with Saint Augustine, that he had to deliver two famous sermons on the matter.[5] Large sectors of the church were scandalized at the appearance of the new Institutes of the 12th century. Attacks and apologias were written,[6] and the pious Reimbald was so moved by the confusion created by the Holy Spirit, that he felt constrained to write his Libellus de Diversis Ordinibus et Professionibus qui sunt in Aecclesia [sic].[7] The mendicants, too, aroused considerable unrest among the faithful, and both Thomas Aquinas and Bonaventure wrote apologias on behalf of their confreres. The Society of Jesus was looked upon with misgivings by earlier orders, since it did not fit into their picture of what the religious life should be. The Vistandine Nuns were enclosed; the Daughters of Charity protected themselves by claiming not to be religious; Mary Ward was finally condemned and imprisoned because she dared to want to establish an apostolic institute for women with a central government. Three centuries were to pass before institutes of simple vows were fully recognized as religious (Leo XIII and the Code of 1917).

3.5.   All of this is understandable up to a certain point. In explaining the sufferings of a number of Founders and Fondresses, Mutuae Relationes observed: "Every authentic charism brings an element of real originality in the spiritual life of the church along with fresh initiatives for action. These may appear unseasonable to many, and even cause difficulties, because it is not always easy to recognize at once that they originate from the Spirit . . . In a genuine charism there is always a mixture of new creativity and interior suffering. The historical fact of the connection between charism and cross, apart from other factors which may give rise to misunderstanding, is an extremely helpful sign of the authenticity of a call of the Spirit (MR, no. 12). The meaning of these words is clear enough. The church often finds it hard to follow the Holy Spirit. Because the Spirit brings new life, while our canons and systems of thought find it hard to press on into the future.

3.6.   We believe that the remembrance of these historical facts and the explanation given them in a document of the Holy See are very much to the point in beginning a process of discernment in faith, peace and communion with the church. Where have we really departed from the fundamental values of the religious life and where, in contrast, has the Spirit of the Lord been leading us away from old models, in order to create new forms of religious life? Mutuae Relationes has told us something that the master teachers of discernment have been repeating for ages: Often, when the Holy Spirit acts in us or in the Church, it is so hard for us to discern his presence and action, that we attribute it to other causes, even those of the opposite spirit. On the other hand, it is far from certain that everything new is the work of the

Spirit. Account must be taken of our weaknesses and limitations. In order to help us situate ourselves--the bishops and religious of the United States--between the Spirit and our own flesh, as we strive to discern the fruits of the Lord from the works of our wounded nature, the pope has sent to the bishops this resume of the church's teaching on the religious life, drawn up by the Congregation for Religious and Secular Institutes.

4. The Content of the Text

4.1.   "Essential Elements" is made up of an introduction and two parts: a longer, doctrinal part and a shorter part containing fundamental juridical norms. The doctrinal part (nos. 5-53) attempts to sum up the essential elements of the church's recent teaching on religious life. The first section of this doctrinal part (nos. 5-12) is devoted to the religious life as a particular form of consecration, while the second section of it (nos. 13-53) explains the various distinctive characteristics of this religious form of life. The text, in an initial list of abbreviations, shows us its main sources: 1) seven conciliar documents (Apostolicam Actuositatem, Ad Gentes, Christus Dominus, Lumen Gentium, Optatam Totius, Perfectae Caritatis and Sacrosanctum Concilium); 2) the decree applying the Council, Ecclesiae Sanctae; 3) Paul VI's Encyclical, Evangelii Nuntiandi and his Apostolic Exhortation, Evangelica Testificatio; 4) the three official documents of the Congregation for Religious and Secular Institutes: Mutuae Relationes, "The Contemplative Dimension of Religious Life" and "Religious and Human Promotion." In the body of the text, moreover, Pius XII's Motu Proprio Primo Feliciter (no. 9), as well as a message of the present Pope (no. 33) are cited. The second part, "Norms," is a resume of the new Code of Canon Law.

4.2.   The document itself, in its introduction, on listing the conciliar, pontifical and curial documents which contain the church's recent teaching on the religious life, tells us that "its doctrinal richness has been distilled and reflected in the revised Code of Canon Law." In fact, anyone who is familiar with the conciliar and pontifical documents on the religious life and now reads "The Essential Elements," will immediately notice that the latter is much nearer the new Code than it is to the Council documents. This is easily explained, not only because those who composed the new text are closer to those who figured in composing the part of the new Code relating to religious, but above all because it is in the new Code that for the first time a common canonical basis had been created for religious and secular institutes and apostolic societies, and where, again for the first time, their differences have been affirmed. This starting from the Code in order to elaborate a theological reflection on the religious life, involves not a few inconveniences. Because it tends to absolutize concepts which in the Code may be functional and many of which have a purely time-bound value, inasmuch as they fix what the church requires today for recognizing a form of religious life, which is not what it required in times past or may require tomorrow. But since the document does not properly aim at being a theological reflection (although it is occasionally forced to enter this field), but rather only a document of guidelines for the present, freedom of investigation is not cut off.

4.3.   We should point out that one source of difficulties that religious of apostolic life (and not only in the United States) may encounter in applying the church's general teaching to our concrete vocation is none other than the new Code of Canon Law. Moreover, these difficulties tend perforce to reappear in doctrinal commentaries deriving from the Code. In the preliminary draft of canons of 1977 there was an attempt to work out a broad typology to cover the rich variety of forms of lives and institutes. Since a good number of religious were upset at not being able to see how they fit in any of the proposed categories, the detailed typology disappeared already in the draft of 1980. In the text that was eventually promulgated, there is an attempt for the first time to include religious, members of the apostolic societies and members of the secular institutes under a common denominator, determining what they have in common, while at the same time distinguishing each kind of institution from the others. This has led to a situation where Carthusians, Discalced Carmelites, Jesuits, Trappists, Sisters of Saint Joseph and Christian Brothers are squeezed into the same little box, canon 607, which attempts to define the canonically constitutive elements of every kind of religious life: a society with public vows, community life, and public witness which is translated into that kind of separation from the world which is proper to the nature and end of each of these institutes. Obviously, both as regards community and as regards this "a mundo separatio," there are many and great differences between a monastic order, an institute specifically founded for intercession (= "contemplation") and orders or congregations devoted to evangelization or to works of social assistance. Each religious institute must therefore read this canon from the point of view of the intention of the foundress or founder and his or her determination concerning the nature, purpose, spirit and character of the institute (cf. canon 577), as recognized officially by the church. This hermeneutical principle must never be forgotten, if we want to avoid confusion in the minds and disarray in the hearts.

5. Elements Common to All Forms of Religious Life

5.1.   In his letter, John Paul II recalls the rich variety with which the religious life appears in the church, thus echoing the statements of the conciliar texts (LG 43b; PC 1). The pope very opportunely recalls that "the essential elements are lived in different ways from one institute to another (no. 3). As always, the common is incarnated in the distinctive, and not separated from it. Even so, however, there are elements which are common to all religious institutes and which the church regards as essential. The Pope goes on to enumerate ten of these elements:

> . . . a vocation given by God, an ecclesial consecration to Jesus Christ through the profession of the evangelical counsels by public vows, a stable form of community life approved by the church, fidelity to a specific founding gift and sound traditions, a sharing in Christ's mission by a corporate apostolate, personal and liturgical prayer, especially Eucharistic worship, public witness, a lifelong formation, a form of government calling for religious authority based on faith, a specific relation to the church.

5.2.   The document of guidelines departs (somewhat strangely, it seems to me) from the list given by the pope. It gives us nine essential elements as opposed to the pope's ten.   While it treats of vocation in connection with consecration, it suppresses "fidelity to a specific founding gift and sound traditions," as an element in itself, and adds in fifth place, "asceticism," which is not mentioned in the pope's letter.   And yet while the pope's letter was dated April 3, 1983, the document was dates almost two months later, May 31, 1983.   We will not dwell on this difference, although it is significant.   Fidelity to the founding charism is a dynamic element, related to the rich variety of charisms referred to in the decree Perfectae Caritatis.   "Asceticism" is a common denominator of every Christian vocation, and is incarnated in a different way in each different vocation, and even more concretely in each of the forms of religious life.

5.3.   Even a cursory glance at the lists given in canon 606, 2-3, in the document and in the pope's letter, reveals that each one of these elements is "essential" for the religious life in quite diverse ways. Some of them are essential constituents of every form of religious life in its very roots and, as such, accessible to theological reflection. Among these we would obviously include: the vocation to this kind of Christian life (a form of discipleship), expressed through the orientation of one's whole existence, by means of celibacy, toward a servitium Dei that goes beyond the initial creation (Genesis), in order to proclaim the errupting presence of the reign of God, and in which, for this every reason, evangelical poverty is manifested in a visible, parabolic form. This type of sequela, created by the Spirit of the Risen Christ, is what has heretofore been called religious life (as it was once called monastic life) and which, since it has also been observed in quite different ways in secular institutes, had to be given a new name in the Code. Such elements already appear among the wandering prophets who, according to the Didache, followed the norms of the Lord, among at least some of the primitive Christian ascetics, among the anchorites and cenobites, among the medieval monks, and so on, until our times. These common constitutive elements, on the radical level discovered by theological reflection and prior to their receiving a canonical configuration, came to be fused with community in the common form of religious life. From another point of view, these radical constitutive elements frequently arise as a demand of a calling to a specific service of God and his church: the vocation to intercession in what we call the contemplative life, and the vocation to apostolic service or charitable works in what we call the apostolic life.

At this same radical level—from which theological reflection must begin, and which is prior to canonical formulation—there appears the element of specific relationship to the church. The Christian religious life is not an exclusively individual relationship to a transcendent God, as it might be in certain forms of monasticism outside Christianity. Rather, it is a reality born in the church and for the church. Vatican II has said as much in more than one document (LG 43, 44, 45, 46; PC 1, 2). Allow me to briefly explain my opinion on this point.

Every form of religious life is ministerial in a deep sense. It is born, as a form of life, for the service of the rest of the church. This is due to the fact, as we have explained elsewhere, that the religious life, in its very root, is nothing more than a "living parable of discipleship."[8] We make our vows not only in the presence of the community, but to the community and, through it, to God, following a sacramental structure (the divine by means of the human) which is typically Christian. And we serve both the church and humanity above all by the public witness of our lives.

5.4.   There are also constitutive elements at the canonical level, and these may vary according to the conditions which the church establishes for the public recognition of this kind of life. Thus, one's vocation must be recognized by the church. Early on, the anchorite novice had to be recognized by his elder; today's hermit must be recognized by the bishop; those who enter an institution must be recognized by it as a member of its communion. Among religious, their commitment to God is converted canonically into the public profession of the three vows of celibacy, poverty and obedience. This way of formulating things is itself canonical, both with respect to the very fact of the vow (until well into the Middle Ages there was no common reference to a vow or vows, not even in the Rule of St. Benedict), as well as with respect to the explicit profession of the three vows. There is no documentary evidence for the vows of chastity, communion and obedience until the middle of th 12th century (eight centuries after the appearance of anchorites and cenobites), and these were changed to chastity, poverty and obedience in the Rule of the Trinitarians (1198), followed by that of the Friars Minor (1221) and the Poor Clares (1252). Innocent IV declared that these three vows are "substantialia cuiusque religionis." In our times, hermits, recognized anew by Canon Law, profess these same three vows, although the vow of obedience arose properly from cenobitic life. It is clear, however, that the vow of obedience takes on a quite different meaning in the eremitical as opposed to the communitarian, form of life. Finally, in the last-mentioned form of life, the call to community and apostolic vocation are canonically converted into a recognized belonging to a community, born of the same charism, and into a sharing in the common mission of the institute.

5.5.   Finally, there is a series of common elements which are essential from another point of view, not for the canonical validity of this form of life, but rather, for its full realization. They are integrating elements which cannot be omitted without mutilating the religious life: fidelity to a specific founding charims and to sound tradition, prayer, and lifelong formation. We should note here that prayer is both an indispensable element in the life of every disciple of Jesus and a connatural expression of any Christian community,

Moreover, continuing formation is a necessity for every human being. It is hard to say how "public witness" fits into one group or another, since much depends on how it is to be understood. It is even harder to understand just what is meant by "a form of government calling for religious authority based on faith."

5.6. We believe that what we have said above offers a sufficient explanation of some of the elements common to all forms of religious life. There is no need to go into further detail on each and every one of them. But there are some whose treatment in the document of guidelines might generate some confusion if taken out of context, namely, the synthesis of the church's recent teaching on religious life, which the text aims at presenting. We will now dwell on those points that might present some difficulty.

6. A Particular Form of Consecration to God

6.1. The document begins its exposition on the religious life with the notion of consecration, which, it states, is "the basis of religious life." Among the documents of Vatican II, _Perfectae Caritatis_ takes as its starting point the concept of the following of Christ, an idea to which it often returns in order to draw its inspiration (_PC_ 1b, 2a, 2e, 5b, 8b, 13a). Nevertheless at the end of no. 1, the decree uses, _en passant_, the expression "lives consecrated by the profession of the counsels" and in no. 5, under the influence of _Lumen Gentium_ explains the self-gift of religious as a "special consecration." On the contrary, chapter VI of _Lumen Gentium_ uses only once the words "following Christ" referring to the early disciples of Jesus to whom he propounded this form of life (_LG_ 44c). The reason for this difference is that _Lumen Gentium_ takes as its starting point and basic concept the more cultic and static act of profession, which it interprets as a full self-gift to God and, on God's part, as a consecration. Even if the priestly vocabulary of "consecration" and "sacred" is rather alien to the early lay monastic circles and to the western medieval monasticism, the idea that nuns and monks belong to God as "maidservants and menservants" goes back to the times of primitive monachate.[9] Culminating a gradual evolution during which _professio_ was transferred from its original meaning—namely the practice of monasticism—to the act whereby one committed oneself to it, Thomas Aquinas treated this act of self-gift as the founding moment of religious life.[10] The Council echoes him and then goes on to explain this self-gift as "a special consecration" which expresses more intimately and more fully one's baptismal consecration (LG 44; PC 5).

6.2. The present document now goes on to treat this concept of consecration as the very "basis of religious life." The reason for this can be discovered in the new Code, which, under the inspiration of PC 1d, has created the phrase "institutes of consecrated life," in order to designate religious, members of apostolic societies and of secular institutes (cc. 573-606). Once more, the continual activity of the Holy Spirit has rendered old molds and ancient nomenclatures obsolete. First, the church spoke of anchorites, then of monks in order to include cenobites, and then of religious in order to include canons regular, mendicants and apostolic institutes. And now it has had to create a larger category and name to include secular Institutes. The designation, "states of perfection," which gained some currency in the time of Pius XII, fell out of favor when it was rejected by the Council. It should be noted, however, that other designations might just as well have been chosen, such as "institutes of evangelical life," or "institua sequelae Christi," (cf. PC) with reference to the specifically Christian practice of the following of Christ and to the significance of these types of life as paradigms or mirrors of life according to the Gospel, which is common to all Christians. The religious life and the life of secular institutes is nothing more than a following of Christ that is institutionalized and made visible in their tenor of life. St. Basil, St. Francis of Assisi and St. Ignatius Loyola--to mention only three epoch-making creative figures--gave high relevance to this concept.

6.3. The concept of consecration as the point of departure for the religious life must be explained to avoid confusing it with the consecration conferred by the sacraments. Baptism is a radical and total consecration of the human being, effected by the anointing of the Spirit and communion with Christ. In this fundamental consecration, the consecrating action of the other sacraments is inserted. A consecration is conferred in those sacraments in which a person is installed by the church in some function or state of life. Ordination is a consecration, but so is matrimony. In the latter, the church--with the spouses acting as ministers--consecrates a relationship of communion, from which a new Christian family community is born. The spousal love that was received from God is now consecrated by him through the church.

6.4.   In what sense is profession--which is not a
sacramental action--a consecration? The Council tells us that
it is a consecration which is rooted in baptism (LG 44, PC 5),
is in some way a more intimate consecration to the service of
God (LG 44) or, if we prefer, is intimately rooted in, and
expresses more fully, the baptismal consecration (PC 5). But
the Council has told us something more. The Council uses the
term consecration in relation to the self-gift made in
profession. Should we understand the term consecration as
being used simply to explain this self-gift, and therefore
meaning it is the religious who consecrate themselves to God's
service by giving themselves to God? This interpretation, in
which "to conserate oneself" would simply mean "to commit
oneself," would be possible since "consecratur" may mean
"consecrates oneself" as well as "is consecrated." It would
be more in the line of Saint Thomas, quoted by the Council,
since Saint Thomas bases his theology of the religious life in
this self-gift or commitment.[11] And Saint Thomas states
explicitly that "religious life is consecrated by the three
vows.[12] The decree Perfectae Caritatis seems to support
this view, when it states: "they have dedicated their whole
lives to God's service. This (dedication) constitutes a
special consecration . . ." (PC 5). There is no doubt that if
we understand "self-gift" and "consecration" as two equivalent
terms, both designating the ation of the religious, we can
understand better that this commitment constitutes a more
intimate consecration (LG 44), in the sense that religious
bring their baptismal consecration (nothing could be more
profound than baptism) to an existential level, to the area of
a life committed to a special service of God.

And yet an answer given by the theological commission to
a remark made by a Father, obliges us to read more deeply into
the text. The Father states that the term "consecrare"
indicates a divine action, while human action should be called
"devovere, mancipare" (commitment, self-gift). The Commission
answered "intimius consecratur (is) sub forma passiva,
subintelligendo a Deo." So, while we commit ourselves, it is
God who consecrates us.[13] Obviously, God is the ultimate
reality who gives sense and value to our self-gift. I think
that we should understand this in two senses. First, it is
God who calls us: our religious life starts not from our
profession, but from his call and grace.

6.5 When we try to apply this concept of self-gift to God as
the act which, on the human side, founds the religious life,
we must bear in mind the specific character of the religious
life professed by apostolic institutes, which are quite

different from monastic institutes, on the one hand, and from contemplative institutes, on the other. In monasticism, the service of God means living exclusively in search of God, under the direction and magisterium of an abbott or abbess, in union with other monks or nuns.

In specifically contemplative institutes, the basic element of prayer, which is of such paramount importance in monasticism, too, becomes a service of intercession on behalf of the church and world (Teresa of Jesus or Therese de Lisieux). In institutes founded for apostolic activities or charitable works, the members commit themselves to God in order to carry out this call to ministry that they have heard. It is not a question of two separate vocations: religious life and ministry. Historically, in fact, the first thing to appear in the consciousness of founders or foundresses has often been an external need of the church and then, as a response to this need, their call to a ministry "to help souls" for a Jesuit,[14] "to serve Christ in the poor" for a Daughter of Charity, "to evangelize the poor" for a Vincentian, Redemptorist, Oblate or Claretian, "to Christianize education and educate the poor" for a Brother of the Christian Schools, "to minister to emigrants" for a Scalabrinian or a Sister of Mother Cabrini-- each of these is not only the first thing which emerged in the consciousness of their founders, but rather, it is what constitutes the central nucleus of the charism from which everything derives. The Brothers of the Christian Schools became religious in order to be able to give themselves fully to their educative mission. The Jesuits and Claretians began as a simple group of companions engaged in the ministry, and ended up as religious. In these cases the service of God is centered on the ministry, and the religious life is born to further this ministry. All of these religious are "sanctified and sent" like Jesus (Jn 10:36), that is to say, chosen by the Father and associated to the Son in his redeeming work. They serve God by committing their lives and persons for the salvation of His sons and daughters.[15]

6.6. Methodologically, the best way to speak of the consecration of apostolic life is to begin by addressing that originating and central element of their charism which is mission. To descend from a generic concept of consecration to God, without reference to the world which the Father so loves that he sent his Son to save it, and these religious in Him, and then to speak only at the end about mission, can clearly cause some confusion. Yet, in the document of guidelines, mission is spoken of precisely in the final paragraph of this first section devoted to consecration. The document avoids this confusion somewhat by recalling the statement of _Perfectae Caritatis_ that apostolic and charitable activity in these institutes belongs to the very nature of the religious life which they profess (PC no. 8; Ess. El., no. 12). However, this affirmation obliges us to re-read and reinterpret all the preceding paragraphs with a more specific and concrete awareness of the religious way of life proper to these institutions. It would have been methodologically more correct and theologically more exact, to start from this founding element.

7. Religious Institutes and Secular Institutes

7.1. In this first section of the document, dedicated to "consecration," there are two paragraphs (nos. 9-10) which attempt to clarify the distinction between the "consecration proper of religious and that of members of secular institutes." Secular institutes live their mission and consecration in the midst of the world and with the means of the world, thus becoming, so to speak, a hidden leaven. In contrast, it is proper to the religious life to be a public witness before the church and the world. This is accomplished by professing life in community and thereby separating oneself from one's own family and former profession. "The presence of the religious is visible, affecting their way of acting, their way of dress and their style of life" (n.10).

7.2. We believe that these paragraphs reveal transparently one of the fundamental concerns of the Holy See regarding the religious life of apostolic communities during the last few years. This concern also emerges in various other sections of the document. They are aimed at reminding us of the difference which exists between the religious life, as a public witness before the world, and the life of secular institutes, whose members are so to speak merged with the rest of the human race. It is both likely and understandable that a certain number of religious consecrated to the apostolate should have felt implelled to adopt a certain tenor of life that is less clearly distinguishable from that of secular institutes. In the first place, we should bear in mind that these apostolic and charitable institutes were born in the midst of and for the human world. This means that they developed a rather positive image of the world. For the world is the place where the sons and daughters of God suffer and need God's grace and is therefore not a place from which they must separate themselves, but rather, a place to be illumined with the Word and mercy of God. In brief, it is the world which God loves and in which Christ still suffers. This new image of the world already appears in the first Franciscans, as can be seen in the text of the Sacrum Commercium, in which a group of Friars Minor, of whom Madonna Poverta had enquired the whereabouts of their friary, pointed to the sweep of the horizon, saying, "This, Lady, is our friary".[16] Recall what St. Vincent de Paul told his Daughters that they should have "for monastery the abode of the sick, for chapel the parish church, for cloister the streets of the city or the wards of a hospital, for enclosure obedience, for the grille the fear of God and for veil holy modesty".[17] Let it not be said that this applies to an apostolic and canonically non-religious community. For something of the same spirit can be seen in Saint Ignatius' insistence that everything should be common and ordinary in his Society.[18]

7.3. In the second place, we should not forget the highly professionalized ministries of many kinds that many of these religious have begun to practice, such as parish ministries, ministries in collaboration with a broad spectrum of different people, counseling, etc. These ministries have introduced many religious into the workaday fabric of society. And this is a source of tensions for them. Paul VI compassionately acknowledged this in Evangelica Testificatio: "Many of you will in fact be obliged to lead your lives, at least in part, in a world which tends to exile man from himself and to compromise both his spiritual unity and his union with God. You must therefore learn to find God even under those conditions of life which are marked by an increasingly accelerated rhythm and by the noise and the attraction of the ephemeral" (ET 33). Recall what St. Ignatius often said as he was laying down the bases for the apostolic spirituality of his companions: to seek God in all things.

7.4. Finally, we should recall that North American society was born with an optimistic vision of the world, a land of liberty and opportunity under the eye of God, where human beings could engage in the pursuit of happiness. Early on, this vision began to influence American Catholic spirituality, as can be seen in the case of Isaac Hecker. And it is significant that this positive vision re-emerged in Thomas Merton toward the end of his life. He who had begun by regarding the Abbey of Gethsemani as "the only real city in America" and had, in Seeds of Contemplation (1949), invited secular Christians to escape from the city as often as they could, eventually came to see--as Teresa of Jesus and Therese of Lisieux had also seen--that the real life and raison d'etre of the contemplative life is "outside" in the "world." An authentic Christian experience corrected his theological prejudices. And Thomas Merton, by becoming interested in the cause of peace and justice during the Vietnam war, revealed himself to be both deeply American and profoundly a disciple of Jesus.

7.5. Nevertheless, the distinction between religious institutes and secular institutes remains. The problem is, to identify precisely where this difference, between secular institutes and religious institutes founded to do apostolic or charitable work, lies. The difference must be sought in the "religious" character of the latter. Essential Elements, harking back to the teaching of Provida Mater Ecclesia, tells us that "of themselves, the counsels do not necessarily separate people from the world." This statement needs to be spelled out. There is no need for us to repeat Karl Rahner's response to Hans Urs von Balthasar on this point.[19] It suffices that we recall the deep meaning of celibacy, according to St. Paul, as a transcending of the things of the world, in order to be occupied with the things of the Lord. This is observed as well by the members of secular institutes who commit themselves to celibacy for the sake of the kingdom of heaven. And it is not valid to counter that they do so by a private vow, because this vow is not merely interior, of the internal forum, but is made in faciem Ecclesiae and is a constitutive element of a state of life in the church. Doubtless, what this means to say to us, is that these members of secular institutes, although theologically they transcend earthly realities, since they place themselves and their very existence on the side of the kingdom of God, nevertheless live in the world, in human society in its this-worldly, empirical sense, dwelling in their own residences (either in their own families or like any other single layperson) and engaged in secular profession (politics, economics, medicine).

7.6. In contrast, we are told that "the very nature of religious vocation involves a public witness to Christ and to the Church." The document goes on to mention the two distinctive elements of religious institutes, in keeping with canon 607,2: the public profession of vows and a stable form of life in community. The juxtaposition of these two statements and the presence of the term "public" in each of them, could be misleading. For a vow to be public, it is simply required that it be received by a superior in the name of the church (canon 1192,1). But it is also clear, beyond the purely canonical sense, that religious life is called upon to give public witness before society and the church. The religious life appears expressly as a prophetic proclamation (LG 44). We have referred to it as a "living parable of discipleship." This is accomplished fundamentally by hermits through their solitude and specifically by members of religious institutes through their incorporation into a community of disciples. Allow us to say that it is the community which allows them to interact dialectically with human society and the church in an attitude of service which is also, in apostolic institutes, an activity.

8. Public Witness

8.1. Here and in a later section (sec.6), the document dwells on the theme of public witness. Witness, both oral and lived, to the grace of the Resurrection, is an essential part of every Christian vocation. By their life, religious must remind others of the common values of the gospel. In the very beautiful closing paragraphs of Evangelica Testificatio, Pope Paul VI reminded us of this and drew from it precisely the necessity for a lively attention to the needs of contemporary humanity (ET 52-53). But religious do this through their type of life which is publicly committed to a service of God that transcends the limits of one's own family and worldly values. Recently Pope John Paul II has also told us, again in a highly inspiring passage, that our life is a special witness of love (RD 14). There has been a continuing development, from the earliest times of Christian monasticism, of a theology and spirituality of monastic life, centered on the witness before the church of the transcendence of faith. But in attempting to apply this doctrine to apostolic institutes, one must take one's starting point from the first, genetically speaking, of its founding charisms. The foundresses and founders of these apostolic communities did not think first of all of creating a type of life that would reveal the passing character of the world, as the anchorites may have done. The first thing that the Holy Spirit set before them was the spiritual, moral or physical suffering of God's children: the souls that need help, the spirits that suffer because of abandonment or lack of education, the bodies tormented by suffering. Their faith spoke to them of God's love for these sons and daughters, and of Christ's identification with the needy, the sinful, the poor, the ignorant, the sick and the abandoned. And they launched forth to serve Christ in them. For this reason they embraced celibacy, a poor life in community and apostolic obedience. Apostolic institutes give this witness radically, through their commitment of service to the needy and through the sacrifice of their own person and life required by this service.

116

8.2. Therefore, rather than "separation from the world" (a monastic concept which must be interpreted as applied to apostolic institutes), what distinguishes us, apostolic religious, is our confrontation with the pagan spirit of a society that accords privileges to some but abandons others (the poor, the orphaned, the elderly) and with the Evil One who oppresses so many hearts and destroys so many families. It is for this reason that we put ourselves beyond some of the fundamental secular structures (family, property) which come from the Creator (multiply, possess). For, this reason, too, we renounce the free disposition of ourselves and enter community. The fact that, as Essential Elements says, our life, our way of acting, our way of dressing and even our recreations should reflect this commitment to be signs of God's love for the needy, is fully understandable. God does not need our sacrifices, nor did Christ attach an absolute value to sacrifice in the abstract. But the sons and daughters of God, and Christ in them, do need them. A simple and austere life, as well as the exercise of control over our affections in relationships, are an unavoidable consequence of our vocation.

8.3. The difficulties arise when we get down to concrete cases. Because the concrete manifestations of this generous spirit of commitment vary in each society and time, and are perceived differently by divergent mentalities. At one time it was a general expression of the monastic spirit that monks and nuns never bathed. At an earlier period there were some who believed they were expressing this spirit by wandering about stark naked in certain desert regions, while others did so by perching, like storks, atop some pillar. Until a short time ago, it was thought to be an expression of religious spirit, that our sisters should be covered from head to toe and leave the house only two by two; that our mail was always opened before we received or sent it; and that the only key to the house was the one hanging on the belt of the porter or portress.

8.4. The document mentions the "manner of dress" as part of witness (no. 10) and somewhat later speaks of the "religious habit." The former seems clear enough, but the latter can give rise to various interpretations. Hence we believe that it is necessary to turn to history, in order to discover the roots of two opposed mentalities. Basil and Augustine asked only that their disciples follow simplicity and a Christian awareness of the body in what they wore, not a specific cut of clothing or uniformity in dress. The habit described in Pachomian sources and in the Rule of St. Benedict was very

117

similar to the clothing worn by the countryfolk of 4th-century
Egypt or 6th-century central Italy. The medieval nuns dressed
like simple women and the Carmelites of Saint Teresa dressed
like Spanish duenas of the people. What distinguished them
was the scapular (originally a working apron to avoid soiling
the tunic) or, in some cases, a religious emblem. The
Daughters of Charity and the Little Sisters of Jesus dress as
women of the people. The Franciscans dressed like the poor
and the beggars of their time: a tunic (trousers were
forbidden), a cord and a hood for protection from the sun or
rain. Institutes of clerics initially adopted the dress of
canons (Premonstratensians, Dominicans) and later, the
scholar's cassock, which finally became the distinctive attire
of the clergy. In most cases, the manner of dress expressed
consecration to God, because it meant adopting the garb of the
poor. Eventually, however, ordinary people changed their way
of dress, while religious continued to dress like the poor of
other centuries, since this way of dressing became somewhat
hallowed by time. What had once been a sign of communion with
the poor, now became a sign of distinction. As early as the
12th century, when the various Orders came into existence, the
various colors and cuts of their apparel came to be a banner
or symbol of the institution. During the last few centuries,
under the influence of a mentality that pushed the distinction
between religious and secular Christians to an extreme, habits
were invented to heighten the difference, even in some cases,
against the very meaning of poverty. Since distinction was
the order of the day, some groups (displaying, one might add,
a rather worldly spirit) created habits for various classes of
religious: superiors in one habit, and poor lay brothers or
sisters cooks wore quite different outfits. Moreover, we know
the 19th-century Church doted on uniformity (Pius IX,
Solesmes, detailed general regulations for religious
Institutes). Uniformity in dress held a great attraction for
them. Today this hankering after distinctiveness is on the
wane, while the desire for simplicity is beginning to prevail.
Besides this, today's communities esteem the variety of
persons who make them up, as the starting point for building
toward their unique vocation and sharing in love. Uniformity
in dress is felt as a burden by not a few religious today.

8.5. What does the church tell us about this? It is well
known that Pius XII already began a movement for the
simplification of religious habits. Number 17 of Perfectae
Caritatis was moving in the same direction. Its object was
not to affirm the value of the habit, which was not under
discussion, but to order that it be "simple and modest..., in
keeping with the requirements of health... and suited to the

times, place and needs of the apostolate," and to prescribe that "habits...which are not in conformity with these norms should be changed." It is significant, however, that this text calls the religious habit "a symbol of consecration." Evangelica Testificatio returns to this theme significantly and with a lively sense of tradition, in the section dedicated to poverty. Pius VI recognizes that certain situations may justify the laying aside of a type of religious dress, but he recalls that according to the Council, the habit of religious men and women should be a sign of their consecration and, as he concludes, "in some way distinguished from forms that are obviously secular" (ET n 22). The criterion of distinctiveness in form and not merely in simplicity, persists here, although in a very limited way: "a formis aperte saecularibus quadamtenus distinguatur.

9. Community

9.1. The document reminds us, opportunely, that belonging to a local community and not just to a family of evangelical life is an essential element of the life proper of religious institutes. We do not say "of the religious life," because the eremitical life, too, is a form of religious life. This is so "normally," the document notes. In effect, religious institutes consecrated to the apostolic ministry or to charitable works, born to respond by some external services to certain needs of the church and humanity, have always appeared as a union of local groups. Canonically, belonging to a local community is one of the fundamental distinctive traits of a religious institute as opposed to a secular institute.

9.2. But it should be noted that while this belonging to a local community is a distinctive element, actual living in the community is only the normal thing and not essential in the sense that the lack of it would destroy the religious life. Canon 665,1, attributes to the major superior and his or her council the faculty to permit a member, for a just cause, to live outside the community, without time limits, for the purpose of "caring for poor health, for the purpose of studies or of undertaking an apostolate in the name of the institute." The fact is, that both the drafters of the document and those of the canon know quite well that in certain cases, especially in a missionary situation, religious are often obliged to sacrifice community life on the altar of the apostolic service to others for which their institutes were founded. This can easily and regularly happen in missions where each priest must take care of an extensive area, or in poor and abandoned parishes which cannot afford to maintain more than one priest.

This fact has become generalized more recently for two reasons: 1) highly specialized or professional ministries which a man or woman religious is called to fulfill in places where there is no community of their institute, and 2) a growing lack of personnel.

9.3. The fact has occured earlier and in a greater number of cases in our country. It can be noted by anyone coming from other countries. Some years back, if one asked the reasons why a religious man or, more often, a religious woman was living alone, sometimes very near a community of his or her institute, one would most likely be told that it was for personal, rather than ministerial reasons. The fact is, that the adaptation promoted by Vatican II led to the dismantling of certain community structures. We are convinced that communities of sisters in the United States were regimented to an extreme rarely found in other countries of the West. Nevertheless it was here that the movement of women's affirmation began earlier, and has since done so much to enrich the Church. Not a few sisters began laying stress on personal development, on professional preparation and perhaps by that very fact on individual ministries over community bonds. This also led, for psychological reasons, and sometimes very strong ones, to a certain phenomenon of dispersion. Years later, closer to our own time, not a few men and women began to feel alone at a certain age, and there has been a return to communion and a tendency to rebuild community in a new way: as interpersonal relationship, which is precisely its central element. Today it is possible for all (we hope) to have a more balanced vision of the relationships between living in community and leaving room for people to breath between commitment to one's own institute and ministry.

9.4. "Essential Element's" reminder of the value and meaning of community life for religious, can be useful to us and we should be grateful for it. The same can be said of its statements of principle concerning the relationship between the style of community and the type of apostolate, and the impact which the latter has on community relationships (no. 22), as well as, theoretically, for the model it proposes of community in diversity, not division, and of unity without regimentation (no. 22). The problems emerge when we arrive at the details: oratory, celebration of the Eucharist, common prayer, common recreations, meals, etc. As one reads these words one tends to get the impression of a rather numerous, more conventual kind of local community, following a more tranquil rhythm than usually prevails in a large number of American communities. Applying this to the American situation is going to call for flexibility. One fact should be recalled: St. Ignatius Loyola obtained the Holy See's solemn approval for a radically apostolic style of community life: flexible, without the divine office (which was not replaced by other devotional prayers), with two shifts at meals, etc. Thus the Church recognized in principle that the apostolic ministry for which these institutes were founded must determine the kind of life they live. However, in the measure to which structures are reduced and flexibilized, there must be an accent on interpersonal encounter, if the religious involved are not to be destroyed psychologically and spiritually. As for the celebration of the Eucharist in one's own community, even though it might not be possible or perhaps advisable to do so frequently in some cases, there is no doubt that it is very effective for community life that the members of a group celebrate periodically (retreat day, community day) the particular bond that unites them.

9.5. We have ventured the opinion that in the United States, especially during the last few years, for the first time in history, a type of radically apostolic women's religious community is becoming generalized. This opinion is confirmed by a sufficiently general phenonemenon that has arisen here. Canons 608-609 tell us and norm 9 of Essential Elements reminds us, that the community should live in a legitimately constituted house and that houses of a religious institute are to be erected "praevio Episcopi diocesani consensu," In not a few apostolic communities of women, the sisters live wherever their ministry requires their presence, and this is normal for an apostolic community, as Essential Elements, no. 21, acknowledges. But the needs of local Churches in the United States have led to a situation where local groups of sisters consecrated to ministries in parishes move readily from one place to another. Not only do individual sisters change, but even whole communities. This is a far cry from the more conventual European experience, where houses are stable for decades and decades. And in not a few institutes, many of these residences do not have either a formal document of foundation from their institute or a written record of the bishop's prior consent. We could say that except for the motherhouse and a few other stable houses, the local groups of women's apostolic institutes dedicated to these mobile ministries may not constitute domus in the full canonical sense of the word. It is perhaps fitting to ask at this point: Do our bishops and superiors prefer to strictly apply the model foreseen in Canon 609 and therefore to undertake the intense amount of administrative paperwork connected with it? There could be a more flexible solution which takes into

121

account the proper character of these local groups of sisters. The Claretians, in the non-too-liberal middle of the last century, included in their Constitutions, approved by the Holy See, two types of legitimately constituted local communities: first, the house or residence erected with the previous written permission of the bishop, and second, what they called a quasi-residence, created for the time required for a certain ministry, for which the spoken permission of the bishop to work in his diocese was sufficient. Some American foundresses as well as some institutes transplanted here have come to call the motherhouse and a few other large communities "houses," while using the term "missions" for these other smaller and more transitory ministerial communities. Naturally, the very least we owe our bishops is to inform them periodically of the location of our communities of whatever sort.

10. Evangelical Mission

10.1. The document devotes a whole section to the mission of religious. It begins by remarking quite opportunely that consecration and mission are closely interrelated, so that it is inferred that every religious is called to cooperate with God in some way for the benefit of God's sons and daughters. In attempting to apply this notion to religious Institutes, there could and perhaps should have been an effort to address, with greater vigor and sensibility, the specifically Christian traits of consecration. When in John 10:36, it is said that the Son was consecrated and sent, the author does not mean that he was consecrated on the one hand (one facet) to the worship of the Father and, on the other (second facet), sent. What he means to say is that the Father calls (i.e. consecrates, in the sense of setting apart for a particular mission) and sends his Son to save the human race. In the same way, Dominicans, Jesuits, Vincentians, Sisters of Loretto, Daughters of Charity and Sisters of Mercy do not feel called to offer worship to God (consecration) on the one hand and, on the other, to serve their brothers and sisters. Saint Thomas had already overcome this dichotomy.[20] We have been set apart by God, associated with the Son by the Father (the experience of La Storta is typical of us all), in order to save his sons and daughters. For us, consecration and mission are two ways of looking at the same reality. It is necessary to repeat this, so as to avoid any confusion about our identity as a particular form of religious life in the church.

10.2. <u>Essential Elements</u> touches on two important points related to ministerial activities. In the first place, there is the question of the institute's fidelity to its founding

122

charism and the need to bring the institute's activities into line with this charism. Charism here, as the document explictly states, means the charism described in the constitutions. Recently we witnessed how lay institutes, above all those of women, and especially in the United States, have been undertaking new ministries that were formerly not open to them in general and to women in particular. Until this century, almost all apostolic institutes of women were devoted exclusively to works of assistance or education (or both), because these were the only activities that a sister was allowed to perform. Faced with the greater possibilities and needs of today, institutes have to examine and analyze the idea of their foundress or founder, to see whether these restrictions were simply imposed upon them by the society of the time. We hope that this re-examination and reformulation was done in the new constitutions. The document warns us of the possible danger of institutes trying to undertake too much, thus dispersing their energies. This is a real danger. On the other hand, however, there are apostolic institutes (clearly the Society of Jesus is one) which have a very broad apostolic charism.

10.3. The second point which the document makes on the theme of apostolate, is the fact that the public ministries of these religious have a public ecclesial character, in as much as they derive from and actualize the institute's mission, which as been recognized by the church. We work in virtue of our baptism and our personal vocation, through the gifts with which the Spirit has endowed each of us, but also, as the document points out, as members of an institute and in its name. In this sense, our apostolate is, as the pope points out in his letter, a participation in the mission of Christ by means of a "corporate apostolate." The document speaks of a "corporate mission," interpreting it as we have just done. But it then broaches the question of the relationship between the work of an individual and that of the other members of the same community. This does not mean that everyone of them does the same thing or that the various gifts of the individual members are not respected (no. 25). But it then adds that, in practice, this "usually" implies working with members of the same institute. The text recognizes that "in clerical or missionary institutes, working alone may only be done with permission of superiors, in order to remedy some exceptional need and for a limited time. At this point one needs to ask what is meant by "working alone." Does it mean living and working alone in the fashion of those missionary institutes just alluded to? If this were the case, this document would be telling us that this could be done only for a limited time and in order to remedy an exceptional need. However, as we have already noted above, Canon 655, although it sets a one-year time limit on the permission major superiors can grant for a stay outside community, nevertheless sets no time limit for such permission, if the object is "to exercise a ministry in the name of the institute." The canon evidently contains a juridical norm that is broader than the criterion which Essential Elements gives us. The reason is, most likely, that the law is obliged to remain within general lines. But Essential Elements points toward a criterion: What type of an apostolate can require that a religious live outside his or her community? That type of apostolate which responds to an exceptional need of the Church. Between the greater breadth of the letter of the canon and the stricter criterion of the document, religious men and women will have to exercise their discernment.

10.4.   Are we to assume, then, that "working alone" means performing a personal ministry while living in community with other sisters or brothers? In the past, religious priests have widely performed such ministries in preaching assignments, spiritual direction, teaching in universities that were not run by their own institutes, publications, animating lay associations, etc. In contrast, lay institutes worked within their own institution, as part of a collective work. But that was largely due to a social mentality that allowed only a priest to act as such a person. Today that mentality has disappeared, and religious brothers and sisters can exercise a broad spectrum of personal ministries, ranging from directing spiritual exercises, to counseling, to developing a ministry as part of a parish team, etc. This is so, above all, in the United States. It is hard to imagine any theological reason why a church text would reserve the possibility of exercising personal ministries to priests. On the contrary, priests—as ordained ministers and as part of a presbyteral college—would seem to be more tied than others. If this were what the authors of the document would like to suggest, namely that only priests, among religious, can carry out personal ministries (we hope not), then many of us would find ourselves before a typical case of ideology, that is to say, a theory built to perpetuate certain discriminatory privileges. Besides, if this hypothetical norm were put into practice (which we do not believe feasible) our dioceses would doubtless suffer greatly on having to withdraw our sisters and brothers from their personal collaboration in many parish teams.

11. Government

11.1   The section on government is one that reflects most clearly the present concerns of Rome regarding recent developments in the religious life, particularly in the United States. It is well known that not only the forms of government in religious institutes, but also, to a lesser degree, the manner of understanding authority, has passed through a number of variations throughout history. It is likewise easy to demonstrate that these changes have been made not only in relation to the charism proper of the institute, but also under the influence of the prevailing form of government in the civil society in which the institutes arose: the medieval abbot or abbess, with their council and chapter; the mendicant orders in the new communal democracies, above all in Italy; the Company of Jesus, against the ideological and political background of the 16th century; the apostolic communities of the 18th and 19th centuries, under the influence not only of the austere spirituality spread by Jansenism, with its allergy to human values, but also as a result of its later reaction against the French Revolution and its consequences. Recent communitarian trends reflect not only the prestige currently enjoyed by democratic systems, but also the weariness of broad zones of humanity under the many dictatorships and authoritarian governments that have arisen in our century.

11.2.   This movement away from a highly personal and authoritarian type of government toward one of dialogue and group discernment, although it has emerged almost everywhere, has been more congenial and natural for North American men and women religious, than for Europeans. Because the former acquired their first vision of the world in a pluralistic and democratic milieu, whereas it has been harder in general for European Christians to accept democracy. While the number of religious who supported Maurras in the old French Republic was significant, it should be remembered that partisans of Mussolini, Franco and Salazar made up nearly all the religious communities in their respective countries. Today, ecclesiology and in particular the interpretation of religious authority in authoritarian terms and of obedience in terms of unilateral submission, is the last redoubt of those who have had a lifelong allergy to the idea of democracy in civil society. The American religious, on the contrary, tends to bring to his or her community a purely functional concept of government as an "administration" subject to careful review every four years. And it is not surprising that, as European religious have been doing for many centuries, the Institutes born in this country have reflected in their new types of government, the system of the civil government, with its distinction of powers.

11.3.   In the United States, somewhat more than ten years ago, another phenomenon began to appear. With the decline and fall of quasi-absolute authority and regimented discipline, some religious found it difficult to rediscover the humane and spiritual meaning that can be attached to the office of leader of the local community. Doubtless the reason for this difficulty lay in the fact that the local leader was understood mainly in juridical and disciplinary terms as the one who formerly made the decisions for the community.

11.4.   This is, in broad strokes, the situation which the document proposes to face. How does it accomplish this? Unfortunately, by a strong imbalance in favor of the personal authority of superiors. This should be noted: It is only in a single, brief phrase in no. 52, after insisting anew on the personal authority of superiors, that the text refers to the "appropriate involvement of the members in the government," to "shared responsibility," and to "subsidiarity." The rest is repeated insistence on the rights/duties of superiors. To this subject, the whole of the long number 49 is dedicated. Number 50 speaks of the council which collaborates with the superiors, but again returns to insist on the fact that authority is invested in the latter. Number 51 offers a rather emasculated view of the (general) chapter, stressing its transitory and temporally limited character, which must be distinguished from the abiding importance of the superior general. It does not state the fact that the general chapter has greater authority than the general does (it can do things that he or she cannot) and that it constitutes, as a greater embodiment of community, a more visible expression of communion (Canon 631). A text of this sort must strike not a few religious as rather puzzling and painful, especially if we bear in mind the great efforts that religious have made to assimilate the praxis of obedience—so different from what they had been used to—that was proposed to them in _Perfectae Caritatis_. Certainly, it is understandable that the text aims at correcting some deviant tendencies, and for that reason tends toward the opposite extreme. But we cannot shake off the suspicion that a more balanced text, better incorporating the various nuances of the conciliar and postconciliar magisterium, would have been much more effective.

11.5.   We can only lament the fact that the document limits its treatment of the office of superior to the level of juridical authority. To know who makes the decisions in community is not the crux of the matter. It is more important to know what a superior has to do. And the constant tradition of the church, visible in the great majority of Rules and Constitutions, has claimed for the superior a highly spiritual ministry of guidance, of exemplarity, of being a sign of the group's friendship and concern toward its individual members. The document passes over this deeper dimension of religious "authority" which is so visible in Mutuae Relationes—in total silence.

11.6.   Moreover, we believe that there are some imprecise statements in the text that are bound to cause confusion. Thus, in no. 49, perhaps with a mind to the situation of major superiors between chapters, we are told that "this religious authority is not shared." But the church has always recognized the authority of the chapters, also on a local level. Certainly, in the Rule of Saint Benedict, even if the abbot is obliged to discuss the most important affairs with his monks, the decision belongs to the abbot[21]. On the contrary in the Mendicant Orders, often the most important decisions are reserved to the community, periodically gathered in chapter.[22] More than this, in the very constitutions that are nowadays being definitively approved by the Holy See, we have been able to discover five different types of treatment of the relationships that obtain between personal authority and community. Attributing certain decisions to a group (chapter), is tantamount to acknowledging a group-authority. There exists, then, a "shared authority" between the members of these groups, according to their constitutions.

11.7.   Another imprecise statement, which is currently being misinterpreted by many, is the affirmation in no. 42, that it is the church that "confers on the institute...the religious authority necessary..." Let us begin by noting that this statement is not found, either in the council documents or in Ecclesiae Sanctae or Evangelica Testificatio. Mutuae Relationes tells us that the authority of religious institutes proceeds from the Spirit of the Lord "in connection with the Sacred Hierarchy," and goes on to explain this statement in the sense it is the hierarchy that has canonically erected the institute and authentically affirmed its specific mission (MR no. 13). Note that the first thing stated is the charismatic origin of this office: the Spirit of the Lord who raises up this new community. Secondly, it is not stated that this authority proceeds from the hierarchy, but in connection with it, because the bishops and the pope, in canonically erecting an institute, give canonically value to its authority.

The new Code of Canon Law tells us, in contrast, that superiors receive potestatem (power) from God through the ministry of the Church (CIC, can. 618). This is a really new statement, without any equivalent in the 1917 Code. We religious should be delighted at this express statement of the ecclesial character of the office of our leaders and chapters. Because it works in two directions: in the direction of necessary communion with the pope and bishops, and in the direction of respect for institutions of evangelical life and for the persons who represent them. We are told that such power is given "per ministerium Ecclesiae." Of course, all authority in the church is given "per ministerium Ecclesiae. It is born, so to speak, from the womb of the church for the good of the church and by means of the church. It is the church who ordains her bishops. In the case of religious institutes, it is this community, this living cell of the church which requires certain ministries of leadership, creates them and elects its ministers. Leadership in our institutes is already an ecclesial fact at this level. Then this authority is publicly recognized by the church, and thus receives canonical value, when the hierarchy officially recognizes the institute and approves its laws--something that it has been doing ever since the 12th century, when the canons regular had recourse to the Apostolic See of Rome in order to insure their institution against feudal lords and even some bishops. Before this, it was the whole church which recognized, without any formal explicit act, the existence of these groups, as a reality closely united to the mystery of the life and holiness of the church.

The document Essential Elements seems to have forgotten the charismatic origin of leadership in religious communities. Every authority in the church is the fruit of a charism of the Spirit. This is true in an even more particular way of authority of religious institutes, because they are communities created by the Holy Spirit beyond the hierarchical structure of the church, for the enrichment of the whole People of God. Essential Elements does not tell us (although it supposes it) that this authority comes from the spirit of the Lord, as Mutuae Relationes states (MR 13) and as Canon 618 affirms. The pneumatic origin seems to have fallen into the shadow. Moreover, Essential Elements states on two occasions (EE nos. 42, 49) that it is the church which "confers" authority. Naturally, we cannot imagine that the redactors of the document are trying to identify the church with the hierarchy in what would be a return to some 19th century ecclesiology. When they say "confers," they are perhaps thinking of the act of canonical erection and therefore of an act of the hierarchy. In the context of tradition, such a statement is acceptable only in the sense that it is through the hierarchy that the church recognizes this internal authority of institutes and gives it public, canonical value. A statement that went beyond this, besides being highly debatable theologically, would reflect a rather suspect ecclesiology.[23]

12. Conclusion

12.1. I have attempted to explain the main points of the document Essential Elements, especially those which most clearly reveal the concerns of the Holy See. These are the points which must serve as the basis of the dialogue between bishops and religious that has been requested by the pope.

12.1.1. We shall have to reflect on the implications of the kind of "public witness" proper to the religious life in our country and our time, since concrete expressions of that witness vary in different times and cultures.

12.1.2. Certainly, we shall have to review whether we have been or are faithful to our profession of community life, bearing in mind, however, that particular relationships exist between community and ministry in the apostolic institutes. Community life is strongly emphasized in the new Code as a common trait of all religious (Canons 607.2; 665.1), as opposed to members of the secular institutes. We must notice also that the new Code supposes that religious live in community with other members of the same institute (Canon 665.1: in propria domu). But while the church's law does not fix any time limit for permission to live outside community in order to carry out a ministerial activity (and therefore permission may be given for the time that is necessary to carry out that ministry) the document says very explicitly that we cannot ask or give that permission to carry out any kind of ministry. Here again a certain discernment is needed.

12.1.3. We may have to see whether we have been able to transcend the purely disciplinary image of the local leader and understand her or him as the person called to represent mutual concern and support, to invite us to communal prayer, discernment, and communication. Only in this way will we be able to understand why the Code affirms that each community

129

(which may be formed by more than one unit) should be entrusted to the ministry of a local leader.

12.2. The document Essential Elements can be useful to us as a summary of the church's current teaching on the religious life and on the traits that distinguish it from other types of Christian life. It contains a series of statements that reveal a certain degree of sensitivity. Others, in turn, sum up statements of the Council. Yet everyone knows that the document has been perceived as something strange by most men and women religious of apostolic life. It is significant how often, at religious meetings and gatherings, the document has been judged to be "monastic" or leaning toward a monastic vision of the religious life. Indeed, certain monastic statements are insinuated here and there. For example, when --clearly overlooking the experience and teachings of St. Ignatius Loyola--it is stated that union with God in prayer is the first duty of religious (Norm 26). The vital need for prayer could surely have been stated in some other way. In paragraph 26 of the doctrinal part, we are offered a definition of the vita apostolica which could have been taken from the polemics of the monks against the canons regular and which takes no account of the semantic evolution of the term as seen in the first documents of the Order of Preachers: "They are genuinely apostolic, not because they have an apostolate, but because they are living as the apostles lived." I hope the redactors of the document will forgive us if we say that our communities are apostolic because we follow Christ in his proclamantion of the Kingdom, with our apostolates and our lives.

12.3. We believe that one of the main sources of difficulty is the fact that the document was composed under the limitations of a mistaken methodology: it descends from a generic concept of religious life (the Code is there for that) and then adds the apostolic aspect, instead of reflectively following the genesis itself of our institutes in the church, in which we have become religious in order to better develop a ministry required by the People of God: Trinitarians, Dominicans, Jesuits, Barnabites, the Institute of the Blessed Virgin Mary, the Company of Mary, La Salle Brothers, Sisters of Mercy, Christian Brothers . . . If this method had been followed, many common concepts would have appeared together with those differences which distinguish them as apostolic institutes. Because our way of understanding and living our consecration, our vision of the world, our public witness and our experience of community life are deeply related to our apostolic mission.

130

12.4.   Finally, the part relating to governance is particularly poor and unbalanced. Its redactors would better have served the pope, the bishops and religious, if they had laid greater stress on the spiritual character of the ministry of authority in the religious life, and if they had not forgotten the communitarian aspects that are most essential to authority and obedience.

12.5.   We hope not to have given the impression that we lack that reverence and docility (in the Latin sense of the term: to be teachable) that we owe to the pope's person and ministry in the church. It is an essential element of our Catholic communion, which we intend to preserve joyfully. I cannot hide the fact that the pope has declared in his address to a group of American bishops on September 18, 1983, that he has "approved" this summary "as guidelines for both the Pontifical Commission and yourselves" (the bishops). I think that what the pope has approved is basically the content, guidelines for the pastoral ministry of our bishops, not every theoretical or technical statement in which these practical orientations have been molded. To pretend the contrary would amount to making the document an act of the pope's magisterium, which it is not, since the pope has not taken full responsability for its whole content, by signing it, in the way he has done with his recent Apostolic Exhortation, Redemptionis donum.

12.6.   On the other hand, we should recognize that the redactors of the document faced a difficult task for two main reasons. First, because they had to summarize the church's teaching on the common essential elements of the religious life, without cancelling the many concrete differences which the Spirit has created in the different families. Second, because it was impossible to compose a doctrinal summary without following one of the various theological views of religious life, which have a legitimate place in the catholic community.

NOTES

1. Th. Matura, The Crisis of Religious Life (Chicago: Franciscan Herald, 1973).
2. J. Alvarez Gomez, La Vida Religiosa ante los Retos de la Historia (Madrid: Instituto Teol. Vida Rel., 1979).
J.M. Lozano, Discipleship: Toward an Understanding of Religious Life) 2nd ed.; Chicago: CCRS, 1983) 100-102. Many

data can be gleaned here and there in the well-known study by R. Hostie, Vie et Mort des Ordres Religieux. Approches Psychosociologiques (Paris: Desclee de Br., 1972, translated and distributed in a limited photostatic edition by Cara: The Life and Death of Religious Orders 1983.)

3. J.P. Dondero, T.D. Frary, New Pressures, New Responses in Religious Life (New York: Alba 1979). Canadian Religious Conference, The Dawn of a New Era (Donum Dei No. 13; Ottawa: CRC, 1968). Confederacion Latinoamericana de Religiosos, Vida Religiosa en America Latina (CLAR No. 20; Bogota, 1976).

4. Canadian Relgious Conference, New Trends in Religious Life (Donum Dei, No. 14; Ottawa: CRC) 1969. J.M. Lozano, "Trends in Religious Life Today," Review for Religious 42 (July 1983) 481-505.

5. Sermons 355-356, De Vita et Moribus Clericorum Suorum: PL 39, 1568-1581.

6. Cf. Anselm of Havelberg, Epistola Apologetica: PL 188, 1132-1138. Rupert of Deutz, De Vita vera Apostolica: PL 170, 611-664. Philip de Harvengt, De Institutione Clericorum: PL 203, 665-1206. The monk Ordericus Vitalis felt obliged to discuss the traits of a vera religio, that is to say, the essential elements of the religious life and to ask whether these elements subsisted in the new Orders: Historia Ecclesiastica, VIII, 25-26: PL 188.

7. Libellus de Diversis Ordinibus . . . (edited and translated by G. Constable and B. Smith; Oxford: Clarendon, 1972).

8. J.M. Lozano, Discipleship 30.

9. Ibid. 85-89.

10. Quodlib. 3, a. 17, ad 6.

11. Cf. J.M. Lozano, Discipleship: Toward an Understanding of Religious Life (2nd ed.; Chicago: CCRS, 1983) 292-295.

12. Contra Impugn. 1.1: Opuscula Theologica (Torino: Marietti, 1954) 8.

13. Schema Constitutionis Dogm. de Ecclesia, p. 156.

14. Julius III, Exposcit debitum (1550): Formula Instituti, no. 1. Constitutiones S.I., nos. 3, 156, 258, 307, 308, 446, 603, 813.

15. S. Thomas Aquinas, 2-2, q. 188, a.2.

16. Sacrum Commercium, ch. 6: St. Francis of Assisi, Omnibus of Sources (Chicago: Franciscan Herald, 1973) 1593.

17. The Constitutions of the Daughters of Charity of St. Vincent de Paul (Paris: Maison Gener. 1954) Ch. 7, p. 33. Cf. The Constitutions... (Paris: 1983) no. 19.

18. Examen Ch. 1, no. 6. Constitutions, no. 580.

19. K. Rahner, "The Layman and the Religious Life,"

Theology for Renewal, Bishops, Priests, Laity (New York: Sheed and Ward, 1964) 147-183. H.U. von Balthasar, "Wesen und Tragweite der Saekularinstitute": Civitas 11 (1955-56) 196-210.

20. 2-2, q. 188, a.2.
21. RB 3.5.
22. Cf., for example, The Rule of Saint Clare, ch. IV, 14-18: Francis and Clare, The Complete Works (New York: Paulist, 1982) 216.
23. The only text, which the partisans of this narrower interpretation have been able to quote, is a statement made by Pius XII in a speech to the Superiors General. This statement, reflecting a tendency of some canon lawyers very influential at that time, must be placed in the context of the whole tradition. Cf, Pius XII to the Superiors General, February 11, 1958: AAS 50 (1958) 153.

Panel of Religious:

            The Experience of the Essential Elements in
                    the Lives of U.S. Religious

a. Margaret Brennan, I.H.M., "Reflections of a Woman
    Religious"

        The task assigned to me in this panel is to share my
experience of the "Essential Elements" in the lives of
American religious women. Because this is a personal
reflection it will very well not be reflective of all
religious congregations nor of all religious within those
congregations. Nevertheless, I believe that the theology and
lived experience articulated here underlies what is the
reality of a significantly large number of women religious in
the United States.

        In general, the "Essential Elements" document presents a
view of religious life which is static, stratified, and based
on a theology of consecration, while the experience of
American women religious, for the most part, is one which
expresses a dynamic, non-hierarchical, prophetic view of
religious life based on a theology of mission.

        In particular, the "Essential Elements" document is
static in that (1) it does not sufficiently take into account
nor allow for further development. Paragraph no. 4 states
that it is "a clarification and restatement of essential
elements" which determine the evolution brought about by
historical and cultural changes. This is not particularly
helpful since many of the elements restated reflect the
ambiguity of those previous statements in many instances. A
study of the history of the Vatican II documents that pertain
to religious life (Perfectae Caritatis and chapter 6 of Lumen
Gentium) attest to differing views of the nature and practice
of religious life among the Church Fathers of the Council.
These differing views, based on differing ecclesiologies are
reflected in the documents making them unclear and even
contradictory in some instances. (2) It describes religious
life apart from the flow of history. It does not allow for a
praxis approach that modifies structures called for by the
signs of these times in which we live--times when radically
new paradigms have surfaced in the church and in society. (3)
It reflects a static world view that is non-evolutionary.

This is seen in paragraph no. 22 where, for instance, the ultimate criteria for judging new works and new ideas is unity rather than the calls of ministry.

Further, the "Essential Elements" document present a stratified view of religious life. Although the following statements need to be nuanced, the document (1) still alludes to religious life as a kind of middle state between the clerical and lay states reflecting a preconciliar elitist conception of religious (no. 7). (2) In general, although allusions to collegial ways of governing are stated, it reflects hierarchical forms of government--monarchical rule, government of one person, general superior, local superior (nos. 49, 50). (3) It places the authentic discernment of founding charisms of the "God-given ministry of the hierarchy" (no. 41) rather than on and in an exercise of mutuality and co-responsibility. It therefore diminishes the prophetic character of religious communities. (4) It is preservative of religious life and does not call religious in their ministry to the empowerment of the laity whom the Spirit is calling to leadership in the church today, nor does it point out that religious life emerged first from the laity.

Finally, the "Essential Elements" document presents a view of religious life that is based on a theology of consecration. (1) It reflects an ontic quality of consecration which separates and stratifies religious from the other People of God. (2) It lacks an appreciation of the reality and autonomy of secular reality as a place of God's self-revelation. Consecration is spoken of in relation to the "absoluteness" of God testified to by detachment and separation which reflects this "absoluteness" (no. 10). (3) It sees the social impact of the vows in terms of a witness to values that challenge society, stressing the being of religious over the doing . . . and stating that "constant evaluation of the use of goods and style relationships in one's own life is one of the most effective ways of promoting the just of Christ at the present time" (no. 36). (4) It describes the vows more as an expression of asceticism and personal consecration than as ways of furthering the mission of the church. (5) It views the consecrated life as separated--as one which reflects a way of life that foretells what is to come hereafter rather than influencing the transformation of society today. (6) It describes public witness in terms of separation from the world and the wearing of a religious habit (no. 37).

135

In contrast to this, the experience of American women religious is one which expresses a dynamic, non-hierarchical, prophetic view of religious life based on a theology of mission. This is evidenced in the lived experience of ministry, authority, lifestyle, and vows.

Theology of Mission. (1) The call to renewal articulated in Perfectae Caritatis and Lumen Gentium was contextualized in the study of other Vatican Documents, particularly the Pastoral Constitution on the Church in the Modern World, the Decree on Missionary Activity and the Declaration on Religious Freedom. Moreover, in the United States, as women religious reflected in the 60's on their role in church and society, they discovered that its context would be one of struggle and turmoil as was evidenced in the cultural and political unrest that characterized life in the United States—the civil rights movement, peace movements, anti-war protests. All of these events had a profound effect on ministry. (2) The experience of the essential elements of religious life is further contextualized in a theology of mission which is (a) critical of a privatized understanding of the Gospel; (b) appreciative of the societal character of the whole of human life and the public nature of Christian ministry; (c) mindful of the universal call to holiness and the responsibility of all the baptized for the mission of the Church—as a result, it tends to de-emphasize distinctions of roles between religious, clergy, laity, and softens the differences between religious communities and other Christian communities which include both married and single persons; (d) envisions the Church's ministry as the transformation of society anticipating and enabling the Kingdom of God within the process of human history. (3) This theology of mission is aware more deeply that religious life does not belong to the hierarchical structures of the church (L. G. nos. 433, 44), but rather to its life of mission and holiness. Within this understanding, women religious have sought to find and experience the meaning of their lives in what this mission and holiness call them to today. (4) Religious re-interpret their lives in terms of the Church in mission and as a result find that their understanding of ministry, their pursuit of holiness, their living of the vows and community life must be grounded in this realization. (5) The lived experience of the teaching in the Pastoral Constitution on the Church in the Modern World, the Decree on the Mission Activity of the Church, the Declaration on Religious Freedom—and more lately from the U. S. Bishops Peace Pastoral and the Canadian Bishops Statement on the Economy, have provided the inspiration for overcoming sacred-secular dichotomies and have led to a diversification of ministries that has gone beyond the confines of institutional and church apostolates in a traditional sense. (6) The missionary character of the church is seen as a question of human liberation leading religious into ministries of advocacy for the poor, social work in government agencies, political lobbying for economic justice, and concerted efforts to work with Christians and non-Christians alike in common efforts to work for nuclear disarmament and the promotion of peace.

Life-Style/Vows. (1) The pursuit of holiness, the profession of the vows, as well as life in community have been deprivatized. (2) Answering the call to serve the marginated led many religious into ministries among the elderly, prisoners, the black community, hispanics, native peoples the oppressed in Latin America—and to live religious life among the people they serve. Large and spacious convents were often relinquished to live in simple neighborhood dwellings open and hospitable to the people. (3) Religious habits and enclosed monastic lives with structured forms gave way to secular dress, while the creation of new forms of community life energized the faith-sharing and life of religious which was often shared with the people.

Authority. (1) The relationship between religious and the world they seek to serve has inevitably created a tension between experience and law. In too many instances its requirements no longer reflect their lived experience. (2) Authority, reflecting the spirit of the Council and the American experience of democracy, has been perceived in terms of mutuality, participation, collegiality, subsidiarity, and the servant role of authority. (3) Moreover, a whole generation of young religious have been formed according to the mandate of Vatican II and a new understanding of religious life. The prescriptions required by many aspects of the new code of canon law and other curial requirements such as those reflected in the "Essential Elements" document reverse in many instances the only experience of religious life these young religious have lived and committed themselves to by referring to that experience as a time of "special experimentation."

Feminism. One more experience of living the essential elements of religious life needs to be reflected upon in which hope, challenge, and tension are experienced. Whereas the Vatican Documents spoke of women only five times, the last twenty years have witnessed in society to the rise of the women's movement, and in the churches to the sharpening lines of a feminist theology. Women religious, whose lives and ministries are dedicated to the mission of the church as it is lived in our society, are increasingly aware that a full participation in its ministries, and a full recognition of their equality is lacking. As a result, they are sensitive to laws and regulations made on their behalf which do not include them in the process of drafting or of their promulgation.

A Final Reflection

The recognition of the place of authority in the church and our respect and loyalty as religious is, I believe, a given. But what is called into question is the need and the appropriateness of both control and close supervision of the life and ministries of religious congregations on the part of the official church which has grown and is reiterated in the "Essential Elements" document.

Paragraph no. 16 of the "Essential Elements" document notes a particular obedience of religious to the Holy Father in virtue of the vow of obedience. This is also prescribed in the new code (Can. 590, 2). It is further recommended that such a clause be inserted explicitly into the vow formula.

This is a new element. And one cannot help but wonder whether its inclusion is out of the need to ensure a loyalty and sense of solidarity with the leadership of the church that might not otherwise be rendered. It further raises the question concerning whether or not religious are or should be more bound in an obedience to the Holy Father than other baptized Christians.

What has been particularly painful in this regard is the fact that for the past twenty years the officers of the Leadership Conference of Women Religious have consistently sought for an opportunity to be received by the Holy Father--to speak with him regarding their commitment and loyalty to the Church--and to share with him the hopes, challenges and tensions of their experience of religious life in theh post-Vatican II Church. These attempts have yet to be realized and to bear fruit.

In Summary

For me, personally, the Essential Elements document did not offer anything new in living out the essential elements of religious life. I had, in reading them, the same feeling as I experienced in the late 60's (some twenty years ago) when we witnessed tension and misunderstanding with SCRIS that culminated and reached crisis proportions in the case of two religious congregations which were pressured into non-canonical status because of an interpretation of these very same "essential elements" which are enjoined on us today. We have not met that situation again--and hopefully we will not. But we have experienced it in the case of individuals in the exercise of political ministry.

John Shea has pointed out that "belief and theology that arise from the religious experience of one generation have the ambition to aid the religious searchers of succeeding generations." (An Experience Named Spirit, p. 76). For this reason alone it would be foolish and temerarious to dismiss the theology of consecration as articulated in the "essential elements" document. It expresses an experience of religious life that developed in other times. A reflection on that experience can be an aid to our own search today as we continue the tradition of religious life--but it cannot be normative.

The Holy Father's concern for American religious women which has initiated the dialogues between congregations and Bishops hopefully will result in greater understanding and in mutual efforts of discernment, collaboration and the enabling the Kingdom of God in our times.

b. James F. Gaffney, F.S.C., "The Religious Brother in the
    Life of the Church"

It has been generally acknowledged that for more than a
decade, religious institutes have been experiencing a crisis.
Personnel statistics would indicate that this crisis has been
slightly more dramatic for religious brothers than for
religious sisters and certainly more so than for religious
priests. The crisis has been one of significance, of
worthwhileness, of identity.

This situation is so serious for brothers that the Sacred
Congregation for Religious and Secular Institutes has chosen
as the topic of exploration for their upcoming plenaria the
place of religious brothers in the church. The crisis for
many brothers, especially those who are members of what the
revised Code of Canon Law terms "Clerical Institutes," is one
relating to their finality and value. More traumatic for many
brothers than the large reduction in their numbers worldwide
has been their struggle to be recognized, affirmed and
acknowledged as a significant presence within the church.

Brothers believe that religious life as a gift to the
church is complete, whole and integral without ordination.
That is, they look upon all religious as being equal in terms
of the meaningfulness of their religious call. Sisters,
religious priests and brothers have all chosen the same way of
life, the same mission and the same basic goals as religious.
The forced classification of religious institutes into
clerical and lay categories (when in reality many view
themselves as truly mixed) adds to the polarization between
religious who are lay and those who are clerics.

Lay religious resent being defined negatively. The
brothers are consecrated lay persons, rather than non-ordained
religious. They live their religious reality and charism as
laity. As such, they give witness to the church as a pilgrim
people, as a community of sisters and brothers. They also
signify the call of all people to holiness and to
participation in ministry according to their gifts. For the
brothers, religious life is looked upon as "the fraternal
life," a reference to the fundamental New Testament model of
brothers and sisters united to promote the Kingdom. Their
religious witness is a public sign of the call to all persons
to be reconciled as daughters and sons of the Father. Their
consecration is prior to any juridical structures. All
vocations are regarded by them as complementary and in service

of the church. As religious, all are equal in terms of sharing the same finality and charism. Those who are ordained have a certain positioning in the church's hierarchical order, but this does not in and of itself speak to the precise meaning of their identity as religious.

For too long, brothers have experienced confusion, resentment, anguish and hurt because of a perceived second-class status. Their work has often been defined as derivative, secondary and auxiliary in nature. They have been regarded as co-adjutors, cooperators, lay helpmates and simple, uneducated appendages. Again, this has been especially for some of those who belong to religious institutes whose members are priests and brothers. But all brothers have been subject to the well-intentioned but demeaning question: "What is wrong with you that you did not go all the way and become a priest?" Besides being somewhat of a personal affront, this query implies a lack of respect for individual, Spirit-in-spired charisms and for lay ministry. It is also a misunderstanding regarding the openness of religious life to having priests and lay persons as members of a structured way of living the evangelical counsels in service of the Kingdom.

All of this is directly contrary to the intentions of many of the founders of religious institutes. It is true that certain institutes were sacerdotal in their nature from their origin. Their history and the place of brothers in them are different from that of most other Institutes. Most founders envisioned themselves as establishing a religious family composed of several or more varied types of membership. The brothers were not seen by them merely as co-adjutors.

Many of these institutes in their foundation were fraternities composed of brothers, some of whom were ordained. priests and brothers alike understood that each was fully a religious. Membership was viewed in terms of communion, service and reconciliation -- not privilege, status and power. Each person was valued not as a worker but for who he was and the gift that he brought to the church as a member of a community seeking to minister and to grow in holiness. The brothers were not looked down upon, ignored, held back from leadership, undereducated or oppressed. The priest members also belonged to the brotherhood and did not view their lifestyle as being the same as that of diocesan priests. Together the religious priests and religious brothers gave witness to the call to all Christians to holiness, conversion and ministry.

141

The regrettable evolution which has occurred is focused most sharply in the denial to brothers in clerical congregations of the right to serve as local, provincial or congregational superiors. This matter will be a fundamental issue at the autumn plenaria being sponsored by SCRIS in Rome. The attitude of most brothers (and of not a few other commentators on religious life) is that religious brothers and religious priests are similar in all ways except for that which flows directly from ordination. Each institute should, then, in accordance with its living tradition be able to indicate if it is lay, clerical or mixed.

When brothers cannot be superiors in clerical congregations, they experience discrimination. They ask what the requirements of the gospel are in terms of righting this perceived wrong. Why is it necessary in all instances for an insult to be received for a brother to be a local superior or a provincial in a so-called "Clerical Institute" (many of which really view themselves as being mixed in composition)? The ministry of the superior is to be an animator, an unifier, a promoter of reconciliation, a communicator, a conflict-resolver, a person who calls the group to its own best aspirations and holds before them the demands of the gospel. In all instances are brothers to be excluded from this role as being automatically less qualified? Cannot the local community or the province or the congregation best discern who is gifted with the charism of leadership? Is leadership being too narrowly and juridically defined?

The reality is that many institutes are reporting that they have brothers who are ideally prepared for this internal ministry. (The related matter of jurisdiction in terms of presentation of candidates for ordination can always be delegated to a priest member of the leadership team.) They indicate that there are brothers who are uniquely gifted to promote a spirit of association, community, collaboration and the handing on of the charism of the group. More than forty institutes in the last several years have asked for equality in governance for all members. They have also sought equality in mission, in rights and in responsibilities. They have requested that each institute be allowed to express its own reality in accordance with its living tradition and not be relegated to narrow juridical categories that reflect status distinctions. However, all but a few have been refused.

The main fear expressed by brothers is concerning a church that might become too highly clericalized, one which communicates indirectly to the laity a status different from the dignity and equality proper to all sons and daughters of the Father. This is viewed as an urgent problem by many. Some religious priests, it is observed, seem to derive their primary identity and sense of purpose from their ordination and not from their religious calling. Bishops are quite correct in indicating difficulty in distinguishing the lifestyle of some religious priests from that of secular clergy.

A number of theologians are pointing to the important service that brothers now provide in focusing on the value, significance and nature of religious life, without distinctions between the ordained and the non-ordained. Brothers are a special charism and vocation of Religious. In fact, brothers can be regarded as protectors of the charism of male religious congregations, not confusing the identity of religious with the ministry of priesthood. The brothers, especially those in lay institutes, also serve a special function in favor of lay ministry and the call to holiness for all lay persons. No wonder that Pope John Paul II has repeatedly urged that bishops, clergy, laity and religious all unite in working to preserve the gift of religious brotherhood for the church.

And what is that uniquely brotherly dimension of religious life that religious brothers can give to the church and to society? In a world torn apart by individualism, nationalism, consumerism and domination, the brothers give effective witness to interdependence and to the communal nature of the church itself. Like the religious sisters, the brothers stand for and promote the common good and the identity that all have as brothers and sisters in the Lord. The appeal of their vocation is as an association for ministry, rooted in prayer and consecration. Their communal life is to strengthen them for ministry, to enable them better to reach out to the poor and needy, to be brothers for others, to unify, to affirm, to develop an attitude of inter-dependence, and to foster universal love and reconciliation. As Pope Paul VI indicated: "Religious are to be for the church what the church is to be for the world."

What do brothers bring to whichever ministry they are privileged to participate in? They bring their own varied experiences of community and interdependence, of unassuming service and of the struggle to communicate and to relate well. They share the benefits they have derived from communal living, that is, their being awakened to their own worthwhileness, healed of some of their deepest hurts, reconciled with those who are different, and challenged when off-base or not actualizing their God-given potential. They also share the reality of divine love, including love for enemies, which they experience in the Eucharist. Their vowed chastity enables them to be free to break down barriers of division and group hatred. Their poverty frees them from possessiveness and the burdens of riches. They vow obedience so as to benefit through their communal life and the mediation of superiors in discerning God's call, increasingly more free of their own whims, blindness and self-centeredness. And many brothers now bring a preferential option for the poor, for doing works of justice and for a gospel way of living. They also remain equally committed to sensitizing the middle class to look upon the poor and needy as brothers and sisters in Christ.

The brothers today recognize themselves as invited to be enablers of the laity and promoters of greater collaboration with their bishops and with the clergy. They are called by vocation to be a leaven and source of unity, spiritual energy and apostolic vitality. Brotherhood implies serving, encouraging, supporting, comforting those in pain, embracing the marginalized, reconciling, being a catalyst for collaboration, sharing the joys of community life, putting aside any special privileges or status, and promoting the interdependence of all people who seek the welfare of humanity.

For the brothers, community is association for ministry. It is rooted in personal and communal prayer and the Eucharist. To lead among them is truly to serve, to unify, to challenge, to listen, to respect, to foster the common good, to share a vision and to suggest ways of realizing it. The brothers know that they are called by vocation to model and promote association, interdependence and unity.

The lifestyle of the brothers, while fundamentally oriented to the apostolate, cannot be fully comprehended just in terms of the works that the brothers do in the church. Rather, it is a matter of how the brothers minister and to what they give public witness. The specific gift of the brothers to the church is that of brotherliness, of a fraternal style of ministry and of a spirit of community, prayer and discipleship -- all focused on the most urgent needs of the church and society. Their brotherly energy is meant to be nurtured by prayer and community and to be shared through ministry. Theirs is community-for-ministry.

All the elements in the lifestyle of the brother are unified by their commitment to serve in the spirit of Jesus Christ. The constitutive elements or components of their lifestyle are interrelated: their faith and zeal; their spirit of association; the fidelity that they maintain to a specific charism and a living tradition; their special concern for the poor; the freedom embodied in their vows; their prayerful reliance on God's providential care and presence; and their apostolic spirituality. They are at once apostles, ministers, men of prayer and people of justice. Whether priest or brother, each religious shares in all of the characteristic components or elements which together and in an interrelated manner constitute the Religious identity which is a gift from God to the Church.

In conclusion, then, what has been the experiences of the brothers during the last ten or fifteen years? We are more enthusiastic than ever before about renewal and the revitalization of our lifestyle. We have gained a much more global perspective on the needs of the church and the world. Many of us have a renewed sense of personal mission in our daily apostolate. We respect the uniqueness and giftedness of each person, while also strengthening our commitment to community and the common good, and to experience brotherhood. Our governmental structures are based on subsidiarity, consultation, collegiality and response to need, but we are not impeded in being able to come to corporate decisions that reflect the mind of the congregation, province or local house. More than ever before, we have been sensitized to the poor, the broken-hearted and the victims of injustice.

It is true that we have lost many wonderful confreres and have not attracted nearly enough new disciples. We have struggled with our identity as religious and equally so as brothers, particularly those in the so-called "clerical congregations." We are burdened with the aging problem, are fatigued at times because of overwork, and feel the lingering effects of grieving for a past that will never reappear. Some of us are still dealing with polarizations and the tensions that result from the interaction of varying perspectives or the difficulty of trying to maintain traditional ministries even as we attempt to respond to the most urgent needs of the poor and needy. Rugged individualism, superficial communication, an inadequate prayer life and the phenomenon of living together in isolation still characterize some of our groups.

Nonetheless, we are hopeful about the future and determined to contribute a uniquely brotherly dimension to the life and mission of the church. We pledge ourselves to greater collaboration and to deeper spiritual ties to our bishops, to our brothers in the clergy, to our sisters in religious life, and to our fellow laity. We are becoming more prayerful and reflective persons. Equally important to us is our role in enabling the laity to emerge as fully participating members of the church. We commit ourselves to be part of an apostolic network of people dedicated to promoting the purpose of the church in communion with the hierarchy. Our hope is to assist all people -- men and women, rich and poor, persons of all colors, creeds and ethnic backgrounds -- in a greater spirit of interdependence and loving unity.

Please pray for us. Please try to understand us. Please challenge and support us in our call to be what the Lord expects of us. And, finally, please promote our vocation as something which you also respect and affirm as an unique gift to the whole church of Jesus Christ, who is our common brother.

c. Richard Rohr, O.F.M., "The Experience of a Priest Religious"

I would like to share with you a bit of the setting out of which I have lived my religious life. I don't think my experience has been typical, for half of my 22 years, mostly in my formation period, has been lived in institutional settings, and the other half lived as the pastor of the lay community in Cincinnati called New Jerusalem. Thus, for the last 13 years, I've been living a really intense community life, but with lay people. Then there are my two vocations, the one to religious life, and the further vocation I received at ordination. That certainly changed the picture in many ways--just recall what we've made of priesthood in the church. Certainly, after ordination, the vocation of priesthood has tended to dominate, even though all my Franciscan spirituality and teaching says that this should not be the case. Certainly St. Francis didn't intend to found a clerical community.

To be honest, I would have to say that my experience in these 22 years has been a very pleasant one, one that has been so positive in relation to my community and to my ministry that it would force me to believe deeply in the religious life. I don't know who to thank for that. I know that it is not everybody's experience.

In reading the Essential Elements document, I can go through it paragraph by paragraph and be saying Yes, Yes; but I know that I am interpreting it all in a very different way and I have no feeling for it. It's just not my experience. I could force it to be, but it isn't. It's all deductive theology. What we really need--and this is something I see happening in a unique way in the American Church, especially among American religious--is a willingness to trust our inductive experience. For me this is a source of great joy and hope, something I'm very anxious to communicate somehow to the Roman church. There is something very rich happening here, something that we are, so to speak, trapped with. That may sound arrogant, or even presumptuous, but there are certain things you know and you can't pretend you don't know them. You can't unknow them. This is not to suggest that we haven't made our mistakes, but I think we know that an awful lot of healthy, free and beautiful things are happening in American religious life.

From the many retreats I give to clergy and religious in this country and elsewhere, I seem to find a lot of religious life which, as someone said, lives on the level of low-key hostility. In a sense, it's constant. But I'm also finding a lot of communities in our country that simply aren't that way. I want to talk very pragmatically here: when I see non-angry people living happy Christian lives together, I have to trust that. I have to say: "Something good is happening there, something hopeful and something free."

Certainly we Americans use the word freedom easily and perhaps even make a god of it, by which we usually mean some kind of political freedom. But the positive side of this American love affair with freedom is a commitment to psychological and spiritual freedom among American religious that I don't find anywhere else. We are not just trying to do the right thing but also, as our Jesuit brothers have taught us in the doctrine of pure intention, trying to do it for the right reason. We are a Church concerned with sifting out the voices. Yes, we want to be obedient, but first we want to be discerning. It seems to me that a person who can learn discernment is going to be the person who is finally capable of true and free and life-giving obedience. That's the kind of obedience I see in religion here.

I was recently the only North American on an international commission in Rome on missions and evangelization. That meeting left me with a feeling of being able to relate much more to my brothers and sisters in American religious life than to the Friars Minor from the other countries. Now whether or not that was a fully representative group, the difference seemed to be more than just cultural. It seemed to be based on this love of psychological and spiritual freedom, this wanting to do something not just because the law says so, but because it is the will of God, what the Lord and the church is telling us to do, and wanting to do it for the right reason. And we don't want to get there and be angry about it. Maybe we take too much time to do that, but I don't think so. I think we've got to trust it and I think we've got to risk going all the way with it.

We can't deny what we now know. Not even a pope can tell me that I can't know things or that I have to deny my experience of what seems to be bringing forth grace and life and the fruits of the Spirit. I have to trust the fruits of the Spirit. But when I read this document on the essential elements of religious life I seem to hear a tone of mistrust, that we can't be free to search for that.

I was allowed and even trained by my religious community to be a searcher. Isn't that a beautiful form of religious life? Isn't that a sign of contradiction to the world? Isn't that counter-cultural in a world which simply gives us the answer which we then spend the rest of our lives protecting or securing? So I can't say, as someone else said today: "If this is written to give bishops some general guidelines by which to understand us, then I guess it is OK." Because I would have hoped for more than that. It doesn't name who I am or where I'm heading, except in a general and sort of pious sense. This is a sense to which I would assent; but then I'd be tempted to say: "So what." We want instead to be honest. We don't want to keep putting our names to things that are just not the truth. Why say pious things that aren't true in a practical and pastoral way? I'd rather learn to trust this life as it is and listen to it, and reflect upon it, and be critical of it. I guess what I am appealing to, and, judging from its documents, what I am not sure the Roman church is capable of, is the more inductive spirituality of religious life that is willing first of all to give its members freedom to fail. Jesus did that. Should religious life be better than the way Jesus discipled his people? --And then reflect upon those failings, and find where the freedom and the grace is emerging, even in experiences of darkness.

A few years ago, our Cincinnati province had a visitator who, after going through the 450 of us, told our chapter that he had found that the most happy and creative men among us, the ones who believed in themselves and who seemed to be making a difference, were men whom he would call inside-outside people. What he meant were men who were very much committed to the Franciscan vision and very loyal to the province, but who had also found creative and faithful ways to live outside it. I guess I have experienced some of that, for religious life has been very good to me, much as a parent is good to a child. It makes the child not leave the parent.

I love religious life, and I am sure I am going to die with an O.F.M. after my name more than, frankly, a Father in front of my name; I'm not sure I need it; and that's not meant to sound rebellious. Religious life has given me a kind of inner authority to trust my experience, to come back as an adult to love, and to give my self to be freely involved as, I hope, a life-giving member of my province. I think I am considered committed to the friars even through I don't live in the friary. I don't say that to brag; I think it's just an objective fact because I've found a way of being in relationship and, I hope, a life-giving relationship to my brothers. It seems to me that that is an understanding that I don't see in this document: an understanding of community as relationship, as a way of relating, as a way of being mutually accountable.

Brothers and Sisters, you know and I know that our houses are filled with people who are doing all according to "the law," but we don't know what is going on inside their hearts. You never get in and they never get out. Is that religious life? Having lived in friaries for 13 years, I know I lived shared life with my brother friars, and I am quite sure they would say the same of me even now when I don't live in a friary. For they do come to share their hearts and souls with me. But I hope I do the same with them.

It is my hope, I guess, that the essential elements of religious life would be at the same time a bit more prophetic than political, and, ironically, a bit more playful. There is something about this document that has us taking ourselves so seriously. Is that really what Jesus is talking about? To be a disciple of Jesus, does it really have to be that heavy? I know I am influenced by Franciscan spirituality, by "Brother Juniper" thinking. But I don't know that seriousness is necessarily the counter-sign that the world needs. I'm not sure that it points to the Kingdom any better than playfulness.

As Father Lozano was talking today about consecrated life, I was much in agreement. It seems that the way to be consecrated is to live a life that embodies choices that clearly challenge the culture, choices which make people say: "Why would you do that? You don't make any sense. You're living in another world." I am thinking of some of the laymen in our community these past years who have given up high-paying jobs in some of the engineering facilities of GE and other companies in Cincinnati because they found their job would be supporting the military complex. These men are just a wonder to their contemporaries and to their peers, and they project an aura of consecration much more than people who walk around in different clothes but who oftentimes are just as trapped in materialism and consumerism as anyone else. I'm not trying to make this dramatic, but I know that living with a lay community has taught me much more about my vow of poverty than the friar's life. Our young couples live from week to week to pay the bills. Experiencing that has taught me a grass-roots, necessary kind of obedience. For if the 250 committed adults and 150 children of the New Jerusalem Community are going to stay together, we just have to be obedient and responsive to one another. Since we are always dying to do our own will, we must constantly by listening to one another and working for a kind of consensus.

Again I find that this has taught me the meaning of my own religious life. The people have said it many times, and I'll just end on that point: We are all going to get converted together, and we are going to be called back to the gospel together. I don't think religious life is going to do it all by itself. We religious are not going to be able to respond to the Lord and to the gospel just as a group, apart from the diocesan clergy, apart from the brothers and sisters, the lay people. For ultimately, it is one church. The emphasis on Baptism has got to continue to be the primary emphasis. All the rest is passing away except our being named as sons and daughters of God. We can show that, and we want to show it in as loud and visible and lovely a way as possible. We can't however do it by separating but, I think, by making choices, clear choices that truly say that we are not going the way of darkness or unfreedom. We are opting for real freedom. And finally, I feel my experience of American religious life has sent me on a search for which I am very, very grateful. It has given me parameters and clear direction that I don't see coming from most parishes or even from the diocesan leadership. But this gospel clarity is also preparing a huge cross for us in the years ahead. Our church leadership is leadership by example and consensus. After all, people don't think themselves into a new way of living, but as religious life has always said, they live themselves into a new way of thinking.

Who They Are and What They Do:
Current Forms of Religious Life in the U.S. Church

by

Marie Augusta Neal, S.N.D.

Since the publication of the decrees of the Second
Vatican Council., religious women and men have pondered the
opening lines of Gaudium Et Spes: "The joy and hope, the grief
and anguish of the poeple of our time., especially of those
who are poor or afflicted in any way, are the joy and hope,
the grief and anguish of the followers of Christ as well" (no.
1). This concern for the poor became ever more explicit as
religious responded to the further directive of this document
which reminded us that: "At all times the church carries the
responsibility or reading the signs of the times and
interpreting them in the light of the gospel, if it is to
carry out its task" (no. 4). Towards the end of the same
document comes a new focus for doing this task: the critical
analysis of culture, the heart of the matter for us today. It
was expressed in these words.

> In each nation and social group there is a growing number
> of men and women who are conscious that they themselves
> are the crafters and molders of their community's
> culture. All over the world the sense of autonomy and
> responsibility increases with effects of the greatest
> importance for the spiritual and moral maturity of
> humankind: This will become clearer to us as we place
> before our eyes the unification of the world and the duty
> imposed on us to build a better world in truth and
> justice. (no. 53)

The introduction of the doing of the justice agenda
rapidly became more focal with this emphasis. Already in
Pacem In Terris we had learned that peace, poverty and human
rights are the central concerns of the committed Christian.
Two years after the Council, in Populorum Progressio, we
further learned that this concern is most effectively
implemented through work for the development of peoples.
After the call to action in Octogesima Adveniens, Pope Paul's
encyclical of 1971, calling for effective political
involvement to right the wrongs of human oppression, the Synod
of Bishops, assembled to implement The Coming Eightieth,
announced:

152

action in behalf of justice and participation in the
transformation of the world fully appear to us as a
constitutive dimension of the preaching of the gospel
or in other words, of the church's mission for the
redemption of the human race and its liberation from
every oppressive situation. (Synod, "Justice in the
World," p.4)

What religious institutes have been doing since the
Council, it seems to me as a result of my research, is
endeavoring to be obedient to this mandate to participate in
the righting of the wrongs of injustice, action now possible
due to changed world conditions but not yet implemented
through our several ministries in the church. Most
congregations of women and of men have in the revision of
their constitutions, centered action and reflection on how to
implement this special option for the poor found in church
documents since Rerum Novarum (1891), but expressed since the
Second Vatican Council with an insistence that those called to
an apostolic spirituality cannot resist, even though the
manner of implementation may radically differ from community
to community (Evangelica Testificatio, nos. 17,18).

Seeking to establish the just society and working for
world peace, focal in the renewed church everywhere, are even
more the concerns of the renewal in religious congregations.
Almost everything that has happened, including the striking
decline in numbers entering and the increase in number of
members leaving, can be explained in the context of this
gospel-rooted mandate to the church to go out and right the
wrongs causing human oppression and then return to place one's
gifts at the altar (Matt 5:23-24). When John the Baptist came
out of the desert preaching repentance those who recognized
their sin and asked what to do to be saved were told, "If you
have two coats, give to them who have none. If you have food,
do the same" (Luke 3:11, 13). One must conclude that if
repentance is constituted by giving to the poor, sin must be
withholding what they need in order to survive. Prior to the
current advances in technology, we could fulfill that mandate
by helping to alleviate the results of poverty, which we did.
Today we are called to eliminate its causes. This focus
requires, as Gaudium Et Spes so well recognized, the apostolic
uses of the sciences, including the social sciences, not to
manipulate and control people, but to participate in human
liberation (no. 5).

The Mandate to Renewal

The document entitled the <u>Pastoral Constitution On The Church In The Modern World</u> embodies the new understanding of our responsibility in history and for history that the holocaust, the dropping of the atom bomb on Hiroshima, and the struggles of Latin American, Asian, and African peoples to extricate themselves from the political hegemony of modern industrial states stirred our consciences to ponder our new understanding of mission. As part of an American people, once we began to realize the potential for good and for evil in our rapidly developing technology and our own involvement in decisions for its uses and abuses in world perspective, we, as religious, sensed a new call to mission.

Religious congregations of men and women, involved as they were in formal education, delivery of health services, social welfare work of all kinds, and pastoral ministry in city, suburb, and rural areas of our own country, and of many mission areas in what are now called third world countries, were moved by this document to full realization that it was our responsibility to use our newly developed professional skills for the liberation of people. We acquired these skills in response to the mandates uttered by Popes Pius XI in <u>Catholic Education</u> (1927), and Pius XII, in his call for a "World Congress on States of Perfection" (1950), and the subsequent generation of the General Congress of Religious, (1950); by the International Conference of Teaching Sisters, September, 1951; by the founding of the Conference of Major Superiors of Women (CMSW) and the Conference of Major Superiors of Men (CMSM); and by the Sister Formation Movement, all of the early 1950's. Each of these reinforced the need to be responsibly educated for our apostolic works. We thus became more vulnerable than most other workers in the church to meeting or defeating the challenge of <u>Gaudium et Spes</u>, with a population, just among the women alone, of whom 67.8% had at least one college degree by 1965 and 28% had master's degrees.. Before this time, we were major culture carriers, but we were becoming culture makers. By 1965 also, the temptation to be successful and effective was already bureaucratizing our apostolic endeavors. Fortunately for the future of the church in the modern world, the decree <u>Perfectae Caritatis</u> mandated us specifically to carry out a renewal of religious life. It declared, in part:

> The purpose of the religious is to help the members follow Christ and be united to God through the profession of the evangelical counsels. It should be

constantly kept in mind, therefore, that even the best adjustment made in accordance with the needs of our age will be ineffectual unless they are animated by renewal of spirit. This must take precedence over even the active ministry. (no. 2)

After this primary guideline, the decree of October 28, 1965, called, "The Decree on the Adaptation and Renewal of Religious Life," indicated the areas of life to be updated. These were the manner of living, praying and working; the manner of government, including a revision of constitutions, directories, custom books, books of prayers and ceremonies and including the suppression of obsolete laws, with all adapted to "the decrees of this sacred synod," (referring of course to the Second Vatican Council) (no. 3). All of these mandates for renewal and the necessary experimentation accompanying them were entrusted to the general chapters of each congregation, to be followed eventually by the approbation of the Holy See or the local ordinary, depending on whether the groups were pontifical or diocesan institutes (no. 4).

Response of the Women

The religious congregations of women responded to this invitation to renew with a remarkable enthusiasm. At their annual meeting in 1965, the Conference of Major Superiors of Women heard, from nine of their own Sisters, a series of analyses of the current world situation that focused on the signs of the times, including the need for a global perspectives; a reexamination of the effects on society of our way of teaching, delivering health services and helping the poor, to determine in whose interests we wre actually serving; the problems of authority involved in planned change; and teh importance of community-making in a world which had become characterized by economic management systems of formal bureaucracy. On the basis of these reflections, the board of the CMSW (now the Leadership Conference of Women Religious) voted the initiation of the Sisters' Survey which began a twenty-year longitudinal study of the changing structures of religious congregations of women in the United States. Thanks to the initiative of women like Sr. Mary Luke Tobin and Sr. Mary Isabel Concannon who are here today, as well as Sr. Mary Daniel Turner.

As the designer and organizer of the several stages of the Sisters' Survey, I can speak accurately to its parts. In 1966 and again in 1982, each of the over 400 congregations of religious in the country received a thirty-two page report to complete, including information on the actual number of members in perpetual vows temporary vows, the number of novices and postulants. Also reported, for each five year segment from 1950 through 1980, were the works that sisters did and do; buildings owned or used, gained and lost; formation programs, content and assessment, requirements for entrance, characteristics of candidates; and plans for the next ten years. Hopes and expectations for the renewal were asked in 1966 and again in 1982, all from the perspective of the administrators of the congregations. I will not burden you today with a full account of these findings, important as they are for assessing the present and planning for the immediate future, because a full report of them is off the press today, June 22, 1984 and will be available to all of you from Michael Glazier, Inc. of Wilmington, Delaware. What I will do, after completing a brief outline of all the parts of the study, is discuss some of the findings, leaving details of what you may want to ask to the time for questions in the discussion period. The coming publication reports on 104,000 sisters and was based on responds by the administration of 342 different groups.

The Second stage of the research was an opinion survey of 649 different questions, sent out in 1967 to 157,000 sisters, 139,000 of whom responded. To a follow-up of that survey in 1980, 65% of a random sample of sisters in twenty different Institutes, 3740 sisters responded. The contemplative nuns and Trappist monks had a separate survey in 1971 based on the same questionnaire. The survey was also used in 1968 to survey the two western provinces of the Jesuits. A parallel study was done in Southern Africa in 1970 and an international one in 1969, in five different languages and including only Sisters of Notre Dame of Namur. In 1969 the publics served by these congregations were surveyed also. A third segment of the long-range study was an analysis of the chapter decrees of 280 of the participating congregations completed in 1974, a further study of chapter decrees in 1977 and a comparison of 20 Constitutions with these decrees in 1983. It is out of the experience of designing, analyzing and interpreting these several pieces of research, assisted by consultors and staff, and attending the general chapters and assemblies of over twenty of these groups that I speak to you today.

The Decrees of the Second Vatican Council, the social encyclicals, and the follow-up studies in the bishops' pastorals of the 1970's on the rights of the poor to the land and on racism, are embodied in the survey items and constitute the framework in which the study was designed and analyzed.

Questions of women's place in the church are also included, as well as a review of sisters' theological positions, opinions on social issues, changes already introduced and planned, and the forms of spirituality that characterize their lives. Commitment to altruism is a basic theme. The research has a point of view, the justice agenda of the church. A main finding is that social justice and peace are not among many agendas but are the core agendas that reflection on the signs of the times makes central to this new era of the church in the world. These agendas are now embodied in the work of the apostolic religious congregations and orders sent to do the works that Jesus did. Even though it is for members of the apostolic congregations and orders a point of tension with old ways, it is the main commitment now. (See Origins, Col. 7, No. 44, April 22, 1978, pp. 690-693.)

Religious Groups in the Church

An historical and canonical note is relevant at this point. The new Canons divide religious life into institutes and societies. Institutes refer to orders and congregations of men and women who take the vows of poverty, chastity and obedience, often referred to as the evangelical counsels. Institutes are divided into religious institutes, that is, groups that take vows and live in community, and secular institutes, men and women who take vows but are free to live alone, or with their families, or in groups of their choice, with a primary focus to be in the world and involved in all its activities. Institutes of religious institutes are also divided into contemplative and apostolic groups. Contemplatives are usually referred to as monks and nuns. A combination style characterizes what are called autonomous monasteries, whose members live both the active and contemplative life, of which Benedictines are the modal case, their primary focus that of being a community as a model for Christian living. Contemplatives, on the one hand, are primarily involved in worship, prayer, and meditation, activities in which all religious participate, but for contemplatives, the order of their lives centers on these activities. On the other hand, "Apostolic action is of the very nature of institutes dedicated to apostolic works. The whole life of the members is, therefore, to be imbued with an apostolic spirit, and the whole of their apostolic action is to be animated by a religious spirit," as Canon 675 states. Benedictines have a tradition that really stands between the enclosed life of the contemplatives and the active life of the apostolic groups, with a focus on community building. This form of religious life constitutes a third emphasis. For apostolic groups, community is _for_ mission; for Benedictines, community _is_ mission.

Considering the canonical divisions, we note that Societies of apostolic life have the requirement to live in community and have the same commitment to the apostolate as have institutes, but they do not take vows. Thus, since Maryknoll men are a society of apostolic life, their priests are secular clergy. They make their binding commitment by oath and they are recognized as a corporate body with constitutions. To fill out further types of commitment to the church in special types of religious callings, we should add another category known from ancient times, but once again a calling popular in the present era, that of hermits, also called anchorites. Hermits take vows or some other form of sacred bonds, do not live in community by definition, dedicate their lives to prayer and solitude, though they agree to give spiritual guidance and counsel to those who seek them out, and lead their form of life directly under the guidance of the bishop. Today, some religious institutes also provide hermitages (Canon 603).

Many of the earlier technical divisions among forms of consecrated life are no longer found in the Canons. The order of virgins is still there, however, (Canon 604). Virgins are consecrated by bishops, may or may not live in community, can live at home and have a "a mystical espousal to Christ". (See _Sponsa Regis_, 1950). This array of forms of religious life is a reminder to all of us that the church has been open at different periods of history to new forms of consecration, as the times called forth new charisms.

At other times, however, the official church has been so closed to new forms that those inspired to initiate new forms were required by Church law to adopt an already existing form of consecrated life rather than follow a new calling. History provides some interesting clarification of present tensions in religious life on this point. A common tension at the present time reflects current concern with the use of the concept "consecrated life". Since the Second Vatican Council affirmed the priesthood of all peoples and the consecration by Baptism to the apostolic life, the laity have expressed some resentment even with the language of the new Canons speaking of a special calling that claims that religious are "linked in a special way to the Church and its mystery," (Canon 573, 574). (Cf. "Religious Life According to the New Code," Jerome Murphy-O'Connor, O.P. _Religious Life Review_). The National Association of Women Religious changed its name to the

National Association of Religious Women to recognize the baptismal consecration of the laity to the mission of the Church as peers with religious institute members.

Another development since 1968 is a response to the fact that some groups have been asked by the church to dispense themselves from their vows and assume non-canonical status. One such group that is still vigorously pursuing apostolic activity in the Church is the Immaculate Heart Community of Los Angeles. Another group called Sisters for Christian Community, founded by Audrey Kopf, recruits former members of many different religious orders and congregations of women. The 1st group has about 300 members; the 2nd about 700 members. Another new development is associate membership. Religious congregations have added this category, which many times includes both men and women, married and single people, and often former members of the group. They share the life, the apostolate and the support of the institute. From this information, it can be seen that new forms of religious life take form from the experience of those hearing a call to do the mission of the church.

The historical distinction between orders and congregations reveals an earlier tension significant again today. I will speak here only of the women's experience. Orders refer to groups founded before 1600 and include members who take solemn vows, that is, vows more binding in that for poverty, for example, no property can be inherited by the individual after the vow is taken. Solemn vows usually require a cloister more binding for women than for men. In fact, after Pope Benedict VIII's Decree, Periculoso, of 1298, cloister was such a stringent ruling for consecrated women that apostolic congregations, founded in the 16th and 17th centuries specifically to work among the new poor in the industrial city, were offered the choice of either returning to the cloister or disbanding as a consecrated group in the church. So binding was this decree that Jeanne de Chantal's Visitations Sisters and Angel Merici's Ursulines changed their original calling to help the poor in order to fit that requirement.

On the basis of this restriction, both groups became convent school teachers, preserving the cloister to remain "real nuns", in the sense of the decree. The Daughters of Charity, however, re-defined themselves as not being nuns and, from the beginning, have renewed their vows annually rather than be confined by the restriction of cloister and solemn vows. The plan of St. Vincent de Paul and Louise de Marillac is encompassed in the following quotation, stated in 1634:

The sisters will have no convent but a hospital, houses of the sick or an asylum; no cell but a hired room, no cloister but the streets of the town; for enclosure they have only obedience, for a grille the fear of God, for veil, holy modesty.

The Daughters of Charity chose to be less than nuns so that they could fulfill legitimately in the church the ministry of nursing which they developed as a dignified profession. Except for the Sisters of Charity, nursing of men was a category of work only for prostitutes until the Sisters of Charity and Florence Nightingale became noted for their service during the Crimean War in 1854.

The Sisters of Charity paved the way for apostolic service in the city. Not until 1900, with the decree Conditae a Christo and the Normae to implement it, was the restriction of cloister lifted, so that women could be recognized as living the consecrated life canonically in the church despite not living within the confines of a monastic seclusion (Ewens). Remember that this same restriction was not placed on men who had the same apostolic vocation of human services and pastoral ministry. We should ponder together the assumptions behind this six hundred year canonical restriction on ministry to the poor placed on women in the church. (As a footnote to this point, there is considerable evidence that the insistence on solemn vows and cloister for women in the high middle ages and later is closely associated with the inheritance practices where the lord of the manor, in dividing up his property among his children to assure their futures, relied on his nun daughters not coming forth later to claim their shares of the estate. With the active apostolate proposed by women in the beginning of the industrial ear, the idea of serving the poor in the city could be best carried out within what we call today "a shelter." Such a building might be sought by an enthusiastic sister from the property of her family. Such a request would upset the plans for dividing the property and, hence, be a threat to an inheritance custom of long standing in the families of nobles and princes. It was mainly from these families that medieval nuns came.--Leyser Page 64). A very pragmatic function indeed!

A further distinction to clarify mission is that between the words nun and sister. The directive of Pope Pius XII, Sponsa Regis, published in 1950, introduced the updating of

160

contemplative cloistered life for nuns. Recognizing that there are few endowments or land grants for the housing and feeding of contemplative nuns to be found in the modern world, and, further, that nuns are as capable as monks of earning their own living, this decree of Pius XII mandated nuns to support themselves by doing work that would not distract them from their contemplative prayer. This new development had an unintended consequence related to the founding of the International Union of Superiors General and the Sister Formation programs, namely, the distinction between works to support monasteries and apostolic work.

In 1950, a major new development in modern religious life began with the introduction of the international gatherings of heads of religious congregations and orders, invited to so do by Pope Pius XII who was deeply concerned about the quality of service religious provided. For him it was a question of justice to assure that the church provide competently trained professionals to do the education, health, and other service work provided by apostolic religious institutes and to assure a healthy psychological development of cloistered religious as well.

These international meetings of heads of religious groups, formation personnel, teachers, treasurers etc. provided assemblies for the critical assessment of the actual functioning of religious consecrated life in the church and in the world. One of the findings that comparative analysis provided was that some of the rules characteristic of religious life and lived by apostolic groups were, in fact, not appropriate to their mission and were intended for monastic life only. In fact, the mission had become for some the work they did to make their living so that they could live the contemplative life. From the perspective of women, one might say they were nuns doing the mission of sisters, or sisters living the life of nuns. The effect of this confusion of mission and fund-raising for furvival was the renewal of religious life to bring the life into line with the different callings.

One of our sisters contemplating this confusion in the discussion of whether sisters should wear religious habits, live in convents, recite the divine office, leave the class room as an obedience to "the bell", or the bedside of a patient for a call to regular prayer, concluded thoughtfully that she was an "ex-nun," that is, that she had been formed for the contemplative life and yet was expected to give primacy to what we had come to call the active life. When the renewal was in process, with focus on the mission so involved in the life of the church in the world, the transformation of unjust structures, the responsibility for education, health work, and social service, as well as pastoral ministry that affirmed the human rights of all peoples to development, imbued with a new realization of the unnecessary exploitation of peoples in the world, sisters became overwhelmed at the responsibilities this placed on them. Those who loved the quiet meditative peace of the monastery garden were no longer at peace. I cited one sister's new understanding of her dilemma because it helps to explain the tension of the years since 1966, the years of activity around renewal, accompanied by a new understanding of mission. Women and men were seeking a spirituality deeply rooted in biblical reflection and meditative prayer but with a prophetic quality able to sustain this commitment to challenge unjust structures.

What becomes clearer with this review is that the form of religious calling arises from the signs of the times. What becomes institutionalized is a function of many pragmatic factors in those times. The vision of the Sisters of Charity, outlined by St. Vincent de Paul and Louise de Marillac in the early 18th century, is only now being implemented in the late 20th century and only because our more shared understanding of mission in the light of social analysis reveals to us that how we live our life of religious dedication is, in fact, part of the cultural pattern that causes the conditions of our world as Gaudium et Spes realized. Everyone, including President Reagan, knows the effectiveness of using God words to get what one wants, even if what is wanted are idols of death rather than the God of Life (See Richard et al, 1983).

The Realities of Religious Life Today

According to the Official Catholic Directory (1983), in the United States at the present time there are 413 Religious Institutes of women and 131 of men. In 1966, there were 459 of women and 126 of men. These include all those who take religious vows and live in community. In the congregations and orders of women there are now 120,699 women; in 1966, there were 181,421, that is, 61,000 more. In men's orders, there are 30,172, down from 35,029 in 1966, 5,000 fewer. Thus the women have declined 33%, the men, 14%. The greatest loss for the men is of brothers (-38%), not of priests (-1%). But the problem of new members is different.

In 1966, there were 21,862 students in seminaries of religious men; in 1983, 4,008. The decline, then, is 82%.

This radical decline is similar for apostolic institutes of women; it is 86%. This latter statistic is not in the Directory. It is from my research and is in the new monograph (Neal, 1984). The corresponding decline in students in diocesan seminaries is 76%. For men's groups, the students include some women studying at the seminaries. We can conclude, then, that the decline in new members is probably similar for institutes of both men and women. It is this reality of decline in new members, more than any other factor, that brings us together. The commitment to the mission affects diocesan seminaries less. They do not have constitutions or mission statements. Priesthood and vows are factors in religious orders of both men and women. But most of all, the problem is related to the radical challenge of mission to a church in a world of greater separation of the rich from the poor when such a separation is no longer a necessity but has become a choice. Groups have to dissociate from the culture of elitism to create a culture of peers. The gospel mandates this, but tradition does not provide guidelines.

Lest we conclude too soon that the apostolic workers in the church are disappearing because no one wants to do this work, let me remind you that the work is being done. Large numbers of laity have responded to the invitations of Vatican II and come forward to do service in the church. Doing this service along with institute members, and sometimes in place of them, is now part of the ongoing normal life of the laity in the institutional church. Religious qua religious are not needed for this work in the same way that they were needed when we were an immigrant church.

Up through 1960 in the United States, we were an immigrant church reaching out for our just share of the resources of society. Today we are an affluent church membership (Greeley). For our new mission, we still need religious institutes. We are faced with the challenge of new immigrants from Africa, Asia, and Latin America in our cities and rural areas and are struggling for an effective response. Our problem, as an affluent church, is more one of letting go than reaching out. This pastoral task is new to us. We are not skilled in it yet (Neal, 1977). Through the work of our missionaries responding to Vatican II, the peoples of the third world are taking up their proper task of organizing to claim their rights as human beings, and using the theologies developed around conscientization and basic Christian communities to do it (Gutierrez, Freire, LADOC). Our task is to work out an effective response to the just demands of the organized poor. As Robert McAfee Brown notes, in Theology in a New Key, this is an ecumenical task, one that we as a catholic church share with the World Council of Churches, one, ironically, that causes some religious people, both in Catholic and other denominations, to categorize our work as "communist". We are all new at these new functions and for that reason the call goes out to different people and from different groups. Revised constitutions and available resources for mission are a critical factor today in determining who comes and who stays.

According to the Catholic Directory, in 1966, 103,832 sisters were teaching; today, 33,310. This is a decline of 68%.. Catholics were 24% of the population in 1966. They are 23% now. Students in Catholic elementary schools have declined from 4.5 million to 2.3 million, a 50% decline. High school students declined 25%, from a million to three-quarters of a million. There are 12% more Catholics today than there were in 1966, but 17% more Americans. We are not increasing in proportion to the size of the total population. Still, there are 6 million more Catholics to serve than there were in 1966.

When sisters speak of the work they want their congregations to do, 77% still put teaching as a top priority; 50% also want work with poor and with homeless women; 55%; social service work of all kinds; 52%, community development. In summary, 60% are ready for work that alleviates the results of poverty; 40% for work that eliminates its causes (Sisters' Survey, 1980). Since both type work needs to be done, there is evidently sufficient will to do what needs to be done. That does not mean sisters can do what they would like to do. A new phenomenon is that of unemployment for sisters, about 6% (Congregational Report, 1982).

The really big difference remains that of the decline in teaching and other direct services. Just as there are fewer teachers, so there are fewer places in which to teach. Elementary schools have declined from 10,962 to 7,969, a 28% decline. There is a 39% decline in high schools, from 2,388 to 1,470. Regarding ownership and control, sisters worked in 189 colleges in 1966 and owned 160 of them. Today, they work in 591 colleges and own 97 of them. They own 63 fewer than they did in 1966. There are 23% fewer Catholic colleges, down from 309 to 238. Ownership is influential in realizing a charism (Avila). This is true also for hospitals. But the vision, or lack of it, for mission of the Boards of Trustees, is a critical intervening factor. People do not join religious institutes to fulfill corporate goals within profit-making systems. They just do the work that Jesus did and, if that does not exist in the institute, they stop coming.

Preparation for Ministry Among Religious Women

There are some interesting changes in preparation for ministry. In 1966, 90,091 Sisters had college degrees of one kind or another; 58% with a bachelor's and 21% more having also a master's degree and 1.7%, the doctorate. Today, there are 98,143 with college degrees, of which 43% are masters and 2% doctors, that means 94% of all sisters now have degrees. Sisters today have a very different academic backgroung from their sisters of 1950 when the Sister Formation movement began. One quarter of the advanced degrees, i.e., master's level, are in education, and 14% in theology. Among new specializations, administrative training ranks highest, at 5.3%. These sisters with this training see their responsibilities in light of their education as well as of their religious formation.

Entering

We look briefly now at who is entering religious congregations of women today in comparison with 1966. Then, 79% entered right from high school, 3% with no high school diploma. Today, 68% have at least a college degree on entering and another 29% some college. These are not the same young women who entered even twenty years ago. Although 71% of congregations still accept young women right from high school, these are not the ones entering now. Furthermore, the formation program is longer; more theology is required; and experience in the mission is also expected before vows are taken. Clearly, the mission being prepared for is differently perceived. It is also a more costly preparation, making the calling of the poor harder to be realized. This is a problem, not a blessing. The training too takes place more in the houses of mission than in a place apart. A different understanding of mission is involved.

Turning now to community living, living in the local community is also quite changed. The old horarium has been adapted to the doing of the mission, as has style of praying, times and types of liturgies, opening the community house to neighbors and friends and issue groups, sharing in local planning and decision-making. This, according to the administrative reports of 1982, is true of over 80% of all places. There is also experimentation with different types of small group living, living in rented apartments, wearing a symbol instead of a habit, depending on what the mission calls for.

Bible reading is characteristic of over 90%, as one would expect, and news watching and reading of 85%. Given the old restrictions from considering the news of the day, this is a new factor. Preferred sources for news run the gamut from very conservative to somewhat liberal. Radical reading is characteristic of fewer than 10%.

Government

The government of religious congregations of women is different from 1966, in keeping with the more peer orientation of member to member and, the data indicates, a new understanding of government for mission inspiring a preference for democratic decision-making. From the 1980 survey, we find that only 9% of the sisters are in groups where decisions are made by a major superior deliberating with her council without participation from the members. Ninety percent prefer participatory decision-making and 67% report that full participation is now a regularly part of their experience (Sisters' Survey, 1980).

Expressions of why this change has been made finds more than preference involved. Seventy-seven percent report a value base to the transition from mother/daughter; subject/superior relationship to sister/sister decision-making. The item with high assent on this topic reads thus:

> The process of participation in decision-making is so important for the poor of the world that no matter the difficulties or inconvenience, we must become skilled in it in governing ourselves so that we will do it well wherever we work. (Item 194)

An unqualified "yes" was given to this item by 55%, a "probably yes" by another 28%.

Participation in Planning

What characterizes changes in the General Chapter is the much greater involvement of members in its preparation--the original intention of Chapters--and the type of content considered. Justice and peace issues are in the forefront of half the Chapters, corporate mission of 63%, quality of community life of 70%. The expectations for the next ten years is an increase in the voice of the sisters in planning, 87%; more involvement in the public sector in a critical way, 58%; and more changes in the style of religious life, 54%. The most pressing need perceived by administrators at this time is determining the relevancy of the gospel to the time, 81%; action in behalf of the oppressed, 62% and social justice, 60%, with the perceived determinant of change, the needs of the human community, 78%. Among the eight highest choices for determinants of change after the needs of the human community comes: ideas of the sisters, 67%, then, human rights issues, 51%; last on the list is directives of the Sacred Congregation, 18%. If we remember that this was asked in 1982, I think we can conclude that at that time administrators assumed that the mandate to incorporate plans for life into the constitutions was moving the determinants to change soon into the "own law" category, with obedience focused on the doing of the mission to which we are sent. Sisters know from their own experience of twenty years that they must pool their skills to generate effective plans and to carry them out.

Asked about problems facing institutes today, most saw declining numbers as the main problem, 55%, with large numbers of elderly a second concern for 45%, and finances in third place for 21%. These immediate and pragmatic problems will overwhelm religious institutes unless enthusiasm for the mission and all the changes it entails brings the affirmation needed to overcome problems, something the history of institutes demonstrates those in vows have done well in the past.

Profile

There is time only for a brief further sketch of who the sisters are. I do not have such information for the brothers. In 1966, 16.5% of all sisters were in initial formation; now 3.7% are; then 8.1% were inactive due to illness and or old age; today, 23.7%. Twenty-seven percent of all sisters today are at least second generation Americans; 41% of their parents were craftsmen or laborers; only 31% had professionals for parents; 56% of the sisters consider themselves working class people. While 45% of their parents had only a grammar school education, 94% of the sisters, as we have seen, have at least one college degree. Fifty two percent come from the east coast, 40% from the midwest and only 5% from beyond the Rockies. The largest number, 46%, are of Irish background;

German, 28%; Anglo Saxon, 19%; Italian, 5%; Polish, .9%. Just 2% come from Spanish speaking backgrounds and less than 1% are from African or Asian heritage. So you see the sisters reflect the church of the past, coming as they do from peoples reaching or already beyond zero population growth. But the church of the future comes from the last named groups and our mission focuses on letting them in.

Conclusions

The pull of professionalism versus mission is a real problem for both women and men religious. The temptation to become the Church of the affluent community faces us in every state. The challenge of the peace pastoral, the Canadian Bishops' pastoral on the economy, the Latin American Church's basic Christian communities, and the reality of the availability of technical solutions to problems of world poverty and the possibility of universal good health care and social security are waiting for our response. A pastoral style and content that address these pressing agendas in a racially unified church with an apostolic and prophetic biblical spirituality would be most welcome. We are glad the monastery is there. We need it, as do all peoples, as a place to which to go apart and rest awhile. However, with our apostolic calling, we need to be about the mission with a cultural framework that affirms our colleagueship and the human rights of God's people working together for the transformation of an unnecessarily unjust world.

Related Questions:

1. Why are some sisters unemployed though many tasks need to be done?

2. Why are diocesan seminaries less challenged by the new direction of mission in the church than our religious institutes of both women & men?

3. Are there Catholic population in the country whom we do not serve as yet?

4. Why is the vocation trend more stable in contemplative than in active institutes?

5. How does the fact that most men in religious institutes are priests distinguish the renewal among priests from that of the sisters?

References

Avila, Charles. Ownership; Early Christian Teaching. Maryknoll, New York: Orbis Books, 1983; London: Sheed and Ward.

Baum, Gregory. The Priority of Labor. New York: Paulist Press, 1982.

Brown, Robert McAfee. Theology in a New Key: Responding to Liberation Themes. Philadelphia: Westminster Press, 1978

Canon Law Society of America, Code of Canon Law (Latin-English Edition), Washington, D.C.: Canon Law Society of America, 1983.

Catholic Bishops of Appalachian Region, "This Land is Home to Me", Pastoral Letter on Powerlessness in Appalachia, Catholic Committee of Appalachia, 1974.

Dorr, Donal. Option for the Poor: A Hundred Years of Vatican Social Teaching. Maryknoll, New York: Orbis Books, 1983.

Ewens, Mary, The Role of the Nun in the Nineteenth-Century America. New York: Arno Press, 1978.

Flannery, Austin, O.P. ed. Vatican Council II: The Conciliar and Post-Conciliac Documents. Northport, New York: Costello Publishing Co., 1975.

Fiorenza, Elizabeth, "Word, Spirit and Power: Women in Early Christian Communities," in Women of Spirit: Female Leadership in the Jewish and Christian Tradition. New York: Simon and Schuster, 1974.

Freire, Paulo, Pedagogy of the Oppressed. New York: Herder and Herder, 1970.

Greeley, Andrew. The American Catholic: a Social Portrait. New York: Basic Books, Inc., 1977.

Gutierrez, Gustavo. A Theology of Liberation. Maryknoll, New York: Orbis Books, 1971.

LADOC, Basic Christian Communities. Washington, D.C.: Latin American Documentation, United States Catholic Conference, 1976.

Leyser, K.J. Rule and Conflict in Early Medieval Society: Ottonian Saxony. Bloomington, Indiana: Indiana University, 1979.

Muckenhirn, Sister M. Charles, C.S.C,.ed. The Changing Sister. Notre Dame, Indiana: Fides Publishers, Inc., 1965.

Murphy-O'Connor, Jerome, O.P. "Religious Life According to the New Code", Religious Life Review

Myers, Sister Bertrand. Sisters of the Twenty-First Century. New York: Sheed and Ward, 1965.

Neal, Marie Augusta SND. A Sociotheology of Letting Go: The Role of a First World Church Facing Third World Peoples. New York: Paulist Press, 1977.

Neal, Marie Augusta SND. "The Sisters' Survey, 1980: A Report", Probe, May/June 1981, Vol. X, No. 5.

Neal, Marie Augusta SND, Catholic Sisters in Transition from the 1960's to the 1980's. Wilmington, Delaware: Michael Glazier, Inc., 1984.

O'Brien, David J. and Thomas A. Shannon. Renewing the Earth: Catholic Documents on Peace, Justice and Liberation. Garden City, New York: Doubleday Image Books, 1977.

Paul VI, Decree on the Mission Activity of the Church (De Activitate Missionali Ecclesiae) (1965), Boston: St. Paul Editions

Paul VI, Ecclesiae Sanctae (1966), Boston: St. Paul Editions.

Paul VI, On the Renewal of the Religious Life According to the Teaching of the Second Vatican Council (Evangelica Testificatio) (1971), Boston: St. Paul Editions.

Paul VI, Decree on the Adaptation and Renewal of Religious Life (Perfectae Caritatis) (1965), Boston: St. Paul Editions.

Pius XI, On Christian Education of Youth, (1929), Boston: St. Paul Editions.

Power, Eileen, Medieval English Nunneries. Cambridge, England: Cambridge University, 1922.

"Report to the Vatican/U.S. Religious Orders Today". Origins April 20, 1978, Vol. 7, No. 44, pp. 690-93.

Richard, Pablo, ed. The Idols of Death and the God of Life. Maryknoll, New York: Orbis Books, 1983.

Sacred Congregation for Religious and for Secular Institutes, Religious and Human Promotion (1978) and The Contemplative Dimension of Religious Life (1980), Boston: St. Paul Editions.

Sacred Congregation for Religious and for Secular Institutes, Instruction on the Renewal of Religious Formation (1969), Boston: St. Paul Editions.

United Nations. The International Bill of Human Rights. New York: United Nations Office of Public Information, 1980.

Wemple, Suzanne Fonay, Women in Frankish Society, Marriage and Cloister, 500-900. Philadelphia: University of Pennsylvania, 1981.

Panel of Bishops:

> History, Teaching, Experience
> and Expectations: What Do Bishops Hope for from
> Religious in the Service of the Church?

a. John F. Whealon, D.D., Archbishop of Hartford

Dear Sisters and Brothers: Father John Lozano ended his presentation by saying "Bishops, this now is your problem." I don't know quite how to respond to that. "Thank you" is not the fitting response. I am reminded of a favorite story of Abraham Lincoln about the man who was tarred and feathered and then ridden out of town on a rail. Later he was asked how he felt. He said: "If it weren't for the honor of it all, I would rather have walked out of town."

We U.S. bishops are the ones who received the much discussed letter from the Holy Father. In time I, a bishop and a recipient, must answer that letter. This conference has been an educational experience indeed that will help the church.

Sister Clare Fitzgerald asked last night why the bishops were not at the side of religious as they went through the past traumatic years. My answer is that not once in twenty years have I been consulted by a religious community before, during or after a chapter change. I would, of course, not ask or expect to be consulted by an exempt religious community. So I was one of the people of God being constantly surprised at what some religious were doing next. At Sister Clare's words, I thought of publicly throwing down the gauntlet and challenging her to a duel. But it would be unseemly for two Connecticut people to duel in Massachusetts.

Now after history, teaching, experience, I give you the reactions, the hopes of one U.S. bishop. I am one of the few remaining U.S. bishops who was at the Second Vatican Council. From my Council background, I tell you that the developments in religious life of which we have been speaking were not all, not in the least, foreseen by the U.S. bishops at Vatican II. I think the origins of these developments are not at all to be found in Vatican II, but rather in sociological trends in U.S. society.

Speaking now as one less wise, as a non-religious, I tell you about five dilemmas which this program has caused for me. To solve those dilemmas I ask your wisdom and help.

Point Number 1: I believe that the presentations of this program did not express the viewpoints of all U.S. religious as I see them. Of the communities with provincialates in the Archdiocese of Hartford which I serve, more than half of the leaderships have told me that they see the papal letter and the ten essentials as expressing their view of religious life, their lived experiences over the past twenty years. And among these religious are some beautiful, vibrant, growing communities. Their voice has not been heard by me during this gathering. Yet they are U.S. religious, and Mother Teresa has spoken for them. I must relate to them also and serve them also. So in this conference, whenever you have used the terms "United States religious" or "religious men and women" in a universal sense, I have been interpreting these words in a partitive sense. My constituency, so to speak, includes a sizeable number of religious who sincerely have a different view of contemporary religious life.

Point Number 2: Some, even much, of the discussion here was an exegesis of the papal letter and accompanying document, separating one from the other, comparing them, studying the literary form, making judgments on the mindset, theology and limitations of the authors. All this I found interesting but really not very helpful. I know from the visit of last September that this question of religious in the United States of America is a major concern of the Holy Father, of a worried Holy Father, and that these documents express his thinking. So I see in these documents only the loving concern of a Father in Christ. I wonder if exegeting the document as legalism is not itself legalism.

Point Number 3: I was very impressed with Father Lozano's statement that before our very eyes a new form of religious life is evolving in the United States, and by the lesson from history that this really is nothing new. But if this is so, and if this is a valid development, then I ask whether this new form of religious life should have a new and different title. If this is quid novum, something new, with new characteristics and new traditions, then should it not in some public way be clearly distinguished from the more traditional religious life? Is this what I should recommend to the Holy Father in responding to his letter?

Point Number 4: I am concerned over the way in which so many religious communities seem to have lost their corporate individualism and specificity in apostolic work. So many religious communities seem to have reached out into various beautiful apostolates, including serving the poor and their needs, including foreign missions. I wonder whether in time this extension of the community will take away from the community its discernible charism and specific apostolate or apostolates. There was a time in our society when we had hardware stores, automobile stores, stationery stores, book stores, candy stores, etc. Now we have K Marts, Caldors, Bradlees, all of them selling nearly everything, and I neither tell nor prefer one from or over the other. I greatly sympathize with superiors struggling to honor institutional obligations while respecting the individual's preferences. But I think that for the good of the community as well as for the good of the entire Church, each community should be perceived as being different from the others, as star differs from star in glory, as one kind of flower is different from another.

Point Number 5: In the background of the papal letter to bishops is the question of religious vocations. That is the major concern of us all. No matter how many good and beautiful things are happening in contemporary religious life, they are sterile if not handed on to the next generation of religious. Indeed the Gamaliel principle is valid, but the digitus Dei, the finger of God, seems now to be moving towards the more conservative, traditional, disciplined groups. In both Protestantism and Judaism the conservatives are at this time growing. With you I wonder about that phenomenon in our Catholic religious life.

As Bobbie Burns said: "Oh that God the gift would give us/to see ourselves as others see us." I saw this conference as not a constructive, positive, happy meeting—ideologically, not socially—because so much of the conference was given to criticism (indeed "resentment" was one verb used) of the Roman congregation and Roman document. Major applause here was given to anti-document protests.

At the present time in the Archdiocese of Hartford we are having RENEW for our parishes, with the expectation that people alienated from parish life will return and find their parish a loving, united, praying community. The church is not fully a united family at this time. There is alienation here. That is our problem. That is a serious problem for bishops.

And that was the point of my beginning; and so, the circle completed, here I end.

b.   John R. McGann, D.D., Bishop of Rockville Center

I am very pleased and grateful to have been invited to this conference of all of us here involved "In the Service of the Church". For me, it is an educational experience that will assist me in formulating my response to the Letter of His Holiness and in my continuing dialogue with the religious communities in our diocese. We are aware that we do not have agreement on everything we have heard during our conference. However, all of us appreciate the opportunity we have had to hear the excellent papers that were so carefully prepared and that continue to produce enlightened discussion among us.

My meetings with the religious of our diocese did not reflect the experience of Archbishop Whealon with regard to the document on Essential Elements. What I heard at those meetings indicated that the document was too monastic in its expression of religious life and did not reflect the experience of the apostolic commitment of those who had obediently undertaken chapters of renewal.

Father Hennesey, in his historical overview, highlighted the importance of history in helping us understand the individual charism of each religious entity, while calling upon us, at the same time, to nurture these charisms that they might adapt and grow and so move as life-giving influences upon the cultural changes that must be faced by the contemporary Church.

I am particularly grateful for the presentations of Father John Padberg and Sister Karen Kennelly. I felt proud as I listened to their recounting the achievements of our young church here in the United States from 1815 to 1965. One of our problems has been that we have not effectively shared this experience with the total church. That we must do, because we are not an American church, but we are the church in America. Father and Sister spoke of the European influence on the origins of religious life in America which helped shape our communities at their beginnings. However, Religious life has developed in the American culture and it is now our task to share with the universal church the tremendous contributions and prophetic vision of the American experience.

It is my judgment that our meeting here has not given sufficient attention to the letter from Pope John Paul II in which he affirms, positively, the development of religious life in our country. Archbishop Quinn and his Commission conveyed this positive interest of the Holy Father to the Leadership Conference of Women Religious, the Conference of Major Superiors of Men, and the National Conference of Catholic Bishops. However, I do not think that the American press presented this positive approach. Father Lozano has described the Essential Elements document as a guideline. I believe then that it is our responsibility to accurately report the positive contribution made by American men and women religious in preserving and, at the same time, developing vowed religious commitment in apostolic communities.

I am in agreement with the caution of Archbishop Whealon that we listen not only to the leadership but also to the total membership of religious communities, including them in our report to the Holy Father and the Sacred Congregation for Religious and Secular Institutes. In undertaking chapters of renewal, I believe it would have been helpful for religious communities to have included bishops, priests, and laity in their effort, so as to enable them to more clearly understand all the changes being undertaken by religious.

Archbishop Quinn has correctly described the work of the Papal Commission and its subsequent listening sessions as "a new moment" for the growth and vitality of religious life in the United States. I am pleased to learn that the bishops and religious superiors of men and women are presently participating in this dialogue. As a former chairman of the Bishops' Committee for Liaison with the LCWR, I know that, whenever there was this kind of shared communication, dialogue improved. We here have recognized the importance of this kind of communication each time we pledged to share in this study in the spirit of Mutuae Relationes. We have to recognize the existence of pluriformity and, at the same time, be certain that our ecclesiology is authentic. On a personal note, I was pleased that the committee invited the bishops, priests, and religious to participate, according to their respective functions, in the Liturgy of the Eucharist as well as in the paraliturgies.

At the recent meeting of the NCCB in Collegeville, Cardinal Dearden made reference to the relationship of the NCCB with the Holy Father and with the Religious Congregations. In discussion that followed, the Cardinal stated that, as President of the NCCB, he had initiated ongoing dialogue that was accomplished through visits to the Holy Father and to the Congregations after our annual meetings. I believe that this present Papal Commission should be concerned about how we can widen and deepen the quality of

dialogue of the religious in the United States with the Holy
Father and with the individual congregations in Rome.

c. John J. Snyder, D.D., Bishop of St. Augustine

I would like to share with you, briefly, my own
experience of religious. Although I cannot call myself a
"brothers' boy," my life has been deeply impacted, influenced
and enriched by sisters. Within the family, outside of my
parents, one of God's greatest gifts to me were two aunts who
were Presentation Sisters. Then there was the experience of
my educational years, my early experience in parish ministry
and later as secretary to two bishops, then Vatican Council II
and my service as auxiliary bishop in Brooklyn, N.Y.

In Brooklyn, my relationship with religious was a
challenging one. It was an association that called me to
growth, causing me to feel the pain of religious from the
perspective of those who were upset by change as well as of
those who felt that things were not developing quickly enough.
All that has had a very positive influence on my own vision of
religious life and church in ministry.

Then, four and a half years ago, I went to Florida and to
a somewhat different experience. For it seems that many of
the issues I encountered in the Northeast are only beginning
to emerge in certain areas of Florida, and I am still trying
to sort through the many factors which account for this.
Possibly we can avoid some of the struggles and pains by
reaching out and opening up opportunities for dialogue. But
in Florida, ours is a much more missionary experience. It is
a growing and dynamic church, one, I think that has a great
potential for vocations. We've seen signs and can sense that
the vocations are out there, but whether we can get the
message out and challenge our young people to opt for this
particular way of living the gospel remains to be seen.

As for expectations, what I must say is that I think I
need the religious to keep me honest. I expect that they will
do that for me in my life, my responsibilities and my
ministry. I expect that they will be open with me and will
dialogue with me. But I also think that we have to be alert
to create opportunities for dialogue.

In St. Augustine, however, we have only one major
religious superior, and in the rest of Florida possibly only
two or three. Thus we are left at a considerable distance in
trying to figure out ways to open up more dialogue with
religious about the future of the church in Florida; we are
only beginning to break ground in that direction. But we were

able to capitalize on the 25th anniversary of the Archdiocese of Miami, and have a day of dialogue between the bishops of the state and the vicars and major superiors or their delegates. Some 120 religious were present. Their response to Archbishop McCarthy's question about repeating the meeting every two or three years was to ask for an annual meeting of two or three days. Longer meetings like this, in which there is also time to come together for prayer, for example the retreats which bishops in the northwestern part of the U.S. have had with major superiors, are necessary in order to create dialogue and build the relationship of mutual understanding and challenge that we need. It can't be done in just a half-hour office interview.

A word that goes through my mind when I think of expectations in terms of religious is integration—integration in the sense mentioned in several of the talks and which flows from the reality of baptism. We are all called in the church to holiness, and perhaps we are going to live it out in different ways. But there is only one type of holiness that we are all called to, laity, priests and religious: the following of Jesus. Somebow we must find ways to integrate our experiences of this following. I think our laity need to know much more about the experience of religious as well as of diocesan priests in our efforts to follow faithfully the spirit of the gospel.

I think we need to develop a vision of church which goes beyond diocese or religious community. This is already happening, in part, but there remains a great need for us to see ourselves as men and women of the church who are willing to make sacrifices for a larger church and not get tied down narrowly to our own turf or responsibility. We also need a better understanding of the relationship of stability and mobility. By stability I don't mean status quo, but what normally exists in a diocese in contrast with the typical mobility of religious life where religious can be on the move to meet new needs, and yet not lose sight of the needs of a diocese and the local church. We need to do more brainstorming and planning together on the future of the church in dioceses and within religious communities.

Thus, much of my expectation here takes the form of a joint exploration. I think of it in terms of our understanding of mutuality and ministry, of our being coworkers in many ways. What I would like to be able to share with religious when they are present in a diocese, is to help them develop a sense of belonging to the diocese, a sense of being part of the diocesan family. This is particularly needed now that we are no longer so caught up with exemption and institutes of pontifical right, now that the bishop has a serious responsibility—without in amy way taking away the individuality or independence of a religious community—to be a leader to and be of service to religious communities. The development of this kind of relationship is something we'd like to see, and I've actually seen it happen. I've seen it happen in Brooklyn. I've seen it, I think, in my present diocese of St. Augustine where religious do feel a much stronger identity with the diocese, the bishop and the diocesan priests. And I see a very healthy bonding taking place that I don't think I sensed in my earlier priesthood where a parish, say, that was conducted by religious was pretty much a parish conducted independently even though very effectively. But my later experience in Brooklyn is that we really were much more co-workers, and we are trying to discover and to learn from one another how we could more fully serve God's people, and how we could do that comparatively rather than just in our own individual ways. I think I would like to work with religious in trying to bring the contribution of their experience of community to bear on this new priority in the life of the church: seeing the church as a community of faith, seeing the parish as a community of faith.

What can the experience of religious community add to our understanding of what we will have to build in the local church? I recall that a short ten or twenty years ago, there were some who were in a sense sounding a death note for the parish; and yet we are now finding there a resiliency and new opportunities. For better or worse, it is on the parish level that the church is experienced, and there are programs for parish renewal that stand right at the top of our diocesan priorities. I feel that our religious can bring to that experience something very valuable and unique; and I would hope that they would feel a part of it whether or not they are in parish work, or directly affiliated with a parish, or working in some other institution. Our diocese is almost entirely, with one or two exceptions, parish oriented. We have very few other institutions. But even in those settings I hope our religious will share this experience, so that they will feel the closeness of their relationship with the laity and with diocesan priests, and so that many of the frictions and divisions that we may have experienced in the past will be healed, and that we will move forward to build the Kingdom more positively.

I see an opportunity here, one that I hope would relate very much to the hunger of our people for a deeper spiritual life and prayer life. For surely, it is not just the priests who are to share their experience of prayer life. Our religious have something valuable to contribute and our people need them. Our people need the background and the knowledge and the lived experience of religious in terms of spiritual direction. There are wide open opportunities here as people take seriously the call of baptism to be a holy people. They need help in that; and I think that the diversity of experience of men and women religious and diocesan priests can only be enriching.

Realistically, I think we also need to touch on something that Bishop McGann mentioned: I mean the hurt, or whatever we want to call it, between diocesan priests and religious, particularly in those situations where the religious may have left the parish school. I think we need a calling to reconciliation and healing, and I think religious superiors and religious leaders and bishops have to work on that jointly so that we strengthen the sense of commitment to the gospel and to discipleship.

In the midst of all this, we can't lose sight of the fact that the diocesan church or local church must necessarily maintain certain basic services, and often become deeply absorbed in them. But there is, on the other hand, the prophetic voice of religious with their greater freedom and mobility to direct attention to specific needs of the church. These religious have an invaluable role to play. If they stir us, that is what they should be doing. We are not always going to enjoy it, We are not always going to welcome it. But without it we're not going to be a dynamic church and we're not going to mature and grow.

The question of vocations: I see vocations flowing from a dynamic and alive church. I don't think we can isolate vocations from the way we live the reality of church. It is in this light that I view things like renewal and programs such as that. Unless that parish comes alive, and unless people really sense their identity as disciples, we can have all kinds of crash programs for vocations, but we will only be pulling them into a vacuum instead of creating something that challenges and excites them to see that the church is willing to stand on its feet and speak about those who are alienated and those who are hurting and those who really need the presence of Christ. In the process we may even alienate some of our members of the church, but I think we just have to take that risk.

182

I think we need to reassure our religious that they can come and discuss with us ways in which we can be of more effective and richer service to them. We need to be called to that. But I think that we are being sensitized more and more to the pastoral service that we have accepted in becoming bishops. Sometimes we can become so absorbed in immediate issues that we lose sight of ways that religious see, ways in which we could be providing better leadership. I hope that we would welcome the opportunity to dialogue with you.

Last night in the panel discussion we were listening to the experience that you have had as religious, and I felt the hurt. Some of it I was already aware of, but other aspects were new to me. I also think that bishops are experiencing some of that hurt too. Not so much when they visited with the Holy Father but in relationship to certain Vatican congregations.

I know that in my interview with the Holy Father he wanted to know about religious. You know what my experience has been. I could only say that I don't know what we would do without them. For better or for worse, the religious have gotten out in front of us and now we are trying to catch up. But you know that there was much, much good that was being accomplished.

I can think also of my own experience of the bishops' conference in Collegeville that Bishop McGann mentioned. I've seen radical changes take place, not in the sense, perhaps, that I could pinpoint actual courses of action, but a sense of becoming a conference--and I've been there for 11 years. Collegeville allowed us, I think, to build relationships. That kind of opportunity will continue to allow us to sense who we are as a conference of bishops. This is going to have a very important role to play in the future of the church in the Unites States, and I welcome the opportunity to be here. I hope that this is a step.

I think back to what Archbishop John Quinn said at our November annual meeting when, on the question of the Commission on Religious Life, someone asked how we were going to interpret the Essential Elements. He replied that he certainly hoped that we would not do less with them than we do with scripture, and we are not literalists when it comes to scripture. I hope we will approach this situation with the same openness and room for the Spirit to move. So thank you.

Structures of the Present:

Reflections of a Canon Lawyer

by

Elizabeth McDonough, O.P., J.C.D.*

It seems to me that the task before me is not an easy one. For nearly two days we have been reflecting on religious life in the context of church. We have addressed it from the perspectives of ecclesial communion, historical evolution, mutual expectations, and practical experience. It is now my dubious—and, perhaps, some would even say lugubrious—honor of assessing the canonical aspects of religious life or, more precisely, the patterns, structures, modes of operation and functions currently recognized in church law. As if the previous presentations were not hard enough acts to follow, I fulfill this task as a minority among minorities. This is true whether you consider me a canon lawyer who is a woman, a canon lawyer who is a religious, a canon lawyer who is not a cleric or, indeed, a canon lawyer who is not a bishop. In addition, the Dominicans present are greatly outnumbered by the Jesuits (which the brethren often say is the correct proportion). Moreover, the time I have been allotted to accomplish my task is twenty-two and one half minutes! I strongly suspect that this last item may represent a harmonious blend of post-Vatican II reverse legalism along with a genuine attempt to keep law in proper perspective. Nevertheless, I am simply delighted to be here because (even if you are a captive audience still present merely because you are curious about the closing banquet) it is an opportunity to say quite clearly that law—especially canon law—does not alter reality, including the reality of religious life.

Let me note at the beginning of this dual presentation that Fr. Gray and I have worked closely together in its preparation and that we share a common theme and a common concern. The common theme of the dual presentation is that the purpose of legal structures and procedures is to help baptized persons to mature and to work for the Kingdom in the

---

* This paper was originally the first part of a double paper: "Structures of the Present and Shapes for the Future." The "Shapes for the Future" part by Howard Gray, S.J. appears below in PART V.

struggling reality of the present world. The concern of the dual presentation is that people who implement legal structures and procedures often demonstrate a mentality of caution or fear or (if you will) lack of imagination or all three which tend to safeguard accidentals and lessen the opportunity for growth and service in the church. That theme and that concern are of importance to both of us, with my portion of the presentation concerning the present and Fr. Gray's portion concerning the future.

Recall for a moment Fr. Hennesey's opening comments about Bishop Carroll and the Baltimore Carmelites. It is a marvelous example of how we act regarding legal articulations and of how important legal interpretation is in real life situations. Bishop Carroll's actions represent a not untypical example of the hierarchy's use of dispensation and exception to serve a pressing apostolic need in what some would call a direct violation of the charism of these nuns. A charism, incidentally, that was insisted upon for them by the hierarchy itself for over five hundred years, especially by Lateran IV, Boniface VIII, Trent and Pius V. But the action of the Carmelites also represents a not untypical example of the response of religious to insist upon remaining faithful to the charism perceived as genuinely theirs in what others would call direct violation of obedience to the highest church authorities. It is a superb example of how law does not alter reality and of how important the interpretation of those involved can be in matters of church law. There could be numerous other examples taken from the historical presentations of yesterday, but time does not allow for more at the moment. What should be clear and what is most important for the purposes of this presentation is that it is not law--nor the decisions of those formulating law--that alters legal reality. Real life is what alters legal reality.

So, too, religious life today will not change because there are no longer definitions of regulars, nuns and sisters in the code or because the categories of consideration have changed through the centuries from monastic life to religious life to consecrated life (or, more precisely, to "life consecrated by profession of the evangelical counsels"). For the most part the two decades of religious life experienced since Vatican II have shaped the contents of the present code far more than any supposed ecclesiastical legislative fiat.

Note that law in the church is fundamentally rationally based or at least that it is not overtly voluntaristic. Canon law takes its definition from the Summa of Aquinas as an

185

ordinance of reason by one who has care of the common good and promulgated (I-II.90.4). Whether one likes or agrees with this definition at the moment is somewhat irrelevant (somewhat because whatever is of importance to people is, indeed, never totally irrelevant) to the fact that this definition has a solid seven-century foundation in its favor and that it is basically a good definition of law. Furthermore, one must admit--at least experientially--that most church legislation is not actually contrary to reason although it may at times very well be contrary to what someone does or does not want to do. Experientially, therefore, it is the interpretation or application of law that appears--and sometimes is--far more "unreasonable" upon occasion than the law itself.

It is important to note that, on the firm foundation of this definition, ecclesiastical law emerges from the philosophical and theological mindset of a former century (one that sought absolute certitude), and from a former church (one that was totally hierarchical and monarchical). I strongly suspect that one cannot really understand canon law unless one learns to think at least a little medievally, and that means--from my experience of medieval manuscripts and commentators--learning how to think obliquely, obscurely and (at times) opaquely.

In addition, this medieval definition is incorporated into a codified system of law. The codified system of law in the church differs greatly from the common law heritage of our North American Anglo-Saxon background. Codified systems enunciate broad principles perceived as universally true for the worldwide visible ecclesial body. But these broad principles require the use of both equity and epikeia. Equity is the "lead measure," that malleable entity adjusting the law to particular situations or tempering the law with mercy in application. Epikeia, although it has had some changes in meaning since being adopted from Aristotle, is understood in canonical circles as action contrary to the words of the law by recourse to a higher law in such a way that one actually fulfills the true intention of the law (with the burden of proof in such cases resting upon the actor). Codified systems require interpretation, application, proper law specifications and exceptions while the norm itself remains intact. In such a system any legal comment that is unnuanced is incomplete and, insofar as it is incomplete, is also partially incorrect. There are no legal actions in the abstract just as there are no moral actions in the abstract.

Common law, on the other hand, is based on an active, temporal alteration of the law by specific decisions in particular situations. It makes no attempt to enunciate general or universal norms to be observed by all. Common law norms change from place to place and time to time as required by ad hoc circumstances. Emerging from a common law heritage and living in a codified ecclesial system causes built-in conflicts of expectations in the approach of Americans to church law.

There is another built-in conflict provided for us by the difference in the "Germanic" and "Roman" approaches towards law. The Germanic approach—reflecting perhaps the German philosophical deontological "ought"—says that "if it is in the law we should be doing it." The Roman approach, on the other hand, is prone to make as many laws as seem necessary (or more, if it makes one happy to have numerous norms) because "The law only applies where it applies."

Given this complexus of medieval mindset and built-in conflicts for ecclesiastical law, it is important to note that law does not alter reality and that the law itself does not change quickly. This is because it is the purpose of canon law in its publically enunciated forms to provide order and stability by intelligent, free and responsible people. As people applying the law we do not always act as if we are intelligent, free and responsible. Indeed, that we are such is a presumption of law obviously contrary to the truth since all are not of equal intelligence, no one is totally free, and there are times at which the best of us would rather not be responsible. But the law presumes this of us, which is a good beginning.

Furthermore, every legal norm is a child of history. As such it is both a point of arrival and a point of departure and is usually a dialectical response to some issue of the times—much like a photo isolating the action in the midst of a sports event. As such, laws must be interpreted in context following the special rules for interpretation (Can. 16). Here we cannot allow ourselves the luxury of legal naivete. Yesterday I made the comment that "Essential Elements" is not a legal document. But as an unnuanced comment what I said is partially incorrect because "Essential Elements" does have legal import by reason of its content—some of which is law strictly speaking, conciliar and codal. Furthermore—as pointed out this morning by Archbishop Whealon—its content represents the considered opinion of the Holy Father and, as such, it simply cannot be summarily dismissed. No, we simply cannot allow ourselves the luxury of legal naivete in the church today.

The law is being interpreted whenever anyone applies or uses the law. Whenever made, however, such interpretations should uphold fundamental Christian values, should basically be a sign of wisdom and should be faithful to the worldwide visible ecclesial community we call the church. Law and its interpretation are a form of communication with theoretical foundations fundamental to their meaning. The meanings of words evolve--although the core content and intent of any law usually perdure as identifiable--and it is this substance of any norm with which we ought to be concerned. It is often easy to ascertain retroactively the historical conditioning and human interpreting of legal norms. The on-going imposition of cloister as the only possible religious life for women for several centuries is a good example from the past. It is less easy to recognize the same phenomenon of historical conditioning and human interpretation in our own era and milieu--but it is there nevertheless. A good current example might be the various ways in which the documents of Vatican II have been understood and implemented in the last two decades.

Now, as if we have not already had enough versions of what may be "essential" to religious life, I have prepared another summary for the purpose of this presentation. It is taken not from Can. 607 or from the letter of John Paul II or from the SCRIS document but from the canons of the code. And it is gleaned from them--in the words of John Paul II in the apostolic constitution, Sacrae disciplinae leges, promulgating the new code on 25 January 1983--"as a complement to the magisterium proposed by Vatican II." With respect to direct content of the present code in the area of "structures/patterns/modalities and functions," the following four part summary emerges empirically (not deductively) from repeated investigation of the canons themselves while having in mind the query "What does this code have to say to us--as a complement to the magisterium proposed by Vatican II--about the apparent essentials of religious life today?"

Basically, there are four elements into which the canons can be grouped. These are: (1) the following of Christ, (2) with public perpetual profession by vow, (3) in an ecclesially approved institute, (4) with incorporation into the universal and local church. These four generic divisions along with canons that seem to relate to them are listed in the Appendix at the end of this paper. There is not time to elaborate on the content or import of each division or canon, but note that

many of the affirmations are very possibly the legal counterparts of the values to which Fr. Lozano alluded so forcefully
yesterday--the sequela Christi (Can. 573), the humble open
dialogue (Can. 601), the witness of religious life (Can. 673).
Basically these canons contain a sound delineation of the
understanding of religious life in the recent past--in the
past because law is always a little behind present experience.
It is not the purpose of law to be prophetic. That is the
role of prophets (and legalists usually stone prophets, or so
it seems). The canons also leave ample room for flexibility
by proper law specifications.

Proper law--or the law that a particular religious
institute enacts in its fundamental and auxiliary codes (by
whatever name these codes or books may be called)--is given a
major role in the '83 code. General law requires
specification at the local level in fifty-three of the one
hundred thirty-one canons dealing directly with institutes of
consecrated life or religious institutes as such. In other
words, in well over one third of the canons, universal
law--that which originates at the level of the Apostolic
See--is recognizing the need for diversity, flexibility,
subsidiarity and participation enunciated by Vatican II.

There have always been and will always be tensions in the
interplay of charism (or vision, if you will) and structure in
the church, but good law--universal and proper--can help to
lessen these. Good law, moreover, can provide a firm
foundation for growth and service. It is the purpose of law
in the church to provide the "skeleton" or stable, functional
base of organization wherin basic interrelationships, rights
and obligations, procedures and necessary structures are
assured. In the church, as in the human body, skeletons are
both facilitating and limiting entities. But, above all, they
should not be our ultimate concern or something is probably
wrong. Although the new code provides the possibility for a
winter of discontent regarding present institutional
limitations and although we may, indeed, wish to be other than
we are structurally, alteration of legal reality occurs not so
much by revolution or wishful thinking as by the regular and
concerted efforts of dedicated people within the system.

Since law primarily concerns actions, the repeated
actions of people are, in fact, the best interpreters of law.
Canon law has and can suffer somewhat in the area of
interpretation. Partly from an essentialist approach that
reduces the importance of customary actions to a legal
nonentity, and partly from occasional reversals of the right

order of values that appear to leave the gospel subordinate to human laws. Again, we cannot afford the luxury of legal naivete. Witness the crusades when with papal legal approbation Christians went about killing a few Moors for Christ (and some Eastern Christian in the process), or recall the inquisition (Dominicans should speak of it only with chagrin) when with papal legal approbation we went about killing bodies to save souls. Legal interpretation occurs whenever the law is actually applied--by anyone. But sound interpretation requires intelligence, prudence, learning and competence--not merely the right to make a decision or the power to apply the law. We are all at times quite prone to subjecting the gospel to human whims, conveniences and errors in legal interpretation. Nevertheless, good law

    --law in which people are primary,
    --law in which authority really is service,
    --law in which relationships have some mutuality,
    --law in which rights and obligations are acknowledged,
    --law in which unity outranks uniformity,
    --law in which actions are reasonable and intentions
      achievable,

such good law can provide prophetic opportunities within the human limitations of our imperfect but indispensable human realities. It is my professional judgment that the '83 code is greatly to be commended--especially in the canons concerning religious life--not only because it has incorporated well much of the vision of Vatican II but also because it is basically good law. That is, it is livable, adaptable, workable law. Our living, adapting and working realistically with it is what can make the future not only different but better. We can expend our energy and use our gifts bemoaning the past or rankling at the present or we can use them to make the future better. The choice--and the responsibility--are ours. It is my personal judgment that if we make the same mistakes as did the Pharisees of Jesus' time in straining out the gnats of following legal norms while swallowing the camels of compromising the gospel the fault lies not in the law (nor in the proverbial stars) but in ourselves.

    In the beginning there was no law, and I am firmly convinced that in the end there will be no law either (at least not as we know it). But we live somewhere "in between." "In between" we can only get to where we are going from where we actually are, by putting one foot in front of the other day after day. Lest we forget in the midst of our daily legal (and other) realities--let me note by way of interim

190

conclusion that we get nowhere at all without the constant help of God. God who is the alpha and the omega. Who is also God of our "in between" (if we allow it). God who is greater than any human law. And God to whom the future, too, belongs.

APPENDIX

Stuctures/Patterns/Modalities Currently Seen as Essential

I. The Following of Christ
   --stable, under influence of Holy Spirit, total dedication (573)
   --as proposed in gospel and proper law (662)
   --God sought and loved above all else in community (619)
   --chastity motivated by an undivided heart (599)
   --poverty motivated by the self-emptying of Christ (600)
   --obedience motivated by desire to be conformed to likeness of Christ in doing God's will (601)
   --adjust lives according to proper law of institute (598)
   --life of prayer, including personal, liturgical (1174), retreat, sound devotions (663,665)
   --aim at continuous worship of God in charity (607)
   --requirements of proper age, health, dispositions (642)
   --formation in Christian and human virtues (652)
   --care for whole person, physically, spiritually, emotionally (619)
   --right to what required to pursue vocation (670)
   --right to privacy, spiritual (607,630) and material (667)

II. Public Perpetual Vows
   --free & deliberate promise to God by vow (607,654,1191)
   --recognized as public by church (1192)
   --mediation of ecclesially approved institute (576)
   --legitimately designated superiors (608,617,622,625)
   --chastity includes perfect continence in celibacy (599)
   --poverty includes dependence and limitations in use of goods (600,668)
   --obedience includes submission of will to legitimate superiors commanding according to constitutions (601)

III. Ecclesially Approved Institute
   --diocesan or pontifical (579,593)
   --juridic personality with perpetuity (113-123,584)
   --administration of goods according to church law (634-640)

191

--right to proper law and internal autonomy (586,587,595)
--right to legitimate apostolic action (611)
--common life (602,607,593)/habit (668)
--identifiable legitimately constituted superiors (608, 626) with authority circumscribed by law (596,617)
--periodic chapters with legislative power (631)
--councils for deliberative/consultative input (627)
--requirements for admission (641-645), formation (646-653) and profession (654-658)
--required procedures for transfer (684-685), exclaustration (686-687), departure (688-693) and dismissal (694-702)

IV. Incorporation in Universal & Local Church
--primary apostolate of witness (673)/spiritual source (675)
--retain and adapt works (677)/apostolic restrictions (672)
--ultimately subject to Bishop of Rome & Apostolic See (590)
--locally subject to Diocesan Bishop in matters of apostolate (678, 679, 682, 683)
--necessity of consultation, cooperation and written agreements (680, 681)

Bishops and Religious: A New Relationship

by

Raymond W. Lessard, D.D.

My role in this presentation is to bring to a close the three days of talks and discussion at this Conference for Bishops and Major Superiors on Religious Life held here at Boston College. It is not my intention to offer a summary of all that was said or even to make an evaluation. Nor do I think it necessary for me to repeat what has already been said elsewhere by others, especially Archbishop Quinn, in explaining the pastoral initiative taken by Pope John Paul II on behalf of religious life in the United States. Rather, I should like to offer some thoughts, suggested indeed by questions and concerns raised by speakers and discussants these past three days, on the pastoral service which the bishops of the United States have now been called to render in their dioceses to religious women and men. Then, I shall attempt to describe in brief strokes the spirit that should characterize the new relationship developing between religious and bishops.

More than once during this conference we heard reference to the considerable task now facing bishops in encouraging "religious, their Institutes and associations to live fully the mystery of the Redemption, in union with the whole church and according to the specific charism of their religious life" (see Letter of Pope John Paul II to U.S. Bishops of April 3, 1983, #3). I think it can be safely said that the rapport between religious and bishops in the past has been generally good; it should probably be admitted, however, that the relationship was based more on a common interest in apostolic works than on a shared concern over the nature of religious life and its renewal. If bishops are to engage now in dialogue with religious on the meaning of their consecrated life as such, it will not suffice just to set up appropriate structures of ongoing communication, however effective, or to limit the exchange to the subject of what religious do in their dioceses. The bishops will have to become familiar not only with the abundant conciliar and post-conciliar literature on the subject of religious life and the rich but complex history of that charism in the church but also with the insights and perceptions that come from the lived experience of religious and the conflicting interpretations of the church's teachings and directives. In other words, the bishops must come to their pastoral service for religious with a firm grasp of what are the expectations of the church and what are the aspirations of religious themselves. Only then will they become effective and discerning participants, according to their proper role as pastors and teachers, in what should ultimately be a "dialogue of salvation."

Part of the task of the Pontifical Commission established by the Holy Father in his letter cited above is certainly to assist the bishops in this learning experience. The Commission will also "facilitate the pastoral work of their brother bishops in the United States " (Ibid. 4) by suggesting procedures that might be followed locally to initiate constructive and ongoing dialogue with religious. What is even more important is the spirit that should characterize the communication and encounter between a bishop and religious in his diocese. At the risk of over-simplification, I would suggest three essential characteristics: a spirit of charity; a spirit of communion; a spirit of joy.

The first criterion of any Christian relationship is that of charity, the goal of our every individual or collective pursuit as followers of Jesus, that loving union with God in Christ Jesus by the power of His Spirit which permits a union among us. If, as the Holy Father suggests in his Jubilee Year letter to religious, Redemptionis Donum, the evangelical counsels sum up the entire economy of salvation (see 9), providing a kind of synthesis of the radical call and content of the gospel, then it can be said that charity is the only adequate summary and expression of that full perfection we seek together. But charity is not only a goal; it is also a necessary trait of the pilgrim on the way and a feature of the pilgrim's every activity. Thus in the authentic renewal of religious life and the particular role which bishops are called to play in that experience, the spirit of charity must reign supreme, characterizing the common search for truth and holiness and making it possible to be respectfully tolerant of differences in gifts and opinions. It is the only trait which will make all participants in the dialogue open to the movement of the Spirit and which, especially in a context of tensions and divisions, of considerable hurt and alienation, will enable them to discern between that which is good and that which is bad.

The second characteristic of the pastoral relationship between bishops and religious is that of communion. Like charity, communion also can been seen as the goal of the journey, that perfect union with Christ and with his people.

But, again like charity, the spirit of communion should be present on the pilgrimage as well. While this characteristic could be considered from a trinitarian perspective, with the Trinity as its ultimate paradigm, or christologically, as an incarnate reality mediated by the human condition in its wholeness, it is for our purposes an eminently ecclesial quality. Our prayerful hope is always that the kingdom of God will be realized, but here and now it is the body of his Son, the church, which is our goal as well as the source of our strength and the context in which we live and work. The very methodology of our discipleship, if one can so state it, must derive from the ecclesial communion; the manner in which we related to each other and work together must be conditioned by the ecclesial communion.

In the conciliar decree, Perfectae Caritatis, we are told that the renewal of religious life involves two simultaneous processes: "a constant return to the sources of the whole of the Christian life and to the primitive inspiration of the institutes, and their adaptation to the changed conditions of our time" (no. 2). Since the sources referred to are preeminently the Scriptures as entrusted to the community of faith, the church, and the original inspiration is a charismatic gift given for the common good of the people of God, it is not surprising that the very next line of the conciliar text directs that this renewal is to take place "under the impulse of the Holy Spirit and with the guidance of the church."

The second process of renewal, adjustment to the times, is similarly ecclesial. The Council's clear call to read the signs of the times is one that seems to have favorably struck contemporary fancy. The call is not, however, to accept and canonize indiscriminately all that is new, but to enter into a serious discernment of changes that have occurred. If we are to testify about "lived experience," we should first of all engage in a much more profound and adequate analysis of our social and cultural scene if our discernment is to be in any way reliable and just. In my estimation, we have barely begun to do that in the United States. I don't want to suggest that nothing has been done, but our efforts risk the judgment of being perhaps superficial or in any case piecemeal.

On this subject, I would identify two syndromes against which we must do battle, two kinds of arrogance that keep us from engaging in any kind of meaningful cultural analysis we so urgently need. The first can be called generational arrogance. Within our own lifetimes, we have moved from the "me" generation to the "we" generation. I am not sure which is worse; in any case, both are bad! It is imperative that we recover a sense of history, so that our sense of communion, yes, our sense of communion possesses a horizontal dimension through time as well as in space, so that we regain that link of connectedness with those who went before us and with the inheritance they bequeathed us. I am pleased that this historical perspective was a key component of the program of this conference.

The second syndrome has been described as national arrogance, the delusion that the American experience has been divinely predestined to lead and teach the rest of the world! We need not deny that the church in the United States has something to offer the universal church; on the contrary, the experience of the church in this land, and specifically, the experience of religious in the United States, has indeed been rich and ought to be shared with the rest of the church. But it would redound to our advantage if we were to shed the cloak of national self-righteousness. For if we are not prepared to admit what may be mistakes or omissions or excesses, then our very credibility is compromised as will be the attractiveness and appeal of that which we want to proclaim to and share with the rest of the world.

I may seem here to have digressed from my original outline and from the immediate context of communion. And yet, these considerations are intimately related to the sense of communion I spoke of above. What the Holy Father had in fact initiated in his pastoral concern and shared with his brother bishops in a spirit of collegial responsibility for religious life in the United States is an experience of ecclesial communion and of a dynamic exchange between the local church and the universal church. An opportunity has been given us to share with the universal church what our experience has been, but this presumes that we are open to what the universal church has to offer us as well.

The third trait that should characterize the developing relationship between bishops and religious is a much more elusive and difficult one to describe, and yet, no less necessary. It is the spirit of _joy_, that gift which is described in Evangelica Testificatio as "an incomparable fruit of the Holy Spirit" (no. 55) of which we have already tasted because we belong to God. It is not only the joy of satisfaction for something of value already possessed but the joy that is part of the journey and the search. It is the delight that comes from the abiding presence of the Holy Spirit assuring us we are not alone in our pilgrimage of discipleship. It is that gratifying sense of respect for the precious goods handed down by earlier generations, the excitement flowing from the discovery of new treasures, the satisfaction of sharing what is possessed with others. It is a joy of and in the Spirit which finds its expression in a youthful restlessness with the less-than-perfect, in celebration of all that is authentically human, in passionate enthusiasm for having been anointed and missioned with the oil of gladness. It is the thrill of being able to transform polarizations and divisions into a fruitful dialectic. And last but not least, it is the pleasure of each others' company, as together we seek the Lord's will and resolve to follow it.

In conclusion, I would like to share with you my own joy and enthusiasm in our common enterprise. Although I may have entertained some fears and misgivings at the beginning, I want to express publicly my excitement for what I have already experienced, both as a member of the Pontifical Commission and as the bishop of a diocese, and for what I have seen happening rather widely in this important sector of the life of the church. Similarly, I would like to share with you my most sanguine hopes for the future of our ministry for bishops, for the future of the church in this country. To some these hopes may seem extravagant but I am confident that if our endeavors are characterized by a spirit of charity, a spirit of communion and a spirit of joy, they already merit the pledge of the Holy Spirit's presence and an anticipation of eternal blessings.

IV

RELIGIOUS LIFE IN THE AMERICAN CHURCH:

THE MEANING AND IMPLICATIONS OF THE PAPAL INTERVENTION

(A Lecture series at the University of San Francisco,
June 20, 27, July 4, 11, 18, 25, 1984)

The Renewal of Religious Life:
Identity and Diversity in Charity

by

John R. Quinn, D.D.

[Editor's note: During the lecture series at the
University of San Francisco, the Pontifical Delegate
adapted to this audience the reflections which he had
previously presented to the NCCB and which are printed
in an earlier section of this book. The following
reflections, a further elaboration on the meaning of
religious life, were initially presented to the
Institute on Religious Life on June 1, 1984.]

It is often said that when treating the church, the
Council adopted as its first theme the church as the people of
God. A look at Lumen Gentium, however, reveals that its first
theme and its first chapter deal not with the people of God,
but with the church as mystery, the mystery of the church.

For the Council, as for the scriptures, the church is the
great mystery of Christ, the whole Christ, the dream of God.
And so St. Paul says, "To me, least of all believers, was
given the grace to preach to the Gentiles the unfathomable
riches of Christ and to enlighten all men on the mysterious
design which for ages was hidden in God, the creator of all.
Now, therefore, through the Church, God's manifold wisdom is
made known to the principalities and powers of Heaven, in
accord with His age-old purpose, carried out in Christ Jesus
Our Lord" (Eph 3:8-11).

The first theme, then, of the Council is not the
structures of the church nor even the mission of the church.
Its first theme is that the church is a great and pervading
mystery which we can know only through the response of faith.
The mystery of the church cannot be fully articulated in human
language nor captured in human categories. The church is not
just one more sociological or historical phenomenon side by
side with all other great human institutions which have made
their mark in history. On the contrary, the church stands
revealed as the great mystery of Christ in us. Our attitude
toward the church and toward its enactments and decisions must
be shaped by our faith in the church as a divine mystery.

As the human Christ was formed by the Holy Spirit in the womb of the Virgin, so the church is formed by the spirit in the womb of history. Though not enclosed by human history, the church is in human history. Thus, despite the transcendent reality of the church as mystery, it is always a pilgrim church. It is the net cast into the sea drawing in all sorts of fish. It is the field planted with good grain and bad which cannot be completely separated until the harvest. But it is not only the holy church in which sinners live, in which there is light and darkness. It is also the church in which tensions exist.

This should not be surprising to anyone acquainted with the New Testament. You have only to read Acts or the two Letters to the Corinthians, or the Book of Revelation to see at once that tensions have accompanied the church's journey from the very beginning. The following words, for instance, were addressed to the church in Corinth less than twenty-five years after the death and resurrection of the Lord: "I have been informed, my brothers, by certain members of Chloe's household that you are quarrelling among yourselves. This is what I mean: one of you will say 'I belong to Paul,' another, 'I belong to Apollos,' still another, 'Cephas has my allegiance,' and the fourth, 'I belong to Christ'" (1 Cor 1:11-12).

Thus a genuine and living faith in the church does not preclude the existence of tensions. Given the profound and almost universal cultural transformation just taking shape at the time, it is not surprising either that the church should have experienced and should continue to experience some major tensions in connection with the Second Vatican Council. Yet the providential character of the Council lies to a great extent in the fact that it was the first Council in the history of the church to be held before the crisis really got underway. But if the church had not had the orientation and sense of direction, and the changes initiated by the Council, the situation today would probably be disastrous and chaotic. The Council, then, was indeed an epiphany manifesting the continuing presence and action of the Spirit in the church.

In calling the whole church to renewal and reform, the Council issued a special call to religious. That call was not to a mere cosmetic reform. For instance "Perfectae Caritatis" states, "The manner of life, of prayer and work should be in harmony with the present-day physical and psychological condition of the members. It should also be in harmony with the needs of the apostolate, in the measure that the nature of each institute requires with the requirements of culture and with social and economic circumstances. This should be the case everywhere . . ." (no. 3)

Speaking specifically of the apostolic religious, "Perfectae Caritatis" continues, "These institutes should adjust their observances and customs to the needs of their particular apostolate. Since, however, the active religious life takes many forms, this diversity should be taken into account when its up-to-date renewal is being undertaken, and in the various institutes, the members' life in the service of Christ should be sustained by means which are proper and suitable to each institute." (no. 8)

These few texts already serve to show that the call of the Council was for a real transformation of religious life and not a mere retouching of a few peripheral factors. I would like to comment on four aspects of that renewal as I understand them from the documents of the magisterium:

1. The Unitary Nature of Religious Life.

2. The Relationship of Religious Life to Culture.

3. The Relationship of Religious Life to the Individual.

4. The Diversity of Religious Life.

And I would conclude with some reflections on the present moment.

1. The Unitary Nature of Religious Life.

In one of his plays, Christopher Fry describes two lovers speaking. One says to the other, "You have gone out into everything I loved before, and everything I loved has come to one meeting place in you." These words describe the total absorption of the lover with the beloved. This is something of what the Council is describing when it states, "The entire religious life of the members should be imbued with an apostolic spirit and all their apostolic activity with a religious spirit." In other words, the Council does not see in religious life a dichotomy between work and prayer, between service and contemplation, between the pursuit of holiness and the works of the apostolate. For the Council, there must be an integration of these, so that prayer becomes apostolic service and apostolic service becomes prayer. It is emphatically clear, of course, that prayer as such, both liturgical and personal prayer, are absolutely fundamental qualities of religious life. (E.E. nos. 28-30) But what the Council is saying is that the life of prayer is not something separate from apostolic service. Prayer is one aspect of apostolic service and apostolic service is one aspect of prayer. Just as faith is the first foundation of our relationship with God and must pervade every aspect of our lives, in a similar way, prayer and the contemplative dimensions must pervade every aspect of religious life. And so I did not say that prayer "leads" to service or that service "leads" to prayer. It is rather that prayer become a permeating atmosphere in which service is given and service becomes a permeating atmosphere in which prayer takes place. Ultimately, both service and prayer are aspects of love, of a single, unitary, orientation toward God, which is charity.

St. Thomas witnesses the faith of the church when he teaches that all the activities of the religious life, prayer, service, asceticism, all converge toward the perfection of love. (Cfr. II-II, Q 186, A 1, Contra)

If religious, then, fail to live the religious life in love and in charity, they fail in its most vital point no matter how perfect all the other things may be. Consequently, our struggles for the Kingdom can really become satanic when charity is absent. For the scriptures clearly teach us that the signs of God's presence in our lives and actions are "Love, joy, peace, patient endurance, kindness, generosity, faith, mildness, and chastity" (Gal 5:22). The Council vision, then, is a vision of integration not diffusion. It is a matter of Christ going out into everything and everything coming to one meeting place in Him.

2. The Relationship of Religious Life to Culture.

The obvious diversity in religious Life was clear long before the Council. Each institute had its own charism and its different history. But the Council enunciates a new source of diversity: "The requirements of culture and . . . social and economic circumstances."

For the Council, culture is not understood simply as the liberal formation and education of the individual as when we speak, for instance, of someone who loves the symphony as being "cultured." Rather culture is understood as the integrated pattern of human activities which constitutes a particular civilization or a particular time. Culture denotes, then, the customs, beliefs, the social forms and moral traits that mark and distinguish one society and its way of life from another so that we can speak of the culture of the middle ages or of the culture of modern India.

The Council, then, envisions diversity not merely from one institute to another, but even diversity within a given institute as its members relate to differing cultures and to differing social and economic circumstances. Attention to culture may not be the primary consideration, but it is not a negligible one.

Since inculturation is something which pertains to the Church, not only in the past but in the present, not only in Asia or Africa, but also in the United States, we have to recognize that there are peculiarities of the American culture which will have an influence on the appropriate renewal of religious life in the United States.

While there are various possibilities, I would like to select two symbols drawn from the American experience which I think typify some important qualities of the American culture. One is the town hall meeting. The town hall is the symbol of the American sense of participation, consultation, discussion and debate. It is an expression of the need to have "ownership" of the final decision once all sides have been heard. A possible weakness of the town hall spirit, of course, is the danger of manipulation which should not be overlooked. Yet an atmosphere of openness in which each one can speak frankly and directly is certainly an element of true religious obedience as long as it does not become a pressure tactic to force superiors to take a certain direction. All this seems to me consonant with Paul VI's Encyclical "Ecclesiam Suam" where he speaks with such beauty and balance about dialogue in the church. This does not mean that there is no final authority or that no one has the power to make ultimate decisions. As Karl Rahner put it, the church is not a fair in which everyone can set up a booth. Yet this aspect of the American character does seem reflected in "Evangelica Testificatio" where we read, "Far from being in opposition to one another, authority and individual liberty go together in fulfillment of God's will, which is sought fraternally through a trustful dialogue between the superior and his (her) brother (sister)." The document goes on to say, however, "This labor of seeking together must end, when it is the moment, with the decision of the superiors whose presence and acceptance are indispensable in every community." (E.T. no. 25)

Another symbol of the American experience which typifies our culture is the pioneer. The pioneer represents the spirit of enterprise, enthusiasm for tackling the unknown, the spirit of discovery and of risk-taking in pursuit of a goal. Of course, the spirit of the pioneer has the possibility also of dissipation and lack of coordination. It is open to the eccentricities of the messianic complex and can be far more geared to self-service and self-interest than to the service of Christ and of others in his name. Nevertheless, if the spirit of the pioneer did not live in the church we would never had had Francix Xavier or Teresa of Avila, Francis of Assisi or Elizabeth Seton. We find a congenial resonance, then, in the words of <u>Mutuae Relationes</u>: "Moreover, the deep upheavals of situations, the growth of human values, and the manifold needs of the world today, press ever more insistently on the one hand for the renewal of many traditional pastoral forms of activity, and on the other for the search for new forms of apostolic presence. In such a situation a certain apostolic diligence is urgently necessary in order to devise new, ingenious, and courageous ecclesial experiments under the inspiration of the Holy Spirit who is by his very nature 'Creator.' A responsiveness rich in creative initiative is eminently compatible with the charismatic nature of the religious life. In fact, the Holy Father, Pope Paul VI, himself affirmed this: 'Thanks to their religious consecration, they (religious) are above all free and can spontaneously leave everything and go to announce the Gospel even to the ends of the earth. They are prompt in acting; and their apostolate frequently excels because of the ingeniousness of their projects and undertakings, which evoke admiration in all who observe them.'" (<u>M.R.</u> no. 19)

Clearly, then, the Council recognizes and affirms the differences in culture and regards these differences as something good and something to be considered in the renewal of religious life.

3.   The Relationship of Religious Life to the Individual.

"The manner of life, prayer and work," says the Council, "should be in harmony with the present-day physical and psychological condition of the members." And so, to the ingredient of culture the Council adds consideration of the physical and psychological condition of the members of the Institute as a factor in renewal. Whatever may be said about the merits of some past forms in religious life, we cannot live in the past. Thus "<u>Evangelica Testificatio</u>" states, "Certainly many exterior elements, recommended by founders of orders or religious congregations, are seen today to be outmoded. Various encumbrances or rigid forms accumulated over the centuries need to be curtailed. Adaptations must be made. New forms can even be sought with the approval of the church." (E.T. no. 5)

And so if we are to follow the Council and take into consideration the "psychological condition of the members" in the context of the American culture, we cannot overlook the fact that American society places a profound value on the freedom of the individual and regards this as linked with respect for the dignity of the human person. Thus, while in the past, there was a much greater emphasis on conformity as one of the marks of the ideal religious, there is rightly today a much greater emphasis on responsible freedom. I use the adjective "responsible" to indicate that truly responsible freedom in religious life has to include the spirit of faith, Catholic faith, a spirit of humility in accord with the gospel of Christ, and a sensitivity to the demands of communion in and with the church.

Obedience properly understood becomes a further definition of responsible freedom. True religious obedience lies not simply in doing what one is told. True religious obedience lies in finding God in doing what one is told. The challenge for the religious is not so much "to obey or not to obey." The great challenge for the religious is to find God in obeying. Where God is there is joy. Obedience, which involves finding God, is true freedom and true joy.

True religious obedience is a form of freedom. It is also a form of maturity. And while it cannot be understood as "mere" conformity, no truly mature person could deny an appropriate place for conformity with rules or directives or expectations. But the nature and number of these should be consonant with the dignity and intelligence of adults and in keeping with the demands of responsible freedom. In this context rules or laws become a sign of respect for the individual but they also contribute to the necessary solidarity among religious and to the common sense of mission and spirit in the community.

Freedom is too often thought of as autonomous self-direction when it should be understood as responsible self-determination in the context of the common good and the purpose of the institute.

207

4. The Diversity of Religious Life.

Diversity has been one of the marks of the church from the beginning. It was precisely diversity which gave rise to the first tensions in the primitive church: The complaints of the Greek-speaking widows against the Hebrew-speaking, unequal treatment. This led to the institution of the Diaconate. A far more significant moment for the whole future history of the church, however, was the tension which arose over the resistance of Greek-speaking converts in the pagan world to adopting the practices of the Mosaic Law. This tension arose from cultural and psychological differences, but it led to some basic and profound clarifications of faith. The spirit was at work in the tension and the diversity, and the church grew in faith, unity, and peace.

Diversity which has been and continues to be a mark of the church is also one of the obvious qualities of religious life in the church. In approving the constitutions of religious institutes the church is in effect approving diversity. She is also doing two other things. She is saying to the whole church and to the members of that institute in particular that this form of life is authenticated as a true path of holiness and that it has a true mission in the church. At the same time the church is endorsing the standard by which the institute is held accountable for fidelity to its way of life before the church. This fact of diversity, then, is one which all religious must come to accept in peace and charity. While in the church diversity must always exist within Catholic unity, it must also exist within charity. It should be expected that, given the call of the Council to such a profound renewal and given the cultural transformation of our times, there would develop a spectrum of forms of religious life within the church, some much more recognizable in terms of past experience, more familiar, but some much less familiar.

There are two extreme positions which can characterize our response to what is new or novel. The first is unreflecting acceptance of the new, a frenetic need, almost pathological, to be in the vanguard, on the cutting edge, but without discernment or reflection. The other extreme fears what is new or novel and suppresses it before it can develop.

Age old wisdom enjoins that serious decisions should never be made in strong emotional states. Panic before the new is not, then, helpful in true discernment. In War and Peace, Tolstoy praises General Kutuzov. The general had greatly disturbed the Royal Court because he did not seem to react strongly enough against the threat of Napoleon. To this Kutuzov replied, "Patience and time. Time and patience." Events proved him right. And so the discernment of the new takes time. It should not be adopted unreflectingly, nor suppressed unreflectingly. Within the church, what is new can be given time if and when the signs of the Spirit are present: love, joy, peace, gentleness, mildness and the rest. Where there is anger, bitterness, factionalism, divisions, this is not the work of the Spirit. The important thing for religious life and for the church is to deal patiently with change and diversity, with the new and untried, but always to insist on the signs of the Spirit. When the signs of the Spirit are not present, then something is very wrong. It is not lacking in significance that one of the most imaginative and innovative of the Apostles wrote not that "the greatest of these is progress" or "the greatest of these is efficiency" but "the greatest of these is love."

5. The Present Moment.

In another year we will observe the twentieth anniversary of the ending of the Council and we will be just fifteen years from the beginning of a new century. Against the background of the Holy Year of Redemption and in the context of this historic moment, the Holy Father has issued a new and imaginative call to the church in the United States. He has called the bishops to a new and deeper interest in religious and called the whole church in our country to a deeper appreciation and understanding of religious life. The response to this call has already brought religious and their bishops closer together and this bond has generated a new spirit of trust and charity which without any doubt will have far reaching effects on the life of the church in this country. In issuing this call to a new relationship between bishops and religious, the Holy Father also desired to strengthen and encourage religious. One of his frequent themes has been to underline for religious and for the church just what a singular gift religious life is. He has stressed recently in the beautiful exhortation on Religious Life the idea of consecration as the foundation of religious life. It is the fruit of the divine initiative. God calls, He acts and He empowers.

Yet consecration in religious life is inseparable from mission. And so the document Essential Elements states, "When God consecrates a person . . . he not only chooses, sets apart and dedicates the person to himself, but He engages him or her in his own divine work. Consecration inevitably implies mission. These are two facets of one reality." (E.E. no. 23)

Also in his letter to the bishops, the pope is conscious of the diversity of religious life and of the particular modality it receives because of the American context: "The Essential Elements," he says, "are lived in different ways from one institute to another. You yourselves deal with this rich variety in the context of the American reality" (Letter no. 3) The pope is also conscious of the lived experience of religious and directs the Pontifical Commission "to consult with a number of religious, to profit from the insights that come from the experience of religious life lived in union with the church." (Ibid. no. 4) Similarly, "Essential Elements" states, "religious life itself is an historical as well as a theological reality. The lived experience, today as in the past, is varied and this is important." (E.E. no. 4)

Yet recognizing that experience is not self-interpreting, the document adds, "at the same time, experience is a dimension which needs to be tested in relation to the gospel foundation, the magisterium of the church and the approved constitutions of the institute." (Ibid.)

* * * * * * * * *

It may be an oversimplification, but it seems to me that the scriptures give two signs of true love. The first is in the gospels. There the sign of love is obedience: If you love me, you will keep my word. (Cf. John 14) In Paul the test of love is the presence of the Spirit, the love of God poured forth in our hearts and manifest in such signs as "love, joy, peace, patient endurance, kindness, generosity, faith, mildness, and chastity" (Gal 5:22) I venture to say that the challenge of this moment for religious in the United States lies in the special call to love, and that where religious communities love in obedience to the word of God and in the signs of the Spirit, God will manifest his power and all things will work together unto good.

The Holy Father speaks of this in his apostolic exhortation on religious life; ". . . of great importance among you is the witness of mutual love, linked to the fraternal spirit of each community, for the Lord has said, 'By this will all know that you are my disciples if you have love for one another."

And in closing, I make my own the pope's prayer that "from Christ, the Redeemer of the world, may the inexhaustible source of your love for the church pour forth." (R.D. no. 15)

The Spectrum of Church Teaching on Religious Life

by

Mary Ann Donovan, S.C.

On Easter Sunday, 1983, John Paul II's letter to the American bishops initiated the current study of apostolic religious life in this country. The process the pope set in motion at that time marks a new era in the relationship between apostolic religious and the American bishops, an era characterized (as Archbishop Quinn has remarked) by the kind of dialogue called for by Paul VI in Ecclesiam Suam. No previous pope has called on the bishops of a country "to render special pastoral service to the religious of your dioceses and your country."[1] While the letter does not precisely delimit the nature of the pastoral care to be exercised, it enumerates several specific recommendations. The introduction of this episcopal responsibility shifts significantly the way bishops relate to apostolic religious. How is that so?

Canon 586 of the new Code assures a true autonomy of life to each institute, especially in governance, and also with respect to the spiritual patrinomy of the institute. The kind of autonomy in question has to do with the inner life of the group. Of course, not even an institute's inner life takes place apart from the great church since religious are, after all, members of the church, and religious life is a way of life directed toward the living out of Baptism. Religious institutes with their proper freedom live and serve within the church. Both the life and service are of concern to the church. The very life of religious is a treasure to the church (as the papal letter again reminds us). The service of religious is directly or indirectly a collaboration in the work of the church. This is certainly of concern to the church. However in the immediate past bishops have exercised little direct care for religious. The pope introduces the new note when he directs bishops to exercise special pastoral care of apostolic religious so that these religious might "live their ecclesial vocation to the full."[2] He is reaffirming the bond between religious and the church. In the reaffirmation John Paul II is entrusting to his fellow bishops in the United States a certain care for that bond. In doing so he introduces a change in the way bishops relate to apostolic religious in this country.

It is too early to predict the outcome of the shift. On the assumption that what has happened in the past is significant for the present it would be helpful to examine the spectrum of church teaching on religious life as that teaching mirrors the changing relationship between ecclesial authority and religious. That story is as long and as complex as the story of the church itself. What follows is of necessity selective, but attends to the principal developments.[3] I will treat the subject in three sections: first, the situation in the ancient church, with the position taken in the Council of Chalcedon; second, the situation that developed in the medieval church, which on the whole is reflected in the position taken in the council of Trent; third, the situation that has been developing in the nineteenth and twentieth centuries, and which is reflected in Vatican II. As a tool to organize the material within each section I will ask three questions.[4] First, what is the situation within which religious life in its various forms develops in the given period? While religious life is a gift of the Spirit to the church, the situation in which that form of life develops is descriptive of the human factors through which the Spirit works. Second, how do the religious of a given era typically express their ecclesial identity? Third, in the period how is religious life viewed from the standpoint of ecclesial authority?

Section 1

The church came into being in the Roman empire, in many ways an ordered world in which birth determined one's place in life. As the church developed a number of factors contributed to the evolution of religious life in its earliest monastic forms. The politics of the empire played a role. For some Christians the desert was an escape from persecution. Once there, a number of them were inspired to remain to seek to live a life of holiness. The effort to avoid physical martyrdom resulted for them in the development of an alternate asceticism. At a slightly later date other Christians fled into the desert to escape the morass of mediocrity spreading in the newly Christian cities. Fervor fueled development of an austere alternate lifestyle.

What led Christians to seek to live the gospel in this way? The work of Origen was important. This Alexandrian teacher offers an optimistic assessment of the powers of human nature to attain sanctity. He stresses the inalienable freedom of human nature as one of the two forces driving fallen humans back to God, providence being the other. That freedom can and must be used to acquire virtue which is won only by discipline. He uses the great metaphors of the journey, of growth, and of struggle to discuss the Christian's return to God. His work inspired generations of ascetics.[5]

A third factor that must be considered is socio-economic. Peter Brown reminds us of the social crisis occurring the the Egyptian villages from which the first monks were drawn. The typical peasant of the time was abrasively independent, seeking to govern his own life in as total as possible a disengagement from the restraints of his neighbors. But complete detachment was out of the question. Economic insecurity, taxation (leveled on the village as a whole rather than on the individual), and the need to cooperate in controlling the water of the Nile "forced households of natural egoists into constant, humiliating, and friction-laden contact and collaboration with their fellows."[6] The situation was acute at the time Egyptian monasticism first flowered. Flight was the instinctive reaction of the farmers, and flight into the desert with escape from insurmountable economic burdens was a route offered by the nascent monastic movement.

Finally, as we move through and beyond the founding period of the third and fourth centuries a fourth factor comes into play: the great migration of peoples from Asia into Europe. Under the impact of this massive relocation the tottering Roman Empire finally collapsed. The subsequent story of monasticism in the West is deeply involved with the recivilization of Europe.

Such is the situation in which religious life developed under the impetus of the Spirit in the ancient church. How did the religious of that era typically express their ecclesial identity? The earliest among them understood themselves as lay people who lived the life of hermits, like the great Antony.[7] Very early, partially under the impact of the need for mutual direction and edification, communal forms of the life developed. For Pachomius, a fourth century founder of cenobitic monastic life in Egypt, the essence of monastic life was conversion of morals.[8] This meant the learning of a new way of life following a complete break with the past. The monk, like the nun in the monasteries directed by Mary, Pachomius' sister, was to leave behind everything of the past: family, friends, property, imperfections, sins. He was to attempt to live a life perfect in morals, with manual work and regular fasting. Obedience to the abbot was critical. While there were daily assemblies and instruction by the <u>Abbot</u>, community life did not have an important role.

<u>Basil</u> <u>and</u> <u>his</u> <u>sister</u> <u>Macrina</u>, who lived in Cappadocia a generation or two after Pachomius, transformed the ecciesial identity of the monk and nun.[9] Monasticism was conceived as a new kind of communal living. Their monasteries expressly intended to help <u>members</u> <u>to</u> <u>live</u> <u>together</u> <u>in</u> <u>charity</u>. Members were to assume responsibility for the spiritual direction of one onother. While solitude had its role as the place where a new spiritual tranquility would be won, members were to experience the new form of community life through mutual spiritual assistance. There is no question that the superior was in charge of the community and the members were expected to accept the superior's regulations.

<u>Benedict</u> <u>of</u> <u>Nursia</u> was the great western monastic founder of the early sixth century, whose sister <u>Scholastica</u> collaborated with him.[10] While Benedict drew on Pachomius and Basil (among others), his basic insight was a bit different. He saw the essence of monastic life as a <u>school</u> <u>for</u> <u>the</u> <u>Lord's</u> <u>service</u>. The fundamental attitude is to hearken to the Master with the heart. To this end the relationship between abbess or abbot and nun or monk becomes one of spiritual parenting implying the duty of spiritual guidance. Yet the group assembled in chapter retains an important role in governance.

For Benedict, Scholastica, Basil, Macrina, and Pachomius the monk or nun was living a particular form of Christian life within the church. The identity of the member of the community might be expressed in terms of conversion of morals, common life in charity, or the school for the service of the Lord. The well-regulated monastery was an ordered society. Just as in late Roman society every person had a place and moved within it, so too was it the case in the monastery. Humanly speaking, this very stability was part of the appeal when the social order collapsed.

Before we move to the middle ages, a question remains. What was the attitude of ecclesial authority toward monastic life in the ancient church? Many individual bishops lived a form of monastic life, and some were also revered as founders. Among the latter were Basil and also Augustine. Gregory the Great, Bishop of Rome, 590-604, was intimately connected with the monastic movement. Prior to his election Gregory was already himself a monk and the founder of monasteries. In this he is the first of a long line of men who came to the

papacy from the religious state.[11] Before and after coming
to ecclesiastical office he acted and wrote in favor of
monastic life. His work helped to shape the dawning middle
ages. However the weight attached to his writing on monastic
life is primarily that which derives from his holiness of life
in combination with his wisdom.

The canons of the Council of Chalcedon in 451 offer the
clearest example of ecciesial authority acting as such toward
religious life on a broad scale. The canons betray both a
sense of the relationship of religious to the church and a
sense of the authority embodied in the Council with respect to
that life. The canons are disciplinary. Canon 4 indicates
both what was expected of monks and what was deplored among
them. What was expected? First, the ideals "Those who truly
and sincerely enter upon the monastic life are to be counted
worthy of suitable honor."[12] Further, they are to be
subject to the bishop, to embrace quiet, to attend only to
fasting and prayer, and to remain in the places in which they
renounced secular life. What is deplored? Monks are not to
busy themselves in ecciesiastical or secular affairs, nor take
part in them, leaving their own monasteries, unless permitted
to do so for any necessary purpose, by the bishop of the city.
Canons 7 and 8 forbid the assumption of secular function or
military service, and place monks who are clerics explicitly
under the bishop's jurisdiction. Canon 16 forbids monks and
consecrated virgins to marry.

What was the difficulty? Why such canons? The history
of the period abounds in lawless monks, wandering from place
to place.[13] Just before the Council for a number of years
monks of disputing parties had roiled the ecciesiastical
waters from Alexandria to Constantinople. The Council knows
itself as authority in the church with power to regulate the
lives of church members, and so it acts to correct the
disturbance. The relationship to the local bishop is seen to
be critical, and is carefully safeguarded. This relationship
will remain central, although with differing nuances, as the
story unfolds.

Section 2

This second section is concerned with the almost one
thousand years between the pontificates of St. Gregory the
Great (590-604) and St. Pius V (1566-1572), so the period
extending from 590 to 1572. In that timespan, three major
developments occurred within religious life with significant

consequences for religious life today. These were the transformation of monasticism, and the emergence of two new forms of religious life, the mendicant orders in the thirteenth century and the clerks regular in the sixteenth century.[14]

Factors transforming monasticism include exemption, new roles for monks, and the growth of true religious orders of congregations. An understanding of the practice of exemption is basic to an understanding of the relationship between religious and ecclesial authority in this period. Exemption concerns removal from the authority of the local bishops. On the one hand wealthy lay patrons increasingly retained influence and privileges in the monasteries. Where this happened, monasteries tended to transfer external allegiance from the bishop to the patron. On the other hand as time passed the pope granted exemption to more and more monasteries, acting sometimes as temporal and sometimes as spiritual lord. This situation applies both to monasteries of men and of women.[15] A further complication affected the men. As larger numbers of monks were ordained, exemption removed from the control of the local bishop men who were exercising priestly functions in their dioceses. Money was involved in terms of profits from the lands, military levies on the dependents of the monasteries, and various benefices. Depending on the relative strength of bishops, pope, abbots and abbesses the potential for conflict was hardly minimal.

In addition to exemption, another factor changing monastic life was the broadening of the monks' participation in missionary activity and in education. Celtic monks like Columbanus were pioneers in the European mission field. It was through mission work that the monks took the first step toward the recivilization of Europe. The second step came through the development of the monastic school. Since recruits often were not literate and literacy came to be required (at least of choir monks) schools were begun. Together with the episcopal schools of the period, the monastic school is the germ of the medieval university. More immediately the monastic schools served as training grounds for bishops. The abbess Hilda provided such fine preparation that five bishops were drawn from her monastery at Whitby.[16]

A third factor transforming monasticism was the growth of true religious orders or congregations. Here this denotes groups of houses following one Rule and related to one motherhouse. Cluny, founded in 910, was the first of these.

The situation which witnessed this transformation of monasticism was the world of feudal Europe. The dominant Rule was Benedictine, so the monastery continued to be seen as the school of the Lord's service. Religious continued to express their ecclesial identity as disciples of Christ, living in a monastery in obedience to the abbot or abbess, with obligation to recite the office in choir. In terms of the social order, monk stood to abbot somewhat as vassal to lord. The abbot, in turn, had various relationships of lordship or vassalage to other abbots, bishops, lords, and the pope.

From the viewpoint of ecclesial authority, it is Pope Gregory VII (1073-1085) who had the most significant effect. Himself a monk, he set out to reform monasticism, and to reform the church on the pattern of a monastic order. Exemption, applied now to entire congregations, was used to strengthen the supreme power of the papacy. After Gregory's time exemption was increasingly abused. The pope tended to see it as a right to intervene freely in exempt monasteries; religious tended to view exemption as total independence not only from the local bishop but also from the pope himself.[17]

Meanwhile, although the economy was still land based, towns (many of which first grew up around the monasteries) were flourishing. The late twelfth and early thirteenth centuries saw a burgeoning of wealth. It was the time of the Crusades, of penitential journeys for the building of churches in northern France, of the communal movement everywhere: in the Midi and in Northern Italy, on the Rhine and in Flanders. With the coming of the Cathari it was also the time of the rise of heresy as a mass movement. In this situation the mendicant orders appeared and swept across Europe.

What is the ecclesial identity of these religious? The mendicants were geared to preach the gospel while living radical gospel poverty.[18] It is true their rules owed much to monasticism. The friars continued to live in common under a superior and to recite the office in choir. However, in contrast to medieval monastic practice, houses as well as individual members depended on alms, members moved from house to house as required, and they engaged in preaching for which they prepared by intense study. Poverty and preaching were key. Granted this internal identity, the founders related themselves to the work of the universal church through the pope. By the thirteenth century the papacy enjoyed true supremacy. The Dominicans in particular made a point of strict obedience to pope and bishop to facilitate the work of preaching and to assure the support of local bishops. Francis of Assisi sought a similar end but went at it differently. He requested a cardinal protector for his order, who was to represent the order at the curia and to the hierarchy, to smooth its path in the church, and to keep from the order any shadow of heresy. (This move alone should give pause to those who accuse the man from Assisi of being lacking in worldly wisdom!)

How did ecclesial authority view the new orders? After initial approval, the great struggles came around the exemption of the mendicants and the question of Franciscan poverty. An issue of equally great significance but fought less fiercely at the time was the role of women in the new orders. The exemption struggle was a fight in which bishops, vicars, and secular clergy on the university faculties took on the mendicants. It lasted one hundred years; ultimately it was resolved in favor of the mendicants who throughout had favored the doctrine of papal primacy. Franciscan poverty raised embarrassing questions, since the friars insisted that the renunciation of property "singly and in common" was an essential element in the way of life Christ Himself had taught His apostles.[19] This was a radical reinterpretation of scripture, calling into question previous exegesis and challenging the way of life of many church people. A series of thirteenth century popes addressed questions raised in efforts to interpret the Franciscan rule approved in 1221. The right and power of popes to act in this way was accepted. The Friars welcomed papal support against their enemies.

Meanwhile where were the Scholasticas and Macrinas of the mendicant orders? Remember that the mendicant charism included radical poverty and the preaching of the gospel. The charism corresponded to the need of the time for witness to poverty and for sound preaching. Both Dominic and Francis founded second orders for women, but social and ecclesial custom alike agreed that these women be cloistered. This ruled out the active side of the mendicant charism. As for poverty, Clare of Assisi's lifelong struggle to obtain approval of her rule with its practice of radical poverty makes moving reading. It was a struggle she won on her deathbed. There the approved original document was brought to her. We are told "she kissed it many times."[20] She won the fight for radical poverty but her nuns were cloistered. Boniface VIII reinforced this provision for all women religious in 1298; for women strict cloister joined to solemn vows was the condition of living in the religious state.[21] In sum, ecclesial authority looked with approval on the mendicants, encouraged their poverty, and supported the ministry of the men.

The move from the thirteenth to the sixteenth centuries is not a progression but a decline; it is a period in which religious life and the church of which it is a part fell ever deeper into the need for reform. These are the years in which western Europe suffered the depredations of the Hundred Years' War; they are the years in which the black plague decimated all of Europe. Now the abuse of exemption escalates to scandalous proportions. Now Chaucer's friar and nun journey to Canterbury. Superiors could hardly initiate reform within congregations as religious could easily remove themselves from obedience to their own superiors; the curia readily granted such exemptions. Here we see the dark side of the close inter-relationship between the church and religious life. At the time, reform of religious life demanded reform of pope and curia. But pope and curia lived as princes, in a style rivaling that of the rulers of the newly emerging nation states. The time was ripe for Luther's call to reform. In this situation in the early decades of the sixteenth century rose another new form of religious life, the clerks regular.

These were ordained male religious who lived by rule and took as their principal task the exercise of apostolic zeal, especially through the practice of the spiritual and corporal works of mercy. Representative of this group are the Jesuits. Bangert points out that Ignatius

> set aside four ancient and key forms of the monastic structure: lifelong residence in one community; decision-making on major issues by individual communities assembled in chapter; the choosing of its superior by each individual community; the chanting of the divine office in choir. Ignatius...elected that detachment, mobility, disposability be the Jesuit marks.[22]

As a key concept Ingatius further insisted that the superior be in every way the spiritual father of the individual subject. How did the founder express the ecclesial identity of the Society of Jesus? John O'Malley writes that the papacy and the Society were joined in Ignatius' mind

> in the scope of their directly pastoral concerns. The approval of the Society and of the Spiritual Exercises by the papacy facilitated the apostolic effectiveness of the Society, and especially made it capable of

transcending diocsan and national boundaries. The pope, as 'universal pastor,' symbolized and helped implement the worldwide vision that animated the Jesuits' concept of their 'missions.' [23]

How is religious life viewed at this time by ecclesial authority? Among the decrees of its twenty-fifth session the Council of Trent promulgated a decree on religious and one on general reform. Recall the difficulty in reforming religious life when cardinals and prelates lived scandalously. These two decrees pair the two levels of reform. The first chapter of the decree on general reform dealt with cardinals and prelates, requiring them to live a simple and frugal life. They were forbidden to use the goods of the church to increase the fortune of their parents and friends.[24] The decree dealing with religious was not a systematic treatise on religious life, but rather a systematic correction of abuses.[25] basically, religious were asked to live according to the rule they accepted on reception into the congregation. Other points of concern were poverty, life outside the religious house, and vows. Nuns were bound by cloister.

In implementing these decrees Pius V invited all women who were living in community in simple vows without cloister to make solemn profession and accept strict cloister.[26] Here he exceeded the requirements of Trent. Even after Boniface VIII groups like the Sisters of Penance, attached to the Dominican Order, had continued to live in common with the three simple vows and no obligation of cloister. Julius II had explicitly permitted this.[27] Following the wish of Pius V, many groups of Ursulines who had been founded as apostolic accepted cloister. In years to come religious life could accommodate neither Francis de Sales and Jane de Chantal's original vision for the Visitandines, nor Mary Ward's movement, nor the Daughters of Charity of Louise de Marillac and Vincent de Paul. The Visitandines were cloistered. Mary Ward's group was suppressed for almost a century. The Daughters of Charity simply did not become religious; they were constituted as a pious association with private vows. In a memorable conference Vincent de Paul told the sisters to bear in mind "that they are not in a religious order, as this state is unsuitable to the duties of their vocation.[28]

Section 3

Vincent spoke to the Sisters not long after the close of the fratricidal wars of religion. One of his great French contemporaries was Descartes, who turned philosophy solidly toward preoccupation with the thinking subject rather than with the objects of thought. Thomas Hobbes and John Locke, English philosophers exposed to Cartesian thought, went on to lay the foundations, Hobbes of naturalism and Locke of liberalism. The rationalism of their day gave way to the age of enlightenment in both France and England. The enlightenment in turn drew to a close with the revolutions of the late eighteenth century. By the opening of the nineteenth century the worlds of philosophy, of science, and of politics had all been turned upside down. The maps of Europe and of the New World had been redrawn. The winds of democracy were blowing through the social order, and religious life in western Europe again lay in ruins. One study maintains:

> On the eve of the French Revolution, worldwide membership in all the men's religious orders stood at approximately 300,000; by the time the Revolution and the secularizations which followed had run their course in France and the rest of Europe, fewer than 70,000 remained.[29]

The Jesuits had been suppressed by the church at the instigation of the Bourbons. Some orders had been suppressed by the state; others died by attrition. The following description of the situation sounds in some ways familiar: "The few scattered religious who remained were old and shell-shocked. Some prophets of doom predicted the demise of religious life as a whole." But note how the passage closes, "in fact, the way had been cleared for a revival and recovery of religious life."[30]

In the nineteenth century situation numerous congregations were founded dedicated to apostolic life, especially teaching. Old orders like the Dominicans and the restored Jesuits devoted vast numbers of their members to that apostolate. Education was a critical need of the time, made more urgent by the combination of immigration (on a scale not seen in the previous fifteen hundred years) with the rise of democracies. In these circumstances many if not most religious found their apostolic identity as educators. Here one meets women like Elizabeth Seton and men like John Bosco. The ecclesial identity of religious was shaped in a church closed to the movement of the times and increasingly centralized on the papacy.

Yet in the church's outlook on religious life the first harbingers of change could be detected. I will single out three. Pius IX was concerned with the quality of candidates for religious life. In a ten year process dedicated to preparation of a document on religious life, it became apparent that one problem was the practice of admitting sixteen-year-old candidates directly to solemn vows. The change suggested by the papacy was to oblige all orders and congregations to permit a three year period of simple perpetual vows before solemn profession. Superiors general were opposed; they feared the loss of vocations and economic damage from the delay of priestly ordinations. The pope convened the superiors general in Rome in 1854 to point out that economic interest simply must cede to the internal reform of the orders. He himself wrote an introduction to the decree enforcing the new arrangement.[31] There he urged on religious the need to insert themselves more in the pastoral ministry through association with the secular clergy. Are there not here foreshadowings both of today's concern for quality over quantity of candidates for religious life, and of the present thrust toward closer collaboration in the apostolate?'

This evidently concerns male religious. What of the women? Numerous women's congregations were founded in the nineteenth century. This is one of the factors that led Leo XIII in 1900 to clarify the status of religious with simple vows; he recognized them as true religious.[32] Following his lead and that of the Norms of 1902, Canon 488 of the 1917 Code identified such congregations of either sex as religious. Their status remains unchanged by the present universal law.

A third indicator of change appears in the early twentieth century. It concerned the education of religious, especially sisters. Sisters in this country began full-scale attendance at institutions of higher learning in 1918 in response to state and regional certification requirements for teachers, and of hospital accrediting agencies for registered nurses. In 1941 Sister Bertrande Meyers, D.C., in her doctoral thesis, "The Education of Sisters," attempted to evaluate the effects on women religious of this large-scale attendance at Catholic and secular colleges and universities. The book revealed widespread dissatisfaction of major superiors with the education of their sisters. In 1950 the Holy See called an international congress of religious men and women to discuss major problems, including the education of sisters. From such beginnings eventuated the Sister Formation movement in this country, and the establishment of Regina Mundi as an international center for the education of sisters in Rome. Such efforts provided preparation for the women religious who have assumed leadership in the years since Vatican II.

On a broader front the 110 years between 1848 and 1958 were marked by the church's hostility to most of what the modern world has to offer. Pius IX condemned the proposition: "The pope can and must try to achieve a reconciliation and a settlement with progress, liberalism, and modern civilization."[33] Leo XIII condemned Americanism, and Pius X modernism. But during the same years increasingly sophisticated historical studies paved the way for the liturgical revival and the renewal of biblical scholarship. The definitive loss of papal temporal power, two world wars, and the unleashing of the atom in effect created a different world. By the mid-twentieth century the time was once more ripe for renewal. It is not surprising that a crowning achievement of John XXIII's council is the pastoral constitution on the church in the modern world.

Vatican II's teaching on religious life marks the conclusion of these two centuries and the turning toward an as yet open future. We are familiar with the principal documents: <u>Lumen Gentium</u> and <u>Perfectae Caritatis</u>, together with Paul VI's <u>Ecclesiae Sanctae</u> which gives the norms for implementation of the renewal required by the two conciliar documents. With these one ought to include Paul VI's exhortation to renewal, <u>Evangelica Testificatio</u>.[34] Vatican II's treatment of religious is in keeping with the Council's character as a pastoral Council. In the dogmatic constitution on the church it described the relation of religious to the church. In the decree on religious life, it called religious to the work of renewal. That work has been the task of the last fifteen to twenty years. Religious men and women have struggled mightily to respond to the call of the church that we might be more nearly and more clearly signs of Christ in our troubled world. The story of that struggle is the subject of Kristin Wombacher's contribution to this volume.

Conclusion

From so sweeping a survey is there a conclusion we can draw? I am more inclined to say there are suggestions for reflection. First, as to the situation in which religious life develops. There are three major forms of religious life: monastic, mendicant, and apostolic. I would suggest reflection on the parallel between the situation, the spirit, the ethos of an age and the form of religious life that developed in that age. We saw an ordered society in empire and in monastery. We saw feudal-style relationships in society and in the transformed monasteries. There was a correspondence between the life and work of the friars and the mass movements of the late twelfth and early thirteenth centuries. Later, as the emerging nation states sent out their generals and explorers, so the church sent out its societies of apostles and missionaries. If this be true, it is also true that the world has changed radically these last two hundred years! What is the new form that will correspond to the new age? May it be found among the Missionaries of Charity? No. Admirable as are Mother Teresa, her Sisters, and their work, this group of missionaries represent the adaptation of post-Tridentine apostolic life to a twentieth century need, and not a truly new form of religious life. In fact the flourishing situation of traditional forms of religious life in the third world countries rather confirms the correspondence between the situation in those countries and the first world situation which originally gave rise, for example, to the women's apostolic congregations of the nineteenth century. While it is apparent that earlier forms of religious life retain validity as they adapt to meet new situations, the question here is whether under the influence of the Spirit the church will be blessed with a form of religious life springing from the situation of the western church in the late twentieth century.

This brings us to a second area for reflection: points at which a changed sense of ecclesial identity is recognizable. Here there are a number of possibilities. Lozano has remarked that study of the new constitutions of women religious reveals a feminist spirituality,[35] a spirituality which I believe has been appropriated and reflected in governmental structures. It is more than simply possible that a transformation of women's apostolic congregations is underway which will rival in significance the transformation of monastic life in the second half of the medieval period. At the same time one must consider the significance of the ecumenical community at Taize, of the hidden apostolates of the Little Brothers and Sisters of Jesus, of the growth of the secular institutes, and of the phenomenon of the "non-canonical" communities. All offer material for discernment of where the Spirit is leading dedicated women and men. Here finally Gamaliel's principle will hold: If an approach is the work simply of women and men, it will fail. If it is of God, no one will be able to overthrow it. . . and its opponents might even find themselves opposing God!

Because religious life is a form of life given by the Spirit for service in, to, and through the church it is of concern not only to its members but also to the broader community of the church and to its bishops. The third area I suggest for reflection has to do with ecclesial authority. It is a direct implication of the shift in relationship between bishops and religious communities in the United States. A review of history reminds us that only in the earlier centuries was relation to the broader church community primarily through the bishop. Through time and the practice of exemption relationship to the great church was increasingly centered on relationship to the papacy. An effect of the papal intervention is to put American religious in more direct contact with bishops. Widening the dialogue at the diocesan level can lead to an appropriate strengthening of the local churches. Whether this will be fruitful for religious life depends (under God) on the trust between the parties, on the quality of the dialogue, and on the type of collaboration that ensues. Be that as it may, as day follows night a new Easter of religious life must follow the Good Friday of these last decades.

NOTES

1. John Paul II, "Letter to Bishops of United States," No. 3, Origins 13 (July 7, 1983),129-133.
2. Ibid. 4.
3. A helpful article covering some of this material is that of M. Batiz, et al.,"Papato," Dizionaria degli Istituti de Perfezione 6, cc. 1120-1171.
4. Use of these questions was suggested by my reading of an unpublished essay by Tom Clarke, S.J.
5. For readable English translations of key works, see Origen (Classics of Western Spirituality; trans. and intro. Rowan A. Greer; New York: Paulist, 1979). Included are "Exhortation to Martyrdom," "Prayer," "First Principles, Book IV," "Prologue to the Commentary on the Song of Songs," and "Homily XXVII on Numbers." See also Origen: The Song of Songs, Commentary and Homilies (Ancient Christian Writers; trans. and notes R.P. Lawson; New York: Newman, 1956). See also H. Urs von Balthsar, Origen. Spirit and Fire: A Thematic Anthology of His Writings (trans. R.J. Daly; Washington: Catholic University, 1984).
6. Peter Brown, The Making of Late Antiquity (Cambridge, Mass: Harvard, 1978) 84.

7. See Athanasius: The Life of Antony and the Letter to Marcellinus (Classics of Western Spirituality; trans., intro. Robert C. Gregg; New York: Paulist, 1980).

8. Louis Bouyer, The Spirituality of the New Testament and the Fathers (trans. Mary P. Ryan; New York: Desclee, 1960) lists the principle sources on Pachomius, pp. 321-325.

9. See W.K.L. Clarke, trans., intro., notes, The Ascetic Works of St. Basil (London: SPCK, 1925).

10. For a helpful edition see Timothy Fry, et al., eds., The Rule of St. Benedict in Latin and English with Notes (Collegeville, Mn.: Liturgical Press, 1981).

11. See "Papato," DIP 6, c.1121,for a list.

12. For the complete text in English, see Stevenson, ed., Creeds, Councils, and Controversies (London: SPCK, 1975) 324-333.

13. Canon 23 refers to "certain clergy and monks" who spend protracted visits in Constantinople "causing tumults, and troubling the order of the Church, and subverting other men's houses." Stevenson 330. Jerome, Ep. 22, offers this description of "a very inferior and little regarded" kind of monk:

> These live together in twos and threes, but seldom in larger numbers, and are bound by no rule, but do exactly as they choose. A portion of their earnings they contribute to a common fund, out of which food is provided for all. In most cases, they reside in cities and strongholds and, as though it were their workmanship which is holy and not their life, all that they sell is extremely dear. They often quarrel because they are unwilling, while supplying their own food, to be subordinate to others. It is true that they compete with each other in fasting; they make what should be a private concern an occasion for a triumph. In everything they study effect; their garb is of the coarsest. They are always sighing, or visiting virgins, or sneering at the clergy; yet, when a holiday comes, they make themselves sick--they eat so much (Stevenson 177).

Note too in Benedict's Rule, c.1, the two groups of monks whose ways the founder considers fitter "to be buried in oblivion than to be the subject of our discourse."

14. Space forbids treatment of the canons regular and the military orders, although one might argue for equally significant consequences deriving from events in the history of these groups.

15. See "Papato," DIP 6, c.1130.

16. See Bede, History of the English Church and People IV 23.

17. See "Papato," DIP 6, c.1132.

18. For sources and literature on the thirteenth century mendicants, see H.-G. Beck et al., From the High Middle Ages to the Eve of the Reformation, trans. Anselm Biggs (Montreal: Palm, 1970) 676-682. In H. Jedin, ed., Handbook of Church History IV.

19. On the whole issue see M.D. Lambert, Franciscan Poverty (London: SPCK, 1961).

20. For the account see Regis J. Armstrong and Ignatius C. Brady, trans. and intro. Francis and Clare: The Complete Works (New York: Paulist, 1982) 209.

21. See constitution "Periculoso."

22. William V. Bangert, A History of the Society of Jesus (St. Louis, Mo.: Institute of Jesuit Sources, 1972) 44.

23. John O'Malley, "The Fourth Vow in its Ignatian Context: A Historical Study," Studies in Jesuit Spirituality 15 (1983) 44.

24. For the complete English text see "Decree concerning reform" in H.J. Schroeder, Canons and Decrees of the Council of Trent: Original Text with English Translation (St. Louis: Herder, 1960) 232-253.

25. For the complete English text see "Decree concerning regulars and nuns" in Schroeder 217-231.

26. See "Circa Pastoralis," May 29, 1566.

27. See bulls of March 14, 1509 and Feb. 27, 1510. For treatment of this subject see E. Jombert and M. Viller, "Cloture" in Dictionnaire de Spiritualite 2 cc. 979-1007.

28. Joseph Leonard, trans., The Conferences of St. Vincent de Paul to the Daughters of Charity 4 (Westminster, Md.: Newman, 1952) 264.

29. Lawrence Cada, et al., Shaping the Coming Age of Religious Life (New York: Seabury, 1979) 38.

30. Ibid.

31. See "Neminem latet,"discussed in DIP c.1165.

32. See "Conditae a Christo, "Dec. 8, 1900.

33. Syllabus of Errors, No. 80; DS 2980.

34. All four documents are conveniently published together in Austin Flannery, ed., Vatican II: The Conciliar and Post Conciliar Documents (Collegeville, Mn.: Liturgical Press, 1980).

35. See John M. Lozano,"Trends in Religious Life Today," Review for Religious 42 (1983), 481-505, with discussion of this question pp. 487-489.

American Religious Life Since Vatican II:
Changes and Continuity

by

Kristin Wombacher, O.P.

Although the title of this presentation refers to American religious life, I shall not be addressing religious life in America. There is no single American experience of religious life. Certainly North America and South America have had very different experiences as have Canada and the United States.

What I should like to do initially is to look at the changes in religious life from four different but related perspectives, each with its own significance and value. In the second part of my remarks, I shall touch briefly on continuity and then attempt to describe religious life in the United States at present. This description will indicate the results of the changes and continuity of the past, the present reality with which we must deal now in order to move with real hope into the future.

In order to set the stage for discussing the change in religious life since Vatican II, let me quote from the Vatican II document, Perfectae Caritatis, Appropriate Renewal of Religious Life, promulgated in October 1965, because, in fact, this was the starting point.

> The manner of living, praying and working should be suitably adapted to the physical and psychological conditions of today's religious and also, to the extent required by the nature of each community, to the needs of the apostolate, the requirements of a given culture, and the social and economic circumstances everywhere, but especially in missionary territory. . . . The way in which communities are governed should also be reexamined in the light of these same standards.

And then at the end of the paragraph, to make sure we got the point,

> This task will require the suppression of out-moded regulations.[1]

The wisdom of the Second Vatican Council, which is truly a prime example of the miraculous power of the Holy Spirit, urged women and men religious out of the medieval cloister era into the contemporary world. In the imagery of John XXIII, the window was thrown open and the spirit of aggiornamento swept through.

Adaptations

And so we began--hesitantly, at first--modifications in prayers, dress, daily practices:

Remember nine psalms and nine lessons at matins after a hard day at work? The format of praying was shortened and varied; modest, meager allowances on a trial basis; talking to one another outside formal recreation, modified veil, raised hemlines, colored shirts, changes in schedule; and the excitement of going to K-Mart alone. These first changes, I will call adaptations. They seemed monumental at the time, but in fact these were the external changes requested and expected by Rome in terms of adapting to the contemporary needs and circumstances of our time and culture. While such adaptations were often very obvious, because they were usually external and very visible, they were really the least significant changes in themselves. Still these minor external adaptations opened more windows and led to many, much more significant changes.

Maturation

For soon our chapters moved beyond the adaptations of externals to much more substantive issues. We turned to writing identity statements. Now, the problem here was that everyone in the congregation was to be included and so polls, questionnaires, committees, study projects, position papers and proposals proliferated. That is, individual opinions were sought, ushering in the breakdown of what I have come to call the "herd mentality." To paraphrase the man-in-the-grey-flannel-suit (it existed in the business world as well), the religious-in-black-brown-and-white habit were no longer a collective entity. This movement toward individuality occurred in other areas as well. It was not always planned--actually, at times it was against the operating norms of the day. But still, little by little religious began slipping away from institutional apostolates to other works--deviants first. Plus, the congregational summer retreat for hundreds gave way to private directed retreats and spiritual direction. In many ways, the herd was out of the corral and wandering far and wide. In this Phase 1 (there are going to be three phases in this second process of change), the emphasis is on increasing individuality and becoming one's self.

In Phase 2, however, which was sometimes following, sometimes concurrent with Phase 1, we sought out and struggled to develop closeness, intimacy, and deep personal sharing. Some tried setting up small experimental living situations--again, deviants first. But the struggle, whether in experimental houses, conventual houses, or in the work-place, was for intimacy, depth-sharing, or at least "depth-listening." And it was, at the time, a very painful struggle. Attempts were also made to introduce a more personal faith-sharing into communal prayer, and if this was not accepted then some religious formed faith-sharing prayer groups. With the onus of particular friendships dispelled, friendships within and without our religious congregations flourished. And so rewarding was this human contact so long forbidden, that many left to live out the relationship or to feel freer to develop such human relationships. Much of our focus or absorption during this second phase was on interpersonal relationships, the quality of our living situation, and primarily within congregational experiences. And so the goal here was intimacy and interpersonal relationships.

In time, though, we moved to Phase 3, and we turned from identity to mission statements. The concern here was with our service to others outside our congregations. Diversity in ministry was by now an accepted fact, and decisions about apostolates were mutually discerned rather than unilaterally appointed. If unilateralness was operative--it was on the part of the individual religious, because at this point no superior would dare. In fact individual religious were often expected to find their own jobs or ministry. Living situations also became increasingly diverse. In the good old days, one could move from convent to convent (naturally with permission and before 6 p.m.), and know exactly what the "horarium" prayer form would be. But no more. More and more individual religious and individual houses began making local decisions. And often these decisions were influenced by ministry. Increasingly the place, time and demands of ministry took precedence over the local living situation. And so in this Phase 3, the emphasis was on mission, ministry, and doing for others.

In all three phases of this second process of change, the pendulum had swung from a "herd" to a "jungle" mentality with individuality at its peak.

This whole second process of change was much more than adaptation. What we did here involved more than the mere external changes spoken of earlier. If I can use as overriding labels: Identity, Search for Intimacy, Mission, I would like to suggest viewing these three phases of this second level of change in terms of maturation. For some time I have mused over the similarity between these three phases of change in religious life and three of Erikson's stages of the human life cycle: --identity formation in adolescence, young adulthood where the task is intimacy, and the adulthood stage where the task is generativity of service for others. If I may be so bold ("bold" isn't the word--it's probably "critical"), I would say that pre-Vatican II religious life, at least in the mid-20th Century was an archaic and childish way of life. And by "childish" I mean passive, compliant and dependent. While the first process of adaptation dealt with the archaic dimension, maturation into adulthood was necessary to deal with the childish dimensions. And so we moved from being passive, compliant, and dependent through various stages of maturation toward becoming active, dynamic, and independent.

Reflecting on the difference between 1964 and 1984, I think it is safe to say that we have grown, both as individuals and as religious congregations. However, let me elaborate somewhat on the three Eriksonian stages here, because it will highlight my attempt to describe religious life in the present in a later part of the paper.

It may be of interest to note that I am going to use a 1982 book that Erikson has written called The Completed Life Cycle. I will presume a familiarity on your part with Erikson's overall theory of human growth and development. It is based on two principles: the epigenetic principle, meaning simply that success in each stage of the cycle depends on the successful movement through previous stages. For instance, if a person has not dealt well with identity, there will be some kind of distortion or difficulty with all the stages that follow. The second point that Erikson also brings to his theory is that human development always takes place within a psycho-social context. What Erikson means by psycho-social context, is that at any stage of development there is always someone else out there, influencing the process. For the infant, it is the mother; in school age, it is the school environment; and as we move on through the three phases I will be talking about, it will be the sub-culture and/or the culture/society the individual lives in. So in adulthood, we do not mature in isolation. We mature in relationship to the society/culture or the sub-culture we are a part of.

Very quickly then, the three stages that we are concerned with tonight:

Identity Formation: Erikson states: "The process of identity formation emerges as an evolving configuration--a configuration that gradually integrates constitutional gains, idiosyncratic libidinal needs, favored capacities, insignificant identifications, effective defenses, successful sublimation, and consistent roles."[2] "The basic pattern of identity will be strongly influenced by the selective acceptance and regulations of the individual's childhood identifications."[3]

During identity formation the whole gamut of roles lies before the individual. They "repudiate" or ignore some, and they "select" and take on others. In this process the young person gradually develops a sense of "who I am" and "where I stand in relation to the world around me." Erikson's stress on the psychosocial context is evident in his insistence that in addition to a sense of "I-ness" and role clarifications, the individual must also develop some sense of a world view and ideological values. Identity then depends on a sense of "I-ness,"--"who I am," and a world view--"where I fit into the world around me." Failure to acquire a sense of identity results in identity diffusion--feelings of confusion, disorientation, and a lack of direction. In identity diffusion, the tendency will be to either fit in with surrounding pressures (that is, take on the identity of other people, which is never really one's own) or to fight continually those around in order to try and clarify one's own sense of self. The identity phase results in either identity formation or identity diffusion.

Intimacy: The young adult who has developed a sense of identity is eager and willing to fuse with others and share with others in sexuality, work, or friendship. A lack of identity makes intimate relating a very fearful experience, leading to isolation or merely superficial relating. Now, while it is true that many psychologists would put emphasis on sexuality as the key element, Erikson talks of intimacy as more than sexual expertise. Erikson states, "The intimacy now at stake is the capacity of commit one's self in concrete affiliations which may call for significant sacrifice and compromise."[4] So, following identity formation, the young adult needs to develop the capacity for intimacy. Failure to develop this capacity leads to "isolation," which is "the core pathology of early adulthood," and a frequent "regressive and hostile reliving of the identity conflict. . ."[5]

Generativity: Generativity includes, of course, procreativity--the actual bearing and caring for children. But Erikson also includes "productivity and creativity."[6] I would like to translate Erikson's "productivity" as "service," because I think it fits more our linguistic description and it is not contradictory to what Erikson means by productivity. Having reached maturity, adults develop a sense of what Erikson calls care: "a widening committment to 'care for' the persons, products/services, or ideas," that one has brought into being.[7] Erikson goes on to say: "Today . . . a new generative ethics calls for a universal care, concerned with all children. . . . Such new caritas, would make the developed (first world) populations offer developing (third world) populations more than just . . . food packages, but some joint guarantee of a chance for the vital development as well as mere survival of every child born."[8] Erikson explains that if adults do not develop a sense of generativity, then they will experience "stagnation, boredom, interpersonal impoverishment. Such persons end up indulging themselves as if they were their own . . . one and only child."[9]

Now my thesis is this: there are strong indications that individual religious and religious congregations have entered the generative stage, and rightly so. As individuals we are adults and hence the adulthood stage is where we ought to be. Plus, religious men and woman, dedicated to the service of others, fit most appropriately in that Eriksonian stage of maturity where life-giving care is the predominant role. As religious congregations, the generative stage is again fitting since Erikson contends that all institutions by their very nature provide in generative ways for successive generations.[10] What he means by that is, an institution can provide a generative, caretaking service in a way no individual can. Principals and teachers come and go but the school goes on. The institution continues to provide service and care even though the individual caretaker may be changed. Pastors and priests may come and go, but the parish continues. So institutions by their nature provide for a continuing and on-going generative care for others. Clearly the generative stage is where we as religious individuals and as congregations should be. But having a mission statement is no proof that we have achieved generativity fully or without distortion, any more than an identification card which says a person is 21 proves identity formation, or a marriage license proves the capacity for true intimacy. Remember, unsuccessful dealing with stages along the way leads to distortion or difficulty in future stages.

In the service of time, I have been very selective from Erikson to illustrate not only the task of the three stages--Identity Formation, Intimacy, and Generativity,--but also to describe the possible distortions that may occur due to incomplete or partial passage through these maturational stages. I will again be selective in order to shed light on the kinds of problems that emerge in the generative stage from the unsuccessful dealing with:

1 - The stage-specific task of generativity.

2 - The intimacy stage.

3 - The identity formation stage.

1. **Problems in generative stage from unsuccessful dealing with generativity:** Erikson states: "Where the experience of generative enrichment fails altogether, regression to earlier stages may occur either in the form of an obsessive need for pseudo-intimacy or of a compulsive kind of preoccupation with self-imagery--and both with a pervading sense of stagnation."[11] Successful identity formation and the successful development of a capacity for true intimacy does not guarantee success in the generative stage. Individuals whose life does not include some kind of service and care for others become increasingly self-absorbed, focused on their own needs and wants, and bored with life in general. Interests tend to narrow and early invalidism or psychosomatic concerns provide an excuse to "receive" rather than "give" care.

Mission, ministry and our commitment to serve others does not prevent religious from experiencing stagnation. There are religious who do not feel their work is life giving, who do not feel that they are really caring for and bringing about life in others. Over time such religious question the value of their service, the value of their commitment and the value of their religious identity.

2. <u>Problems in the generative stage from unsuccessful dealing with intimacy</u>: Again quoting Erikson:

> Intimacy and generativity are obviously closely related . . . For intimacy remains the guardian of that elusive and yet all-pervasive power in psycho-social evolution, the power of communal and personal style: which gives and demands conviction in the shared patterns of living; guarantees some individual identity even in joint intimacy; and binds into a way of life the solidarity of a joint commitment to a style of production/service.

That is, the successful passage through the intimacy stage insures the capacity for true generativity, service, and care for others. But authentic intimacy demands concrete and specific <u>affiliations</u>, "which may call for significant <u>sacrifice and compromise</u>."[12] And it is these affiliations that lead to the capacity for social solidarity which in turn is essential for joint commitments.

In other words, persons who do not deal well with the intimacy stage, may have individual intimate relationships but if they have not dealt with intimacy in such a way that they can affiliate deeply with others, in such a way that they can sacrifice and compromise, in such a way that they can form in solidarity with others, then such persons will not be able to develop a sense of joint commitment in the service and care of others. A good example is the "swinging singles" person who may experience a high degree of sexual intimacy but who does not have the ability to really make an affiliative connection with another person. Such an individual cannot provide an environment in which to bear and raise children in a truly life-giving and generative way. So too, individuals who have difficulty with the sacrifices and compromises necessary to affiliate with others, will have great difficulty in forming social solidarity with others. Therefore they will have difficulty in the generative stage in dealing with joint or true care for others.

This inability to come together in true solidarity is not uncommon in religious life today. There are not a few religious who in their ministry and in other areas of their life are active and contributing "team members." But put them at a community day, chapter, or assembly--and affiliation and solidarity became much more difficult. The next stage may explain why.

3. _Problems in the generative stage from unsuccessful_
dealing with identity formation: The precursor of generativity in the identity stage is wanting to take leadership as
well as followership roles. Erikson states, "Where a person
cannot obey or give orders, he (or she) must make do with a
kind of isolation which can lead to withdrawal."[13]
Erikson's diagram of the life cycle indicates that leader-
ship/followership role clarification needs to have taken place
in the identity formation stage if healthy generativity is to
be achieved.[14] If not, individuals will experience authority diffusion.

One of the tasks of identity formation is the selective
affirmation or repudiation of roles. Is it possible that
religious have repudiated the role of superior and with it
authority and leadership? Erikson says that "role repudiation
results in resisting or fighting such roles or persons as
alien to self, which often result in diffidence, apathy, or
outright defiance."[15].

Evolution

Now at the same time that religious were adapting and
maturing, another process was occurring. I suspect it is this
third process of change that (despite doing what the Vatican
II documents called us to do) occasions some tension between
U.S., religious and Rome. I would like to call this third
process of change "_evolution_." First of all I would like to
point out that the Second Vatican Council was not the real
initial agent of change. The Second Vatican Council happened
because the Roman Catholic Church, like all groups, people,
institutions, nations and cultures is part of the world, part
of creation history, and there subject to the same evolutionary process. Despite the image of an immutable, mono-
lithic, stable church, we all know that the church has evolved
and changed over the years. Surely Vatican II was a major
transition point for the church. McBrien describes it as "the
movement from a Church of cultured confinement . . . to a
genuine world Church."[16] But the "global village" concept
was already a coined McLuhanism in the '60's prior to the
Council, and it described the changes already recognized and
occurring in our world society. My point is, the church and
the world travel the same path. That is, the church is part
of the world, truly a graced and privileged part, but still a
part. And therefore, the Church is also part of God's evolutionary plan. Just as the world society has moved over the
millenia, from tribe/village/clan through city/state/ nation
to the "global village," so too, the church has moved from a

small, local Jewish community-gathering through a national, Western Civilization Roman Catholic church to a world church. Was it a coincidence that the social unrest of the 60's and the dramatic changes of Vatican II happened in the same decade? Was it a coincidence that as religious sought their identity, their rootedness in their founders and foundresses, that the mini-series Roots, which spoke to identity and rootedness, broke all records for viewing audience? I think not! The world and the church are on the same journey. And so, again, women and men religious of the United States, freed from an archaic life style and maturing into more active, dynamic, independent, generative adults, found themselves also in the midst of a worldwide societal shift. In Toffler's words, it is a shift from a "second wave" industrial civilization, where nations were supreme, to a "third wave" technological civilization, where every people, culture, and society share the same backyard. If you have read any of the futurists—Toffler's Third Wave, Naisbitt's Megatrends, Ferguson's Aquarian Conspiracy,—you know that the move from second to third wave is not just another move to bigger, faster, more. Industrialism was much more than an economic, social, or political system. It was a way of life and a way of thinking. In fact, it was primarily a way of thinking. And the real change from second to third wave civilization is a change in thinking, in perceiving, understanding, and conceptualizing.

According to Toffler, the thinking of any civilization is affected by the imagery that explains and gives meaning and understanding to its experience. So, primitive people interpreted natural phenomena as the work of the gods. The imagery of the world, or worldview, (remember, world view is important for identity formation) that was the controlling factor in second wave or Western Civilization was Newtonian Science.[17] I will not go into a lengthy description of Newtonian Science here. Suffice to say that the Newtonian world view was based on a universe that was an understandable and predictable machine. Everything from the heavenly bodies to the smallest atom followed simple and mathematical rules and laws. It was a law-dominated image of the world. And buried within this world view was the implication that people in society, like atoms, also behaved according to fixed laws and each in the same way. So, Darwin came up with laws for social evolution, and Freud came up with laws for human psychology. And in time, Henry Ford came up with replaceable workers on the assembly line, and the Church came up with replaceable religious in the classroom or replaceable priests in the parish. Second wave industrial, machine-like, law-determined thinking, while not the same as, is highly compatible with "passive, compliant, and dependent" childish existence. You simply follow the rules and do as you are told. Toffler insists that much of today's societal confusion is the cultural war between second and third wave. Second wave thinking, based on Newtonian science has been repaced by Einstein's Theory of Relativity, Heisenberg's Uncertainty Principle, and Bertalanffy's General Systems Theory. The result in the third wave world view is that of an "open system." This means that you can't isolate aspects of the universe as you could isolate the atom. The universe is an open system; its parts are always in relationship to one another. It is a play of variables, not isolated predictable atoms, but diverse variables that are no longer subject to predictable laws, but can react in a number of different ways. It is no longer an either/or world, instead there are multiple options that govern our universe. And this reality applies to individuals, groups, organization, and even globalism, i.e., group at a planetary level. The fact is that our 20th century world view has changed. Just when religious needed a clear world view in order to formulate an identity, they had to do it in a society in which the world view was in the midst of a major change.

Now in terms of our topic, the church, being part of the world, was also affected by this change from second to third wave. The Pastoral Constitution on the Church in the Modern World said, "The human race has passed from a static concept of reality to a more dynamic and evolutionary one."[18] McBrien in his book Catholicism, attributes the shift from pre-to post-Vatican II theology to a fundamental shift in methodology (which is really a way of thinking), from classicism to historical consciousness.[19] Classicism--"the philosophical world view which holds that reality (truth) is essentially static and unchanging and unaffected by history. Such truth can readily be captured in propositions or statements (laws) whose meaning is fixed and clear from century to century."[20] Whereas historical consciousness "is a theological and philosophical mentality which is attentive to the impact of history on human thought and action, and which therefore takes into account the concrete and the changeable."[21] In the '50's the emphasis in moral theology was on the individual act (like the isolated atom) to determine whether or not it fell into the category of sin, and if so, whether it was mortal or venial.[22] In other words, an act is performed by some human being in a given context. In a pre-Vatican II perspective, what the context is or who did it are not given the importance they deserve. What we want to look at is whether or not it was sin. And if it was a sin, was it mortal or venial? "Stress was placed on obedience to the law--divine, natural, human. The 'good' is what is commanded by law and therefore conformity, with law is the fulfillment of the good"[23] Back then it was simple. There was no decision. Oh, you did have to make a decision whether you were going to be good or bad. But it was an either/or decision. And in following the laws we remained passive, compliant, and dependent. McBrien goes on to say, though: "The moral theology founded on historic consciousness stresses a personal (I would say, adult) responsibility to God, self, Church, and the wider human community."[24] It does not reject norms and obligations, but norms and obligations never actually embody the values they espouse. And so while values may be absolute, norms to realize the values are relative in the historical situation.[25] Prior to Vatican II, it was a law-determined church and we simply obeyed. Now we have to evaluate the situation, interpret the norms, and make decisions. And all of this requires that we be adult--active, dynamic and independent rather than passive, compliant, and dependent. This evolutionary process, like the maturational process, has brought us to a position which requires adult, mature responsibility and necessitates ongoing evaluation, interpretation, and decision-making.

Transformation

Finally, I would like to identify a fourth process of change, one I'm going to call transformation. John J. McEleney, S.J., in commenting on Perfectae Caritatis, clarifies the documents' distinction between "adaptations," those changes necessary due to the contemporary needs of our time, and "renewal," and interior renovation of the spirit.[26] Now, without doubt, this interior renovation or transformation has been a key characteristic of religious renewal in the United States. Tillard, in speaking to the Inter-American Conferences in 1977, says that, "The main line of religious renewal in North America is the renewal emphasizing prayer and spiritual encounter with God."[27] He contrasts this to the spiritual renewal of South America--different history, different cultural context and therefore a different spirituality-- which is much more focused on the fact that "God is on the side of the poor."[28] He also makes a comment that in the United States, our stress on prayer and spiritual encounter with God is "the mellow fruit of a privileged situation in the socio-economic order."[29].

I would agree with the importance of such interior renewal over the external adaptation. However, I think there is a danger in seeing adaptation, maturation and evolution as secular and human, whereas transformation refers to sacred/divine and consequently is more important. If you are thinking in those terms, that's very second wave thinking-- either/or, the sacred/the secular, the human/the divine. In fact, maturation and evolution are also very interior proc- esses. And depending on how you look at them, both are very sacred/divine, both are a recognition and response to God's call. Maturation certainly is God's call to become fully human, to become fully what God has created and continues to call people as individuals and groups as congregations to be. And God's evolutionary plan is the call to become fully human at a global level, that is, that his Kingdom may come. So, although one could speculate whether or not the transformation process would have occurred without maturation or evolution there is again a second wave danger in thinking that matur- ation and evolution caused transformation, or that transfor- mation caused maturation and evolution. My guess is that they interfaced, interweaved, and mutually reinforced one another. The point is, some individuals may have begun the process at maturation and then with the changes in evolution and transfor- mation all the processes began to reinforce one another. Others may have begun with evolutionary or transformative changes. But eventually all three levels complimented and strengthened one another.

In the third wave thinking, there will always be a diversity of starting points, and the starting point will depend on the individuals and their particular context. But clearly all three of these processes of change are going to interact and reinforce one another. I think it is fair to say that spiritual direction, directed retreats, and the develop- ment of personal prayer life also increased the diversity in our God relationships. And such spiritual development was increasingly compatible with the maturation of individual's responsibility, and also the changes in theology. McBrien records that the regimented piety of 19th century eventually gave way in this 20th century to a more historical under- standing of human existence. Consequently, "spiritualities began to emerge which are more world-centered (Teilhard de Chardin), . . . justice-concerned (Thomas Merton), and more person-integrating (Josef Goldbrunner), without prejudice at all to the traditional contemplative elements."[30] Such spiritual development was strongly incarnational, social justice-minded, biblical, and gospel-oriented.

I call this fourth change "transformation." It is similar to but not the same as metanoia or conversion. It is not a turning away from the world, nor is it the identification and conversion of what is negative. Rather, it is an increasingly in-depth transformation of self, group, world at the very heart of who we are, of who God created and calls us to be.

The key to my presentation with regard to this fourth area is that in developing a personal relationship with God, religious became aware of having their own eyes and ears of faith, their own gospel vision, the ability to see and hear God's call in a wide variety of places, which they experienced. And so, religious were no longer dependent on the "switchboard" approach to God's will through superiors--they could dial direct. And in that direct, unique, personal, spirit-filled relationship, religious often found a passionate drivenness that no superior could ever impel, a joyful spending of self that no law could ever demand, and at times there was even a direction that no constitution ever laid out. However, God did not always go by the book. Remember, He asked a virgin to bear a child. The transformation process, then, is based on a deep personal relationship with God and it adds to the individuality seen in the maturation process of the active, dynamic, independent, generative adult; and to the personal responsibility in the evolutionary process which requires evaluation, interpretations, and adult decision-making. This transformation process means we also have to evaluate, interpret and discern what the Spirit is saying.

And so all three of these processes have brought us to the same place, from being passive, compliant, dependent to now being active, dynamic, independent.

*   *   *   *   *

Let me address continuity. In reading over the essential elements of religious life listed in the document, I think these are basically the same pieces that have traditionally been associated with religious life and that will continue to be seen as essential elements of religious life. I don't know of anyone's trying to do away with God's call, vows, community, public witness, faithfulness to founding gift and sound tradition, personal and communal prayer, asceticism, special relationship to the Church. However, while the same pieces remain, they can be rearranged differently and hence take on different functions, like restructuring/redesigning rooms in a house.

In order to see how they could be rearranged, I would like to look at each of the three processes of maturation, evolution, transformation, as cues for the new arrangement.

First of all, the three processes, were necessary movements away from the childish "herd" mentality. The pendulum swung to what I would now call the "jungle" mentality of independence. But the pendulum is still swinging. It made a brief stop at what I would call pseudo-democracy but it luckily kept on moving. Let me return to my often-quoted authors to discern what religious life must now address in order to continue to mature, evolve, be transformed, i.e., to continue to hear and follow God's call. Erikson, in the introduction to his The Life Cycle Completed, says: "My purpose in referring to (earlier papers) is to indicate in what way . . . the overall theory was working towards and yet stopping short of a systematic attention to the ego's role in the relationship of individuality (where we've left all these three processes) and communality."[31] And Toffler insists that to create a sane society, third wave individuals need community. "Community demands more than emotionally satisfying bonds between individuals. It also requires strong ties of loyalty between individuals and their organization." [32] Toffler explains why a sense of community is absent . . . "because there is little sense of shared mission."[33] And Peter Berger, a Lutheran sociologist of religion, suggests that community is that "plausibility structure" which is essential in order for individuals to remember, nurture and renew their religious experience.[34] So, in restructuring religious life, in rearranging the essentials of religious life, I think community moves from being a piece of it--along with vows, prayer life and ministry, to being the very nature and heart of the reality. And consequently community changes both its appearance and its function. This idea is not original with me. In Chapter 20 of Catholicism, McBrien talks about three models of the church. The pre-Vatican II model for church was the institution. This model sees the church as "hierarchically a society that mediates salvation to members through preaching and teaching the Word and administering sacraments."[35] And the key advantage here is, it gives the church a sense of identity and function. The Vatican II model, which was prevalent during Vatican II itself, was that of a community. This model sees the church as "primarily the people of God whose principal task is the promotion and sustaining of personal growth through their own interpersonal relationships."[36] It was community for its own members--it focused on individuals' own development fostered through interpersonal relationships. Then the third, post-Vatican II model of church, which was spoken of first in the documents themselves (primarily "The Church in the Modern World,"), but was made more explicit in later writings from the synods. This model sees the church as a servant model, "the Church is primarily an agent of social change, whose task is the wise and courageous allocation of its own moral and material resources for the sake of the kingdom"--not just for its members but for all mankind.[37] Do you recognize a pattern of identity, intimacy, and generativity,--from institution, to community-for-itself and then service-to-mankind? McBrien concludes by saying, that a true ecclesiology must include all three models. Thus the church is, he says, "an institutionalized servant community."[38].

With all due respect to McBrien, I'd like to change "institutionalized" to "structured," i.e., a structured servant-community. But this is not a community for itself. It is a community that is truly generative, one that is really focused on service to mankind. My point in this paper has been to show that the moves from the childish (passive, compliant and dependent), from second wave (static, law-controlled, hierarchical institution), from ritualistic, regimented spirituality through increasing degrees of maturation, evolution, and transformation, were necessary differentiations which only paved the way for additional movement. These three processes of change brought us first to be truly active, dynamic, and independent individals. But these changes only laid the foundation and the groundwork for further change. And I think this is where we are today in religious life: Needing to move beyond active, dynamic, and independent, to becoming interactive, resonant, and interdependent persons who operate within a structured, mission-oriented, servant-community--And who then, together, in solidarity, can discern, nurture and theologically reflect on the Spirit's message wherever she may choose to reveal it. But, we can't make that next move alone. We can't go on in the same way that we have been changing. The only way we can move from active, dynamic and independent to interactive, resonant, and interdependent is through the appropriate use of community. No person can do it alone. We came from pre-Vatican II to this present stage, somewhat as individuals, following our own path. And we needed to do that because the task was increasing individuality. But from now on, we will become stagnant--the very characteristic of individuals in the generative stage who are self-absorbed--we will remain static, stuck, and stagnant if we do not really come to understand what community means.

Let me speak to community very briefly: community is not the living situation. It is not all going to Great Americas together, it is not dressing alike, and it is not working in the same facility. Community is the result of our bondedness around a common mission, Christ's mission, the Kingdom, according to the spirit and charism of our founder or foundresses as experienced in this particular group. True and authentic community is essential if we are to continue developing in each of these three processes. If we want to continue to deepen our relationship with God and hear the Spirit, we must understand community. Cardinal Suenens says, in his book on Pentecost, that right after the Resurrection, the risen Lord appeared to individuals, but that since Pentecost, the Spirit and the presence of Christ has been made known through community. We are not going to continue the process of deepening our relationship with God if we continue to do it in privacy and only in our own personal reflections. We must become interdependent. McBrien also speaks to this when he says, "We are radically social beings . . . There is no relationship with God, however intense, profound, and unique, that dispenses entirely with the communal context of every human relationship with God."[39] So, not only is the community essential if we are going to move beyond the present, but the continued evolution of the global village also depends on community. We fool ourselves when we think that community is an element unique to the church or religious life. Community is truly the source of all life. It began in the Trinity and it is the destiny of all life in the Kingdom. Teilhard says, "The world and the universe is caught up in a dynamic evolutionary sweep."[40] "The socialization of community is truly the crucial phase in the whole evolutionary process."[41] In like manner, the maintenance of the life cycle and of the maturation process, also depends on community. Erikson explains that the stages of the life cycle and the structure of human communities are part of one evolutionary development. They have the built-in potential to serve one another. He says, "Communal institutions" (I would say "structured communities," only because of the associations we attached to "institution") can be expected to support the developing potentialities of their members."[42]

We might ask: Why haven't our religious communities done this? Why haven't our communities brought us beyond this development of active, dynamic, independent individuals to becoming interactive, resonant, and interdependent? I think this is where we are now as religious. There are some, no doubt, who need to continue maturing, evolving, and transforming because without such differentiation, they will never be able to come together into community, but will in fact return to the "herd." However, I think for most religious congregations, individuals are in some various "jungle" form. And I think that the causes for this can be found in two main areas:

The first is that there is a sense of _authority diffusion_. I think there is a sense of authority diffusion because, rather than having a clarity regarding leadership and membership roles, we have repudiated authority and in so doing, we have also repudiated a healthy sense of leadership-membership. We don't know how to follow and we don't know how to lead. How often have religious congregations searched madly for leaders, either in their institutions or in their congregations? Remember what Erickson said about the repudiation of authority becoming evident in apathy and defiance to any kind of leadership.

The second cause that I think keeps us in the "jungle" issues from a difficulty with the intimacy stage. Among religious there appears to be an unwillingness to _sacrifice_ and _compromise_ in order to affiliate, to truly affiliate, in order to come together in _solidarity_ with others. There is an undercurrent that sometimes says: "It's either _my way_ or no way."

And so, it may be authority diffusion or an unconscious inability to affiliate/form solidarity that keeps us in a "jungle' situation. As a result, we at times become stuck or stagnant. We need to work on and develop our expertise in bringing about true and authentic community within our religious congregation, and I think we need to start with "me"--not with "him" or "her" or "them" but with "me." In what way do I inhibit community from happening? But, I think it will be _this_ very struggle that will be _the_ most life-giving and _the_ most generative dimension of our ministry and mission. For whatever our apostolate, whether it is parish, education, mental health, hospital, social justice-- (my apologies to anyone I left out)--no matter what apostolate we are in, _in addition_ to the service or care we provide in that place or context, we need primarily to build, to form, to create, and to foster community. That is our unique gift and charism as religious: to bring a sense of community. Was it not Paul in _Corinthians_ who said: "If I speak in the tongues of angels . . . if I give away all that I have, and if I deliver my body to be burned, but have not love . . .?" (1 Cor 13:1-3) And interestingly, Erikson uses _"caritas"_ as that virtue which flows from affiliation and solidarity. So, from our own struggle with community, if truly we would <u>give</u> ourselves to that struggle, if we would be willing to compromise, if we would be willing to <u>sacrifice</u>, then hopefully what we might learn in that struggle is how to assess the quality of community wherever we happen to be, to diagnose its problems, blocks, its limitations. And then involving care and service, with <u>caritas</u> we could facilitate, foster, and work with others to create true life-giving generative communities. And in doing this, then, we would be truly carrying out our mission, Christ's mission, that the Kingdom will come. I think the Kingdom comes little by little. We don't so much build it as we generate and allow it to be caught from one another, for truly the Kingdom of God is contagious.

NOTES

1. <u>Perfectae Caritatis, The Degree on the Appropriate Renewal of the Religious Life</u>, no. 3. Cf. Walter Abbott, <u>The Documents of Vatican II</u> (New York: Guild Press, 1966) 469.

2. E. H. Erikson, <u>The Life Cycle Completed</u> (New York: W. W. Norton Co., 1982) 74.

3. <u>Ibid</u>. 72.

4. <u>Ibid</u>. 70.

5. <u>Ibid</u>. 71.

6. <u>Ibid</u>. 67.

7. <u>Ibid</u>. 67.

8. <u>Ibid</u>. 68. [Parenthetical remark added]

9. E. H. Erikson, <u>Identity: Youth and Crisis</u> (New York: W. W. Norton & Co., 1968) 138.

10. <u>Ibid</u>. 139.

11. E. H. Erikson, <u>The Life Cycle Completed</u> 67.

12. <u>Ibid</u>. 71.

13. <u>Ibid</u>. 70. [Parenthetical remark added]

14. E. H. Erikson, <u>Identity and the Life Cycle</u> (New York: International University Press, 1959) 120.

15. E. H. Erikson, <u>The Life Cycle Completed</u> 73.

16. Richard McBrien, <u>Catholicism</u>, (Minneapolis: Winston Press, 1981) 607.

17. Alvin Toffler, <u>The Third Wave</u> (New York: Wm. Morrow & Co., 1980) 128.

18. <u>Gaudium et Spes, The Pastoral Constitution on the Church in the Modern World</u>, no. 5, cf. Abbott, <u>op. cit</u>. 204.

19. Richard McBrien, <u>Catholicism</u> 941.

20. <u>Ibid</u>. 1238 [Second parenthetical term added]

21. <u>Ibid</u>. 1245.

22. <u>Ibid</u>. 936.

23. <u>Ibid</u>. 936.

24. <u>Ibid</u>. 936. [Parenthetical remarks added]

25. <u>Ibid</u>. 942.

26. Cf. Abbott, <u>op. cit</u>. 464-465.

27. Jean Marie Tillard, "Religious Life Tomorrow," <u>Donum Dei</u> 24, <u>Canadian Religious Conference 1978</u>, p. 149.

28. <u>Ibid</u>. 144.

29. <u>Ibid</u>. 152.

30. Richard McBrien, <u>Catholicism</u> 1095.

31. E. H. Erikson, <u>The Life Cycle Completed</u> 16. [Parenthetical remarks added]

32. Alvin Toffler, <u>The Third Wave</u> 384.

33. <u>Ibid</u>.

34. Peter Berger, <u>The Sacred Canopy: Elements of a Sociological Theory of Religion</u> (Garden City: N.Y.: Doubleday, 1967). A Rumor of Angels: Modern Society and the Rediscovery of the Supernatural (New York: Doubleday, 1969) 48.

35. Richard McBrien, <u>Catholicism</u> 711.

36. <u>Ibid</u>. 712.

37. <u>Ibid</u>. 713.

38. <u>Ibid</u>. 714.

39. <u>Ibid</u>. 1181.

40. Hugh McElwain, <u>Introduction to Teilhard de Chardin</u> (Chicago: Argus Communication, 1967) 58.

41. <u>Ibid</u>. 48.

42. E. H. Erikson, <u>The Life Cycle Completed</u> 31.

Religious Life and the New Code

by

Allan McCoy, O.F.M.

The Catholics of the world are challenged by Vatican II and also by the new Code to accept a new way of thinking, as Pope Paul VI asked of us. This implies a genuine conversion on our part. We ask ourselves whether we are willing to actually enter into a new way of thinking. It will not be easy for any.

This new way of thinking will reflect the new way in which the church looks at itself. Prior to Vatican II we accepted a monarchical image of church. At the Council we were introduced to the image of the community of God's people as the basic image of church. Within that community there were to be various services rendered, by the Holy Father, the bishops, priests, religious and laity. All were going to offer service to that community. If we do not enter into this new way of thinking, the new law of the Code could be disastrous for us and possibly for others.

The law is not primarily prophetic. Do not expect to see in the law a vision of where the church is going. We are not going to find there a reflection of the latest reflections and probing of our theologians and social scientists. Even Vatican II, which is thought of as prophetic in many ways, was basically a summing up the good work that had been done up to that time. Through it we were allowed and encouraged to go on to probe the future. The same with law.

Again, observing the law, this code of law from cover to cover, is no guarantee of eternal life. This is here to help us understand the external structures of the church and the relationships we have within that structure. This is not a moral code. We are to have great respect for it as ultimately reflecting the will of Christ, guiding us now to be the people of God. But it is not to be dealt with as a book of casuistry.

Realizing that we are called to a new way of thinking and that we do not have here a moral code, we can see in the new Code a good piece of legislation, one that is not perfect, but which in many ways is an advance over the code of 1917.

It was not long after the promulgation of the code of 1917 that we had many and serious problems with the legislation itself and with its interpretation. As you know, many decrees came out supplanting the various parts of the code. And so we can expect with this legislation of 1983. We have a good work of human beings regulating the external relationships within the church.

What of religious life in the new code? In the code of 1917 we have a great deal of specific legislation for religious life in general. There was danger that the specific gift of the different charisms of religious communities would be lost to the church. As a reaction to this, the proposed draft of 1977 made an effort to respond to the differing charisms by separate legislation for monastic institutes, separated into monks and comtemplative nuns, then institutes dedicated to apostolic works, separated into canonical institutes, conventual institutes and apostolic institutes. The reaction to these classifications was very negative and that from both women and men religious. The code commission actually discarded this draft after the negative reaction. It is easy to imagine why the formulation of the new code has taken such a long time. As an aside I might mention that when word was first received in this country that a new code of Canon Law was to be prepared, the Canon Law Society of American expressed the desire to slow down the process so that we could not have the new version for some five years. Rather than five years, it has taken 20 years.

In this new code we do see traces of certain models or paradigms. The monastic tradition is reflected in the general legislation for religious as is the so-called apostolic model. But one should not get too excited about the fact that there is some conflict in this. This is an attempt to give us some broad principles through which we can express our different charisms or patrimonies. We are not being forced into a monastic paradigm or into an apostolic paradigm reflecting the sixteenth century apostolic life. Whenever you see these various elements expressed you will find that they are expressed with the proviso that they are to be lived "according to the diffent traditions and patrimonies" of the community. An example of this is the needed <u>separation</u> <u>from the</u> <u>world.</u> It is quite clear that this is according to your tradition. What is that tradition? If here in San Francisco you have a small place in the Tenderloin, this can well be separation from the world. Even though the terms are monastic, the monastic paradigm is not being imposed upon other groups.

You will see in the new code a great stress on community. But realize that this is closely connected with the desire of the Church that we work for the Kingdom of God. In the very beginning of the section on consecrated life you will find that we are called to this work for the Kingdom of God. And this will involve for many of us a deep involvement in the things of this world. What is involved in "working for the Kingdom"? This surely means we as people of consecrated life must be dedicated to the values of the Kingdom of God, the values of human dignity, freedom for every last person on earth, the peace which Christ came to give, justice--social, racial, sexual. In this very first canon we are called to be dedicated to these values. This dedication is to be shown in our announcing this Kingdom and its values, modelling them in our own lives and finally working for the accomplishment of this plan of Christ for all our brothers and sisters. Separation from the world, then, must never mean a backing away from this responsibility for the work of the Kingdom. Your own patrimony or charism will call you to the particular way in which you are to be involved.

Do we as American religious have a particular problem in understanding the law of the Church? The answer is clearly "yes!" I would ask you to reflect on your mentality with regard to law. Sharing as we do with many Anglo-Saxons in a tradition of Common Law we see things quite differently from those brought up in a Roman Law mentality. Also, as Americans, our experience of law is different even from that of others who share our Common Law mentality.

First the Roman Law: that is the tradition of law embodied in the Roman Empire. The church has expressed herself in this way through the centuries. This system is surely reflected in the later feudal system where you have the dependence of the ordinary people on the hierarchy of leadership of the day. The emperor was supreme, then the king, then the duke, then the lord, and finally the villeins and the serfs. One's security depended upon the person at the next level. That person's own self interest was served in protecting each of his dependents. They were the ones who fought his wars, maintained his estates. The benevolent ruler symbolized the structure of society. And this concept is very clear in the Roman Law tradition. In England, however, and later in other parts of Western Europe a change took place that displaced the concept of the benevolent ruler. The leaders of the country came to King John with the clear message that even though he might be a truly benevolent ruler, they were not about to trust themselves forever to his successors. They asked for a bill of rights -- the Magna Carta. Those of us who are in this tradition want to know exactly where we stand before the law. We presume that no matter who is leading us, there are limitations to the ruler's powers and our basic rights can be objectively defended. Efforts were made to get some of this aspect of Common Law into the new code. And there is a section on the rights and the protection of the rights of the individual.

Another important aspect of Roman Law was its permanence. The very description of law was that is was in itself permanent. This was well understood in an empire spread over the known world and with very slow communications. And if a law is to be permanent and to be applied in many different situations, it must be adaptable. The question in the case of Roman Law was "What does the law mean?" and "What does it mean for me now?" In our country we do not ask that question. Our question is, "What does the law say?" If the sign reads 35 miles an hour, there is no one within 50 miles except the policeman, and I'm doing 50 miles an hour I still get the ticket. He merely says "Did you not see the sign?" In Italy the situation would surely be different. If the law is meant to protect people and there are no people to be protected the law has a different meaning. In Roman Law countries people ask, "What does the law mean?" They learn to think with the law, to probe it.

In our part of the world, it is necessary to understand the Roman Law approach. Otherwise we can often do harm to others by a false interpretation, a purely legalistic approach, trying to impose a literal understanding of law, using it as a club to beat others into submission to our way of thinking. Another result of our approach to law, asking only what does it say, is that we multiply laws, enact statutes for every possible occasion. It is hard to realize that last year there were some 50,000 laws and statutes passed in the State of California, in our various townships, cities, and counties as well as the state itself. No one knows what the various laws in our state are, and yet we are presumed to know them.

As American Catholics it is important for us to be freed up as it were, not to be caught in a stiff legalism. This freeing-up will bring us respect for law. This would be a response to the Church asking us to think with the church, to probe, to search.

Another interesting trait of the people of the United States, one we share perhaps with the western Canadians, is that we have a relation to law which is almost one of love. Since we are under the impression that we make the laws, they become, in a sense, our laws. And these laws are somehow sacred to us. They are very especially our own. On the other hand, we also have a strange respect for the one who can break out from all the laws of an area--the outlaws of the West, for instance. Billy the Kid has lived on in our imaginations as a kind of hero. There is a strange fascination with the story of the James brothers. As we expanded into new territory there was an exhilaration in breaking out of patterns of the settled area into a whole new world. We might have to be careful that this temptation does not take over in our regard for canon law. The feeling can come, as we struggle with seeming incongruities of the law--"Well, so what?" Let's get beyond this. It might be well to ponder that this temptation is real for us because of our North American history.

When we turn our attention to the law itself, we find that there are two main groups under the heading of Consecrated Life and the Societies of Apostolic Life. Under the heading of Consecrated Life, the two groups will be institutes, namely religious institutes and secular institutes. Besides these two institutes you have the hermits and the consecrated virgins who are not members of any institute. Religious are those who take public vows in community. Their vows are recognized as such by the church and are taken for the Kingdom of God. Members of secular institutes are living a consecrated life in the world, endeavor to contribute to the sanctification of the world, especially from within (Can. 710). There is very little legislation for hermits or for virgins, except for their acceptance as such by the diocesan bishop.

The Societies of Apostolic Life do not come under the heading of Consecrated Life. They resemble religious, but do not take religious vows. They come together in community to pursue the apostolic purpose proper to each society. Some do take the evangelical counsels through a bond other than a vow (Can. 731) Many of our foreign mission societies would come under this heading. Also, the Vincentian fathers and brothers are members of such a society.

Turning our attention now to religious, we realize that theirs is a call to discipleship in a special way. Every Christian is called to discipleship and all Christians need the freedom to follow Christ in His spirit of poverty, his

253

universalization of love and in his obedience to the Father. Religious take these counsels in a radical way through the vows. In doing so they are pledging themselves to "be to the church what the church is to be to the world" (_Perfectae Caritatis_). Religious are to call the church to the values of the Kingdom of God through the radical commitment of the vows. It is very helpful to remember this as we read the code. It is easy to be so concerned about the obligation to observe the vows that one forgets the great challenge to use them for the Kingdom of God. The basic freedom to be obtained through the vows is all important for the mission of the church itself. Recalling the words of Pope Paul VI that we are to enter into a new way of thinking, we might well reflect that the church itself is here for the promotion of the Kingdom, to preach the Kingdom, model the Kingdom and work for the Kingdom. It will be well for us to watch for this as we review the new legislation.

To accomplish the purpose of religious institutes it is important that community be placed in the center of one's life. We are speaking not merely of common life, important as that might be at various times in the life of a religious. community is much deeper. Community is founded in a deep relationship fruitful to the growth of each member. We find religious who for reasons of work, health or study have to live apart from the common life for a time, who, nevertheless, maintain and grow in a very deep community of life.

The question of religious garb is a difficult one. The sign value of a religious garb is something that is greatly conditioned by time and culture. And the different communities have to express their own insights in this matter. Again, having a religious garb or habit does not mean that one is expected to wear it at all times. The recent regulations from the vicariate of Rome, explaining Pope John Paul II's mandate regarding the clerical attire in Rome, is a clear case in point.

I think it is helpful for us to reflect that the entire church is being asked not just to respect the religious life, but to actively foster and promote the life. All Christians are asked to do this. The religious life is seen as a very valuable part of the church's life and of her efforts for the Kingdom of God. Religious are reminded that their autonomy is safeguarded in the law (Can. 586). This true autonomy of the religious communities is very important for any truly prophetic gift to the church.

In the area of obedience, it is good to reflect that the obedience asked of religious by the Code is an obedience according to the constitutions of each community. The vow of obedience we make to God will be mediated by superiors in the church and in our communities. They are to help us discern the will of God for us in the great decisions of our life.

Again, it is important to remember that as religious we too are called as are the clerics of the church to work in a special way for peace and justice (Can. 287) Some seem to think that the work for the peace and justice of Christ's Kingdom is the special domain of the laity. Is it because this work is beneath the dignity of the clergy or of the religious? Or is it because the work is too dangerous? It would have been strange to hear in the days of persecution: "The laity to the lions, not the clergy." Even though there be certain political positions that are not to be assumed by clergy or religious, we are not absolved from taking our rightful place on behalf of God's people in matters of peace and justice.

Reflections on the Document "Essential Elements..."

by

Michael J. Buckley, S.J.

On June 22, 1983, a letter from the Holy Father to the American Bishops was made public. The letter, dated April 3, 1983, called upon the American Bishops to put themselves at the service of religious life in the United States, to encourage and strengthen it during this period of unprecedented numerical decline. The Pope lists seven ways in which bishops are to accomplish this ministry, ranging from general preaching or teaching throughout the church on the nature of religious life, to direct engagement with religious in Eucharist, preaching, discernment, consultation, and in the "church's universal call to conversion, spiritual renewal, and holiness." In order to facilitate and support this ministry, the papal letter enclosed for the bishops a much longer document entitled, "The Essential Elements in the Church's Teaching on Religious Life as Applied to Institutes Dedicated to Works of the Apostolate."[1] This document was dated much later than the papal letter, May 31, 1983, and the Pope variously described it as "a document of guidelines which the Congregation (SCRIS) is making available to (the bishops)," and "the document on the salient points of the church's teaching on religious life prepared by the Sacred Congregation for Religious and Secular Institutes."[2] The Holy Father described this document once again--this time in his <u>Allocutio</u> to a group of American Bishops on September 19, 1983--in the following way: "As guidelines for both the Commission and yourselves in this important work, I approved a summary of the salient points of the Church's teaching on religious life prepared by the Sacred Congregation for Religious and Secular Institutes."[3]

It is this document that I shall reflect upon in this essay. Obviously, I cannot cover each of its subjects, but I should like to divide my remarks into two major sections:

First: The nature of this document in terms of five
           questions:

  1.   To whom was it sent?

  2.   What was sent--what kind of document is
       it?

256

3. What is its authority?

4. What is its theological qualification--a precision on its authority?

5. How is it to be received?

Second: The content and assessment of some of its components.

Finally: Some concluding remarks on its use in the discussion now underway between American religious and the bishops of the United States.

There are two prenotes which I should like to frame before beginning:

First: Although I have been appointed theological consultant to the Pontifical Commission on Religious life, in these reflections I am offering an analysis and assessment that is merely my own. I speak for no one on the Commission, and I assume the full responsibility for these remarks.

Secondly: As the schematic outline of my remarks suggests, I have drawn a very limited focus for this essay. I propose to offer something of an analysis of the text of Essential Elements itself, not an extended commentary on the history of religious life which stretches out from the Second Vatican Council until the present nor an identification of each of the sources of friction which have emerged during this period, nor even an exegesis and evaluation of each paragraph of the text itself. All of these are important considerations, but so also is an actual analysis of what this single document means and what intrinsic authority it possesses. There is always the danger that one reads a particular set of experiences into the document itself and makes it say what it does not say or assume an importance which it does not claim. I have specified the questions that I want to treat. There are other serious questions which present themselves with equal urgency, but some division of labor is imperative if these reflections are to concentrate upon the document as a whole. Since a more extended outline of this essay might be of some service to its interpretation, I have constructed one and appended it at the end.

Now let us consider the document whose title we have shortened to Essential Elements.

Part I

1. To whom was it sent?

As a beginning, I should like to call your attention to the following point: This "summary document on the salient points on religious life" was not sent officially to the religious, not to their general houses nor to their provincial offices nor to their individual residences. It was sent only to the American Bishops. Many religious resented this procedure, but the resentment misses the essential papal point. The events of recent history easily explain how such a misapprehension could have occurred, and why time was inevitably needed to assess the actual import of this document. The document did not deliver new legislation for religious. It provided a shorthand for bishops, to aid them in their ministry of support and encouragement of religious life in the United States. The religious already have _Lumen gentium_ and _Perfectae caritatis_ from Vatican II, the Apostolic Letter, _Ecciesiae sanctae_, and the Apostolic Exhortations, _Evangelica testificatio_, of Paul VI, soon to be followed in 1984 by _Redemptionis donum_ of John Paul II. They have had a continual stream of documents from the Sacred Congregation for Religious and Secular Institutes: From _Renovationis causam_ of 1969, _Dum canonicarum_ and _Sacris religionis vinculis_ of 1970 to _Mutuae relationes_ of 1978, _La plenaria_ and _Le scelte evangeliche_ of 1981. Add to this the documents formative of each institute, documents that express its foundational charism and embody the evolution of a unique religious tradition, and then top all of these off with the Revised Code of Canon Law, and I think it becomes obvious even to the most sanguine aficionado of Roman prose, American religious do not need another new document from Rome. The pile that confronts them already looms formidable and challenging enough.

By the same token, however, the bishops do need some such a compendium. The prospect that each ordinary should take out the time to assimilate and to master the writings directed to religious could present even the bravest bishop with a disheartening demand. The fact of the matter is that the religious have a history of important documentation that stretches back into the centuries, and the bishops have neither the experience nor the opportunity to gain much command of it. Yet the bishops have been commissioned, papally commissioned, to support and encourage religious life by every means available.

Although there are two places within Essential Elements which could indicate that the document was originally drafted to be sent to bishops throughout the world or to religious universally in the church, this is not what happened. It might be helpful to chart what did happen:

(1) Essential Elements claims to be a response to the requests of religious superiors, chapters, and bishops for directives, and--even further: "In this present text addressed to institutes dedicated to apostolic works, this Sacred Congregation confines itself to a clarification and restatement of these essential elements." Finally: "In drawing up this text, which the Holy Father has approved, the Sacred Congregation for Religious and Secular Institutes wishes to help those institutes to assimilate the church's revised provision for them and to put it in its doctrinal context."[4]

(2) Thus, if one simply reads Essential Elements, one would get the impression that it were directed as a response to requests from bishops and religious throughout the church. There is nothing in Essential Elements that indicates that it is directed to American religious in particular or even to the bishops of the United States. If it had been signed by the Cardinal Prefect of SCRIS and published in Acta Apostolicae Sedis, it would have been promulgated by the congregation to the church in general.

(3) But--and this is critical to note--it was not signed by the prefect and consequently not sent by the authority of the congregation as such. It was taken by the Holy Father and approved to be sent to the American bishops and the Pontifical Commission as "guidelines" or as a "Summary of the salient points of religious life." Naturally LCWR and CMSM received copies of both Essential Elements and of the papal letter. But neither the papal letter nor its enclosure, Essential Elements, was officially directed to them. Neither leadership conference possesses an authority relationship with its members. If SCRIS were going to address them officially in a document sent to this or that religious community, it would have delivered Essential Elements to their general superiors and had them communicate it as an official document sent authoritatively to them. This did not happen. What was this communication to them? It was information about an action of the Holy Father that obviously concerned them.

(4) What seems clear is that the congregation composed a document which attempted to summarize the fundamental points

of previous church teaching on religious life. In this sense, one can understand that is was "addressed to institutes dedicated to apostolic works," but in this same sense also, it would have been addressed to religious throughout the world. Now no one, to my knowledge, suggests that Essential Elements was actually sent to religious throughout the world. The fact of the matter is that the congregation neither took official responsibility for this document by the signature of its Cardinal Prefect nor sent it to anyone. It submitted it to the Holy Father who in turn sent it to the American bishops and the U.S. Pontifical Commission on Religious Life.

(5) Obviously the document has religious life in general in mind, and not exclusively American religious life. The pope is using this document for the purpose which he indicated when he sent it, i.e., of aiding the American bishops to achieve the mandate he had given them: "to render special pastoral service to the religious of your diocese and your country."[5]

2. What was sent?

Placed within this context, the scope of the document Essential Elements becomes considerably clearer. It is directed immediately only to the bishops, and it possesses the value that such a summary can obtain. Let me put this as clearly as I can. This document, issued by SCRIS for the American Bishops at the direction of the Holy Father, was intended only as a summary or compendium of the conciliar and papal teaching found in documents such as Lumen gentium, and Evangelica testificatio, and of the Revised Code of Canon Law. The pope obviously approved the final product, i.e., he found it adequate for the task envisaged--to give the American bishops an authentic overview of consecrated religious life, amply treated only in the source materials from which this compendium was drawn.

It is imperative, then, to recognize that the Sacred Congregation for Religious and Secular Institutes has done something both necessary and very difficult. Such a document was necessary if the American Bishops are to possess a compendium statement of the features or traits that characterize religious life. It is equally difficult because the divergent histories of religious orders, from the uniqueness of their founding gifts to their present pluralism and the nuance involved in their form of Christian life, indicate a living reality that inhibits the precision and distinctions of an abstract index. The insistence or recognition that religious life possesses its own identity

dictated that such a document be issued from the Holy See. As
Lumen gentium taught: "Church authority has the duty, under
the inspiration of the Holy Spirit, of interpreting these
evangelical counsels, of regulating their practice, and
finally of establishing stable forms of living according to
them."[6] Without this kind of insistence upon identity,
religious life would scatter and drift rather than develop.
If the american Bishops are to encourage this life, they must
understand something of its generic identity.

On the other hand, the fluidity and diversity of
religious life over the centuries in which it has evolved, the
special character of each religious community, and the "sound
traditions" which arose in its growth disrupt any attempt at
elaborate or particularized definition. The church in
describing religious life is not dealing with an "essence" or
a "substance" in any but the most metaphorical sense. She is
dealing with a series of relationships, a network of
overlapping and criss-crossing similarities between distinct
communities which bear to one another what Ludwig
Wittgenstein, in his Philosophical Investigations, called
"family resemblances."[7] One religious institute resembles
rather than repeats another, as one member of a family will
carry something of the build, the features, the color of eyes,
the gait, the temperament, and the thousand characteristics
that mark brothers and sisters. No one will carry them all,
but there will be enough to characterize them all, enough to
show a common bond. I think that it is this that the
congregation has attempted in its listing of the "essential
elements." Essential Elements is not a definition through
genus and differentia; it is a collocation of characteristics
realized in highly analogical ways that mark the commonality
among religious institutes.

The identity of religious communities makes it necessary
to attempt this description of what constitutes their
character. The multiform history and contemporary application
of the word "religious life" demands that we attend to this
developing meaning as in the spinning of a thread, one fiber
is progressively added to another. The identity of the thread
does not consist in a single fiber running all the way
through, unaltered in the process, but in the continuity and
in the overlapping of many additional threads, one on top of
another as fiber is twisted on fiber.[8] This has been the
evolution of "religious life" in the church, from the desert
communities to the contemporary American convent. Even the
term "religious life" has had a long history. Only recently
has it become a sub-set of "consecrated life" and

distinguished from "secular institutes." These are critical distinctions, and this document notes the recent advancements of the Code of Canon Law in their registration.

This process of the development of more and more divergent forms of religious life will continue. Periodically there have been attempts of the highest religious authorities in the church to curb this abundance, but to little avail. The thirteenth canon of the Fourth Lateran Council in 1215 absolutely forbade any more of them: "Firmiter prohibemus ne quis de cetero novam religionem inveniat."[9] This prohibition was even more elaborately and insistently repeated at the Second Council of Lyons. Yet shortly after Fourth Lateran, Honorius III approved the new Rule of the Friars Minor on November 29, 1223. Again at the time of Ignatius of Loyola, Cardinal Guidiccioni strongly recommended against the foundation of the Society of Jesus, basing his opposition upon the decrees of these councils condemning the "excessive diversity of religious orders"[10] Alas! In the end neither councils nor curia were able to stem more forms of religious life as clerics regular were followed by the extraordinary growth in the active religious orders of women. Mary Ward might spend some time in the inquisitorial prison or the Visitandines be monasticized, but their initial apostolic inspiration would eventually prevail as through trial and steadfastness this evolving movement disclosed the Spirit which lay as its source and inspiration. So also in our time and in the future! Canon law recognizes that the church will develop more forms within religious life and secular institutes and perhaps even other types of consecrated life to meet the religious needs of the Kingdom of God.[11] This document, then, makes no claim to be a compendium definitive for all times, but to express a contemporary synthesis.

3. What is the authority of this document?

Essential Elements is not legislation, and so does not possess the independent directive authority that goes with the legislation of the church. Even more, it is directed not to religious but to bishops, and its purpose is not to command them but to inform them. What authority does it have as teaching, then, if it has none as legislation?

Since it purports to be a summary, it has the authority derived from the documents which it summarizes. As such a summary it possesses also the authority of the papal approval. Please note, however, that it is not the Pope's document. He sends it, approves it, and recommends it, but does not make it

his own, either as an apostolic exhortation or motu proprio.
Even further, it is not strictly speaking a document of the
congregation. It remains unsigned by the cardinal prefect.
It comes from the congregation, but without the affirmation of
ownership that only his signature would have authorized. It
possesses the character of an instruction, but one that merely
highlights what is in other documents, a summary which is
"prepared" and "made available" to the American bishops by the
SCRIS.

What is the value of such a document? It is twofold, in
my opinion: For the American bishops it gives an overview of
the more authoritative documents on religious life to which it
refers. It is not a comprehensive treatment of religious
life. Like any summary, it is uneven and bears the mark and
the theology of those who selected its components and gave
them their order. It indicates their present concerns and
mindsets, both in the way in which it reports previous
legislation or teaching and in the elements which it chooses
to highlight. For just as there are models by which we
understand the church and revelation, so there are variant
models by which we understand religious life--each of them a
helpful perspective from which to view the elements which
enter into religious life, but none of them adequate to its
mystery. But what is offered to the bishops for their
information is neither the theology of religious life that
lies behind this selection nor the implicit model by which
these elements are united, nor a closure in understanding set
by its limits. What is offered to the bishops are the
elements that are contained, the "essential elements" which
should identify this pattern of life in the church. Secondly,
for religious it possesses the additional value of disclosure.
I should like to underline this point: Essential Elements is
as much a statement about the expectations of the Congregation
for Religious and Secular Institutes as it is a statement
about religious life. It indicates certain constants which
this congregation expects to find in religious institutes
submitting constitutions for its scrutiny and approval. This
is also a major service. It is a very serious act for the
church to approve or to endorse a common way of life. This
approval means that the church recommends this manner of
living as a peculiarly efficacious way of living the Christian
life, of moving to the perfection of that charity which is
identifiable with holiness. This document sketches in broad
brush strokes what the congregation looks for in a religious
rule which it could in conscience recommend to the Holy Father
for all of the Christian faithful.

4. What is its theological qualification?

In light of the foregoing discussion, we can see that this is a very difficult and delicate question. Essential Elements carries both the weight of the documents it summarizes—and is to be judged by the accuracy with which it does this—and also the weight of the general papal approval of its adequacy as a summary of salient points, an approval given without making it a papal statement. In no way does it claim to be an addition to the material it summarizes, let alone a definitional teaching of the church about the dogmatic mystery of religious life. It makes no claim to be in principle irreformable. That is to say, Essential Elements cannot a priori be said to be without error, misstatement or theological inadequacy, and like any statement—even a solemn definition—it is limited and historically conditioned.

Perhaps to relieve the formal consideration of these reflections, I might be able to give some examples of the comparative work that must be done before any assertion of Essential Elements can be given its theological qualification.

"Separation from the world" is a classic concept in Christian spirituality, and it denotes the abiding state of election and separation true of all discipleship: "If you belonged to the world, the world would love its own; but the reason that the world hates you is that you do not belong to the world, for I chose you out of the world."[12] If there is any value in religious life it is not that it adds to this basic Christian stance. It is rather that it is a particularly efficacious way of living it out. The monastic life will do it in one way; the apostolic religious life, in another. The Code of Canon Law recognizes this analogy in its legislation for religious: Religious give public witness to Christ and to the church through "the separation from the world (mundo) which is proper to the character and to the purpose of each single institute."[13] If you read this section in Essential Elements, this analogous realization is dropped. Religious life is contrasted with Secular Institutes in these terms: The members of a secular institute are not separated from the world because "of themselves, the counsels do not necessarily separate people from the world," and these secular institutes are "to communicate the love of Christ through their presence in the world and through its sanctification from within." In contrast: "such is not the case, however, with those whose consecration by profession of the counsels constitutes them as religious."[14] Religious, presumably, are to communicate this same love by their absence from the world and from without! Certainly, the authors of this document would not want so stark, even unreal, a contrast to be drawn between religious communities and secular institutes, but it is not forcing the paragraphs to read them in this manner. A comparison with the documents that Essential Elements is attempting to summarize, however, would obviate this reading as would attention to the later description of the mission of the religious as evangelization. Essential Elements, citing Evangelii nuntiandi, describes evangelization as: "to help bring the good news to all the strata of humanity and through it to transform humanity itself from within."[15] Balanced in terms of its sources and in terms of its later statements, various propositions which might seem exaggerated or positively erroneous often take on a reasonableness that first glance seemed to deny.

Part of this difficulty is linguistic. The English word, "world," translates two different Latin words: "saeculum" and "mundus." The Secular Institutes are called by Primo Feliciter to live "in saeculo" and so to sanctify the world "veluti ex saeculo."[16] The Revised Code speaks of these institutes, therefore, in this way: "Ad mundi sanctificationem praesertim ab intus conferre student."[17] Now, "veluti ex saeculo" is not universal to secular institutes, since it does not apply to those which are clerical or to the clerical members of mixed secular institutes. The hallmark, common to all members, is that they are living "in saeculo." Canon 714 specifies the meaning of this "in saeculo" with the phrase "in ordinariis mundi condicionibus." This in turn specifies "ab intus" of Can. 710, a phrase that John Paul II has used a number of times. The "ab intus" means that the members of a secular institute sanctify the world (mundus) through living in the ordinary conditions of the world (mundi) as opposed to the public witness and fraternal (sisterly) common life and separation from the world (mundo) that is typical of religious. This does not mean that religious live outside of the world or attempt to sanctify it by their absence. It means, very simply, that religious live a kind of life that is publically different from the pattern in which it is ordinarily lived (saeculum). The primitive state of the theology which must draw a clearer distinction between secular institutes and religious is far more responsible for the confusion in these paragraphs of Essential Elements than are its authors. But one cannot extol the evolution of forms of theological transition and development. Suffice to say that the reaction to these paragraphs indicates that much remains to be done on the theology of consecrated life and on the prophetic involvement of religious in the world.

Another example might help clarify this further. Essential Elements asserts about the teaching of the Church on religious life:"Most, recently, its doctrinal richness has been distilled and reflected in the revised Code of Canon Law."[18] The papal letter, dated almost two months before, is more modest and, hence, more promising: "Most recently still, much of this doctrinal richness has been distilled and reflected in the revised Code of Canon Law."[19] Note that Essential Elements speaks absolutely, but the omitted qualification from the papal letter is important in any consideration of the adequacy of the new legislation of the church to express the lived experience of religious. The pope claims considerably less for the Code of Canon Law than the document from the congregation.

For a third example: It is interesting also to compare the papal list of essential elements with that from the Congregation. The fourth essential listed by the Holy Father is "fidelity to a specific founding gift and sound tradition." This generic sense of origins and historical developments is placed in the listing of Essential Elements under the corporate apostolate, and the document develops only the fidelity to a specific founding gift extensively.[20] If a similar individual attention had been given to the nature of "sound tradition" as a distinct heading might have elicited, Essential Elements might have been able to obviate what has become one of the strongest and consistent criticisms of the document: A static treatment of religious life which fails both to situate its principles within an historical context and to assimilate the development of religious life and mission over the centuries and especially over the past twenty years. The papal underlining of sound tradition is not new. It is a direct citation from Perfectae caritatis which maintains that the patrimony of any religious institute is both the spirit and aim of its founder and "each institute's sound traditions."[21]

Further: one might compare paragraph 52 with the two sources it cites, Perfectae caritatis 14 and Evangelica testificatio 25, to realize how critically important this continual return to more authoritative documents is for a proper interpretation of Essential Elements. Or compare the statement in paragraph 51 that "supreme authority in an institute is also exercized, though in an extraordinary manner, by a general chapter while it is session," with Canon 631 which attributes supreme authority only to the general chapter.

These examples could be multiplied any number of times, but they should serve not to discredit the document but to underline its nature and give it nuance and above all to suggest a method of interpretation. It is only a "summary document on the salient points of religious life." Where it offers questions, presents problems, or seems to be inaccurate, the documents from which it draws should be checked. To expect it to be more, to expect (for example) that it would provide a theology of religious life as an encyclical might, or to be a scale against which the particular usages of a religious order would be adequately gauged, would be to place a burden upon it that no such summary can bear. My suspicion is that some of the anger and resentment which Essential Elements has occasioned lies with this failure to understand its summary nature and its very limited primary audience, the American bishops in their work with religious.

5. How is it to be received?

If used for the purpose for which it was written, Essential Elements can prove useful to encourage religious life, to reawaken interest in the more important documents which it is to summarize, and to provide an occasion for religious in the United States to enter into serious conversation with their bishops and the church in the United States. As a matter of fact, this is actually what seems to be taking place. A clearer understanding of its purpose might also make its reception considerably more graceful. How is it to be accepted? By religious? Strictly speaking, this is not a question--it was never officially sent to religious in the first place. What it possesses of the discipline of the church has come to them from many other sources. By the American bishops? Obviously with religious reverence, even though there is no question of the absolute assent of faith, with that fundamental openness and respect due to the Holy See and its congregations and with the attempt to understand it as positively as possible in accordance with the purposes it is to serve. Again, there is nothing remarkable here. This kind of openness and attempt at sympathetic understanding is the condition for any Christian interchange. Four hundred years ago, this primary hermeneutical principle was put as the presupposition for making the Spiritual Exercises: "Let it be presupposed that every good Christian is more ready to save his or her neighbor's proposition than to condemn it. If they cannot save it, let them inquire how it is meant; and if it is actually meant erroneously, let them correct it with charity."[22] Many false battles that have riddled religious histories could have been obviated if this presupposition had been followed. One expects soundness and accuracy, and one attempts to understand another in these terms. But this expectation yields to the actual examination of the text, its purpose, its sources and its general context. Where the document is found faulty, these ongoing discussions can advance their corrections or modifications in love. It is a little silly to savage one another over the best way to live the gospel and the call to the perfection of charity.

Part II

With those general reflections upon the nature of the document, let us spend a bit of time looking at its content, both for an analysis of its structure and an occasional assessment of its statements. Time does not allow more.

Essential Elements is divided into four sections: The Introduction of four paragraphs indicates the sources and purpose of the document and leads into a list of the "essential elements," nine characteristics to be found in those apostolic institutes recognized by the church as religious in the technical or canonical sense of that word. The second section moves progressively toward a definition of apostolic religious life through the successive delimitations of the governing concept of "consecration." The third section takes each of those elements termed "essential" and submits it to a process of "clarification and restatement." The last section reduces these reflections to a set of norms to provide "a comprehensive synthesis of the church's provisions." I think that this division of the text is an important step towards understanding it.

What are the "essential elements," that is, what are those traits and practices which the congregation judges characteristic of religious life and necessarily present if it is to recommend it as a way towards the perfect realization of Christian charity? Certainly, it is not each item in the document. There are a number of things here which religious founders have explicitly excluded in their legislation, whether it be the communitarian Liturgy of the Hours with the Jesuits or a fixed garb with the founders of religious communities from Don Bosco all the way back to the days of early monasticism in the church. All of these particulars occur in the third section, the section which deals with "clarifying the essential elements of religious life through a cluster of instances and practices through which a particular characteristic is realized. The "essential elements" are those listed with some significant variance both in the papal letter and in paragraph 4, the climax of the first section of Essential Elements: "The call of God and consecration to Him through profession of the evangelical counsels by public vows; a stable form of community life; for institutes dedicated to apostolic works, a sharing in Christ's mission by a corporate apostolate faithful to a specific founding gift and sound tradition; personal and community prayer; asceticism; public witness; a specific relation to the Church; a life-long formation; and a form of government calling for religious authority based on faith." These are the elements thought essential to religious life, components which must be present and "without which religious life loses its identity."[23]

I doubt if very many religious would be disposed to quarrel with this list, a modification here and here perhaps. Jesuits might mention that their Constitutions forbid obligatory community prayer and Franciscans would add that their order has never had "corporate apostolate faithful to a specific founding gift," but in general this list meets the requirements of "family resemblances." Religious congregations have manifested these traits over centuries, each in its own way, and their likeness to one another consists in their incorporation of these attributes. I say "each in its own way," because, as the Holy Father indicated, these "essential elements are lived in different ways from one institute to another."[24] The abstract index would be profoundly misleading if it led to expectations of its univocal realization. The founding gifts and the rich tradition of each religious order will particularize a form of community life, the nature of their apostolate, the contours of their practice of prayer. While community, apostolate, and prayer will be common to them all, they will only be analogically common. The Dominican sister will be like the Passionist in that they both pray, but the Dominican and the Passionist will realize the distinctive nature of their charisms in that they may pray in very different ways. Analogy here is not so difficult a concept. A few years ago a popular song expressed the kind of analogy appropriate to the essential elements: "Everything is beautiful in its own way." So also of religious institutes, and "their own way" is that pattern of life that gives them identity and makes their presence within the church unique.

The second section moves to a definition of religious life, and it moves to this definition very much as the sixth chapter of Aristotle's Poetics moved to a definition of

tragedy, i.e., by "gathering up a definition," from those
elements that progressively delimit a central concept.[25]
Here the central concept, taken from Lumen gentium, is that of
consecration: "Christians who pledge themselves to this kind
of life (religious life) bind themselves to the practice of
the three evangelical counsels by vows or by other sacred ties
of a similar nature. They are consecrated wholly to God, to
His supreme love."[26] This choice of "consecration" rather
than discipleship, the governing concept of Perfectae
Caritatis, will tell significantly upon the rest of Essential
Elements. There are apostolic religious orders for whom the
central concept is not consecration, but mission and
discipleship--the sense of call by God comes to them through
the religious needs within the world and the community which
they constitute is one composed of those who share this sense
of mission. Mission literally informs their identity,
specifying both discipleship and consecration. In choosing
consecration as the fundamental and governing meaning,
Essential Elements is following one of the current usages in
the church, and this choice will articulate a corresponding
model of religious life.

The Revised Code of Canon Law uses "consecrated life" as
a general designation for life under evangelical vows or other
sacred bonds whether these are private as in a secular
institute or public as in religious life. Essential Elements
follows this pattern in distinguishing religious life from
that of secular institutes. But in the course of this
distinction, Essential Elements expands considerably the
stipulations of the common law of the church. Canon 607 gives
three marks which distinguish religious from members of a
secular institute: public vows, fraternal (sisterly) life in
common, and that separation from the world proper to the
institute of each. In Essential Elements, public vows become
one of the forms through which public witness of consecration
is given, and this public witness takes a priority in the
definition of the religious. This in turn is identified with
separation from the world in contrast with secular institutes
along the lines previously indicated. Under public
witness/separation from the world are clustered (a) public
vows, (b) a manifest form of community life, (c) separation
from family and career, etc. d) corporate apostolate, and (e)
visibility of presence through distinctive ways of acting,
attire, and style of life.[27] When apostolic religious
criticize the mindset from which this document comes as
monastic, the understanding and pivotal place of "separation
from the world" is what is under attack. By equating it with
public witness and specifying this witness in such tangible,

externally visible detail as it does, <u>Essential</u> <u>Elements</u> is suggesting a physical and cultural separation from the world that many contemporary American religious would understand as more monastic than as descriptive of their lives.

After religious life has been defined in general and the "special founding gifts" and unique spirituality of each has been noted,--only then does <u>Essential</u> <u>Elements</u> introduce the apostolic dimension, and it does so as "a further note." The difficulty inherent in such a procedure is enormous. Religious life seems to be adequately defined, and then over and above this for apostolic religious one adds a further modification: "the participation in Christ's mission is specific and concrete."[28] How can such a procedure carry the dynamism of that solemn statement of <u>Perfectae</u> <u>Caritatis</u> which is cited here, namely that "the <u>entire</u> religious life of such religious should be imbued with an apostolic spirit, and their apostolic activity with a religious spirit."[29] Mission is not something added to the meaning of apostolic religious, as if this form of religious life were basically the same as the monastic or contemplative orders with this additional proviso: that they are required to engage in "apostolic activity and charitable services."[30] As a summary document for use by the bishops, such an understanding of <u>Essential</u> <u>Elements</u> might not be damaging; but as a theoretical statement of the nature of apostolic religious life, it will not do. And it leads to such astonishing assertions as the statement that the local community is "the place where religious life is primarily lived."[31] For the apostolic religious that is simply not true. Religious life is lived as much and as intensely in teaching students in the classroom or in the works of social justice or in sacramental ministry as it is in the domestic life of a religious community. Even more: It is often the case that an apostolic religious is united consciously and affectively with God during these times of religious involvement with the lives of others. Genuine apostolic work often gives this religious a privileged access to God, a conscious union with him, that is only available to him or her at this time.

Let me underline this: I think that it is often the case that an apostolic religious comes into a heightened awareness and love for God precisely <u>within</u> the apostolic activity itself. There is nothing particularly novel about this insistence. The <u>Constitutions</u> of the Society of Jesus, solemnly approved by a succession of popes, stipulate that the general is to be "familiar with God both in his prayer and in all of his activities."[32] The present pope in his address of February 27, 1982, put it very well: "There should be no separation between the interior life and the apostolate. These are the two essential and constitutive elements of the (apostolic) life: They are inseparable and they mutually influence and compenetrate each other."[33]

I pause on this point because it seems to me one of enormous theoretical importance, and the definitional procedures here might lead one to envisage the religious needs of others as something in addition to religious consecration. That is simply not true, nor--and this is important to emphasize--would this document wish to assert this. On the contrary, if you turn to paragraph 23, you will find a statement that attempts to see in a more integrated manner the relationship between consecration and mission: "The choice of a person by God is for the sake of others: The consecrated person is one who is sent to do the work of God in the power of God."[34] Then why spend so much time over the movement towards definition? Because the actual method used to articulate the self-understanding of religious life could mislead one as if a general interpretation of the document would find it idealizing monastic life. The congregation has been insistent subsequent to the publication of this document that this was not its intention, and it seems important to face this objection, to articulate it, and to indicate that it is contrary to the purpose of the authors of Essential Elements.

In the third section, the document takes up each one of the elements previously singled out as "essential." We do not have the time to take each one of them and estimate its meaning and force. A much more important issue is how to interpret this section in general. Many of its subdivisions are filled with ways in which a general "element" can be realized. Is the document asserting that each of these realizations is "essential," that without it "religious life loses its identity"? What are the Franciscans to say about the provisions about stable community life when their spirit essentially embraces the notion of itineracy, or how would the great Jesuit authority on the Constitutions, Jerome Nadal, respond, when he maintained that there were four houses of the Society: Houses of probation, colleges, professed residences and above all the road. "There are the houses of the professed, where the ministries of the Society for the help of souls are exercised. Is there more? Yes, the best: the 'missions' on which the pope or superior sends us, so that for the Society, the whole world will become its house; and thus it will be with the divine grace." There was, for Nadal, a priority among these residences for Jesuits: "The principal and most characteristic dwelling for Jesuits is not in the professed houses, but in journeyings."[35] For the Franciscans before them and for the Jesuits who tried to follow in their footsteps, this was to imitate Christ who had nowhere to lay his head. Further, while there are many insightful, challenging, and even beautiful statements about religious life, there are really quite serious questions to be raised about the theological adequacy of a number of items in Essential Elements: The assertion or presumption that the hierarchy is a model for all religious authority (49), that there must be "personal, religious authority on all levels" as opposed to that shared authority already in practice for centuries in some religious communities (50-52), that the relationship with the Church is to be understood primarily as a relationship with the hierarchy (40-43), that religious garb is worn by all religious (34), that a "common and constant apostolate" previously recognized by the Church cannot be changed without damage to the identity of an institute (25), that community is to be structured in conventual details (19-20), etc.

I think that some of these problems might be softened with a different reading of the third section of the document. Many of these criticisms are leveled at the third section--whether from historians or theologians or from religious themselves--as if the third section was a further listing of essential elements, rather than an attempt to clarify what had been stated in the first section. In reading this section, it is pivotal to understand what function it is to perform. And that purpose is not a listing of a hundred more essentials! This third section seeks for clarification of what has been cited before. The list in the first section was an abstract index; it needs concretion through examples, instances, and explicitation. Each of these nine elements is analogically essential to religious life, granted the modification mentioned above. Each is a component element which must be found in religious communities, but each of these is found in a different way according to the character of the religious institute. Often to indicate ways in which each of these will be realized in a religious community and so to clarify its meaning, the third section gives a series of sub-listings in which each general, abstract topic is concretized. In attempting to explain or to exemplify each "essential element," the document clusters together a number of instructions, laws, and particular usages by which this more general unit is given concretion and embodment. Many of the "essential elements" are treated here, then, as a "cluster-concept," that is, as a concept composed of notes the majority--but not necessarily all--of which will be realized in each case.

Let me give an example. Religious garb is mentioned twice. In paragraph 34, it is one of the seven ways in which the public witness of religious can be given. In the norms under paragraph 37, it figures as a means of witnessing public consecration and the vow of poverty. For the first: What is essential to religious life is public witness. In general, this is not negotiable for religious--except, presumably, in those lands where the political climate is permeated by the persecution of the church. Religious garb is one way of realizing this public character, and Canon Law states that religious should wear the religious garb of their institute. It does not say that each institute should have a distinctive religious garb. Just the contrary. The very next section in the same canon allows for the case in which an order of priests would not have such a distinctive garb; they should wear what the diocesan priests wear.[36] The most obvious next stage would be the question: how about the communities of sisters and brothers who have no distinctive garb? The order of the canon calls for this question, and any knowledge of the history of religious congregations would suggest it. Many religious orders were founded with no provision for such a special mode of dressing. Canon Law does not forbid this, it merely states that the religious should wear the garb prescribed by its proper law. Where their proper law is silent on this, there is no statement from the common law of the Church that additional provision should be made. Essential Elements makes no attempt to impose additional obligations.

There are religious institutes in which the religious garb is so bound up with a graceful history and with the charism of their presence in the Church, that we would all be the poorer if this were to be simply abandoned. There are others, however, who adopted the clothing either of the poor of the time or of the women of the time or of the priests of the time because this enabled a presence or a witness or a mission which would have been otherwise inhibited. Many of these religious congregations have decided that a uniform or a singular mode of dress would be counterproductive. Both decisions have been honored in the Church.[37] As Paul VI put this in Evanglica testificatio: "We recognize that certain situations can justify the abandonment of a religious style of dress. We cannot forget, however, how fitting it is that the dress of religious men and women should be, as the Council

274

wishes, a sign of their consecration, and that it should be in some way (in qualche modo) distinguished from forms that are clearly secular."[38] How then should the presence and value of religious garb be explained? It is one way of realizing what is essential: public witness.

Another example is prayer: The fourth part of the third Section begins with the statement: "Religious life cannot be sustained without a deep life of prayer, individual, communal, and liturgical."[39] But certainly the authors of this document know that the constitutions of the Society of Jesus forbid any obligatory community prayer, and specifically the office in choir.[40] This does not rule out the contemplative dimension from Jesuit life, but it will be realized in another way rather than through the Liturgy of the Hours in common. On the other hand, Essential Elements makes no mention of the Spiritual Exercises of Saint Ignatius, which lie at the heart of the Jesuit's life of prayer. This failure to attend to the prayer characteristic of a particular religious order says nothing against this document, any more than does the inclusion of forms that are foreign to a particular institute. It is an inevitability in the kind of document which this claims to be and an index of the level of generalization of its statements and of their variant realizations.

I stressed at the beginning of these reflections that there was no reason to believe a priori that this summary was necessarily free from error. I do not retract that statement now. But I think that two hermeneutical principles may modify some of the manifold and consistent criticisms leveled against it. In the first section, the principle of analogy: that each of these general principles will be realized by each institute in its own way; in the third section, the understanding of a "cluster-concept," that often the sublisting is an attempt to clarify an essential element with a series of "for instances." The majority of these will obtain in each religious institute but not necessarily all.[41]

There is a third hermeneutical principle fairly constant in the church regarding law and even more appropriate for a document which only attempts to summarize both doctrine and legislation in its guidelines. This document, like any document from the Holy See, enjoys the antecedent reception of good will and the positive interpretation of its statements. If it should happen, however, that a particular factor is included which actually militates against the fidelity to the charism of a particular religious order or which is de facto injurious to its religious life, especially in its mission, recourse can be had to the Holy See and the principles of epikeia followed. This is a normal part of the interchanges with legitimate authority in the Church. The lengthy conversations which the papal intervention has initiated between the bishops of the United States and the religious of their diocese provide an excellent opportunity for such a representation. Nor should such a moment be a priori ruled out. No one put this better than Saint Thomas: "Human acts—which are the subject of laws—consist in individual occurrences which can vary in an infinite number of ways. There is no possibility of laying down a rule of law that would cover every case. Legislators, however, attend to that which happens in most cases and formulate a law accordingly. But in some cases, keeping this law is contrary to the rectitude of justice and to the common good which the law intends . . . In these and similar cases, it is evil to follow the law as it is laid down. It is good, however, letting the letter of the law to be set aside, to follow that which the nature of justice and the general utility demand."[42]

Further: Some understanding of the enormously difficult task which the congregation has set for itself might soften some of the theological criticism. Religious life emerges from the Holy Spirit, inspiring individual persons to live in a particular way and to gather those men or women into a community who experience the same movement and direction by the Spirit. It belongs to the hierarchy to discern or to recognize in time that such an authentic insiration has taken place, that new life has emerged in the church, and to confirm as evangelical the way of life in which this inspiration has already been embodied. Church authority, then, has the responsibility of endorsing a way of life as in accord with the gospels and of recommending it as such to the consideration of Catholics. But the difference, the nuance, the particularities of each of these forms of life are almost infinite. The pope has called the American bishops to the support of religious life, and asked the Congregation for Religious and Secular Institutes to give these bishops a general overview of apostolic religious life. The task was extraordinarily difficult.

The American bishops have used the document in exactly the manner in which it was intended, as a set of guidelines with which to enter into conversations with the religious in their diocese. Where the document is too summary or where its theology falters, it can be supplemented with other more authoritative documents which are either its sources or its complements. The concrete result has been that discussion about religious life--so long sustained only within a religious order or among religious congregations--have been opened to the entire diocese. In the last year, there has been a greater depth and greater breadth in the discussion of religious life throughout the church in the United States than--very probably--at any other time in our history. And the document, Essential Elements, has contributed substantially to this dicussion and to its challenge by giving it a focus upon the characteristics of religious life and a manageable order.

For the difficulty in reading such a document as Essential Elements is that one tends to ask too little or too much from it: too little, in that one fails to comprehend the seriousness with which these "essential elements" are declared or the concrete and grave problems they are addressing; too much, in that one expects a level of theological completeness or immunity from error or concrete precisions that cannot be forthcoming. Of course the document could be considerably better; but it is possible to live profitably with it now if its purpose, nature, individual provisions and inherent limitations are understood. In two ways, the efficacy of this essay of SCRIS could be impaired: either by trivializing its bearing upon contemporary religious life or by exaggerating its provisions into a quasi-infallibility.

Essential Elements is not a ruler to be laid against every religious institute to calibrate its authenticity. That would be to falsify its value, as well as to threaten significant injury to various religious communities and to their foundational charism. For the last time, I repeat: Essential Elements was not sent to religious. But it obviously deals with the life of apostolic religious. It is a strong statement of the elements which are essential to every religious community. As such it can provide a useful instrument by which these communities can continue and even further their own objective evaluation of this period of special experimentation, and widen their dialogue with the church in the United States. Further, it can provide the American bishops with a summary statement on the nature of religious life as background for their encouragement of this life within the church in the United States. Certainly this is the purpose for which it is intended: Not as a theoretical treatise on religious life, but as a compendium to make other teaching available. It is true that one will need both good will and the willingness to consult its sources to employ this summary as a practical tool for the encouragement of religious life and for dealing with the manifold objections to which it is liable. But that is true of many documents, and good will should not be that hard to discover in the church of Christ.

NOTES

1. The papal letter to the American Bishops and the accompanying document, Essential Elements in the Church's Teaching on Religious Life as Applied to Institutes Dedicated to the Works of the Apostolate will be cited by paragraph numbers from text published in Origins: N.C. Documentary Service 13:8 (July 7, 1983) 130-142. The papal letter will be abbreviated to PL and the accompanying document to EE.

2. PL 4.

3. The papal allocution to the American bishops of September 19, 1983 will be cited by paragraph numbers from the text published in L'Osservatore Romano CXXIII:216 (Lunedì-Martedì 19-20 Settembre 1983) 4. Allocutio 3.

4. EE 2, 4, and Conclusion.

5. PL 3. This reading of the intended audience for Essential Elements is confirmed by the following communication from Sister Helen Flaherty, one of the three American delegates to the IUSG: At the annual meeting of the General Council of IUSG (International Union of Superior Generals) in Rome, May 13-17, 1984, the Reverend Basil Heiser, O.F.M. Conv. (Undersecretary of the Sacred Congregation for Religious and Secular Institutes) replied to the question from one of the delegates: "Who wrote the document, Essential Elements? For whom was it written and why?" Father Heiser's answer was: "The Document was written by members of SCRIS. It was meant to be a document of information and clarification for the American Hierarchy, as they began to implement the directive of the Holy Father to study religious life in the United States."

6. Lumen gentium 43. The translation of the documents of the Second Vatican Council and subsequent decrees or instructions of the Holy See is taken from the two volume set, Austin Flannery, O.P. (General editor), Vatican Council II: The Conciliar and Post-Conciliar Documents (Collegeville: The Liturgical Press, 1975) and Vatican Council II: More Post-Conciliar Documents (Grand Rapids: WM. B. Eerdmans Publishing Co., 1982). The documents are cited by paragraph numbers.

7. Ludwig Wittgenstein, Philosophical Investigations. (trans. G.E.M. Anscombe; Oxford: Basil Blackwell, 1972), 66-67.

8. Wittgenstein, op. cit. 67.

9. Joseph de Guibert, S.J. (ed.), Documenta Ecclesiastica Christianae perfectionis studium spectantia (Roma: Aedes Universitatis Gregorianae, 1931) No. 150.

10. Joseph de Guibert, op. cit. No. 151. Guidiccioni favored the reduction of all religious orders to four: Benedictines, Cistercians, Franciscans, and Dominicans. Cf. Paul Dudon, S.J., St. Ignatius Loyola (trans. William J. Young, S.J.; Milwaukee: Bruce, 1949) 258ff.

11. Canon 605.

12. John 15:19.

13. Canon 607, No. 3.

14. EE 9-10.

15. EE 26.

16. Primo feliciter 2.

17. Canon 710.

18. EE 3.

19. PL 3. (Underlining added).

20. Cf. PL 3 and EE 4.

21. Perfectae caritatis 2. Cf. Canon 578.

22. Ignatius of Loyola, Spiritual Exercises, 22. (Grammar slightly altered to avoid sexist language.)

23. EE 4.

24. PL 3.

25. Aristotle, Poetics VI. $1449^b 22$.

26. Lumen gentium 44.

27. EE 10.

28. EE 12. "Apostolic" is used in this essay as a shorthand to designate those institutes dedicated to or engaged in the works of the apostolate. As Canons 673 and 674 suggest, all forms of religious life are apostolic in some way, as indeed are all forms of Christian spirituality.

29. Perfectae caritatis 8.

30. EE 12.

31. EE 20.

32. Constitutions of the Society of Jesus, translated and edited by George Ganss, S.J. (St. Louis: The Institute of Jesuit Sources, 1970) IX 2. No. 723. Nadal records that Ignatius made this compenetration of prayer and activity the focus of apostolic development: "In all things, activities, and conversations, he felt and contemplated the presence of God and the attraction of spiritual things. He was contemplative during the same time that he was involved in activity (simul in actione contemplativus), something which he expressed habitually with the words: we must find God in all things." Monumenta Historica Societatis Iesu, Epistolae P. Hieronymi Nadal (ed. F. Cervos; Madrid: Typis Gabriellis Lopez del Horno, 1905) IV 651.

33. Acta Romana Societatis Iesu XVIII 3 (1982) 731.

34. _EE_ 23. The metaphor of two distinct facets of a single reality, however, still does not do justice to the dynamic identity of mission and consecration for apostolic religious.

35. Cf. John W. O'Malley, S.J., "To travel to Any Part of the World: Jeronimo Nadal and the Jesuit Vocation," _Studies in the Spiritualiy of Jesuits_ XVI 2 (March 1984) 7.

36. Canon 669.

37. For a thorough discussion of the history of religious garb, cf. "Abito Religioso," _Dizionario degli istituti di perfezione_, (ed. Guerrino Pellicia and Giancarlo Rocca; Rome: Edizione Pauline, 1974) I 50-79.

38. _Evangelica testificatio_, No. 22 (Translation mine).

39. _EE_ 28.

40. _Constitutions of the Society of Jesus_ VI. 3.No. 586. Also in contrast to an unnuanced reading of _EE_ would be: "In what pertains to prayer, meditation, and study and also in regard to the bodily practices of fast, vigils, and other austerities or penances, it does not seem expedient to give them (those in last vows) any other rule than that which discrete charity dictates to them." _Ibid_. No. 582.

41. The following paragraphs in the third section seem most open to this interpretation: Community (19-20), Mission (24-25), Prayer (28-30), Public Witness (34-37), and Relation to the Church (40).

42. Thomas Aquinas, _Summa theologiae_ II-II. 120. 1.

OUTLINE

I. Introduction

    A. Papal Letter (4/3/83) and Enclosure of _Essential Elements_ (5/31/84): 6/22/83.

    B. Two Prenotes.

II. Nature of the Document in terms of Five Questions:

    1. To whom was it sent? American bishops and Pontifical Commission on Religious Life.

    2. What was sent? A summary of the salient points of the Church's Teaching on religious life.

        a. Necessity: For the work of the bishops and the Pontifical Commission "to render special pastoral service to the religious . . ."

b. Difficulty: The fluidity and vastly different
forms of religious life.

3. <u>What is the authority of this document?</u>

    a. Not legislation.

    b. A "quasi-instructio" for the American bishops.

    c. Source of its authority:

        1) The instructional and directive documents which it summarizes.

        2) The papal approval of <u>Essential</u> Elements as a summary.

    d. Twofold value:

        1) For bishops: Documentary summary of salient points of religious life.

        2) For religious: Criteriology of SCRIS.

4. <u>What is the theological qualification of its statements</u>?

    a. Abstract

    b. Concrete: Three cases as examples

        1) "Separation from the world"

        2) Doctrinal richness of canon law

        3) List of essential elements in papal letter and in <u>Essential</u> <u>Elements</u>

        4) Comparison of nos. 51 and 52 with their sources.

    c. When problems arise

5. <u>How is it to be received?</u> By religious and by bishops.

III. Content and Assessment of Some Components:

    A.   In General: Outline of the four sections

    B.   In Particular:

        1. Section I (1-4):   What are the "essential elements?"   Analogy   of interpretation. Assessment.

        2. Section II (5-12):   How is "religious life" defined? Assessment. How is "apostolic" religious life defined? Assessment.

        3. Section III (13-53): How is this section to be interpreted? Clarification through "cluster-concepts."

              a.   Abstract

              b.   Concrete--Two cases as examples: religious garb and prayer.

IV. Concluding Remarks on the Use of the Document:

    A.   Four hermeneutical principles.

    B.   Difficulties of the task.

    C.   Use by American bishops.

    D.   Asking too much or too little.

V

TOWARD THE FUTURE

The Bishops and Religious Life

(An Address to the U.S. Bishops, November 15, 1983)*

by

Bette Moslander, C.S.J.

In the few minutes allotted to me I want to share with you what I perceive as some of the best hopes and the greatest concerns of women religious in this country regarding this task in which we are now engaged. Mindful of the grace of Vatican II for the entire church, we are confident that this new call of Pope John Paul II will provide us with the impetus and opportunity to share with you, the bishops of our country, the fruits and the graces of our 20 years of renewal.

Renewal is not a new word for us. We have, since the first challenging months of the Vatican Council been earnestly and faithfully engaged in the renewal urged by that remarkable ecclesial event. We welcome this opportunity to tell the story of our journey in faith over these past 20 years.

1. Our hope is that you will allow us to share with you as we would with brothers and friends. That will require of you open, honest and patient listening. We ask that you hear our story, a story of faith and obedient response to the church. For many of you it will be familiar; but for others, because of reasons both complex and simple, our story is unfamiliar or you hesitate to dialogue openly with us. So often misunderstandings occur simply because we, the members of the church, have not the time, the energy or the opportunity to meet one another as friends. However that may be, we are all of us at a moment of new opportunity. If one of the outcomes of this mandate is conversations at the local level which result in a better understanding, greater trust, stronger bonding and mutual support between the U.S. bishops and women and men religious it will indeed be a great gift to the entire church in the United States.

2. Another hope is that we might dispel some of the confusion and negative judgments that have accompanied the changes of the past 20 years. In any time of great transition it is inevitable that there be (both real and imagined)

---

*Reprinted from Origins 13 (no. 25; 12/1/1983) 430-1.

errors, bad timing, misunderstandings. We have overwhelming evidence to show that the majority of our women are more prayerful, more spirtually alive and more deeply committed to the mission of Jesus Christ and to the church than they were 20 years ago.

Change is never experienced without suffering. We have experienced the loss of many young, dedicated members, especially during the decade of the '60s when the whole societal structure shifted. We continue to experience the loss of many women to active ministry through the natural aging process-a phenomenon not restricted to religious communities. We have experienced the loss of institutions, of prestige and of security. We have suffered judgment and condemnation from those who do not understand or approve of the changes the renewal years have brought to the entire church and to religious life in particular. But we know a new understanding of our lives as apostolic women religious and a revitalized commitment to the needs of people.

A transformation of consciousness regarding the call of the gospel to a life of radical discipleship is taking place among religious. We and the entire church are engaged in a paschal journey--a journey like that of Jesus that leads through death to resurrection. We are not afraid to share our experience of this paschal dying with you for we believe with all our hearts that we have also experienced new life and resurrection in our personal lives and in the life of our communities.

3. A final hope I would express to you today is that in this process the whole church in the United States will be enriched by a deeper understanding as the people of God in this country and in this time. Archbishop Quinn, in his address to the Leadership Conferencee of Women Religious assembly in Baltimore last August, said: "Inculturation is an exigency of the incarnation. It is an indispensable condition for the development and vitality of the church and it is inevitably attended by its share of divisions and struggles and even mistakes."

The entire church here in the United States is an inculturated expression of the gospel of Jesus Christ and the mission of the church, conditioned by time and place. This inculturation in a highly pluralistc, technological, democratic first-world society creates specific modes of responding to the gospel. The church in the United States in general and religious life particularly are coming to a new stage of mature understanding about how to live faithfully true to charism, identity and gospel amid wholly unprecedented circumstances. We are deeply committed to unity with the church and desirous of the understanding of the Vatican. We want to explore with you the impact of our society and culture on the expression of religious life in our country.

We are sincerely hopeful that the mandate of Pope John Paul II to you, the bishops of our contry, will realize these positive outcomes. However, we have some concerns as well and I would like to share these with you now.

1. We are concerned lest this study promote division and polarization within our religious communities and among the various religious congregations. During the past 20 years most communities have worked very hard to communicate, educate, promote participation and unify their members. On the whole most have succeeded in this effort. There has been tremendous growth in the understanding and acceptance of diversity. Authentic unity around charism and mission has been achieved and strengthened with love, patience and courage. However, the heavy imposition of a narrow and fundamentalist interpretation of the "Essential Elements" document to all religious communities without respect for the unique charisms or diverse experiences of the communities may fragment religious communities and bring immense pain and suffering.

Furthermore, during the past 20 years religious congregations of very differing origins and charisms have learned to work together, to share with one another, to collaborate in ministries and renewal processes. We have built a strong and steady network of trust and mutual support. We have learned to love and respect one another. We appreciate the diversity that exists and which reveals even more clearly the whole mystery of Christ. We value the beauty of our diverse expressions of gospel values. We are concerned lest this study promote a certain isolation and separation among us rather than promote our unity. It would be possible for it to drive the wedge of suspicion and antagonism between us. We do not wish to see our efforts toward a more just and human society dissipated or aborted because a rigid and univocal understanding of the "Essential Elements" document places us in judgment of one another.

2. We are concerned lest the study become preoccupied with in-house self-examination and divert us from the very

grave needs of our people and of the world. In the church in the United States we are coming to a deeper understanding of what it means to live the gospel more fully. We have experienced with new intensity that the gospel calls the entire church to a life of justice and peace. Your own conference, bishops, has called the church in the United States time and time again to take up the needs of the poor, the marginated, the alienated. Your pastoral concern for the people and for the world has found expression in such outstanding documents as "This Land Is Home to Me," "Strangers and Guests," "The Challenge of Peace," etc.

Women religious have responded to your conference calls with the same alacrity, generosity and professional competence as they responded to the Vatican II call to renewal. We all know that much remains to be done. We have only begun to respond fully to the call of the synodal document of 1971 "Justice in the World." The educational process on your most recent peace pastoral is barely under way. It would be a disservice to our people here and abroad if our energies, creativity and enthusiasm for these pressing needs were diffused by excessive introspection or non-productive criticism and preoccupation with self-scrutiny.

3. Last, we are concerned lest women in our country look upon this study as another painful example of the inability of the clerical church to receive and honor the experience of women as full members of the church. While the study need not result in negative outcomes for the church in the United States, we must be aware that many women are watching with searching hearts and questioning minds. We are deeply concerned about the women of the church, both within and outside of religious communities.

We hope to build strong and deeper bonds with members of various groups of women, lay and religious, who are creating collaborative structures to work for peace and for justice in our country and in the world. We want this study to bear witness to them that the church is indeed concerned and committed to justice for women in our society and in the church. We want this study to testify that the church respects and values the contribution of women today toward a just society throughout the world.

I thank you for this opportunity to express to you a few of the hopes and concerns of religious women as we undertake this task together.

Shapes for the Future

by

Howard J. Gray, S.J.*

Introduction

Sister Elizabeth McDonough has provided a careful, positive exposition of the structure of the New Code in the section dealing with religious life. Her final set of remarks called our attention to the fact that "good law sets the foundation for evolution and growth by providing the stable base of organization wherein basic interrelationships, rights and obligations, procedures and necessary structures are assured." It is this evolution and growth which I am going to emphasize as I consider the direction--the shapes--which religious life might take in the future.

I am conscious that, in describing the possible future shapes which religious life could assume, I am on the prophetic edge, what Sister Elizabeth has termed the "prophetic opportunities within the human limitations of our imperfect but indispensable human realities. "Let me situate my remarks within a set of emphases which Cardinal Bernardin enunciated in a recent issue of Chicago Studies.[1] In this article, Cardinal Bernardin developed Pope John Paul II's reflections that there were four elements expressive of Vatican II's renewed understanding of the church which are found in the New Code. These four elements are: (1) the church as the people of God and authority as service; (2) the call for mutual relations between the universal church and particular churches; (3) a recognition that all members of the church share in Christ's threefold office of priest, prophet, and king; and (4) the restoration of the entire unity of the church of Christ. Permit me, then, to speak about the future shapes of religious life--its evolution and growth in terms of these four contexts.

---

*This paper was originally given in tandem with that of Elizabeth McDonough, O.P., (see above in Part III) at the Boston   College   conference.

A. The Church as the people of God and Authority as Service

Religious life involves people in its memberships and in its mission. Who, we ask, will be "the people of God" in our future, the people whose talents and needs will shape our identities and our ministries as religious?

A recent study on the context of contemporary and future Church ministry stressed these demographic realities as pivotal in defining the task of the modern Church in the United States:[2]

(1) In 1978 there were more than 12 million Hispanics in the U.S. If undocumented Hispanics are included, then the number could be as high as 15 million or more. This means that Hispanics represent about one-third of the Catholic population of our nation.

(2) Even perhaps more important is the fact that the age profile of the Hispanic population is very young, e.g., twice as many of the Hispanics (38.4 percent) are under 18 years of age, while the total U.S. population has only 19.1 percent under 18 years of age.

(3) Apart from Cuban and Vietnamese refugees, the largest number of immigrants in the past ten years has come from: the Philippines, Korea, Mexico, India, China, the Dominican Republic, Jamaica, and Haiti. The largest percentage of these newcomers is Catholic--or, at least, baptized as Catholic.

(4) American Blacks constituted over 22 million, with 80 percent living in urban areas.

(5) Aging Americans constitute both shifting population, from North to the South or West, and a growing minority.

(6) Native Americans (Indians) continue to represent a national injustice.

If religious life is to be a life lived in reality in our country, it is impossible to consider its future without considering how religious women and men will relate to these people of God and how this emerging reality will, in turn, effect religious life style, recruitment, formation, and apostolic service. One of the crucial tasks of the entire U.S. church is to assume moral, religious, and apostolic leadership in incorporating the culturally marginated of our society into full partnership in our church, i.e., in inviting them and empowering them to act as the people of God. These people represent a rich set of human experiences, suffering, vision, and grace. How the church is "present" to these people will most probably determine whether the church can be present to them.

This "presence" is not the task of religious only. It is the task of all church leadership. Nevertheless, religious communities can contribute significantly to finding ecclesial forms, structures, and programs to meet the needs of our times and to facilitate the process whereby a wholly new group of men and women become--in our context--the people of God. Moreover, religious can facilitate this with reverence for the ethnic, racial, and cultural heritages and experiences of these people.

This social, demographic reality could have profound effects on our future as religious. Formation to learn from others, skills in listening to and in living with someone from a different country, an asceticism of hospitality which welcomes the arrival of people who will make a new church--this kind of formation is not easily begun nor sustained. Opening our religious houses to become community centers of evangelization, education, worship, and fellowship will directly challenge our standard of common life, our level of communication, and our universality. And more critical appraisal of our schools, hospitals, retreat centers, and parishes in order to find ways to take leadership in helping a new generation of Americans take their place in our church and in our culture will be demanding and abnegating. Yet, the first reality that will shape our future is that of adapting who-we-are to who the church in the United States will be and could be. Our "authority" as religious is founded in part on our resources, our professional competence, and institutional sophistication. We must shape these talents to the service of evangelization, incorporation, and accommodation if we are to be faithful to our call to be religious and apostolic.

B. Mutual relations between churches and the universal Church

The experience of North American religious is radically one of charism and culture, two realities which cannot be denied. Simply put, God's Spirit initiates our vocation;

291

United States life gave that charism context, shape, and expression. Religious can discern their charisms and can be critical of their cultures. But they cannot say that these do not constitute their reality before God and other men and women. Just as particular churches--in Boston, Hartford, Detroit, New Orleans, Los Angeles--can rightly claim that they are the church of Christ, so, too, can each religious community claim that it is a community of Christ. Just as particular churches struggle to harmonize collegiality with primacy, religious communities--Dominican, Mercy, Notre Dame, Redemptorist, or Jesuit--have to struggle to harmonize charismatic empowerment with institutional loyalties and responsibilities. This is a dilemma; and it would be dishonest to deny the fact that for many of us there is a concern that conformity could displace communion in religious life. How can this concern move from an inhibition to an opportunity?

The future for us religious is founded, in part, on better sustained communication between local ordinaries and ourselves. That is a truism, of course. However, I do not mean that religious and bishops should talk about salaries, retirement benefits, school jurisdictions, personnel problems, and hospital policies. If local churches are to reflect the radical Christian vocation which they possess as communities, then bishops and religious have to move into religious and/or faith dialogue. If trust, understanding, and apostolic availability are to be the fruit of such dialogue, then we have to find appropriate structures for sharing our prayer, our mutual calls, and our inspirations. Bishops and religious have to donate quality time towards their communion, if the local church is to become a community. We have to mobilize our resources to meet mutual apostolic objectives.

The future beyond the consultations between bishops and religious mandated by the Holy Father has to be one of programmed religious collaboration. This may mean a two-day or three-day time for bishops and religious superiors to pray, to worship, and to work together to confront problems of nuclear madness, urban blight, and pervasive practical atheism.

But, even more, beyond problems lies vision. What do we--bishops and religious--want of our local church? What would happen if we programmed our exchanges so that, beyond getting to know one another, we moved to communal apostolic discernment for the good of the whole church? What if we were free enough to work together to free our imaginations to form

292

apostolic alternatives to meet the needs of the marginated whom I mentioned earlier?

C. All share in Christ's threefold office

Related to this communication between bishops and religious for specifically religious and apostolic collaboration is the further task of lay collaboration with both bishops and religious. The significance of Chapter 5 of Lumen Gentium has come home to many lay Catholics. They hunger for that holiness to which their baptism had oriented them. They want time for prayer, quality eucharistic worships, homilies of substance and challenge, serious discernment about their work, the use of their resources, and their life style. Moreover, through greater participation in parish councils, school boards, and pastoral ministry, many lay people have come to see that the Church is their church.

One of the future shapes of religious life is greater union in life, prayer, shared values, and gifts with lay Catholics. Many of us know that shared ministry in our schools, retreat houses, and parishes becomes mere functionalism if there is not also shared vision and shared life. Granted all the legitimate concern for religious privacy, the future of religious life is not in isolation from but in union with lay people. The theologian David Power has explored the notion of "households of faith in the coming Church," i.e., an alternate model of Christian fellowship through places where serious Christian community can take place.[3] I see the future of religious life as one in which there will be structures in which religious and lay people together explore the meaning of the evangelical life.

D. Restoration of unity

Beyond the Catholic experience of Christianity and belief in God lies a world of committed believers who are not Catholic or not Christian, whose lives are marked by compassion and concern. Ecumenism originates from a religious not a political, sociological, or cultural impetus. Its finality or goal is to restore unity [4] and to cooperate with all men and women of good will to effect "the rightful betterment of this world in which all alike live."[5] Religious have to believe that their religious experience of call, of charism, of evangelical radicality, and of service is a privileged vehicle for ecumenical communication. Religious have to believe that their graced instincts to labor in a variety of socio-professional fields in order to make a world more humane, more just, and more peaceful give witness to the non-believer of their fellowship in caring for our world.

In summary, beyond the present structure of the New Code lies the continued opportunity of Vatican II, an opportunity for religious to move beyond maintenance to create in fellowship with the marginated, bishops, lay Catholics, and non-Catholics new shapes for how we live and work.

The heuristic structure for the future of religious life [6] lies in how we confronted the four elements enunciated by Pope John Paul II. What will help us relate our charisms, resources, and lives to the universality of the Church's challenges and mission? There are, to be sure, structures which we must fashion, attitudes we must develop, and opportunities we must seize. But mostly we must believe in our future, making our own the words of the OT prophet Habakkuk:

> "I will stand at my guard post,
>   and station myself upon the
>   rampart,
>   And keep watch to see what he will
>   say to me,
>   And what answer he will give to my
>   complaint.
>
> "Then the Lord answered me and
>   said:
>   Write down the vision
>   clearly upon the tablets,
>   so that one can read it readily.
>   For the vision still has its time,
>   presses on to fulfillment, and
>   will not disappoint;
>   If it delays, wait for it,
>   it will surely come, it will not
>   be late" (Hab:2:1-3)

NOTES

1. Joseph Cardinal Bernardin, "A Bishop's View," Chicago Studies 23 (April, 1984) 37-44.

2. Joseph Fitzpatrick, "The People," The Context of Our Ministries: Working Papers, Jesuit Conference, 1981, 27-29.

3. Joseph Power, "Households of Faith in the Coming Church," Worship 57 (1983) 237-255.

4. Decree on Ecumenism 4.

5. Pastoral Constitution on the Church in the Modern World 21.

6. Two earlier studies on this notion are: Facts of the Future, Religious Life USA (eds. Ruth McGoldrick, S.P. and Cassian J. Yuhaus, C.P.; Huntington: Sunday Visitor Press, 1976) and Shaping the Coming Age of Religious Life (eds. Lawrence Cada et al; New York: Seabury Press, 1979).

Religious Life in the U.S. - A Guess at the Future

by

Helen Flaherty, S.C.

It seems rather historical to do one's guessing about the future here in San Francisco. The political guesses of last week [the 1984 Democratic National Convention] have now moved on to be tested in the political future of November. I am sure, any guessing we might do this evening concerning the future of religious life in this country, will likewise await the testing of the 21st Century. Perhaps it is the inevitability of earthquake in this city that urges us to move our planning from present to future.

Recently, when I shared with one of my sisters, the fact that I was writing a paper on future guessing about religious life in this country, she immediately asked, "Are we dying or being born?", and I just as quickly responded, "Both." As most of you undoubtedly know, this is probably the fifth transitional period in the structure of religious life since its beginnings in the 3rd and 4th centuries. Of course, it is the first in the United States, and that is the reason for our present tension. Four times the theme of paschal mystery described the changes in religious life.

In the 4th century the movement was from the hermitical to the communal life-style and structure. In the 13th century, the shift from communal to mendicant and preaching activities changed the focus and life-style once again. By the 17th century the spirit of the mendicant and preacher had become institutionalized, and the need for apostolic religious groups to serve the educational, health care and social service needs of the church in Western Europe became apparent. St. Ignatius, St. Vincent de Paul, St. Angela Merici and others formed and identified distinct apostolic charisms and structure. In the 19th century we find the migration of peoples to the United States and elsewhere, causing a need for spiritual and sociological assistance to the immigrants as they adjusted to the trauma of new and liberating forms of government and church.

As in these past four transitions, we in this country are now experiencing as church and as people a shift, a change in life-style and structure resulting from the forces of social, economic and political changes taking place in our society and in our church. It is happening elsewhere in the world also, but not with the rapidity and in-depth analyzation that we are experiencing here. As we approach the year 2000, we come as a group with a history of unprecedented change. For the past 20 years we religious have shared our sufferings, our struggles, hopes, desires and, yes, our visions of the future. I come to this discussion of future as a woman religious, and although I believe there to be many commonalities between the experience of men and women religious during the past 20 years in the United States, I also know there are differences.

For the past 20 years, women religious were asking and searching for responses to such questions as: Who are we personally and corporately? What is our identity to church? To the world? Some were concerned about preserving an identity; others wanted to discover one. Some asked, How are we separate? Others, How are we different? And still others, How are we the same? All of this searching was a real identity question. I believe we are now beginning to hear some of the answers and to describe more clearly the reasons for some of those questions.

Another facet of history which must not be neglected is the United States cultural background and heritage out of which religious life for the future, as in the past, is being shaped and influenced. Jesuit historian James Hennesey, in a meeting of religious and bishops at Boston College recently, states, "American religious life grew up in political and social circumstances vastly different from those which obtained in 19th Century Europe."[1] I believe this difference is just now becoming digested, although not yet totally accepted. Possibly the trauma or tension, if you will, that now exists in even agreeing on the definition of the essential elements of apostolic religious life, lies in the fact that most Americans, particularly clergy and hierarchy, have almost no experiential sense of how deeply the 19th century European context and experience of religious life has shaped total church thinking about this life. American Catholicism in the 18th and 19th century, separated from Europe by an ocean, had its own unique formation influenced by the social struggles for liberty, freedom, democracy, and sometimes basic human survival. The history of religious life in this struggle is just now being written down and analyzed. I think it is significant to note that 65% of European-based communities who came to minister in the United States in the 19th century, are no longer here, and that 70% of the religious congregations serving in the church of the United

States today were founded by Americans in the early and middle 1800's.

In the 1979 publication, Shaping the Coming Age of Religious Life by Cada and Fitz, we are told that religious congregations in the life of the church are not and have never been fixed and static entities. [2] Taken together, they make up an historical process unfolding over time and viewed as a significant social movement, particularly in western civilization. This movement has the usual four significant parts of all social movements: 1) a prophetic response to a need in church or society or both; 2) an institutionalization of that response; 3) a shift or a change of influence by forces for change either inside or outside of the movement thus causing breakdown; 4) numbers diminish, needs shift, structural questions surface and the movement enters transition and possible transformation.

There is a major paradigm shift underway in religious life today; the commonly accepted text for defining or thinking about religious life has changed--not in minor, but in major ways since Vatican II, and we must expect this significant movement of change in the pattern of religious life to continue for perhaps another fifteen or twenty years. Vatican II defined religious life as a charism within the church, a gift of God's Spirit, given for the good of the whole people of God. Johannes Metz enlarged on this and sees religious life with a two-fold function within church: First, an innovative function in which we offer productive models for the church to live within and to influence social, economic, intellectual and cultural situations; and secondly, a corrective role in which we identify dangerous cultural accommodations and compromises and press for the uncompromising nature of the gospel and the imitation of Christ.[3] I believe these definitions to be significant as we move to the future.

Let us take a moment to look first at the external forces in our culture and society that are moving and affecting our future identity. The forces which have shaped religious life in this country in the past twenty years are not too different from the forces that have shaped the whole Catholic church in this country, of which religious life has been a very relevant part. Historically, the variety of physical, social, intellectual and spiritual needs of a largely immigrant people shaped a servant American church amidst a huge ethnic variety. Although the corporate story of women and men religious in the shaping of that church has yet to be written, each congrega-

298

tion since Vatican II has researched and redeemed its own charism and place in that story. One hundred and fifty or sixty years ago, it was not too difficult to recognize, to feel with and to understand the needs of the people of God, for both as religious and as church, we bore a similar label. We were all poor. The challenge of the future is how, from a position of middle-class security and status, can we recognize and respond to the needs of the "new poor" and new refugees among us? How will we assist and collaborate with an American church that in the year 2000 will possibly be 45% Hispanic and 23% Asian?

In a very interesting article in the Spring, 1984 issue of the psychological magazine, Human Development, Joseph Hayden, S.J., describes a possible structure for our guessing about the future. The title of his article was "The Megatrends of Human Development." [4] Briefly, I would like to pinpoint for you what I believe to be "Five Megatrends of Religious Life"--those forces and trends that are now moving us into the future.

1. If we are indeed moving from an industrial-based society to an informational one--the challenge is in the interpretation of this new mass of information so that Christians can avoid the possibility of becoming conforming, non-understanding machines and instead become equipped and motivated to make reflective, responsible moral judgements. We live in a media-addicted culture. Religious educators at every level must collaboratively and creatively face this challenge in the future.

2. High-Tech vs. High-Touch is not just a euphonious slogan, but possibly the most significant challenge that religious for the future may have. The dehumanizing force of technology is eroding the very quality of human relationships --with our God, within our communities, and with all those to and with whom we serve. The religious of the future must be a person who knows how to communicate the truth with authentic, gentle love, regardless of the fascination of the computer, the constant tension caused by mobility, the fragility of human life in the midst of a polluted environment, the intensity of upper mobility in management and its fragmenting results on family. High-Touch is a necessity, not an option, for future religious.

3. As our national economy affects and is affected by world economy, so must the American religious of the future have a global perspective. Several years ago Karl Rahner made

us aware of the need to envision ourselves as a world church, resisting at all times the temptation to isolate ourselves or to reject in any way the movement of Spirit in each part of the total Body of Christ. The American church is experiencing in our lifetime a maturing process. American religious men and women from a heritage and a vantage point of experience, education, freedom and a twenty-year renewal process must now confront a world in its increasing insensitivity to injustice. The cry of oppressed peoples of God in Nicaragua, Africa, the Philippines and many other areas will continue to remind us of our responsibility to strengthen the gifts of total church through collaborative efforts, thus becoming some of the prophetic voices of the future.

4. The hierarchical model of leadership and government has shifted in most religious congregations to a style of participative, collegial responsibility. The decentralization of authority and accountability motivates us to do likewise in our role as ministers. There is strong reason to believe that the church of the future is the church rising from below, not imposed from the top. It can and will happen if we religious share our learned experience and process and enable parish and diocesan groups to emerge with power and vision and self-identity. Interdependent groups or new communities of lay and religious could also become a real possibility for the future. Modeling participative and corporate authority will have a particularly powerful, prophetic impact in this country because, as we know, high value is placed on rights, due process and individual freedom.

5. As the social and economic forces in our culture shift and change population centers and thus human needs, and as our congregational personnel numbers decrease as age increases, the whole possibility and need for many of us to examine how we sponsor, influence and control large educational and health care institutions will be imperative. Again, I refer to collaboration as the mode of the future through intercongregational, inter-lay-religious sharing of ownership and authority. As our American culture moves from institution to self-help, our influence in that culture will be as effective as our structures are flexible. As apostolic women and men religious in these United States we face a future, then, whose cultural forces are dominated by excessive and increasing information and media, interacting with expanding technology having global implications, while human beings themselves tend toward collegial modes of government and self-help.

Religious of the future must clearly identify themselves as self-aware members of the people of God, finding their place in shared ministry, in grass-roots movements, and diverse collaborative linkages with laity, situating this direction within the movements of Vatican II. "We remember that the identity quest of religious surfaced as a consequence of the status shift which rooted religious among the laity. Prior to this structural clarification religious existed somewhere 'in-between' clergy and laity."[5]

This overwhelmingly points to the theological development flowing out of the identity thrust which grounds religious in the people of God: "One same Baptism, one same Call to Holiness, one Spirit Who gifts each for the good of all." Identity in terms of "sameness of mission within the diversity of gifts"[6] is becoming dominant while separateness in terms of status of perfection with its language of separation is losing its significance. Vatican II laid the foundation for the place of the laity in the church as a part of its theological structure. The church is no more church without the laity than it would be church without pope or bishops. In her paper entitled "The Changing Mission of the Church," Doris Gottemoeller, R.S.M. affirms the theological dynamism in this movement of identification among the people of God.[7] She sees it as challenge to religious to enhance the critical importance of the laity within the church.

"Mutuality and shared ministry is grounded," Gottemoeller states, "in a radical sense of the mission we have all equally received in baptismal consecration." Emphasis upon role rather than gifts creates a competitive relationship in ministry. A grounding in mission creates respect for difference, for diverse gifts, and emerges in a sense of ministry which is reciprocal and mutually enriching. Mutuality rooted in mission can greatly contribute to the movement of the laity into their critical place in the structure of the church.

Tom Clarke crystallizes this thinking thus: "God loves to bring salvation to all his people through the anawim, the powerless and oppressed in their midst, as these come to the consciousness of their redeeming mission through the voice of prophets."[8] At the present junction of the church's life, it is the laity who constitute the chosen anawim, in contrast to bishops, priests, and also the professional theologians, who until recently have been drawn all but exclusively from the ranks of the clergy.

Religious have been in an ambivalent position. Theologically and canonically they belong to the laity (in contrast
to the clergy) and they have "enjoyed" the powerlessness of
that situation. But from the perspective of religious
culture, they have been drawn in some respects into the role
of an elite, situated halfway between clergy and the rest of
the laity. With encouragement from Vatican II, they are now
in a better position to reaffirm their links with the rest of
the laity, and so they stand within the body of the anawim
through whom God calls his entire people to renewal.

This movement of solidarity with the laity is being lived
out within the broader context of a movement away from a
religious culture which is oriented to an other-worldly
transcendence and a movement into solidarity with the human in
the context of our world, seeking to explicate the
transcendent dimension from within contemporary culture.

These developments give credence to a statement recently
made by J.M. Tillard, O.P., that, although Perfectae Caritatis
was originally conceived and constructed within the
perspectives of Lumen Gentium, it has come to be interpreted
in the spirit of Gaudium et Spes. Clearly the renewal of
religious life is taking place at the heart of the people of
God, rethinking its life and mission in the world.

Religious are called to make the gospel and the following
of Christ according to the gospel, the supreme rule of their
lives. This means the re-evangelizing of all of its
structures--not just ministry and government, but also
community and prayer, both communal as well as personal. We
witness as never before a national and world community broken
by poverty, injustice and oppression of the multitude, as well
as the yearning for unity, justice and communion which gives
credibility to the transcendent dimension of the human. To
incarnate the sign and sacrament of the world's salvation at
this moment of history calls us into the very heart of the
drama. If we are to become this sign in a language and find
hope, then our sources and resources must be deep and
meaningful and abundant. Daily nourishment from prayer and
community is a vital necessity.

For a moment then, I would like to futurize about some of
the characteristics evolving in these two essential elements
of religious life. I speak in these next remarks, predominantly as a woman religious, who has observed and is
experiencing today within herself two significant changes in
the spirituality, prayer and worship expressions of religious

--these are: (1) a feminization process, or as some say--discovering right brain potential; and (2) an extra-communal dimension. Both of these experiences for many women religious are shaping a new and broader image of God and church, both indicative signs of a spirituality for the future.

Woman's ministerial consciousness and socialization in a church limited until twenty or thirty years ago to private, male-dependent roles, prevented any development or realization of a meaningful feminine spirituality. This is changing. Largely due to the women's movement in this country and the impact of Vatican II, many religious are experiencing today an awakened consciousness that has led to new ways of praising God, personally and in communal worship. New images of God, new symbols and language and models from both scripture and church history are helping them to celebrate and stress the nurturing characteristics of God. Female theologians, spiritual directors, counselors and liturgists have moved us toward a new vision of world and Kingdom and future, and because of this feminine identification the bonding of lay women and women religious is well on its way. Gifted with a new urgency in mission and a new consciousness of self, these religious give hope to a future in which many collaborative modes of prayer and worship are possible within the American church. American women are just now in any significant numbers sensing their credibility and capability in assuming leadership roles in the spiritual renewal of the future.[9]

To explain community, one must see religious life as an integral human life which deals with all spheres of human experience. Thus, we have chosen and will continue to choose certain communal structures which will aid us in channeling this human experience into a meaningful relationship with God and with other human beings. All scriptural images related to church are images of a collectivity--people of God--the mystical body--the Kingdom. Community or corporateness is essential, but I believe we American religious are still struggling with a past of institutionalized corporateness and a present experience in a culture that is in the midst of a massive failure to sustain community or fidelity to significant relationships. Society of the future will not be looking for signs of idyllic saccharine relationships but of a truly human, committed trust and fidelity to the life project of a community-in-mission.

If the future calls us to anything, it calls us to be symbols of hope in an age so heavily burdened with discouragement and despair. To be viable as a symbol to others and attractive to those who may wish to collaborate with us, our life and life-style must be seen as way which confronts life's deepest questions and fulfills life's richest and most profound longings. The question often asked is: Are vows of poverty, celibacy and obedience still at the heart of this questioning and longing? We are living in an in-between period—a time when old symbols and language often fail to communicate and the new ones are not yet found. Does the vow of poverty place religious at the heart of a fundamental human choice between generousity and anxiety? [10] Does it make evident the scriptural sense of all creation as a gift of God to be shared unselfishly by all? How do we grapple with the labels, consumer—middle class—professional? does celibacy symbolize the universal human longing for the fullness of intimacy and generativity, a longing which can never be completely satisfied this side of the Kingdom? And does our vow of obedience speak to those who observe us, giving a voluntary acceptance to authority within community because we see such acceptance as nurturing a deeper faith in God, the supreme authority?

I believe we must address this challenge of vowed life in a humanly integrative way, shaping and motivating our awareness, that the way we live, the way we structure and root our lives in authority-obedience relationships, as well as our responses to local-national-global realities of injustice, our possible solidarity with the poor, our dialogue and questioning of the sinful structures of society—all of these are critical forms of communication. They will reveal very clearly our message to a contemporary nation and world.

Out of all these things is the stuff of the future. If religious life is to be refounded in the next century in this country, largely from the same congregations and church who have carried it through the last century, then, in summary, what are the hopes and concerns that face it?

1. The beginning demographic evidences are among us now. Smaller numbers and older persons. However, this need not be seen as a total disadvantage to anyone, for even as we speak, at least in women's communities, the results of the women's movement among those who realize that marriage and motherhood are not their vocation, are affecting and will continue to affect positively the quality and size of our numbers and the manner in which we collaborate, while an aging population of religious could become natural ministers to a large aging population of Americans.

2. Deinstitutionalization will affect life-style and ministry. However, communal purpose and spirituality will be the unifying factors, as sex and age and even marital status may be options for members. The concern will be the struggle between the concepts of a strong, supportive community or an efficient, capable organization.

3. New ministries must be developed, even sometimes in the shell of the old. It is the religious of the future who must bring the gospel to those many issues which are causing whole new pockets of poor and oppressed peoples, namely, the arms race, exploitation by multi-national corporations with unbelievable profits, supporting excessive consumption by the western world and repressive governments elsewhere. When we begin to confront these, regardless of the cost, religious life will be further renewed.

Our ministries will arise out of real needs and not out of career preparations or successes of the past. Some functions and roles will cease and other functions and roles will change. Again, as I mentioned before, the women's movement will have an effect on the kind of woman and perhaps man who comes to religious life. Also changed will be the manner in which women religious relate to the rest of church. If women remain second-class citizens in a male church, then strong and independent women will find religious life of the future either a life-giving place to be or will shun it as a dignified function of a patriarchal structure. That choice will shape religious congregations and the ministries they are able to provide.

Communities of male religious are facing a role change as well. As the vocation of the laity develops and the clericalization of church is brought more and more into sound theological question, many male religious will have to discover a whole new quality and meaning of religious vocation that will be just as crucial as the identity questions women religious have faced for the past decade. The fact of the matter is, there is really not so much a vocation crisis today as a crisis of significance and spirituality. The future will indeed be different and the differences are necessary. If this generation of religious chooses not to revive the vision, someone surely will, for our country and the world needs these qualities as never before.

I would like to end by sharing with you a reflection by Sr. M. Augusta Neal, S.N.D., a noted sociologist, who just recently published the results of her second major survey of the congregations of women religious in this country. Her first in 1966 was a significant tool used by many congregations in the important background against which to image our future. Her reflection on the new data is:

There is a curious contradiction that becomes evident as we examine pragmatic data concerning declining membership, unemployment of sisters, high costs of housing and transportation, health care, and professional education, on the one hand, and on the other, acknowledge the challenge of the new calls to the mission of assisting the poor to claim their rightful share of these very same resources that have become scarce for us, namely, membership, jobs, health care, housing and education. We have become aware of the mysterious call to obedience to God's will, in imitation of Jesus, to witness to a simple life-style and the generous sharing of our material resources with the oppressed poor. It might seem that as we have moved to this new mission embodying a special option for the poor, we have lost the security that others envied in our lives: the contemplative serenity, a dependable community, care in retirement, and something important and significant to do, i.e., relevant work. Yet, in reality, all these advantages have been heightened, not lost, as we have responded in new ways to the mission of Jesus.

At the present time, the institutional church is finding itself challenged in its official stance as it aligns itself with the liberation struggles, such as those in Central America, where people are organizing to claim their rights to the land and to resist militarily imposed oppression. The church has become a challenge to the State when it challenges the State's stand on justice and nuclear disarmament. This is a new era in the life of the church, one in which our search has brought us perhaps to an ambiguity in knowing who God is, but to more clarity as to where God is, that is, with the poor, as they seek to organize in solidarity to claim their human rights and socio-economic prerogatives. The call to do God's will brings some of our traditional customs into question. How shall we dress, where will we live, where and when will we worship, and how and with whom shall we pray become problems of new concern, subordinate to the mission in which we are called to participate in a radically new way. Like many other people, we long for peace and joyous community, but in addition, we also long to do God's will, manifested to us in Scripture in the Church, and in the signs of the times that new priorities have become manifest. In a world of adequate resources but inadequate use of them, our mission to the poor has very different demands from those it had in a world of manifestly scarce resources and too many people. War no longer appears as an acceptable option for the solution of over-population, now that preference for it as such a solution has been raised to full consciousness and rejected as such.

Although critical social action becomes a manifest need, preference for traditional skills is still manifest in our choice of training for mission, if not in our choice of ministry itself. Transitions require time, reflection, prayer, choice, and planning. What we have learned reluctantly is that shared responsibility does not obtain without shared authority, and we have been mandated to share responsibility by those who manage our affairs. By asking our administrators to be accountable for choices made, we have become aware of how very difficult altruistic choice is for us when we have power. But we are learning about the roots of conflict and, with that, valuing more highly the making of community. As community makers, we are learning the essentials of dialogue but we are also learning how rare a skill that is when command can supersede consensus. We do not yet have evidence that we really are inventing new models for effective action to change oppressive realities, but we do know that trying to do so is an essential part of our mission.

Congregations with diverse charisms are dividing up the diverse tasks that need to be done and finding collaboration a powerful mechanism for effective action, but this has scarcely begun. Models of caring and responsible acting have long been a religious agenda, but how one can fit such agenda into a changing world and continue the mission of Jesus is still a dilemma. That God will continue to call persons to religious life we recognize as a reality and that life is made holy by means of vows which express in a starkly clear way the directives of the Gospel, we affirm and highly value. Community life

and corporate commitment to mission are a necessity.
Personal and communal prayer and asceticism are a
necessity. Public witness has shifted from that of
physical appearance to stance on social issues.
Fostering a specific relationship with the Church as
people of God is a constant part of our new efforts
toward making community, and the experience has
confirmed the need of life-long formation.

A form of government calling for religious
authority based on faith is affirmed in our response
to a call to do God's will. Where our new insights
have led us, however, is to the discovery that
religious authority, that is, authority that binds us
together with God's people and God's mission, is far
more demanding of participation in decision-making
than we ever realized before. Doing this effectively
is still a mystery of the life of the Church today,
one to which we bind ourselves in loving and faithful
obedience.

One of our clearest models for religious life and
Church of the future is a South American tragedy that
occurred four years ago; one archbishop, Oscar Romero,
and four women: Maura Clark, Ita Ford, Dorothy Kazel,
and Jean Donovan. All dimensions of the Church and
Religious Life are found in this fivesome and their
martyred witness challenges us today. They represent
one of the earliest and one of the most recent
congregations of religious women, the Ursulines and
the Maryknoll Sisters, and the new vocation of lay
volunteer, together with a supportive pastoral Bishop.
Where our religious callings are sending us remains a
mystery; where our Church and the forces of our times
are moving us is becoming clearer.[11]

My optimistic Irish heart says that in that
comtemplative-apostolic perspective, we can and will face a
new future.

NOTES

1. James Hennesey, S.J., "To Share and to Learn" (See
above in Part III).
2. Lawrence Cada, S.M., Raymond Fitz, S.M., Gertrude
Foley, S.C., Thomas Giardino, S.M., and Carol Lichtenberg,
S.N.D. de N., Shaping the Coming Age of Religious Life (New
York: Seabury Press, 1979) 11.

3.   Johannes B. Metz, <u>Followers of Christ</u> (New York: Paulist Press, 1978) 11.

4.   Joseph J. Hayden, "Megatrends of Human Development," <u>Human Development</u> 5.1 (Spring, 1984) 15.

5.   Margaret Ann Leonard, L.S.A., "Appendix 3. A Synthesis of Six Essays," <u>Starting Points</u> (Washington, D.C., An LCWR Publication, 1980) 142.

6.   <u>Ibid</u>.

7.   Doris Gottemoeller, R.S.M., "The Changing Mission of the Church," <u>Starting Points</u> 15.

8.   Leonard, <u>op</u>. <u>cit</u>. 143.

9.   Sandra M. Schneiders, I.H.M., "Women's Experience and Spirituality," <u>Spirituality Today</u> 35.2 (Summer, 1983) 100.

10.   E. Edward Kinerk, S.J., "Religious Vows, Past and Present," <u>New Catholic World</u> 22.1349 (Sept/Oct, 1982) 212.

11.   Marie Augusta Neal, SND de Namur, <u>Catholic Sisters in Transition</u>. (Wilmington, Delaware: Michael Glazier, Inc., 1984) 76-79.

Essential Elements in Church Teaching on Religious Life

from the

Vatican Congregation for Religious and for Secular
Institutes

Introduction

1. The renewal of religious life during the past 20
years has been in many respects an experience of faith.
Courageous and generous efforts have been made to explore
prayerfully and deeply what it means to live consecrated life
according to the gospel, the founding charism of a religious
institute and the signs of the times.

Religious institutes dedicated to works of the apostolate
have tried, in addition, to meet the changes required by the
rapidly evolving societies to which they are sent and by the
developments in communication which affect their possibilities
of evangelization. At the same time, these institutes have
been dealing with sudden shifts in their own internal
situations: rising median age, fewer vocations, diminishing
numbers, pluriformity of lifestyle and works, and frequently
insecurity regarding identity. The result has been an
understandably mixed experience with many positive aspects and
some which raise important questions.

2. Now, with the ending of the period of special
experimentation mandated by Ecclesiae Sanctae II, many
religious institutes dedicated to works of the apostolate are
reviewing their experience. With the approval of their
revised constitutions and the coming into effect of the newly
formulated Code of Canon Law, they are moving into a new phase
of their history. At this point of new beginning, they hear
the repeated pastoral call of Pope John Paul II "to evaluate
objectively and humbly the years of experimentation so as to
recognize their positive elements and their deviations" (to
International Union of Women Superiors General 1979; to Major
Superiors of Men and Women Religious in France, 1980).

Religious superiors and chapters have asked this Sacred
Congregation for directives as they assess the recent past and
look toward the future. Bishops, too, because of their

special responsibility for fostering religious life, have asked for counsel. In view of the importance of these developments, the Sacred Congregation for Religious and for Secular Institutes, at the direction of the Holy Father, has prepared this text of principles and fundamental norms. Its purpose is to present a clear statement of the church's teaching regarding religious life at a moment which is particularly significant and opportune.

3. This teaching has been set forth in our times in the great documents of the Second Vatican Council, particularly Lumen Gentium, Perfectae Caritatis and Ad Gentes. It has been further developed in the apostolic exhortation Evangelica Testificatio of Paul VI, in the addresses of Pope John Paul II, and in the documents of this Sacred Congregation for Religious and for Secular Institutes, especially Mutuae Relationes, "Religious and Human Promotion," and "The Contemplative Dimension of Religious Life." Most recently, its doctrinal richness has been distilled and reflected in the revised Code of Canon Law. All these texts build on the rich patrimony of preconciliar teaching to deepen and refine a theology of religious life which has developed consistently down the centuries.

4. Religious life itself is a historical as well as a theological reality. The lived experience, today as in the past, is varied and this is important. At the same time, experience is a dimension which needs to be tested in relation to the gospel foundation, the magisterium of the church and the approved constitutions of an institute. The church regards certain elements as essential to religious life: the call of God and consecration to him through profession of the evangelical counsels by public vows; a stable form of community life; for institutes dedicated to apostolic works, a sharing in Christ's mission by a corporate apostolate faithful to a specific founding gift and sound tradition; personal and community prayer; asceticism; public witness; a specific relation to the church; a life-long formation; and a form of government calling for religious authority based on faith. Historical and cultural changes bring about evolution in the lived reality, but the forms and direction that the evolution takes are determined by the essential elements without which religious life loses its identity. In the present text addressed to institutes dedicated to apostolic works, this sacred congregation confines itself to a clarification and restatement of these essential elements.

I. Religious Life: A Particular form of Consecration to God

5. Consecration is the basis of religious life. By insisting on this, the church places the first emphasis on the initiative of God and on the transforming relation to him which religious life involves. Consecration is a divine action. God calls a person whom he sets apart for a particular dedication to himself. At the same time, he offers the grace to respond so that consecration is expressed on the human side by profound and free self-surrender. The resulting relationship is pure gift. It is a covenant of mutual love and fidelity, a communion and mission, established for God's glory, the joy of the person consecrated and the salvation of the world.

6. Jesus himself is the one whom the Father consecrated and sent in a supreme way (cf. Jn 10:36). He sums up all the consecrations of the old law, which foreshadowed his own, and in him is consecrated the new people of God, henceforth mysteriously united to him. By baptism, Jesus shares his life with each Christian. Each is sanctified in the Son. Each is called to holiness. Each is sent to share the mission of Christ and is given the capacity to grow in the love and service of the Lord. This baptismal gift is the fundamental Christian consecration and is the root of all others.

7. Jesus lived his won consecration precisely as Son of God: dependent on the Father, loving him above all the completely given to his will. These aspects of his life as Son are shared by all Christians. To some, however, for the sake of all, God gives the gift of a closer following of Christ in his poverty, chastity and obedience through a public profession of these counsels mediated by the church. This profession, in imitation of Christ, manifests a particular consecration which is "rooted in that of baptism and is a fuller expression of it" (Perfectae Caritatis 5). The fuller expression recalls the hold of the divine person of the Word over the human nature which he assumed and it invites a response like that of Jesus: a dedication of oneself to God in a way which he alone makes possible and which witnesses to his holiness and absoluteness. Such a consecration is a gift of God: a grace freely given.

8. When consecration by profession of the counsels is affirmed as a definitive response to God in a public commitment taken before the church, it belongs to the life and holiness of the church (cf. Lumen Gentium 44). It is the church which authenticates the gift and which mediates the

313

consecration. Christians so consecrated strive to live now what will be in the after life. Such a life "more fully manifests to all believers the presence of heavenly goods already possessed here below" (ibid). In this manner these Christians "give outstanding and striking testimony that the world cannot be transfigured and offered to God without the spirit of the beatitudes" (Lumen Gentium 31).

9. Union with Christ by consecration through profession of the counsels can be lived in the midst of the world, translated in the work of the world and expressed by means of the world. This is the special vocation of the secular institutes, defined by Pius XII as "consecrated to God and to others" in the world and "by means of the world" (Primo Feliciter, V and II).

Of themselves, the counsels do not necessarily separate people from the world. In fact, it is a gift of God to the church that consecration through profession of the counsels can take the form of a life to be lived as a hidden leaven. Christians so consecrated continue the work of salvation by communicating the love of Christ through their presence in the world and through its sanctification from within. Their style of life and presence are not distinguished externally from those of their fellows Christians. Their witness is given in their ordinary environment of life. This discreet form of witness flows from the very nature of their secular vocation and is part of the way their consecration is meant to be lived (cf. Perfectae Caritatis 11).

10. Such is not the case, however, with those whose consecration by the profession of the counsels constitutes them as religious. The very nature of religious vocation involves a public witness to Christ and to the church. Religious profession is made by vows which the church receives as public. A stable form of community life in an institute canonically erected by the competent ecclesiastical authority manifests in a visible way the covenant and communion which religious life expresses. A certain separation from family and from professional life at the time a person enters the novitiate speaks powerfully of the absoluteness of God. At the same time, it is the beginning of a new and deeper bond in Christ with the family that one has left. This bond becomes firmer as detachment from otherwise legitimate relationships, occupations and forms of relaxation continues to reflect God's absoluteness publicly throughout life. A further aspect of the public nature of religious consecration is that the apostolate of religious is in some sense always corporate.

Religious presence is visible, affecting ways of acting, attire and style of life.

11.   Religious consecration is lived within a given institute according to constitutions which the church, by her authority, accepts and approves. This means that consecration is lived according to specific provisions which manifest and deepen a distinctive identity. The identity derives from that action of the Holy Spirit which is the institute's founding gift and which creates a particular type of spirituality, of life, of apostolate and of tradition (cf. Mutuae Relationes 11). Looking at the numerous religious families, one is struck by the wide variety of founding gifts. The council laid stress on the need to foster these as so many gifts of God (cf. Perfectae Caritatis 2b). They determine the nature, spirit, purpose and character which form each institute's spiritual patrimony, and they are basic to that sense of identity which is a key element in the fidelity of every religious (cf. Evangelica Testificatio 51).

12.   In the case of institutes dedicated to works of the apostolate, religious consecration has a further note; the participation in Christ's mission is specific and concrete. Perfectae Caritatis recalls that the very nature of these institutes requires "apostolic activity and charitable services" (Perfectae Caritatis 8). By the fact of their consecration, the members are dedicated to God and available to be sent. Their vocation implies active proclamation of the gospel through "works of charity that are entrusted to the institute by the church and are to be performed in her name" (ibid.) For this reason, the apostolic activity of such institutes is not simply a human effort to do good but "an action that is deeply ecclesial" (Evangelii Nuntiandi 60). It is rooted in union with the Christ who was sent by the Father to do his work. It expresses a consecration by God which sends the religious to serve Christ in his members in concrete ways (cf. Evangelii Nuntiandi 69) corresponding to the founding gift of the institute (cf. Mutuae Relationes 15). "The entire religious life of such religious should be imbued with an apostolic spirit, and all their apostolic activity with a religious spirit" (Perfectae Caritatis 8).

II. Characteristics

1. Consecration by Public Vows

13. It is proper, though not exclusive, to religious life to profess the evangelical counsels by vows which the church receives. These are a response to the prior gift of God which, being a gift of love, cannot be rationalized. It is something that God himself works in the person he has chosen.

14. As a response to the gift of God, the vows are a triple expression of a single yes to the one relationship of total consecration. They are the act by which the religious "makes himself or herself over to God in a new a special way" (Lumen Gentium 44). By them, the religious gladly dedicates the whole of life to God's service, regarding the following of Christ "as the one thing that is necessary, and seeking God before all else and only him" (Perfectae Caritatis 5). Two reasons prompt this dedication: first, a desire to be free from hindrances that could prevent the person from loving God ardently and worshipping him perfectly (cf. Lumen Gentium 44). The vows themselves "show forth the unbreakable bond that exists between Christ and his bride the church. The more stable and firm these bonds are, the more perfect will the Christian's religious consecration be" (ibid.).

15. The vows themselves are specific: three ways of pledging oneself to live as Christ lived in areas which cover the whole of life: possession, affections, autonomy. Each emphasizes a relation to Jesus, consecrated and sent. He was rich but became poor for our sakes, emptying himself and having nowhere to lay his head. He loved with an undivided heart, universally and to the end. He came to do the will of the Father who sent him, and he did it steadily, learning obedience through suffering and becoming a cause of salvation for all who obey.

16. The distinguishing mark of the religious institute if found in the way in which these values of Christ are visibly expressed. For this reason, the content of the vows in each institute, as expressed in its constitutions, must be clear and unambiguous. The religious forgoes the free use and disposal of his or her property, depends through the lawful superior on the institute for the provision of material goods, puts gifts and all salaries in common as belonging to the community, and accepts and contributes to a simple manner of life. He or she undertakes to live chastity by a new title,

that of the vow, and to live it in consecrated celibacy for the sake of the kingdom. This implies a manner of life that is a convincing and credible witness to a total dedication to chastity and which forgoes any behavior, personal relationships and forms of recreation incompatible with this. The religious is pledged to obey the directives of lawful superiors according to the constitutions of the institute and further accepts a particular obedience to the Holy Father in virtue of the vow of obedience. Implicit in the commitment to the institute which the vows include, is the pledge to live a common life in communion with the brothers or sisters of the community. The religious undertakes to live in fidelity to the nature, purpose, spirit and character of the institute as expressed in its constitutions, proper law and sound traditions. There is also the willing undertaking of a life of radical and continuous conversion as demanded by the gospel, further specified in the content of each of the vows.

17. Consecration through profession of the evangelical counsels in religious life necessarily inspires a way of living which has a social impact. Social protest is not the purpose of the vows, but there is no doubt that the living of them has always offered a witness to values which challenge society just as they challenge the religious themselves. Religious poverty, chastity and obedience can speak forcefully and clearly to today's world which is suffering from so much consumerism and discrimination, eroticism and hatred, violence and oppression (cf. "Religious and Human Promotion" 15).

2. Communion in Community

18. Religious consecration establishes a particular communion between religious and God and, in him, between the members of the same institute. This is the basic element in the unity of an institute. A shared tradition, common works, well-considered structures, pooled resources, common constitutions and a single spirit can all help to build up and strengthen unity. The foundation of unity, however, is the communion in Christ established by the one founding gift. This communion is rooted in religious consecration itself. It is animated by the gospel spirit, nourished by prayer, distinguished by generous mortification and characterized by the joy and hope which spring from the fruitfulness of the cross (cf. Evangelica Testificatio 41).

19. For religious, communion in Christ is expressed in a stable and visible way through community life. So important is community living to religious consecration that every

religious, whatever his or her apostolic work, is bound to it by the fact of profession and must normally live under the authority of a local superior in a community of the institute to which he or she belongs. Normally, too, community living entails a daily sharing of life according to specific structures and provisions established in the constitutions. Sharing or prayer, work, meals, leisure, common spirit, "relationships of friendship, cooperation in the same apostolate, and mutual support in community of life chosen for a better following of Christ, are so many valuable factors in daily progress" (Evangelica Testificatio 39). A community gathered as a true family in the Lord's name enjoys his presence (cf. Mt 18:25) through the love of God which is poured out by the Holy Spirit (cf. Rom 5:5). Its unity is a symbol of the coming of Christ and is a source of apostolic energy and power (cf. Perfectae Caritatis 15). In it the consecrated life can thrive in conditions which are proper to it (cf. Evangelic Testificatio 38) and the ongoing formation of members can be assured. The capacity to live community life with its joys and restraints is a quality which distinguishes a religious vocation to a given institute and it is a key criterion of suitability in a candidate.

20. The local community, as the place where religious life is primarily lived, has to be organized in a way which makes religious values clear. Its center is the eucharist in which the members of the community participate daily as far as possible and which is honored by having an oratory where the celebration can take place and where the blessed sacrament is reserved (cf. Evangelica Testificatio 48). Time for prayer together daily based on the word of God and in union with the prayer of the church as offered especially in the Liturgy of the Hours, support community life. So also does an established rhythm of more intense times of prayer on a weekly and monthly basis, and the annual retreat.

Frequent reception of the sacrament of reconciliation is also part of religious life. In addition to the personal aspect of God's pardon and his renewing love in the individual, the sacrament builds community by its power of reconciliation and also manifests a special bond with the church.

In accordance with the proper law of the institute, moreover, time is provided for daily private prayer and for good spiritual reading. Ways are found for deepening the devotions particular to the institute itself, especially that to Mary, the Mother of God. The needs of the institute as a whole are kept before the members and there is an affectionate remembrance in prayer of those members who have already been called from this life by the Father.

The fostering of these religious values of community life and the ensuring of a suitable organization to promote them is the responsibility of all the members of the community, but in a particular way it is that of the local superior (cf. Evangelica Testificatio 26).

21. The style of community life itself will relate to the form of apostolate for which the members have responsibility and to the culture and society in which this responsibility is accepted. The form of apostolate may well decide the size and location of a community, its particular needs, its standards of living. But whatever the apostolate, the community will strive to live simply, according to norms established at institute and province level and applied to its own need. It will build into its way of living the asceticism implicit in religious consecration. It will provide for its members according to their needs and its own resources, always bearing in mind its responsibilities toward the institute as a whole and toward the poor.

22. In view of the crucial importance of community life, it should be noted that its quality is affected, positively or negatively, by two kinds of diversity in the institute: that of its members and that of its works. These are the diversities of Saint Paul's image of the body of Christ or the council's image of the pilgrim people of God. In both, the diversity is a variety of gifts which is meant to enrich the one reality. The criterion for accepting both members and works in a religious institute, therefore, is the building of unity (cf. Mutuae Relationes 12). The practical question is: Do God's gifts in this person or project or group make for unity and deepen communion? If they do, they can be welcomed. If they do not, then no matter how good the gifts may seem to be in themselves or how desirable they may appear to some members, they are not for this particular institute. It is a mistake to try to make the founding gift of the institute cover everything. A gift which would virtually separate a member from the communion of the community cannot be rightly encouraged. Nor is it wise to tolerate widely divergent lines of development which do not have a strong foundation of unity in the institute itself. Diversity without division and unity without regimentation are a richness and a challenge that help the growth of communities of prayer, joy and service in witness to the reality of Christ. It is a particular

responsibility of superiors and of those in charge of formation to ensure that the differences which make for disintegration are not mistaken for the genuine value of diversity.

3. Evangelical Mission

23. When God consecrates a person, he gives a special gift to achieve his own kind purposes: the reconciliation and salvation of the human race. He not only chooses, sets apart and dedicates the person to himself, but he engages him or her in his own divine work. Consecration inevitably implies mission. These are two facets of one reality. The choice of a person by God is for the sake of others: The consecrated person is one who is sent to do the work of God in the power of God. Jesus himself was clearly aware of this. Consecrated and sent to bring the salvation of God, he was wholly dedicated to the Father in adoration, love and surrender, and totally given to the work of the Father, which is the salvation of the world.

24. Religious, by their particular form of consecration, are necessarily and deeply committed to the mission of Christ. Like him, they are called for others: wholly turned in love to the Father and, by that very fact, entirely given to Christ's saving service of their brothers and sisters. This is true of religious life in all its forms. The life of cloistered contemplatives has its own hidden, apostolic fruitfulness (cf. Perfectae Caritatis 7) and proclaims to all that God exists and that God is love. Religious dedicated to works of the apostolate continue in our time Christ "announcing God's kingdom to the multitude, healing the sick and the maimed, converting sinners to a good life, blessing children, doing good to all and always obeying the will of the Father who sent him" (Lumen Gentium 46). This saving work of Christ is shared by means of concrete services mandated by the church in the approval of the constitutions. The fact of this approval qualifies the kind of service undertaken, since it must be faithful to the Gospel, to the church and to the institute. It also establishes certain limits, since the mission of religious is both strengthened and restricted by the consequences of consecration in a particular institute. Further, the nature of religious service determines how the mission is to be done: in a profound union with the Lord and sensitivity to the times which will enable the religious "to transmit the message of the incarnate word in terms which the world is able to understand" (Evangelica Testificatio 9).

25. Whatever may be the works of service by which the word is transmitted, the mission itself is undertaken as a community responsibility. It is to the institute as a whole that the church commits that sharing in the mission of Christ which characterizes it and which is expressed in works inspired by the founding charism. This corporate mission does not mean that all the members of the institute are doing the same thing or that the gifts and qualities of the individual are not respected. It does mean that the works of all the members are directly related to the common apostolate, which the church has recognized as expressing concretely the purpose of the institute. This common and constant apostolate is part of the institute's sound traditions. It is so closely related to identity that it cannot be changed without affecting the character of the institute itself. It is therefore a touchstone of authenticity in the evaluation of new works, whether these services will be done by a group or by individual religious. The integrity of the common apostolate is a particular responsibility of major superiors. They must see that the institute is at once faithful to its traditional mission in the church and open to new ways of undertaking it. Works need to be renewed and revitalized, but this has to be done always in fidelity to the institute's approved apostolate and in collaboration with the respective ecclesiastical authorities. Such renewal will be marked by the four great loyalties emphasized in the document, "Religious and Human Promotion": "Fidelity to humanity and to our times; fidelity to Christ and the Gospel; fidelity to the church and its mission in the world; fidelity to religious life and to the charism of the institute" (13).

26. The individual religious finds his or her personal apostolic work within the ecclesial mission of the institute. Basically it will be a work of evangelization: striving in the church and according to the mission of the institute to help bring the good news to "all the strata of humanity and through it to transform humanity itself from within" (Evangelii Nuntiandi 18); "Religious and Human Promotion," introduction). In practice, it will involve some form of service in keeping with the purpose of the institute and usually undertaken with brothers or sisters of the same religious family. In the case of some clerical or missionary institutes, it may sometimes involve working alone. In the case of other institutes, working alone is with the permission of superiors to meet an exceptional need for a certain time. At the end of life, the apostolate will be for many a mission of prayer and suffering only.

But at whatever stage, the apostolic work of the individual is that of a religious sent in communion with an ecclesially missioned institute. Such work has its source in religious obedience (cf. Perfectae Caritatis 8 and 10). Therefore, it is distinct in its character from those apostolates proper to the laity (cf. "Religious and Human Promotion" 22; Apostolicam Actuositatem 2, 7, 13, 25). It is by their obedience in their corporate and ecclesial works of evangelization that religious manifest one of the most important aspects of their lives. They are genuinely apostolic, not because they have an "apostolate," but because they are living as the apostles lived: following Christ in service and in communion according to the teaching of the gospel in the church he founded.

27. There is no doubt, that, in many areas of the world at the present time, religious institutes dedicated to apostolic works are facing difficult and delicate questions with respect to the apostolate. The reduced number of religious, the fewer young persons entering, the rising median age, the social pressures from contemporary movements are coinciding with an awareness of a wider range of needs, a more individual approach to personal development and a higher level of awareness with regard to issues of justice, peace and human promotion. There is a temptation to want to do everything. There is also a temptation to leave works which are stable and a genuine expression of the institute's charism for others which seem more immediately relevant to social needs but which are less expressive of the institute's identity. There is a third temptation to scatter the resources of an institute in a diversity of short-term activities only loosely connected with the founding gift.

In all these instances, the effects are not immediate but, in the long run, what will suffer is the unity and identity of the institute itself, and this will be a loss to the church and to its mission.

4. Prayer

28. Religious life cannot be sustained without a deep life of prayer, individual, communal and liturgical. The religious who embraces concretely a life of total consecration is called to know the risen Lord by a warm, personal knowledge, and to know him as one with whom he or she is personally in communion: "This is eternal life: to know the only true God and Jesus Christ whom he has sent" (Jn 17:3). Knowledge of him in faith brings love: "You did not see him,

yet you love him; and still without seeing him you are already filled with a joy so glorious that it cannot be described" (1 Pt 1:8). This joy of love and knowledge is brought about in many ways, but fundamentally, and as an essential and necessary means, through individual and community encounter with God in prayer. This is where the religious finds "the concentration of the heart on God" ("The Contemplative Dimension of Religious Life" 1), which unifies the whole of life and mission.

29. As with Jesus for whom prayer as a distinct act held a large and essential place in life, the religious needs to pray as a deepening of union with God (cf. Lk 5:16). Prayer is also a necessary condition for proclaiming the Gospel (cf. Mk 1:35-38). It is the context of all important decisions and events (cf. Lk 6:12-13). As with Jesus, too, the habit of prayer is necessary if the religious is to have that contemplative vision of things by which God is revealed in faith in the ordinary events of life (cf. "The Contemplative Dimension of Religious Life" 1). This is the contemplative dimension which the church and the world have the right to expect of religious by the fact of their consecration. It must be strengthened by prolonged moments of time apart for exclusive adoration of the Father, love of him and listening in silence before him. For this reason, Paul VI insisted: "Faithfulness to daily prayer always remains for each religious a basic necessity. Prayer must have a primary place in your constitutions and in your lives" (Evangelica Testificatio 45).

30. By saying "in your constitutions," Paul VI gave a reminder that for the religious prayer is not only a personal turning in love to God but also a community response of adoration, intercession, praise and thanksgiving that needs to be provided for in a stable way (cf. Evangelica Testificatio 43). This does not happen by chance. Concrete provisions at the level of each institute and of each province and local community are necessary if prayer is to deepen and thrive in religious life individually and communally. Yet only through prayer is the religious ultimately able to respond to his or her consecration. Community prayer has an important role in giving this necessary spiritual support. Each religious has a right to be assisted by the presence and example of other members of the community at prayer. Each has the privilege and duty or praying with the others and of participating with them in the liturgy which is the unifying center of their life. Such mutual help encourages the effort to live the life of union with the Lord to which religious are called. "People

have to feel that through you someone else is at work. To the extent that you live your total consecration to the Lord, you communicate something of him and, ultimately, it is he for whom the human heart is longing" (Pope John Paul II, Allotting [Altoetting?-Ed.]).

5. Asceticism

31. The discipline and silence necessary for prayer are a reminder that consecration by the vows of religion requires a certain asceticism of life "embracing the whole being" (Evangelica Testificatio 46). Christ's response of poverty, love and obedience led him to the solitude of the desert, the pain of contradiction and the abandonment of the cross. The consecration of religious enters into this way of his; it cannot be a reflection of his consecration if its expression in life does not hold an element of self-denial. Religious life itself is an ongoing, public, visible expression of Christian conversion. It calls for the leaving of all things and the taking up of one's cross to follow Christ throughout the whole of life. This involves the asceticism necessary to live in poverty of spirit and of fact; to love as Christ loves; to give up one's own will for God's sake to the will of another who represents him, however imperfectly. It calls for the self-giving without which it is not possible to live either a good community life or a fruitful mission.

Jesus' statement that the grain of wheat needs to fall to the ground and die if it is to bear fruit has a particular application to religious because of the public nature of their profession. It is true that much of today's penance is to be found in the circumstances of life and should be accepted there. However, unless religious build into their lives "a joyful, well-balanced austerity" (Evangelica Testificatio 30) and deliberately determined renunciations, they risk losing the spiritual freedom necessary for living counsels. Indeed, without such austerity and renunciation, their consecration itself can be affect. This is because there cannot be a public witness to Christ poor chaste and obedient without asceticism. Moreover, by professing the counsels by vows, religious undertake to do all that is necessary to deepen and foster what they have vowed, and this means a free choice of the cross, that it may be "as it was for Christ, proof of the greatest love" (Evangelica Testificatio 29).

6. Public Witness

32. Of its nature, religious life is a witness that

should clearly manifest the primacy of the love of God and do so with a strength coming from the Holy Spirit (cf. Evangelica Testificatio 1). Jesus himself did this supremely: witnessing to the Father "with the power of the Spirit in him" (Lk 4:14) in his living, dying, rising and remaining for ever the faithful witness. In his turn he sent his apostles in the power of the same Spirit to be his witnesses in Jerusalem, throughout Judea and Samaria and indeed to the ends of the earth (cf. Acts 1:8). The subject of their testimony was always the same: "Something which has existed since the beginning, that we have heard and we have seen with our own eyes; that we have watched and touched with our hands; the Word, who is life" (1 Jn 1:1) Jesus Christ "the Son of God, proclaimed in all his power through his resurrection from the dead" (Rom 1:5).

33. Religious, too, in their own times, are called to bear witness to a similar, deep, personal experience of Christ and also to share the faith, hope, love and joy which that experience goes on inspiring. Their continuous individual renewal of life should be a source of new growth in the institutes to which they belong, recalling the words of Pope John Paul II: "What counts most is not what religious do, but what they are as persons consecrated to be Lord" (Message to the plenary assembly of the Sacred Congregation for Religious and for Secular Institutes, March 1980). Not only directly in works of announcing the gospel, but even more forcefully in the very way that they live, they should be choices that affirm with confidence and conviction: We have seen the Lord. He is risen. We have heard his word.

34. The totality of religious consecration requires that the witness to the gospel be given publicly by the whole of life. Values, attitudes and lifestyle attest forcefully to the place of Christ in one's life. The visibility of this witness involves the forgoing of standards of comfort and convenience that would otherwise be legitimate. It requires a restraint on forms of relaxation and entertainment (cf. Ecclesiae Sanctae I, 2; Christus Dominus 33-35). To ensure this public witness, religious willingly accept a pattern of life that is not permissive but largely laid down for them. They wear a religious garb that distinguishes them as consecrated persons, and they have a place of residence which is properly established by their institute in accordance with common law and their own constitutions. Such matters as travel and social contacts are in accord with the spirit and character of their institute and with religious obedience. These provisions alone do not ensure the desired public

witness to the joy, hope and love of Jesus Christ, but they offer important means to it, and it is certain that religious witness is not given without them.

35. The way of working, too, is important for public witness. What is done and how it is done should both proclaim Christ from the poverty of someone who is not seeking his or her own fulfillment and satisfaction. In our age powerlessness is one of the great poverties. The religious accepts to share this intimately by the generosity of his or her obedience, thereby becoming one with the poor and powerless in a particular way, as Christ was in his passion. Such a person knows what it is to stand in need before God, to love as Jesus does and to work at God's plan on God's terms. Moreover, in fidelity to religious consecration, he or she lives the institute's concrete provisions for promoting these attitudes.

36. Fidelity to the mandated apostolate of one's own religious institute is also essential for true witness. Individual dedication to perceived needs at the expense of the mandated works of the institute can only be damaging. However, there are ways of living and working which witness to Christ very clearly in the contemporary situation.

The constant evaluation of use of goods and of style of relationships in one's own life is one of the religious' most effective ways of promoting the justice of Christ at the present time (cf. Evangelii Nuntiandi 39), of those denied the right to birth and life, of unjustified restrictions of human freedom, of social inadequacy that causes suffering in the old, the sick, and the marginalized: These are present continuations of the passion which call particularly to religious who are dedicated to apostolic works (cf. "Religious and Human Promotion" 4d).

37. The response will very according to the mission, tradition and identity of each institute. Some may need to seek approval for new missions in the church. In other cases, new institutes may be recognized to meet specific needs. In most cases the creative use of well-established works to meet new challenges will be a clear witness to Christ yesterday, today and forever. The witness of religious who, in loyalty to the church and to the tradition of their institute, strive courageously and with love for the defense of human rights and for the coming of the kingdom in the social order can be a clear echo of the gospel and the voice of the church (cf. "Religious and Human Promotion" 3). It is so, however, to the

extent that it manifests publicly the transforming power of Christ in the church and the vitality of the institute's charism to the people of our time. Finally, perseverance, which is a further gift of the God of the covenant, is the unspoken but eloquent witness of the religious to the faithful God whose love is without end.

7. Relation to the Church

38. Religious life has its own place in relation to the divine and hierarchical structure of the church. It is not a kind of intermediate way between the clerical and lay conditions of life, but comes from both as a special gift of the entire church (cf. Lumen Gentium 43; Mutuae Relationes 10). In particular, by being an outward, social sign of the mystery of God's consecrating action throughout life, and by being this through the mediation of the church for the good of the entire body, the religious life in a special way participates in the sacramental nature of the people of God. This is because it is itself a part of the church as mystery and as social reality, and it cannot exist without both these aspects.

39. It was this dual reality that the Second Vatican Council underscored in insisting on the sacramental nature of the church: at once necessarily a mystery, invisible, a divine communion in the new life of the Spirit; and equally necessarily a social reality, visible, a human community under one who represents Christ the head. As mystery (cf. Lumen Gentium 1), the church is the new creation, vivified by the Spirit and assembled in Christ to come with confidence to the Father's throne of grace (cf. Heb 4:16). As social reality, she presupposes the historical initiative of Jesus Christ, his paschal going to the Father, his objective headship of the church he founded and the hierarchic character which proceeds from that headship: from his setting up of a variety of ministries which aim at the good of the whole body (cf. Lumen Gentium 18, cf. Mutuae Relationes 1-5). The twofold aspect of "visible social organism and invisible divine presence intimately united" (Mutuae Relationes 3) is what gives the church "her special sacramental nature by virtue of which she is the visible sacrament of saving unity" Lumen Gentium 9). She is both subject and object of faith essentially transcending the parameters of any purely sociological perspective even while she renews her human structures in the light of historical evolutions and cultural changes (cf. Mutuae Relationes 3). Her very nature makes her at once "universal sacrament of salvation" (Lumen Gentium 48): a

visible sign of the mystery of God, and hierarchical reality; a concrete divine provision by which that sign can be authenticated and made efficacious.

40. The religious life touches both aspects. The founders and foundresses of religious institutes ask the hierarchical church publicly to authenticate the gift of God on which the existence of their institute depends. By doing so, the founders and those who follow them also give witness to the mystery of the church, because each institute exists in order to build up the body of Christ in the unity of its diverse functions and activities.

41. In their origins, religious institutes depend in a unique way on the hierarchy. The bishops in communion with the successor of Peter form a college that jointly shows forth and carries out in the church-sacrament the functions of Christ the head (cf. Mutuae Relationes 6, Lumen Gentium 21, Perfectae Caritatis 1, 2, Christus Dominus 2). They have not only the pastoral charge of fostering the life of the Christ in the faithful but also the duty of verifying gifts and competencies. They are responsible for coordinating the church's energies and for guiding the entire people in living in the world as a sign and instrument of salvation. They therefore have in a special way the ministry of discernment with regard to the manifold gifts and initiatives among God's people. As a particularly rich and important example of these manifold gifts, each religious institute depends for the authentic discernment of its founding charism on the God-given ministry of the hierarchy.

42. This relationship obtains not only the the first recognition of a religious institute but also for its ongoing development. The church does more than bring an institute into being. She accompanies, guides, corrects and encourages it in its fidelity to its founding gift (cf. Lumen Gentium 45) for it is a living element in her own life and growth. She receives the vows made in the institute as vows of religion with ecclesial consequences, involving a consecration made by God himself through her mediation (cf. Mutuae Relationes 8). She gives to the institute a public sharing in her own mission, both concrete and corporate (cf. Lumen Gentiumm 17; Ad Gentes 40). She confers on the institute, in accordance with her own common law and with the constitutions that she has approved, the religious authority necessary for the life of vowed obedience. In short, the church continues to mediate the consecratory action of God in a specific way, recognizing and fostering this particular form of consecrated life.

43. In daily practice, this ongoing relation of religious to the church is most often worked out at diocesan or local level. The document _Mutuae Relationes_ is entirely devoted to this theme from the point of view of present-day application. Suffice it to say here that the life and mission of the people of God are one. They are fostered by all according to the specific roles and functions of each. The unique service rendered by religious to this life and mission lies in the total and public nature of their vowed Christian living, according to a community founding gift approved by ecclesiastical authority.

8. Formation

44. Religious formation fosters growth in the life of consecration to the Lord from the earliest stages, when a person first becomes seriously interested in undertaking it, to its final consummation, when the religious meets the Lord definitively in death. The religious lives a particular from of life, and life itself is in constant ongoing development. It does not stand still. Nor is the religious simply called and consecrated once. The call of God and the consecration by him continue throughout life, capable of growing and deepening in ways beyond our understanding. The discernment of the capacity to live a life that will foster this growth according to the spiritual patrimony and provisions of a given institute, and the accompanying of the life itself in its personal evolution in each member in community, are the two main facets of formation.

45. For each religious, formation is the process of becoming more and more a disciple of Christ, growing in union with and in configuration to him. It is a matter of taking on increasingly the mind of Christ, of sharing more deeply his gift of himself to the Father and his brotherly service of the human family, and of doing this according to the founding gift which mediates the Gospel to the members of a given religious institute. Such a process requires a genuine conversion. The "putting on Jesus Christ" (cf. Rom 13:14, Gal 3:27, Eph 4:24) implies the stripping off of selfishness and egoism (cf. Eph 4:22-24, Col 3:9-10). The very fact of "walking henceforth according to the Spirit" means giving up "the desires of the flesh" (Gal 5:16). The religious professes to make this putting on of Christ, in his poverty, his love and his obedience, the essential pursuit of life. It is a pursuit which never ends. There is a constant maturing in it, and this reaches not only to spiritual values but also to those which contribute psychologically, culturally and socially to

the fullness of the human personality.

As the religious grows toward the fullness of Christ according to his or her state of life, there is a verification of the statement in Lumen Gentium: "While the profession of the evangelical counsels involves the renunciation of goods that undoubtedly deserve to be highly valued, it does not constitute an obstacle to the true development of the human person but by its nature is extremely beneficial to that development" (Lumen Gentium 46).

46.   The ongoing configuration to Christ comes about according to the charism and provisions of the institute to which the religious belongs.   Each has its own spirit, character, purpose and tradition, and it is in accordance with these that the religious grow in their union with Christ.   For religious institutes dedicated to works of the apostolate, formation includes the preparation and continual updating of the members to undertake the works proper to their institute, not simply as professionals, but as "living witnesses to love without limit and to the Lord Jesus" (Evangelica Testificatio 53).   Accepted as a matter of personal responsibility by each religious, formation becomes not only an individual personal growth, but also a blessing to the community and a source of fruitful energy for the apostolate.

47.   Since the initiative for religious consecration is in the call of God, it follows that God himself, working through the Holy Spirit of Jesus, is the first and principal agent in the formation of the religious.   He acts through his word and sacraments, through the prayer of the liturgy, the magisterium of the church and, more immediately, through those who are called in obedience to help the formation of their brothers and sisters in a more special way.

Responding to God's grace and guidance, the religious accepts in love the responsibility for personal formation and growth, welcoming the consequences of this response which are unique to each person and always unpredictable.   The response, however, is not made in isolation.   Following the tradition of the early fathers of the desert and of all the great religious founders in the matter of provision for spiritual guidance, religious institutes each have members who are particularly qualified and appointed to help their sisters and brothers in this matter.   Their role varies according to the stage reached by the religious, but its main responsibilities are: discernment of God's action; the accompaniment of the religious in the ways of God; the nourishing of life with solid doctrine and the practice of prayer; and, particularly in the first stages the evaluation of the journey thus far made. The director of novices and the religious responsible for those in first profession have also the task of verifying whether the young religious have the call and capacity for first and for final profession. The whole process, at hatever stage, takes place in community. A prayerful and dedicated community, building its union in Christ and sharing his mission together is a natural milieu of formation. It will be faithful to the traditions and constitutions of the institute, and be well-inserted in the institute as a whole, in the church and in the society it serves. It will support its members and keep before them in faith during the whole of their lives the goal and values which their consecration implies.

48. Formation is not achieved all at once. The journey from the first to the final response falls broadly into five phases: the prenovitiate, in which the genuineness of the call is identified as far as possible; the novitiate which is initiation into a new form of life; first profession and the period of maturing prior to perpetual profession; perpetual profession and the ongoing formation of the mature years; and finally the time of diminishment, in whatever way this comes, which is a preparation for the definitive meeting with the Lord. Each of these phases has its own goal, content and particular provisions. The stages of novitiate and profession especially, because of their importance, are carefully determined in their main lines by the church in her common law. All the same, much is left to the responsibility of individual institutes. These are asked to give details concretely in their constitutions for a considerable number of the provisions to which common law refers in principle.

9. Government

49. The government of apostolic religious, like all the other aspects of their life, is based on faith and on the reality of their consecrated response to God in community and mission. These women and men are members of religious institutes whose structures reflect the Christian hierarchy of which the head is Christ himself. They have chosen to live vowed obedience as a value in life. They therefore require a form of government that expresses these values and a particular form of religious authority. Such authority, which is particular to religious institutes, does not derive from the members themselves. It is conferred by the church at the time of establishing each institute and by the approving of

its constitutions. It is an authority invested in superiors for the duration of their term of service at general, intermediate or local level. It is to be exercised according to the norms of common and proper law in a spirit of service, reverencing the human person of each religious as a child of God (cf. Perfectae Caritatis 14), fostering cooperation for the good of the institute, but always preserving the superior's final right of discerning and deciding what is to be done (cf. Evangelica Testificatio 25). Strictly speaking, this religious authority is not shared. It may be delegated according to the constitutions for particular purposes but it is normally ex officio and is invested in the person of the superior.

50. Superiors do not exercise authority in isolation, however. Each must have the assistance of the council whose members collaborate with the superior according to norms that are constitutionally established. Councilors do not exercise authority by right of office as superiors do, but they collaborate with the superior and help by their consultative or deliberative vote according to ecclesiastical law and the constitutions of the institute.

51. Supreme authority in an institute is also exercised, though in an extraordinary manner, by a general chapter while it is in session. This again is according to the constitutions, which should designate the authority of the chapter in such a way that it is quite distinct from that of the superior general. The general chapter is essentially an ad hoc body. It is composed of ex officio members and elected delegates who ordinarily meet together for one chapter only. As a sign of unity in charity, the celebration of a general chapter should be a moment of grace and of the action of the Holy Spirit in an institute. It should be a joyful, paschal and ecclesial experience which benefits the institute itself and also the whole church. The general chapter is meant to renew and protect the spiritual patrimony of the institute as well as elect the highest superior and councilors, conduct major matters of business and issue norms for the whole institute. Chapters are of such importance that the proper law of the institute has to determine accurately what pertains to them whether at general or at other levels: that is, their nature, authority, composition, mode of proceeding and frequency of celebration.

52. Conciliar and postconciliar teaching insists on certain principles with regard to religious government which have given rise to considerable changes during the past 20

years. It laid down clearly the basic need for effective, personal, religious authority at all levels, general, intermediate and local, if religious obedience is to be lived (cf. Perfectae Caritatis 14; Evangelica Testificatio 25). It further underlined the need for consultation, for appropriate involvement of the members in the government of the institute, for shared responsibility and for subsidiarity (cf. Ecclesiae Sanctae II, 18). Most of these principles have by now found their way into revised constitutions. It is important that they be so understood and implemented as to fulfill the purpose of religious government: the building of a united community in Christ in which God is sought and loved before all things, and the mission of Christ is generously accomplished.

Mary, Joy and Hope of Religious Life

53. It is especially in Mary, Mother of God and Mother of the Church, that religious life comes to understand itself most deeply and finds its sign of certain hope (cf. Lumen Gentium 68). She, who was conceived immaculate because she was called from among God's people to bear God himself most intimately and to give him to the world, was consecrated totally by the overshadowing of the Holy Spirit. She was the ark of the new covenant itself. The handmaid of the Lord in the poverty of the anawim, the mother of fair love from Bethlehem to Calvary and beyond, the obedient virgin whose yes to God changed our history, the missionary hurrying to Hebron, the one who was sensitive to needs at Cana, the steadfast witness of the foot of the cross, the center of unity which held the young church together in its expectation of the Holy spirit. Mary showed throughout her life all those values to which religious consecration is directed. She is the mother of religious in being mother of him who was consecrated and sent, and in her fiat and magnificat religious life finds the totality of its surrender to and the thrill of its joy in the consecratory action of God.

III. Some Fundamental norms

The revised Code of Canon Law transcribes into canonical norms ·the rich conciliar and postconciliar teaching of the church on religious life. Together with the documents of the Second Vatican Council and the pronouncements of successive popes in recent years, it gives the basis on which current church praxis regarding religious life is founded. The natural evolution necessary for ordinary living will always continue, but the period of special experimentation for religious institutes, as provided by the motu proprio Ecclesiae Sanctae II ended with the celebration of the second ordinary general chapter after the special chapter of renewal.

Now the revised Code of Canon Law is the church's juridical foundation of religious life, both in its evaluation of the experience of experimentation and its looking to the future. The following fundamental norms contain a comprehensive synthesis of the church's provisions.

I. Call and Consecration

§1. Religious life is a form of life to which some Christians, both clerical and lay, are freely called by God so that they may enjoy a special gift of grace in the life of the church and may contribute each in his or her own way to the saving mission of the church (cf. Lumen Gentium 43).

§2. The gift of religious vocation is rooted in the gift of baptism but is not given to all the baptized. It is freely given and unmerited; offered by God to those whom he chooses freely from among his people and for the sake of his people (cf. Perfectae Caritatis 5).

§3. In accepting God's gift of vocation, religious respond to a divine call: dying to sin (cf. Rom 6:1), renouncing the world and living for God alone. Their whole lives are dedicated to his service and they seek and love above all else "God who has first loved us" (cf. 1 Jn 4:10; cf. Perfectae Caritatis 5 and 6). The focus of their lives is the closer following of Christ (cf. Evangelica Testificatio 7).

§4. The dedication of the whole life of the religious to God's service constitutes a special consecration of the whole person which manifests in the church a marriage effected by God, a sign of the future life. This consecration is by public vows, perpetual or temporary, the latter renewable on expiration.. By their vows, religious assume the observance of the three evangelical counsels; they are consecrated to God through the ministry of the church (Can. 607 and 654); and they are incorporated into their institute with the rights and duties defined by law.

§5. The conditions for validity of temporary profession, the length of this period and its possible extension are determined in the constitutions of each institute, always in conformity with the common law of the church (Can. 655-658).

§6. Religious profession is made according to the formula of vows approved by the Holy See for each institute. The formula is common because all members undertake the same obligations and, when fully incorporated have the same rights and duties. The individual religious may add an introduction and-or conclusion, if this is approved by competent authority.

§7. Considering its character and the ends proper to it, every institute should define in its constitutions the way in which the evangelical counsels of chastity, poverty and obedience are to be observed in its own particular way of life (Can. 598, 1).

II.   Community

§8. Community life, which is one of the marks of a religious institute (Can. 607, 2), is proper to each religious family. It gathers all the members together in Christ and should be so defined that it becomes a source of mutual aid to all, while helping to fulfill the religious vocation of each (Can. 602). It should offer an example of reconciliation in Christ, and of the communion that is rooted and founded in his love.

§9. For religious, community life is lived in a house lawfully erected under the authority of a superior designated by law (Can. 608). Such a house is erected with the written approval of the diocesan bishop (Can. 609) and should be able to provide suitably for the necessities of its members (Can. 610, 2), enabling community life to expand and develop with that understanding cordiality which nourishes hope (cf. Evangelica Testificatio 39).

§10. The individual house should have at least an oratory in which the eucharist may be celebrated and is reserved so that it is truly the center of the community (Can. 608).

§11. In all religious houses according to the character and mission of the institute and according to the specifications of its proper law, some part should be reserved to the members alone (Can. 667, 1). This form of separation from the world, which is proper to the purpose of each institute, is part of the public witness which religious give to Christ and to the church (cf. Can. 607, 3). It is also needed for the silence and recollection which foster prayers.

§12. Religious should live in their own religious house, observing a common life. They should not live alone without serious reason, and should not do so if there is a community of their institute reasonably near. If, however, there is a question of prolonged absence, the major superior with the consent of his or her council, may permit a religious to live outside the houses of the institute for a just cause, within the limits of common law (Can. 665, 1).

III. Identity

§13. Religious should regard the following of Christ proposed in the gospel and expressed in the constitutions of their institute as the supreme rule of life. (Can. 662).

§14. The nature, end, spirit and character of the institute, as established by the founder or foundress and approved by the church, should be preserved by all, together with the institute's sound traditions (Can. 578).

§15. To safeguard the proper vocation and identity of the individual institutes, the constitutions of each must provide fundamental norms concerning the government of the institute, the rule of life for its members, their incorporation and formation, and the proper object of the vows (Can. 587). This is in addition to the matters referred to in III, 14.

§16. The constitutions are approved by competent ecclesiastical authority. For diocesan institutes this is the local ordinary; for pontifical institutes, the Holy See. Subsequent modifications and authentic interpretations are also reserved to the same authority (Can. 576 and 587, 2).

§17. By their religious profession, the members of an institute bind themselves to observe the constitutions faithfully and with love, for they recognize in them the way of life approved by the church for the institute and the authentic expression of its spirit, tradition and law.

IV. Chastity

§18. The evangelical counsel of chastity embraced for the kingdom of heaven is a sign of the future life and a source of abundant fruitfulness in an undivided heart. It carries with it the obligation of perfect continence in celibacy (Can. 599).

§19. Discretion should be used in all things that could be dangerous to the chastity of a consecrated person (cf. Perfectae Caritatis 12; Can. 666).

V. Poverty

§20. The evangelical counsel of poverty in imitation of Christ calls for a life poor in fact and in spirit, subject to work and led in frugality and detachment from material possessions. Its profession by vow for the religious involves dependence and limitation in the use and disposition of temporalities according to the norms of the proper law of the institute (Can. 600)

§21. By the vow of poverty, religious give up the free use and disposal of goods having material value. Before first profession, they cede the administration of their goods to whomsoever they wish and, unless the constitutions determine otherwise, they freely dispose of their use and usufruct (Can. 668). Whatever the religious acquires by personal industry, by gift or as a religious, is acquired for the institute; whatever is acquired by way of pension, subsidy or insurance is also acquired for the institute unless the proper law states otherwise (Can. 668, 3).

VI Obedience

§22. The evangelical counsel of obedience, lived in faith, is a loving following of Christ who was obedient unto death.

§23. By their vow of obedience, religious undertake to submit their will to legitimate superiors (Can. 601) according to the constitutions. The constitutions themselves state who may give a formal command of obedience and in what circumstances.

§24. Religious institutes are subject to the supreme authority of the church in a particular manner (Can. 590), 1). All religious are obliged to obey the Holy Father as their highest superior in virtue of the vow of obedience (Can. 590, 2).

§25. Religious may not accept duties and offices outside their own institute without the permission of a lawful superior (Can. 671). Like clerics, they may not accept public offices which involve the exercise of civil power (Can. 285, 3; cf. also Can. 672 with the additional canons to which it refers).

VII. Prayer and Asceticism

§26. The first and principal duty of religious is assiduous union with God in prayer. They participate in the eucharistic sacrifice daily insofar as possible and approach the sacrament of penance frequently. The reading of sacred scripture, time for mental prayer, the worthy celebration of the Liturgy of the Hours according to the prescriptions of proper law, devotion to the Blessed Virgin, and a special time for annual retreat are all part of the prayer of religious (Can. 663, 664 and 1174).

§27. Prayer should be both individual and communitarian.

§28. A generous asceticism is constantly needed for daily conversion to the gospel (cf. Poenitemini II-III, 1, c). For this reason, religious communities must not only be prayerful groups but also ascetical communities in the church. In addition to being internal and personal, penance must also be external and communal (cf. "The Contemplative Dimension of Religious Life" 14; cf. Sacrosanctum Concilium 110).

VIII. Apostolate

§29. The apostolate of all religious consists first in the witness of their consecrated life which they are bound to foster by prayer and penance (Can. 673).

§30. In institutes dedicated to works of the apostolate, apostolic action is of their very nature. The life of the members should be imbued with an apostolic spirit, and all apostolic activity should be imbued with the religious spirit (Can. 675, 1).

§31. The essential mission of those religious undertaking apostolic works is the proclaiming of the word of God to those whom he places along their path, so as to lead them toward faith. Such a grace requires a profound union with the Lord, one which enables the religious to transmit the message of the incarnate word in terms which today's world is able to understand (cf. Evangelica Testificatio 9).

§32. Apostolic action is carried out in communion with the church, and in the name and by the mandate of the church (Can. 675, 3).

§33. Superiors and members should faithfully retain the mission and works proper to the institute. They should accommodate them with prudence to the needs of times and places (Can. 677, 1).

§34. In apostolic relations with bishops, religious are bound by Canons 678-683. They have the special obligation of being attentive to the magisterium of the hierarchy and of facilitating for the bishops the exercise of the ministry of teaching and witnessing authentically to divine truth (cf. Mutuae Relationes 33; cf. Lumen Gentium 25).

IX. Witness

§35. The witness of religious is public. This public witness to Christ and to the church implies separation from the world according to the character and purpose of each institute (Can. 607, 3).

§36. Religious institutes should strive to render a quasi-collective witness of charity and poverty (Can. 640).

§37. Religious should wear the religious garb of the institute, described in their proper law, as a sign of consecration and a witness of poverty (Can. 669. 1).

X. Formation

§38. No one may be admitted to religious life without suitable preparation (Can. 597, 3).

§39. Conditions for validity of admission, for validity of novitiate, and for temporary and perpetual profession are indicated in the common law of the church and the proper law of each institute (Can. 641-658). So also are provisions for the place, time, program and guidance of the novitiate and the requirements for the director of novices.

§40. The length of time of formation between first and perpetual vows is stated in the constitutions in accordance with common law (Can. 655).

§41. Throughout their entire life, religious should continue their spiritual, doctrinal and practical formation, taking advantage of the opportunities and time provided by superiors for this (Can. 661).

XI. Government

§42. It belongs to the competent ecclesiastical authority to constitute stable forms of living by canonical approval (Can. 576). To this authority are also reserved aggregations (Can. 580) and the approval of constitutions (Can. 587, 2). Mergers, unions, federations, confederations, suppressions and the changing of anything already approved by the Holy See, are reserved to that See (Can. 582-584).

§43. Authority to govern in religious institutes is invested in superiors who should exercise it according to the norms of common and proper law (Can. 617). This authority is received from God through the ministry of the church (Can. 618). The authority of a superior at whatever level is personal and may not be taken over by a group. For a particular time and for a given purpose, it may be delegated to a designated person.

§44. Superiors should fulfill their office generously, building with their brothers or sisters a community in Christ in which God is sought and loved before everything. In their role of service, superiors have the particular duty of governing in accordance with the constitutions of their institute and of promoting the holiness of its members. In their person, superiors should be examples of fidelity to the magisterium of the church and to the law and tradition of their institute. They should also foster the consecrated lives of their religious by their care and correction, their support and their patience (cf. Can. 619).

§45. Conditions for appointment or election, the length of term of office for the various superiors, and the mode of canonical election for the superior general are stated in the constitutions according to common law (Can. 623-625).

§46. Superiors must each have their own council, which assists them in fulfilling their responsibility. In addition to cases prescribed in the common law, proper law determines those cases in which the superior must obtain the consent or the advice of the council for validity of action (Can. 627, 1 and 2).

§47. The general chapter should be a true sign of the unity in charity of the institute. It represents the entire institute and when in session exercises supreme authority in accordance with common law and the norms of the constitutions (Can. 631). The general chapter is not a permanent body; its composition, frequency and functions are stated in the constitutions (Can. 631, 2). A general chapter may not modify its own composition but it may propose modifications for the composition of future chapters. Such modifications require the approval of the competent ecclesiastical authority. The general chapter may modify those elements of proper law which are not subject to the authority of the church.

§48. Chapters should not be convoked so frequently as to interfere with the good functioning of the ordinary authority of the major superior. The nature, authority, composition, mode of procedure and frequency of meeting of chapters and of similar assemblies of the institute are determined exactly by proper law (Can. 632). In practice, the main elements of these should be in the constitutions.

§49. Provision for temporal goods (Can. 634-640) and their administration, as well as norms concerning the separation of members from the institute by transfer, departure or dismissal (Can. 684-704) are also found in the common law of the church and must be included, even if only in brief, in the constitutions.

Conclusion

These norms, based on traditional teaching, the revised Code of Canon Law and current praxis, do not exhaust the church's provision for religious life. They indicate, however, her genuine concern that the life lived by institutes dedicated to works of the apostolate should develop ever more richly as a gift of God to the church and to the human family. In drawing up this text, which the Holy Father has approved, the Sacred Congregation for Religious and for Secular Institutes wishes to help those institutes to assimilate the church's revised provision for them and to put it in its doctrinal context. May they find in it a firm encouragement to the closer following of Christ in hope and joy in their consecrated lives.

From the Vatican, on the feast of the Visitation of the Blessed Virgin Mary, May 31, 1983

LIST OF EDITORS AND CONTRIBUTORS

(in alphabetical order)

Margaret Brennan I.H.M., associate professor of pastoral theology and director of continuing education at Regis College, Toronto, is a former superior general of the Congregation of the Immaculate Heart of Mary, Monroe, Michigan, and a former president of the Leadership Conference of Women Religious.

Michael J. Buckley, S.J., associate professor of systematic theology and spirituality at the Jesuit School of Theology at Berkeley in the Graduate Theological Union, is the theological consultant to the Pontifical Commission on Religious Life in the United States.

Robert J. Daly, S.J. is professor of systematic theology and chairperson of the department of theology at Boston College.

Mary Ann Donovan, S.C. is associate professor of historical theology with an emphasis upon patristics at the Jesuit School of Theology at Berkeley in the Graduate Theological Union.

Clare E. Fitzgerald, S.S.N.D., adjunct professor in the School of Education and director of the Catholic School Leadership Program at Boston College, is a former president of the Leadership Conference of Women Religious.

Helen Flaherty, S.C., one of the three American delegates to the International Union of Superior Generals, is the past president of the Leadership Conference of Women Religious and the present superior General of the Sisters of Charity of Cincinnati.

James Gaffney F.S.C., is vice president of the Conference of Major Superiors of Men, provincial of the Chicago Province of Christian Brothers, and president of the Christian Brothers National Conference.

Howard Gray, S.J., former dean and professor of spirituality at the Weston School of Theology in Cambridge, MA, is provincial of the Detroit Province of the Society of Jesus.

James Hennesey, S.J., former vice provincial of the New York Province of the Society of Jesus, and author of American Catholics: A History of the Roman Catholic Community in the

United States, is a professor of Church History at Boston College.

Karen Kennelly, C.S.J., author of The Peace and Truce of God and numerous biographical essays on American Women Religious, is Province Director of the Sisters of Saint Joseph of Carondelet, St. Paul Province.

Raymond Lessard, D.D., member of the Pontifical Commission on the Study of Religious Life in the United States, is Bishop of Savannah, Georgia.

John M. Lozano, C.M.F., consultor to the Congregation for the Causes of the Saints, and author of Discipleship: Towards an Understanding of Religious Life, is superior of Claret House and professor of spirituality in the Catholic Theological Union, Chicago.

Allan E. McCoy, O.F.M., a past president of the Conference of Major Superiors of Men and of the Canon Law Society in the United States, is the executive director of the Franciscan Conference and a member of the committee of religious for the Pontifical Commission on the Study of Religious Life in the United States.

Elizabeth McDonough, O.P., consultant to several religious congregations, is assistant professor in the Department of Canon Law at the Catholic University of America.

John R. McGann, D.D., member of the Administrative Committee of the N.C.C.B., of the Administrative Board of the U.S.C.C., and of the United States Catholic Bishops Advisory Council, is Bishop of Rockville Center, New York

Marie Augusta Neal, S.N.D., author of Catholic Sisters in Transition from the 1960's to the 1980's, and member of the Sub-Committee of the Bishops' Committee on the Study of Religious Life in the United States, is Professor of Sociology at Emmanuel College, Boston.

John W. Padberg, S.J., specialist in the history of religious orders, is professor of church history and president at the Weston School of Theology in Cambridge, MA.

John R. Quinn, D.D., Archbishop of San Francisco, is the Pontifical Delegate appointed by the Holy Father to guide the efforts of the American Bishops to render religious in the Unites States "special pastoral service."

Richard Rohr, O.F.M., founder and Pastor of the New Jerusalem Community in Cincinnati, is active in retreats and workshops for church leaders and is well known for his tapes.

John J. Snyder, D.D., member of the Commission on Marriage and Family Life of the U.S.C.C., and of the Advisory Committee with Handicapped Persons of the U.S.C.C., is Bishop of St. Augustine, Florida.

John F. Whealon, D.D., chairman of the Ecumenical Interreligious Affairs Committee of the N.C.C.B., and co-chairman of the Episcopalian-Roman Catholic Ecumenical Dialogue, is Archbishop of Hartford, Connecticut.

Kristin Wombacher, O.P. is a clinical psychologist at Napa State Hospital as well as the director of its Psychological Internship Program. She has focussed much of her work not only on individual psychotherapy and group therapy with religious, but also on workshops and lectures on the integration of psychology and spirituality.